Who's Not Working and Why

Over the last quarter-century, the U.S. labor market has experienced some disturbing trends. Despite apparent economic prosperity, joblessness among less-educated prime-age males is rising and, in addition, an increasing number of university graduates are taking "high-school jobs." Moreover, except for a thin layer of university-educated workers, most in the labor force are experiencing stagnating or falling real wages. Simultaneously, the inequality of wages is increasing within most groups.

Using an entirely new approach that takes account of the cognitive skills of U.S. workers and the detailed occupational structure of the labor force, Frederic L. Pryor and David L. Schaffer explore the underlying causes of these trends. To explain both employment and wages, they demonstrate that what a worker knows is becoming increasingly more important than a worker's formal education. They also present evidence that because of differences in wages between men and women, women are replacing men in many occupations. Finally, they synthesize these and other labor market characteristics to explain the increasing inequality of wages.

The authors have written this empirical study in non-technical language for those concerned with labor market problems and policies. For specialists they analyze a variety of technical issues in the appendices.

Who's Not Working and Why

Employment, Cognitive Skills, Wages, and the
Changing U.S. Labor Market

FREDERIC L. PRYOR   and   DAVID L SCHAFFER
Swarthmore College   *University of Wisconsin*
                                          at Eau Claire

CAMBRIDGE
UNIVERSITY PRESS

HD
5724
.P78
2000

#3965914*

PUBLISHED BY THE PRESS SYNDICATE OF THE UNIVERSITY OF CAMBRIDGE
The Pitt Building, Trumpington Street, Cambridge, United Kingdom

CAMBRIDGE UNIVERSITY PRESS
The Edinburgh Building, Cambridge CB2 2RU, UK
40 West 20th Street, New York, NY 10011-4211, USA
10 Stamford Road, Oakleigh, Melbourne 3166, Australia
Ruiz de Alarcón 13, 28014 Madrid, Spain
Dock House, The Waterfront, Cape Town 8001, South Africa

http://www.cambridge.org

First published 1999
First paperback edition 2000

Printed in the United States of America

Typeset in Times Adobe

A catalog record for this book is available from the British Library

Library of Congress Cataloging in Publication data
Pryor, Frederic L.
    Who's not working and why : employment, cognitive skills, wages, and the changing
U.S. labor market / Frederic L. Pryor and David L. Schaffer.
    p.   cm.
    Includes bibliographical references and index.
    1. Labor market—United States. 2. Skilled labor—Supply and demand—United
States. 3. Life skills—United States. 4. Cognitive learning—United States. 5.Wages—
United States. I. Scaffer, David L., 1958– . II. Title.
    HD5724.P78   1998
    331.12'0973—dc21
                                                                    98-39048
                                                                    CIP

ISBN 0 521 65152 2 hardback
ISBN 0 521 79439 0 paperback

For Mil and Claire

For Andrea

Contents

List of tables and charts   *page*   *ix*
Acknowledgments   *xiii*

Introduction
1 The Changing Labor Market   1

Employment, Cognitive Skills, and Job Displacement
2 Cognitive Skills, Education, and Other Determinants
     of Employment   19
3 Upskilling and Educational Upgrading of Occupations   47
4 Labor Force Displacement Mechanisms   74

Wage Levels and Distribution
5 Wage Levels   102
6 The Distribution of Hourly Wages   137

Alternative Approaches
7 Five Misleading Theories about Joblessness   170
8 Notes on Subjective and Institutional Factors   205

Implications and Interpretations
9 Final Observations   216

Appendix Notes
1.1: The Current Population Survey Data   234
1.2: Unemployment and Labor Force Non-Participation of
        the Prime-Age Population   234
1.3: Determinants of Employment in 1971 and 1994   237
2.1: The Data from the National Adult Literacy Survey   240
2.2: Notes on the Education Variable in the Current
        Population Survey   243

3.1: Imputing 1994–95 Census Occupation Codes for the
      March 1971 and 1972 CPS Samples   248
3.2: Biases in the Data on Occupations   249
3.3. Skill Ratings and Structural Changes in Skills   250
3.4: Occupational Deskilling by Educational Tier   253
3.5: More Data on Years of Education and Occupation
      of Prime-Age Workers   255
4.1: More Data on years of Education and Occupation
      of Prime-age Workers   257
4.2: Using the Biproportional Matrix Technique
      for Decomposition   260
4.3: Further Decomposition of the Structural Changes   263
5.1: More Data on Median Hourly Wages   264
5.2: Estimating Hourly Wage Data   266
5.3: The Impact of Other Cognitive Skills on Wages   269
5.4: Wage Regressions at Different Points in Time   271
6.1: More Charts on Wage Distributions   272
7.1: The Impact of Immigration on the Employment of
      Native-Born Workers   274
8.1: Determinants of Hiring Criteria and of Labor Force
      Composition   276

Bibliography   280

Name Index   292

Subject Index   295

List of Tables and Charts

Tables

2.1: Functional Literacy Scores of the Prime-Age Population
by Education in 1992 24

2.2: Explaining Average Literacy Test Results of the Prime
Working-Age Population in 1992 28

2.3: Functional Literacy, Employment Status, and Education of
the Prime Working-Age Population in 1992 35

2.4: Partial Discrete Changes in Employment Probabilities of
the Prime Working-Age Population 39

3.1: Average Annual Changes in the Educational Levels of the
Population and the Employed Work Force Compared to
Similar Changes in the Educational Intensity
of Occupations 50

3.2: Major Occupations Ranked by Changes in Average
Education 55

3.3: Percentage of Employed Workers With a University
Education in High School Jobs 62

3.4: Years of Education and Occupations of Prime-Age
Workers, 1971 and 1995 64

3.5: Weighted Average Functional Literacy Scores and Jobs of
the Prime Working-Age Population in 1992 66

3.6: Structural Shifts in Skill Characteristics of the Four
Educational Tiers 70

4.1: Distribution of the Prime Working-Age Population by
Employment Status and Occupational Tier versus
Gender, Race, and Education 78

4.2: The Hypothetical 1995 Matrix and the Derived
"Aggregate" Changes 82

4.3: Structural Changes in the Distribution of the Prime
Working-Age Population Between 1971 and 1995 88

4.4: Some Relevant Data on the Who of Structural Changes 95

ix

4.5: Some Relevant Data on the How and When of
      Structural Changes   97
5.1: Median Hourly Real Wages of Prime-Age Workers,
      1970 and 1994   104
5.2: Median Weekly Wags of Full-Time, Prime-Age Workers
      by Education and Average Functional Literacy Scores
      in 1992   107
5.3: Regression to Explain Weekly Wages of Full-Time,
      Prime-Age Workers in 1992   112
5.4: Impact on Wages in Each Occupation of an Individual's
      Cognitive Skills and Education   118
5.5: Determinants of the Changes in Real Hourly Wages of
      Prime-Age Workers by Occupation   126
5.6: Largest Prediction Errors of Wage Changes of
      Prime-Age Workers, 1971–72 to 1994–95   130
6.1: Changes in the Generalized Entropy Measure of the
      Inequality of Hourly Wages of Employed Prime-Age
      Workers   145
6.2: Decomposition of Changes in the Theil Entropy
      Measure of Wage by Gender, Race, Education,
      and Occupation of Prime-Age Workers   148
6.3: Changes in Wage Inequality Within and Between
      Occupational Tiers and Detailed Occupations of
      Prime-Age Workers   152
6.4: Some Characteristics of the Largest 38 Detailed
      Occupations in Tier 4   156
6.5: Determinants of the Fraction of Prime-Age Female
      Workers in Tier 4 Occupations   158
6.6: Major Occupations in Tier 4 with the Highest Median
      Wages in 1993–94   161
7.1: Trends in Labor Market Turbulence, Mid 1950s
      through 1990   175
7.2: Gross Rates of Job Creation and Destruction in the
      Manufacturing Sector   176
7.3: Hypothetical Changes in Production, Productivity, and
      Employment of All Employed Workers with
      Different Levels of Education, 1971–1991   179
7.4: The Impact of Skill Intensity of Production on the
      Change in Net Exports   186
7.5: Hypothetical Changes in Trade, Production, and
      Employment of Workers With Different Levels
      of Education   190

7.6: Share of Immigrants in the Employed Labor Force, 1979 and 1995   196

7.7: Jobless Rates of the Prime-Age Population in Central Cities, 1971 and 1995   201

8.1: Important Factors in the Hiring of Front-Line Workers   207

9.1: A Summary of the Major Arguments Made in This Book   218

9.2: Indicators of the Growth of Population, Labor, Capital, and Investment   224

A1.1: Unemployment of the Prime Working Age Population as a Percent of the Total Cohort   235

A1.2: Non-Participation Rates in the Labor Force of the Prime Working Age Population as a Percent of the Total Cohort   238

A1.3: Estimated Employment Probabilities of the Prime-Age Population, 1979 and 1987   241

A2.1: Education by Race and Gender of the Less Educated Population in Prime Working Age as a Percent of Relevant Cohort, 1964–1994   246

A2.2: Partial Discrete Changes in Employment Probabilities of the Prime Working-Age Population When NALS Scores are Excluded From the Regression   247

A3.1: Structural Upskilling for Various Skills Among Employed Prime-Age Workers   252

A3.2: Characteristics of Jobs Held by Less Educated Workers in Their Prime Working-Ages in 1971 and 1995   254

A3.3: Years of Education and Occupations of Prime-Age Workers, 1979 and 1987   255

A4.1: Comparison on the "Scaled-Up" 1971 Matrix to the Actual 1995 Matrix   257

A4.2: Decomposition of Structural Changes into Proportional Employment Component and Occupational Shifting Component   263

A5.1: Median Hourly Wages of Prime-Age Workers, 1978 and 1986   264

A5.2: Average Weekly Wages in 1992 of Different Occupations of Full-Time Prime-Age Workers as a Function of Particular Occupational Characteristics   270

A5.3: CPS Wage Regressions in 1994 Dollars   271

A8.1: Determinants of Hiring Criteria   277

A8.2: Labor Force Composition as a Function of Hiring Criteria   278

Charts:

1.1: Percentage of Males in Prime Working-Ages Without
      Employment   8
1.2   Percentage of Females in Prime Working-Ages Without
      Employment   8
2.1: Prime-Working Age Population by Level of Education,
      1964–1994   42
5.1: Male Unemployment Rates by Highest Level
      of Education   134
5.2: Female Unemployment Rates by Highest Level
      of Education   134
6.1: Overall Wage Distribution, Prime-Age Workers   146
6.2: Comparison of Median Wage Distribution Across
      Detailed Occupations in Tier 4   154
6.3: Male and Female Wage Changes in Tier 4 Occupations   164
6.4: Net Displacement of Men by Women in Tier 1
      Occupations   167
9.1: Joblessness Among Prime-Age Men and Women   221
A6.1: Overall Wage Distribution of Prime-Age Workers   272
A6.2: High End of the Wage Distribution of Prime Age Workers 273

Acknowledgments

In writing and researching this book, we have received a great deal of help from others whom we would like to thank.

For supplying and helping us with data and computer programs, we are grateful to Robert Feenstra, Maury Gittleman, Wayne Gray, Zenita Jones, Andrew Kolstad, John Priebe, Daniel Shapiro, John Stinson, Richard Vernizky, and Lynn Weidman.

For reading the entire manuscript we appreciate the help of Zora Pryor and Charles LaMorte, as well as Susan Hodge, who carefully edited the manuscript. For reading individual chapters we would also like to thank Martin Asher, Richard Ball, Linda Bell, John Caskey, Richard Cooper, Seth Cooper, Janet Ceglowski, Richard DuBoff, Steven Golub, Robinson Hollister, Harry J. Holzer, Philip Jefferson, Mark Kuperberg, Michael Leeds, Chris Mazingo, Lawrence Mishel, Stephen A. O'Connell, Daniel Pryor, Bryan Ray, Andrea LaMorte Schaffer, William D. Schaffer, Chad Stone, Elliott Sulcove, and Chris Tilly. Audree Penner skillfully turned our manuscript into camera-ready pages.

We received with gratitude useful comments after presentation of various parts of this book to audiences at the Atlantic Economic Society, the Economic Research Division of the Social Security Administration, Haverford College Faculty, Kalamazoo College, Kiev-Mohyla Academy; Lyon College, Oglethorpe University, Swarthmore College, Suffolk Univerity, Tri-College Summer Economic Seminar, University of Delaware, University of North Carolina at Wilmington, University of Pennsylvania, University of Wisconsin at Eau Claire, and Washington and Lee University

Finally, we received partial funding from the Swarthmore College Faculty Research Fund, for which we are grateful.

We offer the usual disclaimers of responsibility of our mistakes for all of those who generously gave their time and advice to us. Unfortunately, we bear the full responsibility for any errors.

CHAPTER 1

The Changing Labor Market

The period from 1970 to 1996 represents a time of dramatic change in the U.S. labor market. The manufacturing sector has been shrinking and restructuring while the service sector has been growing. Jobs of all types have moved out of the inner cities and into the suburbs. Increased international trade and competition has helped some industries expand their domestic output while others have been forced to scale back, shut down, or move their facilities abroad. Well-educated employees with decades of experience have become as fearful about layoffs as younger less-educated workers. Legal and illegal immigration has continued at high levels, creating more competition for many entry-level jobs. The technology changes associated with the computer revolution have continued to modify the nature of many jobs. Women have become just as likely as men to get a university degree, and almost as likely to seek paid work. The financial rewards to the most successful workers in the labor market have grown dramatically, while those to most other workers have shrunk. The quality of public education, at least in many urban areas, has declined precipitously.

These phenomena have received wide attention in both the academic and popular press. Hardly a month goes by without a new book appearing – by an economist, a sociologist, a business executive, or a journalist – attempting to explain why these changes are occurring and what they mean for the future.[1] Our book follows in this tradition – but with a few key differences.

First of all, most previous work in these areas focuses on one or two poten-

---

[1] Recent books include: Barlett and Steele, America: *Who Stole the Dream?* (1996); Danziger and Gottschalk, *America Unequal* (1995); Frank and Cook, *The Winner-Take-All Society* (1995); Holzer, *What Employers Want: Job Prospects for Less-Educated Workers* (1996); Levitan, Gallo, and Shapiro, *Working But Poor: America's Contradiction* (1993); Mishel, Bernstein, and Schmitt, *The State of Working America, 1996-1997* (1997); Perelman, *The Pathology of the U.S. Economy: The Costs of a Low-Wage System* (1996); Thurow, *The Future of Capitalism* (1996); Wilson, *When Work Disappears: The World of the New Urban Poor* (1996); Wolff, *Top Heavy: A Study of the Increasing Inequality of Wealth in America* (1995).

Recent collections of articles include: Bhagwati and Kosters, editors, *Trade and Wages: Leveling Wages Down?* (1994). Danziger and Gottschalk editors, *Uneven Tides: Rising Inequality in America* (1993); Farley, editor, *State of the Union: America in the 1990's*, Vol. 2, (1995); Ginzberg, editor, *The Changing U.S. Labor Market* (1994); Solmon and Levenson, editors, *Labor Markets, Employment Policy, and Job Creation* (1994).

tial explanations and then tries to document their importance. For example, one study focuses on increased international trade while another deals with spatial mismatch between jobs and workers – the jobs are in the suburbs while many unemployed workers are in the cities. Or one explores the increasingly rapid pace of technological change while another focuses on the large number of recent immigrants. We set out to look at all of these potential causes simultaneously, and to use a careful analysis of economic data to determine the relative importance of each. However, along the way, we encountered some surprises. We found that many of these changes are related. We determined that the standard explanations cannot explain the magnitude of these changes. We discovered that several factors which have been ignored or dismissed by others may, in fact, be catalysts driving these changes.

How do we reach conclusions different from most others? Part of the answer lies in the data underlying our analysis. We use Current Population Survey (CPS) data from 1970 through 1996 which have been very carefully modified so that education, employment, and wages in individual detailed occupations (3-digit or 500-category) can be tracked for the entire period. These provide us a way of looking at the labor demand side of the market that is missing in most studies. We also use National Adult Literacy Survey (NALS) data from 1992, which enable us to look at the skill levels of individuals independent of their education or occupation.

Part of the explanation for our different results also lies in the conceptual framework that we develop. Our abundance of data on detailed occupations enables us to develop a concept, called "education intensiveness," to classify each of these detailed occupations into four broad categories or "tiers." This concept is very fruitful in helping us to identify some of the primary labor market mechanisms affecting this quarter century of changes in the labor market.

Finally, part of the explanation for our different results lies in the analytical approach we use. Rather than relying on a single method, such as a standard type of regression analysis, we look at the data in a variety of ways. Of course, we make extensive use of regression analysis, but we also use two relatively less familiar techniques – one to separate the changes in employment into aggregate versus structural changes (Chapter 4), and the other to decompose the changes in wage inequality into those between various categories and those within particular categories (Chapter 6).[2] We also examine much of the data at the individual detailed occupations level to see how the changes occurring may differ across jobs within the same broad tier.

---

2   Although these two analytical techniques are very different and are used for very different types of analysis, both are associated with the work of Henri Theil.

An Outline of Our Story

We believe that the most important transformations of the labor market over the last quarter century can be most easily understood by focusing on four interrelated changes: (1) the rising joblessness of prime-age males, particularly among the less educated; (2) the increased number of university educated workers in "high-school" jobs; (3) the significant increase in wage inequality within and across well-defined demographic groups and occupations; and (4) the increasing average rate of economic return to an investment in a university education.

This book focuses on the implications of a surprising, but crucial fact for the labor market and the four trends just described: Jobs for less-educated workers have increased faster than the population with the corresponding educational credentials while, simultaneously, jobs for more-educated workers have increased slower than the more-educated population. Thus, contrary to arguments proposed in the popular press and technical literature, joblessness of less-educated workers is not linked to the disappearance of low-skilled jobs, a phenomenon often erroneously attributed to the impact of foreign trade or technical changes.

We carefully document these relative changes affecting low-skilled jobs and potential workers. As a result of such changes, low-skilled positions are increasingly filled by workers whose educational credentials exceed job requirements. In other words, over the last quarter-century there has been a considerable downward occupational mobility dramatically reducing the probability that workers with particular educational credentials obtain employment in occupations commensurate with their years of schooling; not surprisingly, they are accepting jobs requiring less education. In brief, university graduates are taking high-school jobs.

In the following chapters we show that such downward occupational mobility is facilitated by three key mechanisms. First, hourly wages within and across many occupations exhibit downward wage stickiness.[3] A decrease in wages occurs when the labor supply increases for a particular occupation, but there is also some excess supply which does not disappear quickly. Second, the labor market is increasingly sorting workers by their cognitive skills. Using data from the National Adult Literacy Survey we can separate the inde-

---

3 Possible explanations for this wage stickiness include the impact of minimum wage laws, the impact of firms following efficiency wage policies to maintain high productivity and the prevalence of implicit contracts allowing labor demand to vary more easily along the quantity dimension than the wage dimension.

pendent influences of education and cognitive skills to show that workers experiencing downward occupational mobility generally have lower cognitive skills than others with the same educational credentials. "Years of education" is an imperfect indicator or measure of cognitive skills, which are becoming more important as a determinant of employment. Third, growing numbers of educated women have been filling jobs previously held by men, particularly in those jobs requiring considerable education and skills.

The combination of wage stickiness and the various job displacement mechanisms underlying downward occupational mobility results in significant changes affecting the lower end of the occupational scale. Workers with some education have crowded into jobs requiring relatively few years of schooling at a faster rate than these jobs increase. As a result, wages in low-education occupations are falling. Moreover, the least-educated workers are leaving the labor force entirely, especially when the actual wages approach the legally mandated minimum wage.

Changes occurring at the other end of the occupational scale are more complex. Although there are more university graduates than university-level jobs, average wages in such jobs have risen. Averages, however, are deceptive. Our investigation concludes that technical change has affected the wage premium for high cognitive skills, since the demand for these skills has risen faster than the small group of university graduates possessing them. Thus, one subgroup of university graduates has received increasing wages over time, while university graduates with average or lower-than-average cognitive skills have experienced falling or stagnant real wages (even those not experiencing downward occupational mobility).

Employment trends have important implications on the distribution of wages, which are becoming increasingly unequal according to most measures. Many previous studies have shown that the greatest changes in wage inequality occur within broad occupational groups, rather than between them. We find similar trends for most narrowly-defined occupational groups, except for those requiring substantial education. The causes of increasing wage inequality differ, however, in the low- and high-end occupations.

Our study identifies three factors affecting the increase in wage inequality occurring within occupations requiring relatively little education. First, a modest decrease in the real minimum wage has resulted in many workers receiving lower real wages than ever before. Second, a large decrease in the rate of unionization over the last quarter-century has meant a decrease in organized labor support for wage equality. Finally, downward occupational mobility has resulted in a broader distribution of both education and cognitive abilities within the low-education occupations which, in turn, has generated a broader distribution of wages.

For jobs requiring a university education, we show that four mechanisms have resulted in greater wage inequalities: Wages in the health care and legal professions have dramatically outpaced those in others. Further, a substantial displacement of men by women working at lower wages has occurred, particularly in the middle-wage professions. In addition, the increasing wage inequality is enhanced by technological change that leads to an increase in the demand for workers with higher cognitive skills. Finally, a movement toward "winner-take-all" wage-setting has also occurred which has led to small groups within certain occupations obtaining extra-high wages.

Our explanation of these changes is quite different from that of others and is likely to be met with some skepticism. The co-authors have different political views and pursued no ideological agenda in carrying out this research. As previously noted, we were initially surprised at many of our findings. Our conclusions, however, are supported by the lengthy empirical analysis presented in this book. When we propose a theoretical explanation, we also provide the facts underlying the theory.

Dimensions and Long-Run Trends in Joblessness

The starting point for our analysis is joblessness among men and women. This lack of employment has economic consequences such as loss of production and income. Scholars in various disciplines have shown it also has significant social implications, especially for those formerly employed. These include a decline in physical and mental health, increased rates of suicide, higher admission rates to mental hospitals, more divorce, more child abuse, lowered self-esteem, more alcoholism and severe depression, greater helplessness and, quite likely, more crime.[4] Different studies also indicate long-term unemployment among specific groups of workers exacerbates a decline in concentration and effort, not to mention loss of job skills.

We leave detailed exploration of these economic and social implications to others. Nevertheless, these social costs justify our attention in this book to joblessness and the importance of understanding its underlying causes. Our focus

4   Warr (1987, especially Chapter 11 and 12) and Mallinckrodt and Fretz (1988) have useful bibliographies showing the relationship of unemployment to the different social variables cited in the text. This literature on the social consequences of unemployment is vast and features both time-series and cross-sectional studies carried out on both a macro-level (for instance Brenner's (1973) study of aggregate trends and admissions to mental hospitals), and a micro-level. Although unemployment is often tied to crime, macroeconomic relationships are difficult to interpret, particularly because isolating such effects requires complicated simultaneous equation models. Nevertheless, most studies show the expected positive relation between unemployment and crime. The literature is reviewed by Chiricos (1987) and Freeman (1994). Microeconomic evidence is even more likely to show a positive and significant positive relation between high unemployment and low wages on the one hand and criminal behavior on the other (Freeman, 1996-b). Nevertheless, some contrary evidence is also available (Kim *et al.* 1989).

is not on the lack of employment arising from cyclical or other short-term causes (which are relatively well understood), but on the factors underlying long-term, structural joblessness, where general understanding is less developed.

Dimensions of Long-Run Joblessness

The first task in approaching the problem of joblessness is to define the group of individuals to be observed, and the measure of joblessness for that group. Since we explore long-run changes, we focus our attention on prime working-age men and women. These are men and women ages 25 through 49 who have completed all of their formal education, acquired some work experience, and have not yet begun the transition toward retirement.[5] By looking only at prime working-age men and women, we avoid confusing the core problems of joblessness with two types of special problems associated with age. Young persons who have completed secondary school or university may have special difficulties securing employment commensurate with their education. Older workers in their fifties and sixties may experience health-related employment problems. Moreover, due to the availability of pensions, Supplemental Social Insurance, and other sources of income, many older workers have voluntarily chosen early retirement.

The second task is to choose a measure of long-run joblessness for prime working-age men and women. During previous decades, those addressing problems of joblessness have focused most of their attention on unemployment, rather than withdrawal from the labor force. Unemployment is defined as those without employment who are "actively looking for work," and the conventional belief is that most unemployment is involuntary.[6] In contrast, non-participation in the labor force is generally considered voluntary. However, for men in their prime working years, non-participation in the labor force is more likely to be involuntary; most men in their prime working-ages would

---

5 Most economists define prime working ages as beginning somewhere between ages 20 and 30, and ending somewhere between ages 50 and 55. We choose to look at persons age 25 through age 49, although our calculations suggest that the choice of beginning and ending ages does not affect our results in any substantive way.

6 The Current Population Survey (CPS) defines people as employed if, for a given month's period, they work for any length of time for monetary payment, or if they are engaged at least 15 hours a week in unpaid work in a business or farm owned by a member of their immediate family. Cohany, *et al.* (1994) provide a fuller definition. People are considered unemployed if they have no employment but have actively looked for work in the past four weeks, or have been laid off and have evidence that they will be recalled. For prime-age workers the new labor force survey methods introduced in 1994 raised the unemployment rate about 0.3 percent; and the participation rate in the labor force, about 0.1 percent.

choose to work for pay if able to find an acceptable job. For this reason, economists designate prime working-age men who are neither employed nor actively looking for work as "discouraged workers". Given this, we believe the best measure of long-run male joblessness – the excess supply of labor among men compared to the available jobs- is the fraction of prime working-age men who are not employed. This includes all meeting the conventional definition of unemployed, as well as those not in the labor force.

For women, the choice of definitions for long-run joblessness is less obvious. Certainly many prime working-age married women are "voluntarily" out of the labor force to raise young children and to take responsibility for household tasks. However, recent data suggest many of these women would join the workforce – and send their children to daycare – if the "right" job became available. In order for such women to join the labor force, a job must have the flexibility needed to accommodate parenting responsibilities. This additional requirement makes it less likely that married women will find the right job, and so they are more likely to be out of the labor force than their husbands. Whether this is a "voluntary" or "involuntary" is a difficult question that we cannot answer here. The changes in the workforce behavior of married women have been so dramatic over the last quarter-century – especially the group that formerly chose not to work for pay outside the home – that we definitely want to include them in our analysis. Thus, we apply the same definition of long-run joblessness to both men and women.

Over the last third of a century the nature of long-run joblessness among those in the prime working-ages has changed dramatically. In the mid-1960s, the number of unemployed prime-aged men exceeded those who had withdrawn from the labor force. By the 1990s, however, those who have withdrawn from the labor force – many are designated as "discouraged workers" – considerably outnumber those classified as unemployed.[7] Among prime-age

In response to objections raised against the "standard definition" of unemployment, the Bureau of Labor Statistics calculates several alternative measures. A narrow definition of unemployment considers only the long-term unemployed, those workers who have been unemployed 15 weeks or more. By way of contrast, an expanded definition (formerly called series U-7) includes as unemployed those seeking full-time jobs one-half of those seeking part-time jobs and one-half of those employed part-time for "economic reasons" (the worker wanted a full-time job) plus all "discouraged workers" (those declaring they want work, but have not actively looked for work in the past month). Bregger and Haugen (1995) discuss the various definitions of unemployment and how they changed as a result of the 1994 revisions to the CPS questionnaire.

Since this study focuses primarily on total joblessness, we do not need to worry about the line separating the unemployed from those who have completely withdrawn from the labor force.

7   In Appendix 1.2 we provide relevant data by education, race/ethnicity, and year for both unemployment and those who have completely withdrawn from the labor force. Subsequent to the calculation made for Charts 1.1 and 1.2, the percentage of jobless men and women fell respectively about 1.3 and 2.1 percentage points between March 1995 and March 1999. Although the jobless rate among prime-age, high-school dropouts was considerably more than the average, the jobless rates in 1999 for these two groups were respectively 22.8 and 48.6 percent, so that the problem still remained serious.

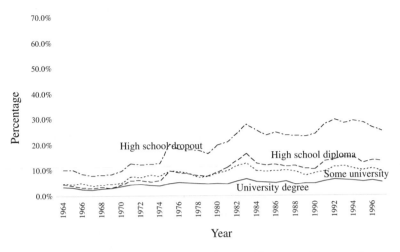

Chart 1.1: Percentage of ales in prime working-ages without employment

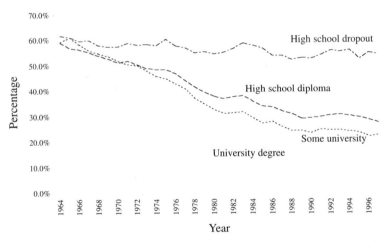

Chart 1.2: Percentage of females in prime working-ages without employment

women the percentage of those without formal employment outside the home has always been greater than those unemployed, since many stayed home to fulfill home-making or child-rearing responsibilities. Nevertheless, the difference in number between the unemployed and those out of the labor force has dramatically narrowed over the last 30 years.

This shift in the composition of joblessness has many important economic implications. At the macroeconomic level, it suggests that the "natural rate of unemployment" has changed. This might occur because employers can draw upon a much larger pool of jobless workers at a given level of unemployment. At the microeconomic level, it directs our attention to the possibility that the problem of joblessness might be considerably more severe among certain sub-groups than traditional indicators of unemployment suggest. For example in the mid-1900s roughly one-fourth of the white male prime-age workers without a high school diploma had no job; among black male prime-age workers with a similar education, the percentage was roughly one-half.

Joblessness Over the Last Three Decades: A Few Descriptive Statistics

How severe is the problem of joblessness? Charts 1.1 and 1.2 allow us to see how it has evolved over the last third of a century by illustrating the separate jobless rates for men and women, differentiated by their level of formal education. These calculations are based on samples of 60,000 to 120,000 people from the data files of the March Current Population Survey (CPS) of the various years.[8] These labor force data refer to the status of the respondents during the week before the interview. We define the jobless (or non-employment) rate as the total number of jobless divided by the total population in the relevant age/education category.

For both men and women, the rates of joblessness are inversely related to level of educational achievement. Thus university graduates have the lowest rate of joblessness, and high school dropouts have the highest. Over time the trends were less favorable for the less-educated than for the more-educated, although the pattern was different for men and women. More specifically, the rates of joblessness for men increased faster for the less-educated men than those with more education. For women, the rates of non-employment fell more slowly for those less-educated than for more-educated women.

Trends and differences between non-employment rates are more dramatic when we separate the educational groups by race. For men with less than a high school degree, the situation appears especially worrisome. For instance, between 1971 and 1995 the jobless rate of white men increased

---

8 In Appendix 1.1 we present a brief description of the Current Population Survey (CPS) and in Appendix 1.2 we provide a more detailed break down of the data presented in Charts 1.1 and 1.2. Although the CPS is the standard source of many key labor force statistics used by the government and private researchers, the data are not completely standardized over the period under investigation. At appropriate places in this study we discuss how we achieve (or do not achieve) comparability for particular statistics.

13.6 percentage points (from 11.9 percent to 25.5 percent); for black men, the jobless rate increased 30.7 percentage points (from 17.0 percent to 47.6 percent). For white men with just a high school diploma, the non-employment rate increased 6.1 percentage points; for black men, 8.7 percentage points. (See appendix tables A1.1 and A1.2.)

Although women as a whole experienced decreasing jobless rates, similar differences occurred when race is considered. Between 1971 and 1995 the jobless rate of white women with less than a high school diploma decreased 9.3 percentage points (from 60.5 percent to 51.2 percent); for black women in the same education group, the jobless rate increased 5.6 percentage points (from 52.0 percent to 57.6 percent). For white women with just a high school diploma, the jobless rate decreased 25.2 percentage points; for black women, it increased 0.4 percentage points.

At the other end of the educational spectrum, the non-employment rates for both white and black men with a university degree rose only slightly between 1971 and 1995. For women university graduates, the situation again depended on race. The jobless rate of white women decreased 25.5 percentage points, while for black women the rate decreased only 4.2 percentage points. It must be added that by 1995, the employment rate of black women was still higher than the rate of white women. Thus, employment rates for white educated women were catching up to those of black women.

At this point it is useful to note some similarities and differences among unemployment rates which have received more public attention. The unemployment rate is much more volatile than the rate of joblessness. The two rates are, however, similar in that both are higher for the less-educated than for the educated, and are also higher for blacks than for whites. Nevertheless, unemployment trends for men and women are roughly similar, in contrast to rates of joblessness.

But the greatest difference between unemployment and total joblessness lies in their respective long-run trends. In the late-1990s we might wonder whether it is worthwhile worrying about unemployment in the United States since the rates have been at a 30-year low. Moreover, in contrast to the European continent, the unemployment situation in the United States. looks even better.[9] By focusing attention on total joblessness, however, we can identify some serious problems, particularly among less-educated males.

---

9   In the decade of the 1960s, for instance, the unemployment rate in the United States was more than 1.7 times as high as in the industrialized European members of the O.E.C.D. In the decade from 1984 through 1993, however, the U.S. had an unemployment rate roughly two-thirds of these other nations. If we compare not just the European members but all members of the O.E.C.D. (the 19 European members plus Australia, Canada, Japan, and New Zealand) to the U.S., the U.S. unemployment rate was 1.9 times higher in the 1960s and about five-

The focus of this book provides a different perspective on the labor market than most studies, and suggests some policy prescriptions that differ from those derived from exclusive attention to unemployment.

Key Causal Factors: Cognitive Skills, Education, and Gender

Cognitive skills, education, and gender play important roles in our analysis of joblessness and wage inequality. It is useful to briefly review some major questions we address by describing how we interpret these factors.

Cognitive Skills

Although cognitive skills measured in terms of functional literacy and education are related, they focus on two quite different dimensions of human capital. Cognitive skills reflect our ability to use reading, writing, and calculating skills to solve problems. Education is partly an indicator of what we know, and partly a formal credential attesting to the number of years of formal schooling we have had, and the examinations we have successfully passed. As noted earlier, formal years of education is a very imperfect measure of cognitive skills. As a result, cognitive skills and education play separate and quite distinct roles as determinants of employment and wages.

As a measurement of cognitive skills we use a definition of functional literacy taken from the National Adult Literacy Survey. In Chapter 2 we examine the distribution of functional literacy in the prime age population and investigate its determinants. Although formal education plays an important role, a number of demographic and social variables also have considerable causal impact. We also show that functional literacy is one of several key determinants affecting employment and wages. In particular, it has a large and statistically significant effect on both employment and wages independent of years of education.

sixths as high in the decade from 1984 through 1993.

The unemployment rate in most O.E.C.D. nations generally show an upward trend since the 1970s, while the U.S. unemployment rate has been essentially flat. From the mid 1960s to the mid 1990s, the growth of jobs in the United States was considerably faster than the growth of the potential labor force, while in Europe the converse was the case.

The data underlying these generalizations come from O.E.C.D. (annual, 1993 and 1996).

Education

Charts 1.1 and 1.2 show dramatic differences of non-employment rates by level of education. Nevertheless, we must be careful about making inferences from such data because all other causal factors of joblessness are not held constant. For instance, aside from education, factors such as race/ethnicity, age, family structure, family background, and literacy all play causal roles in explaining joblessness. In the next chapter and in Appendix 1.3 we carry out a statistical analysis of employment status testing more than 50 different explanatory variables. Nevertheless, the general conclusions are roughly the same as those drawn from a simple glance at our two charts – the greater the education, the lower the joblessness.

We draw some important conclusions that are considerably less intuitive when we look at education, occupations, and changes in the job structure over time. The salient fact, as noted previously, is that those jobs requiring a high school education or less have increased at a faster rate than the number of prime-age workers having commensurate educational credentials. On the other hand, jobs requiring more than a high school education have increased more slowly than the prime-age workers with the appropriate education. We develop this argument in detail in Chapter 3.

The downward occupational mobility arising from these changes in the relative supply and demand for jobs requiring particular educational credentials has created a cascading displacement effect, whereby workers with higher education displace workers with less education. This, in turn, provides a major piece of evidence that some of the explanations about the causes of joblessness of less-educated workers are simply myths. These considerations also allow us to disentangle the major causal forces underlying the inverse relation between years of education and joblessness. We should emphasize that the displacement effect does not tell us why the jobless rate among men is increasing.

Gender

In Chapter 4 we demonstrate that a major determinant of the displacement effect has been the rapid entry of women into the labor force from 1971 to the early 1990s. This is most dramatically seen in comparisons of predicted and actual employment by gender and education in occupations classified by the workers' required education.

The overall replacement of men by women has been accelerated by three factors. (a) Women have disproportionately entered the fastest-growing occupations, particularly those requiring more education. (b) Women with the same education and functional literacy receive, on the average, lower wages than men. This enhances their desirability as job candidates for profit-maximizing enterprises. (c) Among high school dropouts or those with just a high school diploma, women have somewhat higher cognitive skills along the prose and document scales indicating useful skills for lower-level clerks.

Employment and Wages

Employment trends, of course, are linked in many different ways to wage trends. We tie the various strands of our argument together by examining wage trends between 1971 and 1995 in Chapter 5, and the increasing wage inequality in Chapter 6.

We begin by showing that median real wages have increased for those with a university degree who are in jobs requiring such an education. By contrast, median real wages have either stagnated or have fallen for all other groups. We also show the strong influence various causal influences such as functional literacy, gender, and race have on wages.

If our surprising claim is correct – that the number of jobs requiring a university education is increasing at a slower rate than those who have the commensurate education – then why are the average wages of university graduates increasing rather than decreasing? The key to solving this puzzle is the fact that economic returns to cognitive skills, independent of education, have increased. This is the most important manifestation of what many call "skill-biased technical change."

As a result, although the number of university graduates has increased at a faster rate than the jobs held by those with degrees, the number of workers with requisite cognitive skills has not has not grown as fast. Thus, those with such cognitive skills have received a rising wage premium. These skills, of course, are difficult for employers to determine until the job candidate has worked for them. Since competition for those with high cognitive skills is fierce, employers must pay a premium for university graduates, at least until they can establish the actual capabilities of these new employees. Those not making the cut may experience downward occupational mobility. Those possessing the highest functional literacy have raised the average wages of all university graduates, at least in jobs appropriate for those with degrees.

At the same time, downward occupational mobility has increased the supply of workers competing for jobs requiring lower educational credentials. This shift in the supply of workers has exceeded the rising demand for those with the commensurate education. High school dropouts caught in this cascading displacement effect have been pushed out of the labor force. Not surprisingly, relative real wages among those with less education have also fallen.

The increasing wage premium to those combining a university education with high cognitive skills also plays an important causal role in the increasing wage inequality. When looking at wages in occupations sorted according to the necessary educational requirements, we observe that both average wages and wage inequality have increased most among the college-educated workers in jobs requiring the highest cognitive skills. Further, we show that the increasing wage inequality at the top is a more significant factor affecting the overall increase in wage inequality than the widening average wages earned by those with different educational levels.

Myths about the Causes of Increasing Joblessness

One or more of five common explanations (myths) are offered in the popular press and the technical literature to explain the trends in joblessness that we have briefly described:

• Increasing non-employment of the less-skilled is the result of skill-biased technical change that has lessened the demand for less-educated workers and increased the demand for more-educated workers. Such technical change has not only led to the elimination of many low-skill jobs but has also lowered the wages of those workers who manage to hold such jobs.

• Increasing non-employment of the less-skilled is the result of growing internationalization or globalization of the economy. This refers to the rising ratio of foreign trade to GDP and the increasing openness of the economy. The key are the type of work-skills embodied in traded products. Allegedly, the U.S. has experienced a rising share (compared to production) of low-skill-intensive imports from developing nations, and a falling share (compared to production) of low-skill intensive exports. Because of the low wages in countries competing with U.S. production, the workers in these industries have been unable to find work elsewhere.

• Increasing non-employment of the less-skilled is the consequence of immigration policies and the rising number of poorly-educated foreign workers. Because they are willing to accept low wages, these immigrants have displaced low-skilled native-born workers.

• Increasing non-employment of the less skilled is the result of structural changes in U.S. consumption and productivity that have favored goods and services produced by more-skilled labor. Some analysts claim the joblessness resulting from these changes is exacerbated by two factors: the increasing sclerosis of the U.S. economy, and the decreasing mobility of labor from regions having a surplus of workers to areas experiencing labor shortages. The labor mobility phenomenon is also tied to the next argument.

• Increasing non-employment of the less-skilled is the result of the rising spatial mismatch of jobs and population. Jobs are now increasingly located in the suburbs or outside the central cities of metropolitan areas. For various reasons, less-skilled workers are not moving sufficiently quickly to these new job locations; because they live in the city, they cannot easily reach these work places or even learn about job openings. Concentration of jobless ness in certain parts of the central city has also influenced attitudes about work internalized by others living in these areas, and this has contributed to the problems.

In Chapter 7 we turn to an empirical examination of these five arguments often used to explain long-term labor market trends. Although each has a grain of truth, we show that they are not the major causal factors underlying the trends in joblessness and that our approach has greater explanatory power. In Chapter 8 we examine the influence of "subjective factors" such as work attitudes, and soft-skills like communication abilities, on the sorting and displacement mechanisms in labor markets. We find that these factors have little impact on our results.

The Data

In this book we draw conclusions quite different from those found in others. In major part, these differences arise because we use two quite unique databases that allow a new perspective on the operations of the labor market:

The most widely used data set to analyze labor markets in the U.S. is the Current Population Survey (CPS). This survey is administered by the Census Bureau and is based on interviews with adults living in more than 50,000 households each month. The survey collects detailed information about the current employment situation of the adult members in the household, including a job description (if they are employed), the employer's industry, and the number of hours worked. These numbers are used to calculate the national unemployment rate figures released by the federal government. Each March the standard CPS questionnaire is supplemented by additional questions which collects information about each adult's employment during the previous calendar year, including total earnings. The data from these March CPS surveys is most commonly used to analyze changes in the U.S. labor market.

One of the most important pieces of information collected – at least from an economist's point of view – is the description of each person's job. Based on this description, analysts categorize each worker as being in one of approximately 500 detailed occupations.[10] These detailed occupations help

10 Some examples of the 500 detailed occupations: financial managers, construction inspectors, aerospace engineers, physicians, economics teachers, elementary school teachers, photographers,

define unique labor markets. Unfortunately, in 1982–83 the Census Bureau dramatically changed the definitions of most of the 500 categories. For example, of all the individuals categorized as "economists" under the old system, 72 percent would still be classified as economists under the new system. Of the other 28 percent, about half would be classified as "management analysts" and half as "accountants and auditors". For individuals categorized as "jewelers and watchmakers" under the pre-1982–83 system, 50 percent would be "camera, watch, and musical instrument repairers" while 41 percent would be "precious stones and metals workers". The other nine percent are scattered across three other categories.[11]

Although this well-publicized change in classification was meant to improve information about the details of the U.S. labor market, it introduced serious comparability issues. It is difficult, if not impossible, to track employment, unemployment, and wages for any particular detailed occupation from 1970 through 1996 because the definition of most detailed occupations has changed. This has forced economists to rely heavily on aggregate labor market data when analyzing the trends of the last 30 years. Not surprisingly aggregate labor market data make it difficult to discern movements across occupations, which we find to be so important.

How did we circumvent this difficulty? We acquired a very detailed set of statistical estimates made by a team of economists and statisticians at the Census Bureau for the purpose of estimating a set of most likely post-1982–83 occupations for any individual in a pre-1982–83 sample. These estimates were based upon a set of observations from the 1970 Census which were analyzed again by the Census Bureau in the 1980s to assign each working individual a post-1982–83 occupation code to go with their pre-1982–83 code. An enormous statistical model was then estimated from this double-coded sample. The model uses a wide range of data about pre-1982–83 workers – their original occupation category, the industry of their employer, their earnings, their hours of work, their age, gender, and race, the region of the country they live in, and a few other factors – to generate a set of probabilities about which post-1982/83 occupation they should be assigned. For those with considerable patience, we present the details in appendix 3.1.

Using this model and these estimates, we were able to generate a set of most likely post-1982–83 occupations for every individual in every CPS

licensed practical nurses, motor vehicle and boat sales workers, secretaries, postal service mail carriers, police and detectives in public service, bartenders, farm workers, automobile mechanics, carpenters, dressmakers, bakers, punching and stamping press machine operators, laundering and dry cleaning machine operators, production testers, bus drivers, crane and tower operators, construction laborers, stock handlers and baggers.

11   For more examples, see U.S. Department of Commerce, Census Bureau (1989).

before 1982 – a major task. After doing so, we created a consistent series of data for 500 different occupations from 1970 through 1996 incuding employment, unemployment, average hourly wages, and average education levels. Our data series make it possible, for the first time, to track the economics of individual occupations over this entire time period.

The second unique data set used in our study is the National Adult Literacy Survey, a massive 1992 survey administered to a cross-section of U.S. adults to determine their ability to read, write, and perform arithmetic operations used to solve problems of everyday life.[12] We discuss this database in considerable detail in Chapter 2. This database was used to derive measures of functional literacy, which provide us with key information about individuals and various subgroups in the labor force such as those who are jobless, or workers employed in particular occupations. This database, which is only beginning to be used by economists, allows us to separate the different effects of literacy and education, and to match both with occupation.

We derived our measure of cognitive skills from this database for several reasons. First, the survey focuses on what we believe to be critical cognitive skills for holding jobs in a modern industrial economy. In recent years these skills have received increasing media attention, particularly in the aftermath of low U.S. student scores recorded for international standardized tests. Of course, other cognitive skills are important in performing various occupations, but we have chosen to focus on what we believe to be the most important. Second, the survey contains valuable economic data about the respondents, including detailed occupational and industrial information. This allows us to link the results to information about the labor force gleaned from the Current Population Survey. Third, the sample is large and is nationally representative when we use the weights supplied in the survey results. These factors enable us to consider a broader number of subgroups than can be examined in other studies. Finally, we are using a measure that is not inherent in the genes of individuals, but is a function of the quantity and quality of education they have experienced. In short, policy measures can be taken to improve such skills.

We also draw upon other standard databases. For those interested, we describe all of the sources and our various estimation techniques in excruciating detail in various appendices.

Final Observations

In the final chapter we turn to two remaining tasks. First, we examine whether the labor market mechanisms that have operated over the last

---

12 A key document describing this survey is by Kirsch, *et al.* (1993). In later chapters we describe this database in greater detail.

quarter century will continue in the future. For instance, the displacement mechanism of men by women arises from the increasing labor force participation rate of women. We provide evidence, however, that such a labor force phenomenon is slowly ending. In the future, the major share of rising employment rates among women will result from their rising levels of education, rather than from an increase in labor force participation independent of education.

We then look briefly at some policy implications. Since our conclusions about the determinants of joblessness are so unlike those of others, the policy conclusions that can be drawn from them are also quite different. Although the purpose of this book is analysis of causes rather than specification of corrective measures, we also show how many of the commonly-argued remedies for joblessness, if implemented, should turn out to be ineffective. We also discuss why creating jobs, the key to reducing joblessness, raises some unique difficulties.

The rising jobless rate among prime-age males represents a fundamental failure of the economic and educational systems. Such joblessness represents a powerfully destructive force to those unfortunate enough to find themselves involuntarily caught in this situation. When this phenomenon is combined with declining real wages for most male and female workers, dramatic increases in wage inequality, and unused skills, the situation is even worse.

If economic history in the late twentieth century proves that a centrally planned economic system does not work, then the economic history of the twenty-first century may make the same judgment on market economies unless we solve these problems. The first and most crucial step is to understand who is not employed and why. This is our purpose for writing this book.

CHAPTER 2

Cognitive Skills, Education, and Other Determinants of Employment

In this chapter we begin to present the empirical evidence to support the hypotheses described in Chapter 1. The starting point for our analysis is joblessness versus employment. What determines an individual's probability of obtaining employment? Is it race or ethnicity or education or cognitive skills? Why, for instance, is joblessness so much higher among African-American men than white men? Is it location? Why is joblessness higher in the center city than in rural areas? Is it parent's background – or age – or gender?

Although we cannot answer fully such questions, in this chapter we look behind the raw data presented in Chapter 1 to isolate the factors that determine an individual's probability of being employed. We look at all of the factors mentioned above, but our particular focus is on the impacts of cognitive skills and formal education, two factors that play crucial roles throughout the rest of this book. We show that our particular measure of cognitive skills – a person's average score on the National Adult Literacy Survey (NALS) – is partly related to years of formal education, but also has a strong independent component. We demonstrate how cognitive skills and years of education both have a separate and positive impact on a person's probability of being employed. Other things equal, a person with fewer cognitive skills is less likely to be employed. In later chapters we show how cognitive skills are related to other aspects of the labor market such as downward occupational mobility and wages.

In the last section of the chapter we also deal briefly with some problems occurring when measuring the educational level, since many people do not answer questions truthfully about their education when asked by employers or survey takers. We find that much of the criticism against the commonly used educational statistics is misdirected and that, for our purposes, the self-reported data on education are useful. Turning briefly to trends in education of the prime working-age population, we find a rapid upgrading of educational credentials over the last few decades. Nevertheless, this has not resulted in a rise in employment rates among men over time that we might expect from our statistical analysis of employment showing that, at a single point in time, employment rates rise with years of formal education.

Cognitive Skills and Functional Literacy:
An Overview

It is clear that general cognitive skills are developed over time and may be affected by many factors. Likely contributors include: years of formal education, quality of formal education, effort put forth by the student, education environment in the family, and native intelligence. Since our focus here is on employment, we are interested in the specific set of cognitive skills useful for obtaining and holding a job. We believe that this set of skills is well proxied by a recent test of "functional literacy" developed by the Educational Testing Service (ETS), and utilized as part of the National Adult Literacy Survey (NALS) of 1992.

In the first section below, we discuss various tests of cognitive skills and why we believe the ETS-designed test of functional literacy is the most appropriate measure for the study of employment. Then we explore the determinants of functional literacy, showing that it is correlated not just to the level of formal education but also to race/ethnicity, gender, mother's education, and other factors.

What is Functional Literacy?

Many economic studies focusing on the determinants of employment or wages combine employment data over time with information about high-school grades or the results of standardized tests taken in high-school. Sometimes these studies look at employment of groups of people, using aggregative results from such tests as the National Assessment of Education Progress, the Iowa Test of Educational Development, and the Scholastic Aptitude Test. Other studies focus on the employment status of individuals and apply the results of such tests as the Armed Forces Qualification Test (AFQT), the Armed Services Vocational Aptitude Battery, the General Aptitude Test Battery, the Wechsler Adult Intelligence Scale, or the Raven Progressive Matrix Test.[1]

For the study of employment trends the use of these tests raises some difficulties. Most of these tests were taken before a person entered the labor force and, unfortunately, they provide no information about what knowledge or skills are retained in later life when employed. Further, in many cases not all

---

1   Hunt (1995) reviews many of these various tests, what they measure, and some of their correlates with performance.

groups of adult workers have taken these tests so they cannot be used to generalize about the population as a whole. Finally, these tests measure a variety of attributes ranging from general intelligence to very specific aptitudes that may have little to do with employment in general.

Lacking a battery of different test scores available for the population as a whole to use in determining their usefulness in predicting employment status, it is necessary to select the most appropriate test on some other basis. It seems to us that functional literacy, which is the ability to use reading, writing, and arithmetic skills in real-life situations, would yield the most useful information about the ability to obtain and maintain employment, particularly if it is measured at the same time that employment status is determined.

Fortunately, the results of such a test of functional literacy are available, namely the National Adult Literacy Survey (NALS). The Educational Testing Service administered this test in 1992 to a nationwide cross-section of the adult population which, unlike some other such surveys, includes high-school dropouts.[2] The questions are more open-ended than in standard multiple-choice tests; they cover a variety of contexts; and they focus on the skills necessary to carry out ordinary tasks requiring brief written and/or oral responses. The database containing the scores also includes sufficient information about various demographic and employment characteristics of the tested population so that information about functional literacy can be used to analyze employment, wages, occupational choice, and a variety of other economic questions. A major drawback of the survey is that it covers only one year, 1992, so that we must infer changes over time by looking at scores of different age groups, which is a tricky exercise.

The NALS tells us what adults can do with written information and distinguishes three scales of functional literacy.[3] Prose literacy comprises "the

2   Trained interviewers visited and administered the tests in the homes of the respondents, who were paid. The raw data of the NALS come from the National Center for Education Statistics, but they are not responsible for our use of their data. A similar type of test for functional literacy has been used in several previous studies, for instance, Kirsch and Jungeblut (1986) and Kirsch, Jungeblut, and Campbell (1992). Specialists at the Educational Testing Service, the organization which devised and carried out the NALS, tell us that the results of these previous tests cannot be easily compared with the NALS because of technical differences in the sampling procedures. A variant of this type of test has been used in an international comparison of functional literacy by the OECD (1995), and its scores are also not directly comparable with those of the NALS.
     We present a brief description of the NALS data in Appendix 2.1.
3   In this discussion we draw upon Campbell *et al.* (1992) and Kirsch *et al.* (1993). The NALS speaks only of "literacy" but we have added the modifier "functional" to distinguish this test from the old-fashioned literacy tests that focus only on the ability to read, rather than comprehension.

knowledge and skills needed to understand and use information from texts including (newspaper) editorials, news stories, poems, and fiction." One question, for example, requires the respondent to summarize the main argument from an op-ed article. Document literacy comprises "the knowledge and skills required to locate and use information contained in materials that include job applications, payroll forms, transportation schedules, maps, tables, and graphs." One question, for example, asks the respondent to complete an employment application and another requires the interpretation of a line graph. Finally, quantitative literacy comprises "the knowledge and skills required to apply arithmetic operations, either alone or sequentially, to numbers embedded in printed materials, such as to balance a checkbook, complete an order form, or calculate the amount of interest from a loan advertisement." One question, for example, asks the respondent to determine the cost of a particular meal, to calculate what change should be returned, and what a 10 percent tip should be. Many of the questions are, of course, more difficult. Nevertheless, it is depressing to see the low average scores recorded on these three scales.[4]

4   Given the high correlation between the three scales it seems legitimate to ask exactly what each scale is really measuring. We could argue that the skills of functional literacy used in daily life are the same for prose as for quantitative problems, an approach that flies in the face of the common notion that quantitative skills are "different." We could also argue that all three scales really measure something more basic.

We have our doubts that the NALS measures innate intelligence *per se*. Underlying our considerations is the reasonable assumption that average intelligence is roughly the same in the industrialized nations in which NALS-type literacy tests were given. The fact that many nations with lower average schooling than the U.S. scored considerably higher in such tests suggests that not just the quantity, but the quality of schooling are the crucial variables underlying differences in the NALS scores. Of course, on an individual basis people with higher innate intelligence could score higher with fewer years of education because they would learn more quickly. Additionally, general attitudes toward literacy skills taught in school influence the NALS scores.

An even more subtle problem of interpretation also arises. Those constructing the test tried to include only those problems relating to everyday situations. Some argue, however, that pencil and paper tests do not measure many of the skills used in everyday life since competency in such skills are based on "field-methods" or "methods-derived-from-context," rather than the type of learning acquired in school. For instance, Lave (1988) reports her experiments showing no significant correlation between performance in solving pencil-and-paper "best-buy problems" and performance in solving "best-buy problems" when the respondents are actually shopping in a supermarket (p. 57). She also cites a considerable literature providing other instances where those skillful in solving everyday math problems performed poorly on pencil-and-paper tests with questions focusing on the same types of problems.

It could be argued that employment status is directly related to functional literacy as measured in the NALS study, if it were necessary to pass a certain pencil-and-paper test to obtain a job. If this conjecture is true, we would have to modify our interpretations of Tables 2.3 and 2.4.

A much more important consideration, however, is that literacy skills measured by the NALS are directly related to job performance when the nature of the work is sufficiently varied or

Although these prose, document, and quantitative scales are different, the scores of the individual respondents along these three scales turn out to be highly correlated: More specifically, all these correlation coefficients of the scores of the three scales are 0.84 or above. Moreover, regressions linking the scores of the three functional literacy scales to the same explanatory variables yield roughly the same results. For simplicity, therefore, we use the average of the scores along these three scales as our variable, rather than the scores on the individual scales.

Levels of Functional Literacy

Table 2.1 presents some weighted averages of the functional literacy scores of men and women by level of education. Such data yield two immediate conclusions.

• The averages are low and hardly seem consistent with active participation in the heralded "information age." For instance, roughly 40 percent of prime working-age Americans cannot interpret instructions from a simple appliance warranty, take and use information from a bar graph depicting source of energy and year, or calculate the total costs of purchased items from an order form in a catalogue. Only about five percent can compare two metaphors used in a poem, use information in a table to complete a graph, or determine total costs including shipping on an order form for items in a catalogue.[5] These low average scores should not be surprising because American school children have scored lower on standardized tests than those of most industrialized nations for many years. Although such examinations are different from the functional literacy test, these results tell us something depressing about the relative quality of American schooling and we should not be startled at the low functional literacy skills that these students carry over to the work place in their adult life.

International comparisons of functional literacy are only beginning. For instance, according to a seven-nation functional literacy study by the OECD, a higher percentage of American adults scored lower than 225 in the documentary and quantitative tests than any other nation except Poland.[6] The United States did rank somewhat better in the percent of adult scoring above 325.

changing so that the employee does not have time to develop "field-methods" for solving the problems at hand. It is the relation between these vital literacy skills in a changing world and job performance that is the focus of our analysis.

5   These results are drawn from various tables in Kirsch *et al.* (1993) and refer to the population from 25 through 54.

6   OECD (1995). According to newspaper reports (for instance, Simon (1995)), the study originally included more nations. For unknown reasons Ireland participated in some manner, but no results for that nation are included. The French actually carried out the study but its government

Table 2.1: *Functional Literacy Scores of the Prime-Age Population by Education in 1992*

Scale	Men				Women			
	Prose	Document	Quantitative	Average	Prose	Document	Quantitative	Average
Highest level of education								
High-school dropout	235	236	237	236	239	238	231	236
GED (high-school equivalency)	272	271	277	273	281	277	275	278
High-school diploma	275	274	283	278	282	275	277	278
Trade/vocational school	288	291	295	291	288	285	286	286
Some university	305	305	311	307	310	303	305	306
B.A. or B.S.	331	325	335	330	333	323	325	327
Graduate degree	345	340	347	344	342	334	335	337
Total	295	293	300	296	296	290	290	292

category includes those with some graduate training, but without a graduate degree. For each scale the following descriptions give some idea about what level of literacy the scores indicate.

Prose skills on NALS scale. Prose scale 225: Underline meaning of a term given in a government brochure on supplemental social security income. Prose scale 275: Interpret instructions from an appliance warranty. Prose scale 374: Compare two metaphors in a poem.

Document skills on NALS scale. Document scale 230: Locate intersection on a street map. Document scale 277: Identify information from a bar graph depicting source of energy and year. Document scale 378: Use information in a table to complete a graph including labeling axes.

Quantitative skills on NALS scale. Quantitative scale 238: Calculate postage and fees for certified mail. Quantitative scale 278: Use a calculator to determine difference between regular and sale price from an advertisement. Quantitative scale 383: Determine shipping and total costs on an order form for items in a catalog.

For the sample of 13,889 observations, the weighted standard deviations range from 64 to 67. For the two sexes the standard deviations range from 66 to 70 for men and from 62 to 65 for women. We have included in the averages only the scores of completed tests.

Depending on the scale, however, nine to sixteen percent more Swedish adults than Americans achieved scores higher than 325. We know, of course, that a higher percent of Americans have university degrees and we believe that the average degree of native intelligence is not greatly different in the two countries. Therefore, it seems likely that the difference in the quality of primary and secondary education in the two countries, combined with differences in student motivation and informal learning at home, underlie the contrasts in functional literacy between Swedes and Americans. The importance of the quality of formal education must always be kept in mind in interpreting differences between racial groups in America.

• As we might expect, the degree of functional literacy is directly related to the highest level of formal education obtained. Among the less-educated, which this study defines as a person with a high-school diploma or less, high-school dropouts scored dramatically lower than those with a high-school diploma or its equivalent. Further, women scored slightly higher than men on the prose and document scales, but not on the quantitative scale. These differences in the prose and document scales are more marked in the regression analysis when other determinants are held constant. They are also of crucial importance in determining who obtains the low-level clerical jobs that are available in the central cities of most metropolitan areas.[7] With respect to functional literacy, the GED and the regular high-school degree are roughly equivalent, a phenomenon explored in greater detail below.

The Determinants of Functional Literacy

Given the present state of knowledge, we can specify the determinants of an indiviual's functional literacy only on an intuitive basis. We clear-

refused to allow its results to be released with those of the other nations. This may be related to the fact that French adults scored only marginally better than Poles and were second from the bottom. Claude Thélot, a director of the French Ministry of Education, said that the tests, which were quite similar in design to those used in the NALS, were invalid because they were influenced by "Anglo-Saxon culture." This decision later unleashed a furor in France (*Le Monde,* January 24, 1997).

An example of the relative performance of U.S. school children is shown in U.S. Department of Education (1993), p. 54, which shows 13-year-old children in the U.S. scoring second to last of 15 nations participating in an internationally standardized mathematics test. Hanushek and Kim (1995) summarize a variety of international studies of primary and secondary pupils by the International Association for the Evaluation of Educational Achievement (IEA) and the International Assessment of Educational Progress (IAEP). According to the different ways they make their estimates, the U.S. pupils rank 42 out of 87, 43 out of 90, or 22 out of 27 in the achievement tests.

7   The need for these skills in the central city is documented by Holzer (1996), who surveyed employers on these matters.

ly need to include as explanatory variables such basic demographic variables as education, gender, race/ethnicity, and age. Such variables, we must be quick to add, are not necessarily causally related but are proxies for variables more difficult to measure. The race/ethnicity variables are defined as: non-Hispanic white, non-Hispanic black, Hispanic, and "other," a small and heterogeneous category that includes Native Americans, Aleuts, Eskimos, Pacific Islanders, Asians and those of mixed race. Other obvious variables correlated with functional literacy are place of birth (in the U.S.A. or abroad), region of residence, and parents' educational background. For instance, although the scores of a particular ethnic group might be lower, this might be attributable to a lower degree of education of the parents of these people, rather than to their ethnicity *per se*. Although family background variables obviously play an important role in determining a person's functional literacy, we are unfortunately limited in our exploration of these matters by the paucity of such information in the data set.

The exact formula or functional form of the relation between particular casual variables and functional literacy scores is unclear. To sidestep these specification problems, we express each variable or characteristic as a set of alternative categories. For instance, instead of using years of education completed as a variable, we divide people into six discrete education categories.

Table 2.2 presents the results of this calculation. The variable to be explained is the average functional literacy score, which combines the prose, document, and quantitative scores of each person in the sample. The sample size is large and the explanatory variables account for about 46 percent of the variation in these test scores, a highly respectable degreee of explanatory power for cross-section regressions of this type.

This type of approach requires us to select one category within each set of alternatives to use as the basis of compairsion for the other categories in the set. Then, the impact of each alternatives is measured relative to the impact of the reference category. For instance, in the set of alternatives referring to educational level, having a high-school diploma and no additional education is the reference category. The calculated coefficient of -32.17 for the high-school dropout indicates that such a person would typically score 32.17 points less on the NALS than a person with just a high-school diploma.

The level of functional literacy is related, as expected, to the highest level of formal education, with high-school dropouts scoring the lowest and those with at least one graduate degree scoring the highest. Except for those with a GED, who do not score significantly differently from those with a regular high-school diploma, all of the calculated regression coefficients are statistically significant. This result parallels a similar conclusion of others.[8] As we show below, however, this does not mean that those with a GED have similar

---

8   Kaplan and Venezky (1993) use the same database and obtain roughly similar results. Experi-

Table 2.2: *Explaining Average Literacy Test Results of Individuals in the Prime Working-Age Population in 1992*

	Calculated coefficients	Standard errors
Dependent variable = average of scores on the three NALS scales		
Intercept	+286.47*	1.41
Highest educational level: High-school diploma is basis of comparison		
High-school dropout	-32.17*	1.23
GED (high-school equivalency)	-1.18	1.80
Trade or vocational school	+8.29*	1.48
Some university	+24.95*	0.96
B.A./B.S.	+44.35*	1.07
At least one graduate degree	+55.99*	1.38
Gender (female = 1; male = 0)	-0.10	0.68
Race/ethnicity variables: White, non-Hispanic is the basis of comparison		
Black, non-Hispanic	-39.28*	1.17
Hispanic	-24.36*	1.43
Other races/ethnicities	-21.83*	2.11
Place of birth (foreign born = 1, native born = 0)	-19.54*	1.48
Highest education of mother: High-school diploma is the basis of comparison		
High-school dropout	-7.97*	0.85
Some university	+6.69*	1.04
At least one university degree	+4.25*	1.15
Region of residence: Northeast is the basis of comparison		
South	+0.095	0.968
Midwest	+2.93*	1.04
West	+6.26*	1.07
Live in metropolitan area (1= yes; 0 = no)	+1.42	0.84
Age: 25–29 is the basis of comparison		
30-34	-0.49	1.03
35-39	+3.03*	1.01
40-44	+0.63	1.08
45-49	-3.35*	1.15
Adjusted coefficient of determination	.4606	
Sample size	11,721	

Notes: An asterisk denotes statistical significance at the .05 level. The trade and vocational school training is after high-school. The calculated coefficients indicate the impact on the functional literacy scores when the explanatory variable changes from 0 to 1. The weighted mean of the scores is 297.4 and the weighted standard deviation is 49.65. Both the average and the standard deviation are smaller than in other regressions reported below because a number of cases were omitted, a situation arising because data on mother's education were not available in a number of cases. The data come from the National Adult Literacy Survey. The observations are weighted by the population weights provided in the sample, although the results from unweighted regressions are not much different.

employment rates. Although those taking additional education after high-school in trade or vocational schools score higher on the average than those with just a high-school education, we must not interpret this result to mean they receive higher wages than someone with only a high-school diploma.

Of the different independent variables, education is the single most important in explaining functional literacy. To gain a rough idea of this effect, we can calculate two additional regressions, the first using only the education categories as independent variables, and the second using all but the education variables. In the former the coefficient of determination, which represents the explanatory power of the regression, is 0.35; in the latter, 0.25.

The results show that for the sample as a whole, the differences in test scores of men and women are not statistically significant. By recalculating the regression with dummy variables indicating gender, education, and race, we find that both white and black women with a high-school diploma or less have an average score higher than men, other factors remaining the same. The data presented in Table 2.1, which do not hold all other factors constant, only hint at this result. This conclusion provides one important clue for explaining why less-educated women seem to be replacing men with the same education in the labor force, a phenomenon we explore in detail in Chapter 6.

The race/ethnicity variables are statistically significant determinants of functional literacy. Although the respondents self-identified their race/ethnicity, the interviewer made the final determination. Since a special dummy variable for whether the person was born abroad is held constant, the results for Hispanics cannot be attributed to place of birth.

Other things being equal, non-Hispanic blacks score about three fifths of a standard deviation below non-Hispanic whites. This difference is considerably smaller than the results from the Armed Forces Qualification Test (AFQT), where, according to Neal and Johnson (1996), blacks score about a standard deviation below whites. The gap in functional literacy between blacks and whites is also roughly the same at all educational levels.[9]

We can only speculate about the causes of these racial/ethnic differences since little direct evidence is available. Several possible explanations come to mind: (a) The quality of schooling received by many African-Americans living in central cities is worse than whites in the suburbs. As noted above, school

mentation with various functional forms of this regression make little difference to the major conclusions. Kaplan and Venezky also review the work of Cameron and Heckman (1993) and other studies in this literature. As shown in Tables 2.3 and 2.4, we find differences between employment rates of those with a regular high-school diploma and with a GED, although this effect depends in part upon the specific sex-race/ethnic group under examination. In Chapter 5 (Table 5.3) we find no statistical difference in wages of those with a GED and those with a regular high-school diploma.

9   This result conflicts with O'Neill's (1990) calculations from the AFQT showing that the white/black gap in scores increased with a rising level of education.

quality factor helps to explain international differences in functional literacy between white Americans and Europeans. Although many argue that measurable differences in school quality have little impact on various types of test scores, several recent studies suggest that non-measured differences in high-schools may appear to have a significant impact.[10] (b) The fact that the tests are written in standard English that may not be spoken often in some homes of the minority population might also have an influence on the race/ethnicity differences in scores. (c) Inner-city African-Americans taking the test may have also been affected by adverse "neighborhood-effects."[11] (d) In carrying out studies on racial differences, some have also found that test-stress is more serious among African-Americans than Whites.[12] (e) Finally, we might note that the degree to which the test itself contained some type of racial bias is not known, but it should be noted that the Educational Testing Service devised the test and they have some sensitivity to such issues.

Hispanics score slightly more than half a standard deviation below non-Hispanic whites, holding constant other factors including whether the person is foreign- or native-born. Since the "other race/ethnicity" group is quite heterogeneous and, moreover, is relatively small, the calculated coefficient has little meaning even though it is statistically significant. Those born abroad also have lower functional literacy, other things being equal, although this may be due to language difficulties.

In so far as both employment and wages are related to functional literacy, part of the differences in average wages between members of different race/ethnic groups may be attributable to these differences in literacy of the group, rather than to discrimination or to social factors related to individuals. This conjecture receives statistical support in the discussion below.

10   Both Grogger (1996) and Betts (1996) find little impact on AFQT scores of such measurable indicators of the quality of schools attended by the test-takers such as teacher/student ratios or percentage of teachers with MAs. Grogger notes, however, that by placing dummy variables for specific schools (and by limiting the sample only to those where at least two people in the sample attended the same high-school), he has a significant increase in explanatory power. Betts also includes such dummy variables in his regressions, although the exact impact of these dummy variables on the coefficient of determination is not clear.

11   Both Betts (1994) and Grogger (1996) show that scores on the AFQT are inversely related to the percentage of minority students in the school attended by the subject. Neighborhood effects can have an influence through the impact both on attitudes toward school work in general and test-taking in particular.

12   For instance, Steele and Aronson (1995) show that among Stanford undergraduates taking a verbal ability test, African-American students who took the test under non-threatening conditions (for instance, they were told that the tests was to explore psychological factors in solving verbal problems or they were not asked to specify their race/ethnicity on the personal information form) did better than those who were told that the test measured ability or who were required to specify their race/ethnicity. Holding SAT scores constant, the differences between Whites and Blacks were much smaller or negligible under the first set of conditions than the second.

As noted above, background variables are important in determining attitudes toward school and the acquisition of functional literacy. Unfortunately, the sample has little such information except for the education of the mother or stepmother, and father or stepfather. It can be argued that the mother's influence on the functional literacy of the children is greater than the father's because she usually spends more time with them. Moreover, since it is more likely that children in single parent families live with their mother, the education of the father is irrelevant in many such cases. Indeed, in a considerable number of these cases, the education of the father is unknown. We focus, therefore, only on the education of the mother or stepmother as an explanatory variable.

Table 2.2 also shows this parental education variable has a small but significant influence on functional literacy. Curiously, those with mothers with some university education scored slightly higher than those with mothers with a university degree, although the difference is not very great.

The region of residence also has a small but significant impact. Other things held constant, those from the Midwest and West outscore those living in the Northeast and South. Although this probably reflects differences in the schooling systems, other causal factors may also be at work. In these calculations functional literacy is not significantly different for those living inside or outside metropolitan areas.

Finally, Table 2.2 shows several differences by age, although these age effects are small and irregular. Those between 35 and 39 score slightly but significantly higher than those between 25 and 29. By way of contrast those between 45 and 49 score slightly but significantly lower than those in their late twenties. None of the other age coefficients are significant.

These statistical results for the age variables suggest no marked long-term deterioration of the educational system. That is, if our calculations are correct, then despite the baneful influence of television and modern pop culture, Americans are not becoming more illiterate. Of course, their specific knowledge, work attitudes, or analytic skills not measured by the test might be changing, and these are not reflected in our data.

These results about the relation between age and functional literacy are quite different from those of others studies which suggest that cognitive skills should be higher for the cohort in their forties than in their thirties.[13] Differences from our results found by other researchers may arise from the fact that these other studies are based on tests of formal math skills given to young peo-

Like these Stanford undergraduates, those taking the NALS were paid. It is unclear, however, whether the "stereotype threat" analyzed by Steele and Aronson to account for the differences they found was as important, especially since the NALS was given to adults who were established in the labor force. The testing environment (see footnote 2) was also different.

13   The trends in SAT scores are well known, but, of course, a significant portion of the population does not take this test. Bishop (1991, Figure 5.1) presents data from the Iowa Test of Edu-

ple who were either in high school, or not many years beyond high school. By way of contrast, the NALS test was given to people of all ages and, in the quantitative part, presents real-life problems requiring simple mathematics and skills in quantitative inference. These skills, we believe, are more important indicators for a person's performance in the economy than the ability to solve standardized math problems. More indirect approaches for determining time trends in cognitive skills using data on wage differentials are also available, but they yield conflicting results.[14]

The key result of this analysis is that both education and race/ethnicity have separate impacts on functional literacy. Formal education is, however, the most important causal variable.

Some Limitations to the Analysis

The regression analysis carried out in Table 2.2 to isolate the determinants of functional literacy raises several methodological problems:[15]

First, because functional literacy might be correlated either with other cognitive abilities (e.g., general intelligence) or attitudes, the calculated coef-

cational Development, which is given to a broader group of the population (but excludes some high-school dropouts). These show a fall in high-school test scores starting in the mid 1960s (a cohort roughly 45 in 1992, when the NALS was given) and continuing until the late 1970s (a cohort roughly 30 in 1992), when it began to rise again. Using the results of a mathematics test given to respondents in two surveys (National Longitudinal Study of the High-school Class of 1972 and the High-school and Beyond), Murnane, Willett, and Levy (1995) show that the 1972 cohort of high-school graduates (who were 38 in 1992) had higher math scores than the 1980 cohort of high-school graduates (who were 30 years old in 1992). Contrary evidence is, however, available from the National Assessment of Educational Progress (for instance, Mullis, *et al.,* [1994] or NAEP data reported in Bureau of the Census (annual) showing little change in high-school scores in reading, writing, mathematics, and science over the past quarter-century. Reconciling these conflicting time-series results with our cross-section results is difficult and a complete analysis of the problem would raise some fascinating issues.

14   If wages reflect in part how much people have learned in school, then we might indirectly approach the problem of the declining educational quality by looking at wage differentials between those with different education and experience. Unfortunately, various studies of such wage differentials do not hold enough factors constant to exclude vintage-effects (the supply and demand situation for people with different education at specific times) and other statistical nightmares. As a result, studies presenting relevant data on such matters, for instance, Blackburn, Bloom, and Freeman (1990), Juhn, Murphy, and Pierce (1993), Katz and Murphy (1992), Kosters (1991), Murphy and Welch (1992) and Pierce and Welch (1994) yield quite different conclusions about trends in cognitive skills. As Gary Burtless (1991) ruefully observes, "Drawing strong inferences about (changes in) the quality of schooling from time series data on relative wages is difficult."

15   This exercise is similar to those designed to explain the scores of the Armed Forces Qualifi-

ficients might be biased ("omitted variable bias"). That is, the calculated coefficients reflect not just the role of the corresponding variables on functional literacy, but also the indirect effect of these omitted variables on the other causal variables correlated with functional literacy. Because we have neither a theory nor the data to tell us how to separate the impact of these different cognitive abilities and attitudes, we cannot make appropriate corrections and instead, simply calculate a reduced form model that shows the total effect – direct and indirect – of education on functional literacy, while leaving the mechanism a bit uncertain.

Second, certain problems about the direction of causality arise. For instance, functional literacy may determine what type of occupation a person can pursue which, in turn, may have an impact on that person's functional literacy. Farm hands have, for example, little opportunity to exercise and improve their literacy skills. We have tried to circumvent this problem by omitting those independent variables where causal relations can run in both directions although, we must add, experiments that included these variables did not greatly change the results. Although some endogeneity exists for the schooling variables (that is, high functional literacy is both a result and a cause of the higher levels of achieved education), we do not believe that the causation running from functional literacy to education is very strong. After all, many primary and secondary schools often promote students to higher levels who have not mastered the materials of the previous class level. We might add that 15 to 20 percent of those graduating from a four-year university score in the lowest 40 percentiles of the various functional literacy scales, which hardly indicate that high functional literacy is necessary to graduate from even a university.[16]

In sum, we do not believe that such problems prevent us from gaining important insights about employment and wages when using functional literacy scores as one of the explanatory variables. So let us turn first to employment; we analyze the impact of functional literacy on wages in Chapters 5 and 6.

Statistical Analysis of Determinants of Employment

We can now get to the heart of the employment/joblessness problem. The first step is to present data showing the relationship of employment status to functional literacy, education, and gender without holding any other factors constant. Then we carry out a regression analysis to investigate the separate impact of these and other underlying causal factors.

cation Test, for instance, the study by Neal and Johnson (1996).
16   The data underlying this statement come from Kirsch, *et al.*, (1995), pp. 116-8.

Functional Literacy Scores and Employment

Table 2.3 reports data on average literacy test scores by employment status, education and gender. Several conclusions immediately follow from these results.

Most importantly, employed men scored higher than unemployed men, who in turn scored higher than those out of the labor force. Further, men with full-time employment had higher functional literacy than those with part-time work. The underlying causality, however, is uncertain: That is, it is unclear whether low functional literacy is the reason why certain men are not employed, or whether a situation of less than full-time employment leads to a loss of functional literacy (a use-it-or-lose-it approach to human capital). On the surface, the former explanation seems more likely, but the evidence available to us does not allow a definite conclusion to be drawn.

For women the comparisons between functional literacy scores of those with different labor force situations are somewhat different from those for men. The unemployed also scored lower than the employed. Those out of the labor force, however, scored higher than the unemployed; and those working part-time had roughly the same degree of functional literacy as those with full-time jobs. Of course, this is because many prime-age women take part-time employment or are out of the labor force for reasons of child care, a factor having little to do with their functional literacy or employability.

In comparing the results between men and women, the results of those with full-time employment are roughly the same at each level of education. For cases other than full-time employment among the less-educated – those with a high-school diploma or less – an important difference occurs. In most employment categories among the less-educated the functional literacy of women is higher than for men.[17] Since employers can test functional literacy, it seems likely that such literacy in part determines one's place in the queue for employment. As a result, less-educated men stand more toward the end of the line than women. In later chapters we present considerable evidence of head-to-head competition for jobs among men and women with the same education. This difference in functional literacy skills among those with less education who are not working is undoubtedly an important factor why women at this educational level are replacing males in a variety of jobs, and why the rate of non-employment among less-educated men has been rising in the last quarter-century.

17 The two exceptions are the unemployed with a high-school diploma or the equivalent (GED).

Table 2.3: *Functional Literacy, Employment Status, and Education of the Prime Working-Age Population in 1992*

Average of the three functional literacy scores:

Highest level of education	Men Employed Full-time	Part-time	Unemployed	Not in labor force	Women Employed Full-time	Part-time	Unemployed	Not in labor force
High-school dropout	243	218	228	208	244	249	235	226
GED (High-school equivalency)	275	278	264	266	282	282	257	278
High-school diploma	280	261	268	264	282	283	253	276
Trade/vocational school	296	275	271	238	292	295	275	272
Some university	308	315	296	294	308	311	285	303
B.A. or B.S.	332	317	331	301	328	334	322	321
Graduate degree	346	348	297	297	339	343	317	322
All	302	276	271	263	300	300	264	276

Notes: The various samples for the GED scores are small. All averages are weighted. The underlying data come from the National Adult Literacy Survey.

Determinants of Employment

By employment status we mean the employment situation (full- or part-time) of the respondents during the week preceding the survey. We select the distinction "working" and "not-working," rather than the more usual distinctions between employed and unemployed or between those in and out of the labor force because it seems conceptually more appropriate for our purposes, especially with regard for prime-age men. Furthermore, our distinction sidesteps the ambiguities in distinguishing between the unemployed and the persons out of the labor force.

The key questions we wish to explore are the separate impacts on employment status of cognitive skills and education. Such an exercise requires the use of a dummy variable indicating employment status and a logit regression technique (where the variable to be explained has a value of either zero or one). Since the coefficients of such regressions are difficult to interpret and because most of our explanatory variables are categorized variables, we present calculations of "partial discrete changes" instead. These indicate the changes in the probability of employment if, for one particular chartacteristic, a person's category is altered from the reference category to the alternative under examination, while holding all other characteristics at their mean values. We must emphasize that these are somewhat different from the more common "mean probability derivatives (MPDs)," which show the impact of a change in the employment probability of one particular independent variable is increased by one unit while all other independent variables are at their mean values.[18]

The determinants of employment are well known and require little explanation. To isolate different possible causal factors, we calculate the employment regressions separately for prime-age men and women.

The impact of functional literacy is particularly important to explore. If two persons with the same education, gender, race/ethnicity, and age are compet-

---

18   More exactly, the usual economic interpretation of the MPD with regard to X is the change in the dependent variable if all independent variables are at their mean value and if X is increased by one unit above its mean value. With multi-category dummy variables, however, it is problematic to interpret the regression coefficients directly by considering just a unit value change in one coefficient. For instance, looking at the coefficient for black, this would imply a movement from a situation where the sample averages are, say, black = 15 percent, other race/ethnicity = 5 percent, and, implicitly, white = 80 percent to black = 115 percent, other = 5 percent, and, implicitly, white = -20 percent.
Our statistic compares a movement from, say, black = 0, other = 0 (and implicitly white = 1) to black = 1, other = 0 (and, implicitly, white = 0). We interpret this as the change in probability that would occur if a white person, with the average non-racial characteristics of all persons, were changed to a black person, but still with the same other non-racial characteristics as before.

ing for a job, the one with the higher functional literacy is more likely to get the job if any type of written test is given. Moreover, such a person is more likely to retain the job if functional literacy is an important skill for success-fully fulfilling it. Although it seems clear that a person with lower functional literacy is more likely to stand toward the end of the job queue, the real question concerns the quantitative impact of this factor.[19]

Since more-educated people have a choice of a greater range of jobs than less-educated people, the probabilities of employment should rise with educa-tion. Those living in booming regions or in metropolitan areas should have greater job opportunities than those living in depressed areas or in small towns. Racial/ethnic biases can influence employment, despite fair employ-ment laws. For example, information about available jobs may vary by racial/ethnic group, as may location of residence and availability of transporta-tion. (We show in chapter 7, however, that the location effect is not very large.) Other characteristics varying by racial/ethnic group include unmea-sured attitudes toward work and the availability of unreported employment in the underground economy.

We also include a dummy variable indicating whether a person was born abroad. For this variable, however, prediction is difficult because several off-setting causal factors are at work. On the one hand, we would expect the for-eign-born to have a lower probability of employment because of their poorer knowledge of the English language. Moreover, their contacts or sources of information about the labor market may also be less than those of the native-born. On the other hand, many immigrants have arrived to take advantage of employment opportunities in the United States (and would search vigorously for jobs), so we would expect them to have a higher rate of employment. The data presented below suggest that the second set of considerations is slightly stronger.

Finally, some have argued that men living alone are less likely to be employed than married men while, on the other hand, the reverse would be true for women living alone. For this reason we include a variable indicating whether a person is unmarried and living alone.

In Table 2.4 we present the results of our statistical calculations showing the effects of the different explanatory variables on the probability of employ-

---

19 It is possible that some reverse causation exists, namely that actual employment leads to high-er functional literacy since such skills are honed and improved on the job. Although we do not believe this endogeneity to be very important, one way to explore such an effect would require taking into account the length of non-employment. A certain type of self-selection bias also occurs. Unfortunately, the NALS database does not include sufficient information to explore these matters.

The results that we obtain are quite similar in many respects to those of Rivera-Batiz (1995), who separately examined the impact of the prose and quantitative scales.

ment for men and women. Unfortunately, few regression studies of individual labor force or employment status we have seen have a high degree of explanatory power, and our regression results prove no exception.[20]

A key result for both men and women is that functional literacy has a positive and statistically significant impact on employment that is independent of formal education.[21] More exactly, if functional literacy is one standard deviation higher than the mean, men and women have respectively a 3.5 and 7.2 percent greater probability of employment.[22] The fact that the impact of functional literacy on employment is greater for women than for men is consistent with our results in Chapter 5 that wages are positively related to functional literacy, and with the well-established result that female labor supply is more sensitive to wage rates than male labor supply.

Table 2.4 shows that employment probabilities generally rise with the level of education, but the relationship is irregular. Of course, education has not only a direct effect when functional literacy is held constant, but also an indirect effect because it influences functional literacy (Table 2.2). When this is taken into account, the relationship between education and employment probabilities becomes more linear. Other things being equal (including functional literacy), high-school dropouts and those with a GED have lower employment probabilities than those with a high-school diploma who, in turn, have lower employment probabilities than those with a college degree. Attendance at a trade or vocational school has little impact in comparison to high-school graduates, and only women with some university training have significantly higher employment probabilities than those with just a high-school diploma.

Although most of these results seem intuitively plausible, the lower employment probabilities of those with a GED than those with a high-school

---

20   Another problem with the regression must be noted. The data refer to 1992 which was a year of mild recession, with the unemployment rate averaging 7.5 percent for the year. Although some of the calculated coefficients might be somewhat different in a more "typical" year, we are more interested in the causal relationships (whether a calculated coefficient is statistically significant), and these should be the same in most years.

21   At this point we must point out a possible case of two-way causation between employment and functional literacy that arises because certain companies provide educational programs to their employees which, in turn, might raise their functional literacy. Unfortunately, we do not have the proper data to take either this or other possible cases of endogeneity into account. Although we do not believe these relations to be quantitatively very important, we must note that in the case of functional literacy, the calculated coefficient linking it to employment may have an upward bias.

22   In interpreting this result, two offsetting biases in these coefficients must be noted. First, because the measurement of functional literacy is not perfectly correlated with actual functional literacy, the calculated coefficient for functional literacy in this regressions in Table 2.4 are understated. Second, because functional literacy may be correlated with other cognitive skills related to employment, the calculated coefficient for functional literacy may be overstated. Unfortunately, we have no way of knowing which bias is stronger, although we doubt whether either bias is very strong.

Table 2.4: *Partial Discrete Changes in Employment Probabilities (PDCEP) of the Prime Working-Age Population*

Dependent variable: Working (=1), not working (= 0)

	Calculated coefficients	
	Men	Women
	PDCEP	PDCEP
Literacy score (Change if scores are one standard deviation higher)	+3.5%*	+7.2%*
Highest educational achievement		
(high-school diploma is basis of comparison)		
High-school dropout	-5.0*	-12.6*
GED	-10.3*	-6.1*
Trade/vocational school	-2.6	+0.7
Some university	-1.4	+3.1*
B.A. or B.S.	+0.8	+3.5
At least one graduate degree	+6.3*	+13.1*
Race/ethnicity variables		
(White, non-Hispanic is basis of comparison)		
Black, non-Hispanic	-3.5*	-0.6
Hispanic	+1.7	+1.4
Other races/ethnicities	-3.5	-8.7*
Place of birth (foreign born = 1; native born = 0)	+1.7	+2.4
Region of residence (Northeast is basis of comparison)		
South	+4.5*	+3.2*
Mid-West	+3.1*	+4.5*
West	+1.2	+3.6*
Live in metropolitan area (yes = 1; no = 0)	-0.5	-1.1
Age (age 25-29 is the basis of comparison)		
Age 30-34	-0.4	+0.4
Age 35-39	-1.1	+2.4
Age 40-44	-1.9	+2.2
Age 45-49	-2.6*	+5.6*
Never-married person living alone (yes = 1, no = 0)	-6.1*	+12.0*
Pseudo R^2	.1049	.1109
Sample size	6085	7789

Notes: The coefficients represent the percentage change in the probability of employment if the dummy variable for the variable moves from 0 to 1 (or, for the literacy score coefficients, whether the variable changes one standard deviation). An asterisk designates statistical significance at the .05 level. For each block of variables, the "comparison variable" is designated.

These are weighted regressions with the population weights provided by the data set. The pseudo R^2 is the Nagelkerke adjusted generalized R^2 (SAS Institute, 1995). The data come from the 1992 National Adult Literacy Survey. NALS scores range from 0 to 500 with a mean of about 297 and a standard deviation of about 50.

diploma is surprising, especially since we hold functional literacy of the two groups constant and, on average, the two groups are roughly similar in this respect. It is possible employers might perceive – rightly or wrongly – that those with a GED are less satisfactory workers than those with a high-school diploma. Or those unable to obtain employment for reasons having little to do with their level of education might acquire a GED in the vain hope that this might help their employment chances. Or some with a GED might have earned this high-school equivalency credential in prison, and they might be disadvantaged in the job market as a result of this particular life-circumstance. Unfortunately, the NALS database does not permit further exploration of these or other conjectures.

The impact of race/ethnicity on employment probabilities depends upon gender. Among men, non-Hispanic Blacks have a 3.5 percentage point lower probability of employment than white non-Hispanics, a difference which is statistically significant. The differences in employment probabilities between other racial/ethnic groups and white, non-Hispanic are not significant. For women, by way of contrast, the race/ethnicity variables play no statistically significant role except for those of other races/ethnicities, a category so small and heterogenous that no meaningful conclusion can be drawn. These various conclusions are not novel and a number of other studies show similar results.

The impact of the other causal variables can be quickly summarized. Both men and women who are born abroad have slightly higher probabilities of employment, but the results are not statistically significant. This result has relevance to the debate about the impact of immigration and the common assertion that immigrants prefer to collect welfare, rather than work. For both men and women, most areas seem to offer greater employment possibilities than the Northeast. Surprisingly, living in a metropolitan area has no impact on the probabilities of employment.

For men between 25 and 49, age has no statistically significant impact on employment. It appears that their employment probabilities are roughly the same for prime-age workers of all ages. For women, by way of contrast, the probabilities of employment increase with age. Such a result undoubtedly reflects the fact that younger women are more likely to have pre-school children at home and, as a result, cannot easily accept employment.

Finally, unmarried men living alone (that is, without children or spouses) have a lower probability of (declared and gainful) employment than other men, a conclusion that confirms some sociological theorizing on these matters. For women, on the other hand, the reverse is true. We suspect this means men living alone are more likely to pursue non-conventional and alternative sources of income such as hustling or crime than women living alone, but without additional evidence we can only speculate.

To conclude this part of the analysis, several general remarks are in order. Most statistical studies of the determinants of employment do not have a variable reflecting functional literacy. Such an omission yields results indicating that employment is considerably more sensitive to education than our results, a phenomenon occurring because education and functional literacy are positively correlated.[23] Similarly, for men the race variable has a considerably larger effect on employment when functional literacy is omitted from the regression. For women, the partial discrete change coefficient of the race variable is actually negative, rather than positive. These results occur because in the regression omitting functional literacy, the race coefficient is partly picking up the effect of the lower functional literacy of certain race/ethnic groups. In other words, this missing variable problem biases the results and magnifies the impact of both education and race/ethnicity.

While this statistical exercise unearths a number of interesting and useful determinants of employment status, the two key conclusions for this study can be stated simply: First, functional literacy has an impact on the probabilities of employment independent of the level of formal education and a variety of other causal variables as well. For any given level of education, those with lower functional literacy are more likely to be toward the end of the job queue. Second, omission of functional literacy in analyzing the determinants of employment biases the calculated coefficients.

Trends in the Level of Formal Education of the Prime Working-Age Population

Given the importance of education as a determinant of employment, we need to have some idea of the trends in schooling. Although such data are readily available, certain problems of consistency and accuracy of the series arise, matters discussed in detail in Appendix 2.2. In this discussion we present some relevant data, discuss briefly their significance, and then identify an important inconsistency between these trends and our statistical results exploring the determinants of employment.

The Basic Data

Chart 2.1 shows the share of the non-institutionalized, civilian, prime working age population at different levels of education. As expected, the share

---

23 We present the results of calculations comparable to those in Table 2.4 but without the variable for cognitive skills in Appendix 2.3. These remarks summarize the major differnces between the two sets of calculations.

of those with a high-school diploma or less has declined steadily over the years. Conversely, the share of those with some college or a college degree has steadily increased. The zags in the series after 1992 arise from a slight change in the way the survey-takers asked the education question. For the use to which we apply the data, this should not make much difference.

The prime-age population has experienced an increase from an average of 12.0 years of education in 1971 to 13.6 years in 1994. This increase, however, has occurred at different rates among the various subgroups. In the mid 1960s and early 1970s white and black prime working-age men had a lower share of those with just a high-school diploma or less ("less education") than women. By 1994, however, white and black women caught up. In the mid 1960s whites had a lower share of those with less education than blacks. Although these shares declined for both groups, the percentage gap has remained. More details are supplied in a Table A2.1 in the appendices.

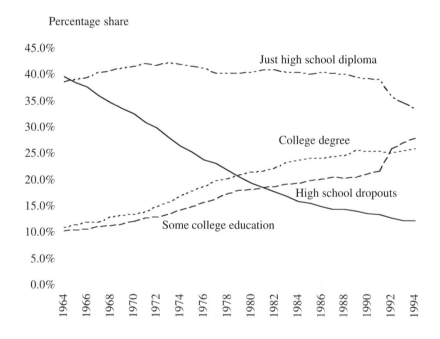

Chart 2.1: Prime working-age population by level of education.

Educational Ugrading and Upskilling

Much of the discussion in further chapters of this book deals with specific occupations and the relation between the education of the labor force and the educational requirements for the different occupations. For this discussion it is crucial to keep in mind several important distinctions.

• *Educational upgrading.* The educational requirements of many jobs seem to have increased, a phenomenon we call "educational upgrading" or just "upgrading." It is often argued that as a result of skill-biased technical change, many particular occupations require increasingly more knowledge and thus more education. If this occurs, we designate the phenomenon as "real" educational upgrading. Nevertheless, the average education of those in particular occupations may increase because of credential creep, a phenomenon independent of job performance or requirements. For instance, officials at a factory of Corning Inc. in Alfred, New York, recently announced that workers with just a high-school diploma will not even be considered for employment, regardless of what they know or can do (Wiegand, 1997). The average education in an occupation can also increase because of a general rise in the educational level of the labor force. We call these phenomena "pseudo" or "apparent" educational upgrading.

It is also possible that the structure of occupations has shifted toward those specific occupations requiring more education. We call this "structural" educational upgrading. To gain some idea about the magnitude of this change, it is useful to decompose the year-and-a-half increase in the average education of prime-age employed workers between 1971–72 and 1994–95. Looking at 500 different occupations and using a simple shift-share analysis, we find that educational upgrading *within* the different occupations was much more important than structural upgrading.[24] More specifically, the increase of the average level of education *within* the individual occupations accounted for 1.20 years, or 79.5 percent of the change in educational level. The structural change in occupations toward jobs requiring more education accounted for an increase of only 0.31 years of average education, or 20.5 percent of the total change. At this point, of course, it is unclear whether the increase of average education within occupations represents a real or a pseudo educational upgrading, but we leave this for discussion in the next chapter.

---

24 In this shift-share analysis we calculate the change in the average educational level occurring within individual occupations simply by assuming that the number of workers in each occupation in 1971–72 increased at the average rate for the whole sample. With these results for 1994–95 we then determined the "average education."

• *Upskilling.* The skill (or ability) requirements of many jobs seem to have increased, a phenomenon we refer to as "upskilling." It is increasingly claimed that, within many detailed occupations, skill-biased technical change has increased the demand for workers with higher skills, independent of their level of education. Upgrading of an occupation can occur without upskilling, especially where the job does not truly require more actual work skills, but the employer wants workers with higher educational credentials. Similarly, upskilling can occur without upgrading. For instance, employers may be increasing efforts to hire workers with problem-solving abilities or communication skills, independent of what they actually know, or their educational level. Although we can distinguish real, pseudo, and structural versions of upskilling, as defined above, in this essay we deal only with real upskilling.

Real educational upgrading and real upskilling are related when, with additional education, workers acquire additional skills that are necessary for the job. But jobs may change so that they require more functional literacy without any additional general knowledge, or the reverse. Although such polar cases may be rare, upskilling and real educational upgrading usually occur in different proportions in the various occupations and they should not be confused. Moreover, as we show in Tables 2.2 and 5.3, they have independent impacts on employment and wages.

We emphasize this distinction because, as we show in later chapters, the two concepts are particularly important in disentangling the different changes occurring in the labor markets at the top and bottom ends of the occupational ladder. For instance, in the next chapter we show that those occupations requiring the least education have not experienced much real educational upgrading or upskilling. By way of contrast, educational upgrading of many occupations at the top end has been slight, but the upskilling occurring in some of these occupations has been considerable. We provide more evidence of this in Chapter 5, and in Chapter 6 we show that such a change has led to increased wage differences across these high-end occupations.

An Apparent Contradiction Between Cross-Section and Time Series Results

Table 2.4, which focuses on the employment situation at a single point in time (1992), shows a positive relation between education and employment. Chart 2.1 shows an increasing level of education over time. We would, therefore, expect that employment levels should rise over time. But the data presented in Charts 1.1 and 1.2 in Chapter 1 (as well as the tables in Appendix A1.2) show, at least for men, that the situation is the reverse of what we would expect.

The resolution of this apparent contradiction, which is pursued in subsequent chapters, is complicated. In the next chapter we show that, contrary to the conventional wisdom, fewer jobs for prime-age workers with high levels of education have opened up than those possessing the requisite educational requirements. At the same time, more jobs have opened up for those with few educational qualifications than those workers having the corresponding level of education. As a result, an important downward occupational mobility has taken place, so that workers with more education are displacing those with less education. That is, these more-educated workers are holding jobs for which they are educationally overqualified and, as a result, much of the educational upgrading is apparent rather than real. A key mechanism underlying this movement is the displacement of male by female workers, a phenomenon we examine in Chapter 4.

Summary and Conclusions

From this study of employment status, several simple yet important conclusions can be drawn:

• Functional literacy is correlated with education, the educational background of a parent, residence in certain regions or in metropolitan areas, and immigrant status. Among those with a high-school education or less, women usually have higher functional literacy along the prose and document scales; the picture is mixed along the quantitative scale.

• In comparing different age cohorts and holding other factors constant, no marked trends in functional literacy are apparent.

• Holding education constant, functional literacy among men in the prime working-ages is strongly correlated with employment status. Those with full-time jobs have higher functional literacy than the unemployed, who have higher functional literacy than those not in the labor force. Although employed women have higher functional literacy than those who are not employed, the scores of the unemployed are lower than the scores of those not in the labor force.

• Although they are correlated, functional literacy and education have independent influences on employment status. In later chapters we show that this is also true for the choice of occupation, and weekly wages.

• Once functional literacy is held constant, the independent impact of race on employment is considerably reduced. It is the schooling process leading to the acquisition of functional literacy that is the key policy variable. Since functional literacy skills can be learned, we are not talking about innate intelligence.

• Other variables influencing employment are education, region, age, and whether a person is an immigrant.

• The highest level of formal education of those in the prime working-ages has steadily increased between 1964 and 1995. For whites, educational levels of men and women have converged and in the mid 1990s are essentially the same. For African-Americans, women have caught up and by the mid 1990s surpassed men in their average level of education.

This type of analysis approaches the problem from the supply side. It does not tell us anything about the demand for the various skills of job seekers or the manner in which these determinants of employment actually play out in the labor market. These are topics pursued in the following chapters.

CHAPTER 3

Upskilling and Educational Upgrading of Occupations

The previous chapter focuses on the supply side of the labor market; in this chapter we begin to discuss the demand side. Much of our analysis here is about the ability, skill, and knowledge "requirements" of particular jobs. In particular, what are the requirements of existing jobs? How have these changed over the past quarter-century? Have the requirements of less-skilled jobs increased, making it difficult for less-educated persons to satisfy them? Have the requirements of more-skilled jobs also increased, making advanced training and high-skill levels more important than ever?

These questions do not seem difficult to answer. Certainly most discussions in the popular press suggest that the answer to the last two questions is "yes." In other words, the assumption is made that it has become more difficult for less-educated persons to meet the requirements for less-skilled jobs, and for more-educated persons to meet the requirements for more-skilled jobs. Thus, it is essential that everyone should acquire more education and skills than in previous generations. Those who do not are likely to be jobless, underemployed, or working for very low wages. According to this view, it is not surprising that high-school dropouts have such a high jobless rate. The solution to this problem is to encourage more education and training. The empirical analysis in this chapter, however, shows that there are some fatal flaws in this argument.

In the first section we present data supporting a key finding of this book – one that immediately challenges the standard story. We use our unique CPS data set on detailed occupations to show that the number of jobs requiring relatively low levels of education has increased considerably faster than has the number of prime-age persons with the corresponding low educational levels. At the same time, the number of jobs requiring high educational credentials has increased more slowly than has the number of prime-age persons with the corresponding high educational levels. As a result, downward occupational mobility has occurred.

In the second section we explore two questions raised by this surprising finding. First, could these results be due to an upskilling of individual occupations, rather than a shift in the occupational structure? Our evidence suggests that this structural effect has not been critically important. Second, to what degree has the shift in the occupational structure been tied not just to higher educational requirements but also to higher skills in other areas as well? We use several databases to attack this question.

The third section provides a case study of the downward occupational mobility discussed above, namely college-educated workers taking "high-school jobs." We document this phenomenon and show that it is those college-educated workers with functional literacy little better than the average high-school graduates who end up in these lower-level jobs.

In the final section we examine some of the implications of our findings on a more microeconomic basis. In particular, we look at the impact of these aggregate trends for individual groups of occupations. We also explore how our results suggesting a surplus of skilled workers can be reconciled with the complaints of many corporate executives that they cannot find high-skilled workers to hire.

The Myth of the Disappearance of Low-Skilled Jobs

The most difficult aspect of analyzing the demand for low- and high-skill workers is in determining which jobs should be considered low-skill and which high-skill. Most previous work in this area attempts to divide jobs into two or three "skill" categories by grouping detailed occupations into high-skill and low-skill groups. The basis for this grouping is usually a subjective analysis of the amount and kinds of education and training involved in preparing for a job in a particular occupation. Because of our unique CPS data set on detailed occupations and the characteristics of the people in them, we have the possibility of defining our skill categories in a more objective way.[1] In particular, we group all of the 500 detailed occupations into four large categories, or tiers, based on the "educational intensity" of each occupation. We define the educational intensity of an occupation as the average years of formal schooling completed by prime working-age persons in that occupation in a given year.

There are advantages and disadvantages to this approach. The main disadvantage is that we have data only on years of formal education with no data on

---

1   The sophisticated BLS methodology we use for ensuring that the detailed occupation categories are comparable over the entire 1971 through 1997 period has been mentioned earlier. Many of the details are discussed in Appendix 3.1.

There is no way to test statistically the validity of this imputation methodology outside of the double-coded sample used to developed it. However, before using the imputed data, we looked carefully at the time-series characteristics of each detailed occupation over time, (especially between 1982 and 1983) and saw no signs of the discontinuities which would appear if the imputation method was faulty. Our extensive work with the data in preparing this book has also revealed no abnormalities and has strengthened our belief that the imputation methodology works well.

years of informal or on-the-job training. Thus, our approach focuses on only one of the factors that relate to the skill requirements of an occupation.[2] The main advantage is that our groupings are determined empirically. If the average years of formal education in a particular occupation is high, then it belongs to the same group as other occupations with highly-educated workers. This allows us to analyze more clearly such questions as: Do some occupations have higher average levels of education today than in 1970? Has the relative ranking of occupations by education intensity changed over the last quarter-century? Do changes in the education intensity of an occupation necessarily translate into changes in the requirements of jobs in that occupation?

The empirical implementation of these definitions is hindered by the standard-base-year problem. Since the education intensity of most occupations changes over time, which year's numbers should determine the four broad categories or tiers? After some experimentation, we settled on using the data from the beginning of our time period, 1971 and 1972 (an average for two years is taken to increase the size of the sample). Tier 4 designates those occupations where the average level of education of employed, prime-age workers in 1971 and 1972 is greater than 14.5 years. Tier 1 designates those occupations where the educational intensity in 1971 and 1972 is 10.5 years or less. Tiers 2 and 3 designate occupations with intermediate educational intensities.

How does the choice of base year influence our results? The answer to this involves an important empirical result: the ranking of 500 detailed occupations by education intensity in 1995/96 is very similar to the ranking in 1971–72. In fact, once we define our four tiers based on the numbers from 1971 and 1972, we find that 73 percent of the detailed occupations remain in the same tier in 1995 and 1996. The other 27 percent of the detailed occupations move up or down by one tier. The largest movement is between the less education-intensive tiers – 1 and 2. The least movement is between the most education-intensive tiers – 3 and 4. Most of the detailed occupations that switched tiers over this time period were near the border between two tiers initially, and crossed over to just on the other side.[3] This remarkable stability in relative levels of education-intensity levels over a quarter century occurred when average educational levels changed markedly. This points to a fairly inflexible, hierarchical aspect of the U.S. labor market, a result con-

2   There are also some problems about the accuracy of detailed occupation reporting by participants in the CPS surveys. We discus this issue further in Appendix 3.2. In this study, our method of grouping occupations into four broad tiers by education intensity should minimize the impact of all but the very largest reporting errors.

3   Another way to see this is to note that the educational intensity of various occupations in the two years is highly correlated (the coefficient of determination is .78; the Kendall rank order coefficient is .71), even though the average level of education is significantly higher in the later years.

Table 3.1: *Average Annual Changes in the Educational Levels of the Population and the Employed Work Force Compared to Similar Changes in the Educational Intensity of Occupations*

Highest level of formal education	1971 to 1979	1979 to 1987	1987 to 1995	1971 to 1995
Panel A: Total prime-age population				
High-school dropouts	-3.1%	-1.4%	-0.7%	-1.7%
High-school diploma	+1.4	+3.0	-0.8	+1.2
High-school diploma or less	-0.3	+1.7	-0.8	+0.2
Some college	+6.4	+4.7	+5.7	+5.6
At least one college degree	+7.3	+5.0	+2.8	+5.0
More than a high-school diploma	+6.9	+4.8	+4.2	+5.3
Total	+2.0	+3.0	+1.7	+2.2
Panel B: Total prime-age employed				
High-school dropouts	-3.3	-1.8	-0.9	-2.0
High-school diploma	+2.6	+3.6	-0.6	+1.8
High-school diploma or less	+0.5	+2.2	-0.7	+0.7
Some college	+7.7	+5.1	+5.9	+6.2
At least one college degree	+8.0	+5.3	+2.8	+5.4
More than a high-school diploma	+7.9	+5.3	+4.2	+5.8
Total	+3.1	+3.6	+1.9	+2.9
Panel C: Educational intensity of occupations, 1971–72 classification				
Tier 1: 10.5 years or less	+1.1	+2.4	+1.5	+1.7
Tier 2: 10.5 to 12.0 years	+2.2	+2.7	+1.4	+2.1
Tiers 1 and 2	+1.6	+2.6	+1.5	+1.9
Tier 3: 12.1 to 14.5 years	+4.5	+4.5	+2.0	+3.7
Tier 4: More than 14.5 years	+4.9	+4.1	+3.0	+4.0
Tiers 3 and 4	+4.6	+4.4	+2.3	+3.8
Total	+3.1	+3.6	+1.9	+2.9
Panel D: Educational intensity of occupations, 1994–95 classification				
Tier 1: 10.5 years or less	-3.5	+5.1	+1.5	+1.0
Tier 2: 10.5 to 12.0 years	+1.3	+2.1	+1.7	+1.7
Tiers 1 and 2	+0.9	+2.3	+1.7	+1.6
Tier 3: 12.1 to 14.5 years	+3.3	+2.1	+3.1	+2.8
Tier 4: More than 14.5 years	+4.6	+7.4	+0.0	+4.0
Tiers 3 and 4	+3.6	+3.8	+2.0	+3.1
Total	+3.1	+3.6	+1.9	+2.9

Notes: The underlying data come from the Current Population Surveys of March in 1971, 1972, 1979, 1987, 1994, and 1995. The data include those immigrants answering the survey and, at least for the U.S. Census, this includes roughly 60 percent of undocumented Mexican immigrants (Borjas, Freeman and Lang, 1991).

firming the findings of sociologists about the stability of the rankings of occupational prestige.

With these ideas in place, we turn to addressing the growth rate of labor demand. We use the number of people employed in each occupation tier as a measure of the demand for labor in that market or tier. Panel C of Table 3.1 shows that the number of jobs in the least education intensive, tier 1 occupations (defined in terms of the 1971–72 classification) increased at an annual rate of 1.7 percent from 1971 to 1995. Jobs in tier 2 occupations increased at a somewhat more rapid 2.1 percent annual rate. The combined growth rate of jobs in tier 1 and tier 2 occupations is 1.9 percent. Clearly the number of jobs in occupations which rank near the bottom in average levels of education has been growing albeit more slowly than occupations requiring more education.

What about labor supply? We use the number of prime-age people (or employed people) at each particular level of education as a measure of the labor supply. Panel A of Table 3.1 shows that the number of high-school dropouts has decreased at an annual rate of 1.7 percent. The number of persons with just a high-school diploma has grown at an annual rate of 1.2 percent. For both groups combined, the growth rate has been 0.2 percent per year. All of these growth rates are lower than the comparable ones for labor demand. The results are similar if we look only at prime-age employed people (Panel B).

This surprising conclusion is an important finding because it indicates an apparent increase in excess demand for low-skilled workers. That is, in terms of the relevant supply and demand for labor, low-skilled jobs are not disappearing, at least if we assume that the jobs in these occupation tiers are *not* experiencing a dramatic real upskilling and/or real educational upgrading. Panel D shows the same result when educational intensity is defined in terms of the 1994–95 data: those with just a high-school diploma or less increased 0.2 percent a year, while jobs with the corresponding educational intensity increased 1.6 percent a year.

It is also noteworthy that the growth rate of well-educated prime-age persons, those with at least some college, has been greater than the growth rate of jobs in the most education-intensive occupations, tiers 3 and 4. In other words, the number of prime working-age persons with either some college or a college degree increased considerably faster than the number of jobs with a high degree of educational intensiveness. This excess supply has two interpretations: (a) Well-educated workers are taking jobs that do not require all of their educational credentials, a phenomenon we label "downward occupational mobility." This is also associated with "credential creep." (b) Or well-educated workers are taking jobs in less education intensive occupations that are experiencing real educational upgrading – an explanation that we explore below and refute.

There is, of course, some correlation between the knowledge requirements of an occupation and the average education of those pursuing it. Nevertheless, the correlation is by no means perfect because of different rates of credential creep in the various occupations. Such creep occurs because employers may use years of formal education as a signal for some skill or attribute of the job candidates that is difficult or expensive to determine directly. The problem of credential creep is exacerbated because the average level of education is rising over time. Thus, for various reasons a rising educational intensity of a particular occupation may be unrelated to the actual requirements of the job, a phenomenon designated as pseudo educational upgrading in the previous chapter.

The lesson from this type of statistical exercise is clear: Contrary to popular opinion, but consistent with the results of several other economists such as David Howell (1997), low-skill jobs are not disappearing, at least in comparison to those with the corresponding educational credentials. The assertions that the decline in employment rates of the less-educated adult population is due either to a disappearance of low-skill jobs due to the rising technological level, to foreign trade, or to immigration, are based on an assumption about the disappearance of low skill jobs that does not correspond to reality. The real questions are quite different: Is real educational upgrading of these low-skilled jobs occurring? What is the mechanism at work by which workers with high educational credentials are channeled into occupations requiring lower educational credentials? How and why are less-educated workers being shoved completely out of the labor market? And why are real wages rising in the top job tiers and falling in the bottom job tiers? These questions receive attention both in this chapter and in the following chapters.

Skills and Education, Especially at the Low End of the Occupational Scale

The calculations in Table 3.1 focus only on increases in the education of workers, with no attention paid to upskilling or to real and pseudo educational upgrading. For those low-skill occupations with the greatest increase in average education, it is important to determine whether these changes represent upskilling, real educational upgrading, or merely pseudo-upgrading. Using various types of evidence we argue below that upskilling and real educational upgrading are highly unlikely.[4]

---

4   Some such as Pryor (1996, Table A.7) or Howell and Wolff (1991) document the shift in the occupational structure in terms of specific labor force skills. Neither study considers, however, the possibility of upskilling within individual occupations.

Real Upgrading and Upskilling of Given Occupations

In this discussion we explore the impact of cognitive skills, although other skills may be relevant for wage and employment determination. For an indicator of the average cognitive skills of workers in the various occupations, we use functional literacy, a measure that is unfortunately available only at a single point in time. For upskilling, that is, *changes* in the required cognitive skills of any given occupation, we must use an indirect approach.

Previous approaches to the problem: Considerable anecdotal evidence about the upskilling of particular occupations can be found. For instance, some secretaries are increasingly assuming the tasks of administrative assistants, which require more cognitive skills, although their job titles may not change (McKenzie, 1997). Unfortunately, systematic evidence for these matters is scarce.

Several studies in the economic literature focus on this problem of upskilling for the entire occupational structure. Most, such as those by Spenner (1983, 1988), rely on comparisons between the skill requirements for the individual occupations that are recorded in various editions of the U.S. Department of Labor's *Dictionary of Occupational Titles* (DOT). Although these studies show changes in certain occupations, they also find little net change in the skill requirements for an average occupation. The major problem with this approach is that the compilers of DOT do not appear to review the skill requirements of every occupation in each edition. Moreover, questions arise about the temporal consistency of the criteria used by the DOT experts to judge the skill ratings (not to mention the cross-section consistency between the ratings of occupations in different industries).

It is also possible to ask managers (or workers) whether required skills are increasing. This type of analysis is carried out, for instance, by Peter Cappelli (1996), who utilizes data from a sample of 2,945 manufacturing and non-manufacturing enterprises from the Census Bureau's survey of the Educational Quality of the Workforce. He focuses on the answers to a question asking managers whether the skills required to perform general entry-level jobs have risen over the past three years. Although a majority reported an increase, the meaning of these results are unclear. Skills and education are conflated and, moreover, it is unclear whether the managers were reporting a change in the skills for individual occupations or a change in the occupational distribution toward those requiring more skills.

Cappelli (1993, 1996) has also tried another approach by utilizing information from the files of the Hay Associates, the world's largest compensation consulting firm. The database reports on 94 production job titles across a sample of 93 manufacturing establishments in 27 U.S. communities in the period from 1978 to the mid 1980s. Cappelli concludes that some upskilling has occurred in entry-level production, but not clerical, jobs.

A *microeconomic perspective:* To investigate the relationship between upskilling and real educational upgrading, we need to take a closer look at specific occupations. An obvious first step is to determine which occupations in our list of 500 occupations have experienced the greatest educational upgrading and then to ask ourselves two questions: Is such upgrading real or apparent? Does such upgrading also reflect upskilling? To avoid sampling problems and to deal only with the most familiar jobs, we focus only on those occupations having 100,000 or more workers in both years, which leaves us with 179 occupations. Our conclusions are not changed, however, if a much lower cutoff limit is used instead.

Table 3.2 shows the 30 occupations with the largest changes in educational intensity (that is, educational upgrading). All but one of these 30 major occupations required less than a high-school diploma in 1971–72. Moreover, one-third of the listed occupations had an educational intensity of less than a high-school diploma in 1994–95.

In perusing this list, we can subjectively distinguish three groups of occupations: In the first and largest group, we place those we believe not to have experienced any type of occupational upskilling or real educational upgrading over the last few decades. These include sawing machine operators, timber cutting and logging operators, vehicle washers, truck drivers, driver-sales workers, construction workers, firefighting occupations, guards and police – excluding public service, automobile mechanics, sales workers – apparel, janitors and cleaners, maids and housemen, and so forth. In these cases the educational upgrading is apparent, not real, and little or no occupational upgrading occurred.

In some of these occupations the nature of the technology used by workers has changed, but not in a way that requires more skill or education. For example, modern cash registers have scanning devices, inventory logs, automatic coupon processing, itemized printouts, and high-speed connections to credit card approval and bank withdrawal centers and they are vastly more sophisticated technologically than those of 30 years ago. Yet they are in most ways easier to use than those of previous generations. They require only very minimal numeracy and literacy skills on the part of sales clerks. Similar arguments can be made about the newer sophisticated alarm and monitoring systems used by security guards, or the newer computerized diagnostic devices used by automobile mechanics.

A second and much smaller group includes occupations where both real upskilling and real educational upgrading has probably occurred. These include farmers, licensed practical nurses, and possibly production coordina-

Table 3.2: *Major Occupations Ranked by Changes in Average Education of Prime-Age Workers*

Occupation code	Years of education			Occupation
	Average		Change	
	1971–72	1994–95		
727	8.76	11.47	2.71	Sawing machine operators
496	8.69	11.31	2.62	Timber cutting and logging occupations
738	8.89	11.44	2.55	Winding/twisting machine operators (textile industries)
599	9.86	12.27	2.41	Construction trades, not elsewhere classified (n.e.c.)
856	9.41	11.68	2.27	Industrial truck and tractors equipment operators
887	9.41	11.68	2.27	Vehicle washers and equipment cleaners
473	10.80	12.95	2.15	Farmers, except horticulture
433	10.77	12.90	2.13	Food preparation supervisors
855	9.68	11.78	2.10	Grader, dozer, and scraper machine operators
853	9.90	11.95	2.05	Excavating and loading machine operators
883	10.06	12.10	2.04	Freight, stock, and material handlers, n.e.c.
804	10.17	12.20	2.03	Truck drivers
806	11.24	13.27	2.03	Driver-sales workers
469	11.29	13.29	2.00	Personal service occupations, n.e.c.
207	11.59	13.58	1.99	Licensed practical nurses
534	10.99	12.95	1.96	Heating, air-conditioning, refrigeration mechanics
869	9.30	11.24	1.94	Construction laborers
809	10.96	12.89	1.93	Taxicab drivers and chauffeurs
417	11.90	13.82	1.92	Firefighting occupations
426	11.30	13.22	1.92	Guards and police, excluding public service
505	10.42	12.33	1.91	Automobile mechanics
756	10.25	12.14	1.89	Mixing and blending machine operators
507	10.48	12.37	1.89	Bus, truck, stationary engine mechanics
264	11.75	13.63	1.88	Sales workers, apparel
549	10.63	12.49	1.86	Not specified mechanics and repairers
748	9.39	11.25	1.86	Laundering and dry cleaning machine operators
766	10.47	12.33	1.86	Furnace, kiln, and oven operators, excluding food
453	9.76	11.59	1.83	Janitors and cleaners
363	12.12	13.94	1.82	Production coordinators
449	9.47	11.28	1.81	Maids and housemen, except household

Notes: The occupational and educational data for the 500 occupational categories are averaged for 1971 and 1972, as well as for 1994 and 1995. The average increase of education of workers in the period was 1.51 years. In the table only those occupations with more than 100,000 workers in both years are included. Totals may not add because of rounding. n.e.c. means not elsewhere classified. The data come from the March Current Population Surveys for the respective years. The conversion of the 1971–72 occupational codes to the 1994–95 occupational codes is discussed in Appendix 3.1 and, in more detail, in Pryor and Schaffer (1997).

tors. We must emphasize, however, that the proportions of real educational upgrading and real upskilling vary in these various cases.

A third group consists of those occupations which are too heterogeneous to hazard anything but a guess about changes in skill requirements. These include, for instance, construction trades, not elsewhere classified (n.e.c.), personal service occupations, n.e.c., and not specified mechanics and repairers. In most of these cases, however, it seems likely that the educational upgrading was mostly apparent, rather than real, and also that little upskilling occurred.

It is clear that the greatest educational upgrading occurred at the low end of the occupational ladder. We must conclude that, in most of these occupations, this represents a pseudo upgrading that, moreover, was not accompanied by any real upskilling. Thus, among these low-skill occupations at any point in time, many workers have more than the necessary education or cognitive skills needed for the job.

In closing this discussion about upskilling and real educational upgrading, two warnings must be issued. First, it is important to keep these results about occupations separate from our discussion about the educational requirements of industries. Nevertheless, as we show in our discussion in Chapter 7, changes in the structure of consumption and production are *not* a major cause of educational upgrading. We have also investigated the impact of changing productivity within individual industries and the subsequent change in the structure of employment with similar negative results. The major shifts within the occupational structure have come as a result of changes within, not between, particular industries.

Second, we must be careful in generalizing our conclusions about upskilling and real educational upgrading based on Table 3.2 alone to the economy as a whole because of the changing relative importance of different occupations. In particular, there has been a shift of the labor force into those occupations requiring more education and skills ("structural upgrading"). Moreover, some individual occupations not included in Table 3.2, particularly those in the middle and high end of the occupational scale, may be experiencing either real upgrading and upskilling.

To increase our understanding about where upskilling has occurred, we tried a simple thought-experiment. We went through the list of 500 occupations and subjectively assessed (that is, on the basis of what we know or could guess about these occupations) whether the cognitive skills, as measured by functional literacy required to carry out each occupation, have increased significantly in the last quarter-century. In drawing the line on "significant changes" we adopted very liberal criteria.

Such an exploratory exercise has the sole purpose of isolating some stylized facts that can be investigated and explained more rigorously in later chapters. From this exercise an extremely useful observation emerges: Jobs in education-intensive occupations (based on the 1971–72 classification) are more likely to have experienced upskilling. What this means is that necessary cognitive skills are increasing most rapidly in those occupations associated with high levels of education. This seems consistent with the commonly-believed proposition that more-educated workers are more flexible and more capable of acquiring new skills. It also suggests the occurrence of skill-biased technical change, at least among those occupations with the greatest educational intensity.[5]

This exploratory thought-experiment also leads to two other conjectures of great relevance to our general approach that we investigate in later pages: First, the demand for cognitive skills has increased faster than the supply of educated workers with high cognitive skills. Second, the demand for university-educated workers with average cognitive skills has increased more slowly than the number of persons with these attributes, because the real demand increase is for those with high cognitive skills. Both hypotheses rely crucially on the distinction between upskilling and educational upgrading. We test and find supporting evidence for both conjectures in Chapter 5. Finally, such results give some important clues about why wage increases are occurring fastest among certain occupations in tier 4, a matter explored in much greater detail in Chapters 5 and 6.

Other evidence: Using data from the Panel Study on Income Dynamics, Sicherman (1991) reports that about 40 percent of the workers report that their jobs require much less education than they actually have. Unfortunately for our purposes, his sample consists of workers from 16 to 60, including many young workers who have taken temporary jobs while searching for employment more closely matching their education level. The question, of course, is also somewhat nebulous and can be interpreted differently by various respondents. Nevertheless, his results are supportive of our hypothesis.

Zemsky, Johnson *et al.* (1996) also report that 61 percent of their sample of young workers wanted more challenging work, which suggests that these workers were not working up to their educational or skill potential.

Implications for Employment and Wages

If we are correct that in most cases the educational upgrading of jobs requiring relatively little education in 1971–72 has been more apparent than

---

5   Our results on these matters are also consistent with the finding of Juhn and Murphy (1995) that the relative demand for highly-skilled workers, in contrast to moderately-skilled workers, increased dramatically in the 1960s.

real, then one clear inference can be drawn: The downward occupational mobility that we document has created fierce competition for these low-skill jobs. In the simple textbook world of supply and demand, this should lead to a reduction in wages sufficient to eliminate the excess supply of workers. However, as we discussed briefly in Chapter 1 our empirical results suggest that there is enough downward wage stickiness – both within and across detailed occupations – to keep wages from decreasing by more than a small fraction of the amount necessary to restore equilibrium. Certainly one of the causes of this wage stickiness, especially in low-paying jobs, is the minimum wage law. In addition, for low- and high-paying jobs, firms are reluctant to lower wages too much and risk increases in turnover or in reduced morale that would lead to shirking.

In the absence of large wage reductions, credential creep is almost inevitable in those occupations experiencing a flood of job applicants. Employers set up educational screens to reduce the number of applicants they must consider. We suspect, for instance, that this has been the case for such governmental jobs as firefighters or prison guards, where the average levels of education between 1971–72 and 1994–95 increased respectively 1.92 and 1.81 years (the latter occupation does not meet the 100,000 cut-off limit and is not included in table 3.2).

If the least-educated workers are displaced by those with higher educational credentials, they have nowhere else to work. This mechanism underlies the falling rate of employment among less-educated males from 1971 to the present. For less-educated females, the employment rate has remained relatively constant, rather than rising, as it has for women with more education.[6]

The downward occupational mobility of educated workers causes an increase in the supply of persons competing for low-skill jobs, and this, in turn, creates a downward pressure on wages. We must be careful in interpreting the results from Table 3.1 that show an excess demand for less- educated workers, because the downward occupational mobility of more-educated workers changes the effective supply of workers seeking these jobs. This shift in effective supply has more than offset the apparent excess demand and, as a result, wages for jobs at this end of the occupational ladder have stagnated or fallen. We discuss these matters in detail in Chapters 5 and 6.

---

6 Differences in the behavior of employment rates of less-educated men and women over time appear to be influenced by two additional factors: (a) Women's wages are lower, so employers prefer to hire them rather than men; (b) Among those with just a high-school diploma or less, women have somewhat higher functional literacy than men (Chapter 2).These generalizations are drawn from the National Adult Literacy Survey and concern literacy skills related to reading and writing of prose and to the interpretation of documents, but not to quantitative skills. Such results mean, for instance, that less-educated women would make more desirable employees than men with a similar education for such jobs as lower-level clerk positions requiring considerable paperwork and merely standard arithmetic.

The major message is simple: It is *not* skill-biased technical change in the less education-intensive, tier 1 and 2 occupations that is directly responsible for the fall of wages and employment among the less-educated. Rather, the primary cause is the downward occupational mobility of more-educated workers that arises from the failure of the economy to absorb workers with higher educational qualifications. It is now time to look at this phenomenon in greater detail.

Downward Occupational Mobility: University Graduates in High-School Jobs

The existence of a certain downward occupational mobility in the United States leads to a puzzle: If the university-educated are flooding the job market in such numbers that many must take jobs previously held by those with just a high-school diploma, then why are the wages of these university-educated workers rising when a surplus should lead to falling wages? This particular question has been the focus of a recent debate between Daniel E. Hecker (1992, 1995) of the U.S. Department of Labor and John Tyler, Richard J. Murnane, and Frank Levy (1995).

Our approach to this puzzle is straightforward. We first briefly summarize the state of the debate about university-educated workers taking high-school jobs. Next we define "high-school jobs" so as to attack the problem systematically and then present data on functional literacy, employment levels, and wages for workers with different levels of education in various occupations. These data show that it is the university graduates with relatively low functional literacy that are experiencing such downward occupational mobility. Those university graduates with functional literacy commensurate with their education retain the top tier jobs. Finally, in Chapter 5 we show that among these graduates, those in occupations requiring particularly high functional literacy have obtained the highest wages.

The State of the Debate

Daniel F. Hecker (1992, 1995) opened the debate by arguing that an increasing number of university graduates were taking high-school jobs. Unfortunately, he used highly aggregated occupation data. He also introduced data from the Recent College Graduates Survey into the discussion indicating that almost 40 percent of the graduates awarded B.A. degrees in 1984 and 1986 reported they thought a university degree was not needed to obtain the job they held a year after graduation. Since, as some have pointed out, it takes many graduates several years to find employment suitable to their talents, the relevance of this evidence is not entirely clear. He argued these data indicate a surplus of university graduates in relation to the number of available jobs, a position consistent with the Department of Labor's oft-stated prediction that the U.S. job outlook for the university-educated as a group is not as rosy as commonly believed.[7]

Hecker then faces squarely the difficult and crucial question: If there is a surplus of university-educated workers, why are the wages of the university-educated rising? He proposes and then refutes two possible explanations.

First, it is possible that many university graduates learned little from their university education and do not qualify for jobs requiring university-level skills. As a result, they finally take jobs in occupations where most workers have fewer years of education than they. Hecker uses aggregate trends in SAT and Graduate Record Examination scores to argue there is no evidence of declining average skill levels of university graduates that would encourage a rising number to take high-school jobs. Moreover, he claims (1992, p. 8) that it is not clear "why employers would place so many of these admittedly less-qualified university graduates in jobs that do not require university-level skills if they had vacant university-level jobs." By way of contrast, we argue below that this explanation is indeed the key to the paradox and that Hecker's rebuttals are not germane to the crucial points.

Second, Hecker's classification of occupations on which he bases his empirical analysis may bias his results. For instance, his classes of service occupations or administrative support occupations cover a wide variety of jobs requiring different skills and education and, as a result, his calculations raise difficulties for his argument. For our highly disaggregated database, however, this is less serious a problem.

Hecker's explanation for the increasing wage gap between high-school and university graduates revolves around a restructuring of the economy and the decline of high-wage jobs for blue collar workers. In this regard he cites approvingly a conclusion by Lawrence Mishel and Ruy A. Teixeria (1991) that the relative return to education increased in the 1980s primarily because of declines in the real wages of the less-educated, not because of increasing real wages for the more-educated.

John Tyler, Richard Murnane, and Frank Levy (1995) bring additional data, particularly regarding wages, into the argument. They make two major points.

First, recent increases in the proportion of university-educated workers in high-school jobs have occurred primarily among older workers rather than younger ones. They provide evidence that although male university-graduates

---

7   Bishop (1996) reviews a number of Department of Labor projections of job growth in various occupations. After showing that many of these projections diverged considerably from what actually happened, he analyzes various sources of possible errors.

between 45 and 54 have experienced an increase in high-school jobs, this has not been the case for women in the same age cohort or for men and women between 25 to 34. Unfortunately, they rely on the same highly-aggregated data used by Hecker to make this argument. Our data in Table 3.4 show a very different picture.

Second, university graduates holding high-school jobs receive more than the average wages in these occupations. A key point is that in many occupations, if not most, the work can be performed by people with different levels of formal education. That is, employers face a choice of hiring high-school graduates at a given wage, or university graduates at a higher wage; presumably the latter have higher marginal productivities. We show that, within a typical occupation, the wage gap between university graduates and those with just a high-school education has risen over the years (shown in Chapter 6). So the university-educated in high-school jobs are not necessarily receiving wages identical to those high-school graduates in the same jobs. Bishop (1996) also stresses this phenomenon when he argues that more years of education usually have some payoff, regardless of the job. We also show evidence of this phenomenon in Chapter 5.

On a number of issues the participants of the debate are not listening to each other. In our empirical discussion we ask a simple question: Which university graduates end up in high-school jobs?

Some Crucial Definitions

To attack these problems systematically, it is necessary to develop some objective criteria for defining a high-school job.

In Table 3.3 we present data showing the changing share of university-educated workers in high-school jobs, where three alternative definitions of high-school jobs are presented. In Panel A of the table we show percentages of those with a university degree with jobs in occupations where the average level of education is less than or equal to 12.0 years. In Panel B we present data where the cutoff is 13.0 or fewer years; and in Panel C, the cutoff is 14.5 or fewer years. These different calculations allow us to determine the degree to which the definition of high-school jobs influences the conclusions.

We agree with both Hecker and Tyler *et al.* that the greatest degree of downward occupational mobility occurred in the 1970s. In many details, however, our conclusions differ from those drawn in the other studies under discussion.

The calculations in the first column for "all workers" parallel similar estimates by Hecker. With Hecker's methodology, however, the results show a large increase in the number of university graduates in high-school jobs between 1970 and 1980, with very little increase after 1980. We obtain simi-

Table 3.3: *Percentage of Employed Workers with a University Education in High-School Jobs*

Panel A: Narrow definition of high-school jobs

Year   Jobs in tier 1 and 2 occupations
          (where the average education of workers was 12 years or less in 1971–72)

	All	Prime-age (25-49)	Men 25-34	Women 25-34	Men 45-54	Women 45-54
1971	7.1%	5.7%	6.3%	3.8%	6.3%	7.0%
1979	9.9	9.7	13.1	8.2	7.9	6.8
1987	10.7	10.4	14.3	9.0	7.7	5.6
1995	10.1	9.6	12.5	6.7	10.1	6.4

Panel B: Intermediate definition of high-school jobs

Year   Jobs in tier 1 and 2 and part of tier 3 occupations
          (where the average education of workers was 13 years or less in 1971–72)

	All	Prime-age (25-49)	Men 25-34	Women 25-34	Men 45-54	Women 45-54
1971	23.7%	22.1%	21.5	16.0%	27.2%	24.8%
1979	30.6	30.0	33.1	29.0	30.2	23.7
1987	34.5	34.0	37.5	33.2	32.5	26.8
1995	34.8	34.0	36.6	31.8	38.5	26.2

Panel C: Broad definition of high-school jobs

Year   Jobs in tier 1, 2, and 3 occupations
          (where the average education of workers was 14.5 years or less in 1971–72)

	All	Prime-age (25-49)	Men 25-34	Women 25-34	Men 45-54	Women 45-54
1971	40.8%	40.3%	41.2%	33.7%	44.6%	35.8%
1979	50.2	49.4	53.9	49.9	48.5	39.9
1987	54.7	54.9	58.1	59.6	51.5	45.0
1995	55.4	55.0	56.9	56.3	56.9	45.2

Notes: The data come from the Current Population Surveys for March 1971, 1979, 1987, and 1995.

lar results when we use the narrowest definition of high-school jobs (Panel A). That is, the percentage of university graduates in high-school jobs increased most between 1971 and 1979. This increase tapered off between 1979 and 1987, and declined slightly between 1987 and 1995 (although it was still higher than the 1979 level). If we use either of the two broader definitions, however, the deceleration of growth in the percentage of university graduates in high-school jobs appears but is much weaker, at least until 1987.

It is also striking that the results for prime-age workers alone are very similar to the results for the entire employed population. This seems to contradict the assertion by Tyler, Murnane, and Levy that there was a differential effect based on gender and age, and that the phenomenon was only for men from 45 to 54, many of whom had difficulty obtaining work commensurate with their education after they were laid off. To address this issue more directly, we calculated the percentages for the same sex/age subcategories as those reported by Tyler and his collaborators. They found that between 1979 and 1989, the percentage of university graduates in high-school jobs actually decreased for all of these four groups with the exception of men ages 45 to 54. For most subcategories we find that this percentage increased from 1979 to 1987. It seems unlikely that the difference in endpoints accounts for the difference in results.

Using the narrowest definition of high-school jobs (Panel A), the percentage of university graduates in high-school jobs declined for all groups from 1987 to 1995 except for older men and women. This is similar to the findings of Tyler *et al.* However, if we use either of the broader definitions, a different scenario appears. The numbers improve for the same three groups, but only by a small amount, and they certainly do not fall below their 1979 values. Such results cast some doubt on the strong assertion of Tyler, Murnane, and Levy that only older men have experienced this type of occupation downgrading.

In Table 3.4 we disaggregate these data for prime-age workers to show the number of workers with various levels of education in the occupations classified by educational tier in 1971 and 1995.

Reading across the rows in Parts A and C we see the percentage of those in occupations of a particular educational tier who have various levels of education. In 1971, for example, 2.9 percent of the workers in tier 2 occupations (where the average education was 10.6 to 12 years) had a university degree; by 1994 this rose to 9.0 percent.

Reading down the columns in Parts B and D, we see the percentage of those with a given education who are pursuing occupations in various educational tiers. For instance, in 1971 4.5 percent of all employed persons with a university degree were in tier 2 occupations; in 1994 this rose to 6.6 percent. Such data confirm the phenomenon discussed by Hecker in a dramatic fashion,

Table 3.4: *Years of Education, and Occupations of Prime-Age Workers, 1971 and 1995*

Tiers defined by average education of those in occupation in 1971–72	Educational tier of occupation				Total
Highest educational attainment	Tier 1 10.5 years or less	Tier 2 10.6–12.0 years	Tier 3 12.1–14.5 years	Tier 4 > 14.5 years	
Part A: Percentage by rows: 1971					
High-school dropout	58.3%	34.9%	11.0%	1.4%	28.5
Only high-school diploma or equivalent	36.4	51.8	49.4	9.4	41.4
Some university	4.5	10.5	23.0	11.6	13.4
University degree	0.8	2.9	16.7	77.6	16.7
Total	100.0	100.0	100.0	100.0	100.0
Part B: Percentages by columns: 1971					
High-school dropout	54.1	32.0	13.3	0.6	100.0
Only high-school diploma or equivalent	23.2	32.7	41.2	2.9	100.0
Some university	8.9	20.5	59.4	11.2	100.0
University degree	1.2	4.5	34.6	59.7	100.0
Total	26.4	26.2	34.6	12.9	100.0

Part C: Percentage by rows: 1995

High-school dropout	26.1	12.0	2.4	0.5	8.9
Only high-school diploma or equivalent	49.2	45.9	28.2	5.7	32.5
Some university	20.4	33.1	37.0	13.4	28.9
University degree	4.3	9.0	32.4	80.3	29.6
Total	100.0	100.0	100.0	100.0	100.0

Part D: Percentages by columns: 1995

High-school dropout	58.2	29.5	11.5	1.0	100.0
Only high-school diploma or equivalent	30.1	30.9	36.1	2.9	100.0
Some university	14.1	25.0	53.2	7.7	100.0
University degree	2.9	6.6	45.5	45.0	100.0
Total	19.9	21.9	41.6	16.6	100.0

Notes: Parts A and C show the share of workers with different occupations engaged in occupations with different average degrees of education of practitioners in 1971. Parts B and D show the percentage of workers with a given education who are engaged in occupations where the average level of education of practitioners in 1971 varied. The data come from the Current Population Surveys for March 1971 and March 1995. We present similar data for 1979 and 1986 in Appendix 3.5.

Table 3.5: *Weighted Average Functional Literacy Scores and Jobs of the Prime-Age Workers in 1992*

| | | | Occupational tiers | | |
Average level of education of job in 1971-1972	Tier 1 10.5 years or less	Tier 2 10.6–12.0 years	Tier 3 12.1–14.5 years	Tier 4 >14.5	Total
Highest level of education					
High-school dropout: averages	232	249	266	—	244
(Standard errors)	(2.8)	(3.1)	(3.9)		(1.9)
High-school diploma: averages	267	285	293	301	283
(Standard errors)	(1.4)	(1.3)	(1.2)	(4.1)	(0.8)
Some university: averages	291	301	313	326	308
(Standard errors)	(2.3)	(1.7)	(1.0)	(3.0)	(0.8)
University degree: averages	301	316	331	343	335
(Standard errors)	(6.0)	(3.1)	(1.1)	(1.1)	(0.8)
Total: averages	264	286	311	338	301
(Standard errors)	(1.2)	(1.0)	(0.7)	(1.0)	(0.5)

Notes: The table reports the weighted average scores of the three scales of functional literacy for full-time, prime-age workers. These scores run from 0 to 500 and the original sample came from a 1992 nationwide survey. For this table the total sample size is 7931 people. High school diploma includes those with a GED or with a high-school diploma plus additional trade/vocational schooling. The results for the northeast and southwest corners of the table are not reported because these subsamples are too small for the results to have much meaning. The table is calculated from the raw data of the National Adult Literacy Study and differs slightly from a previously published version of this table because of small changes in classification and sample selection.

although we focus only on prime-age workers and he includes the entire labor force. The general upgrading of the occupational structure of the labor force is supported by relative fall of the share of jobs in the lower occupational tiers and the corresponding rise in the share of jobs in the higher occupational tiers.

Enter Functional Literacy

Underlying most of the debate is the assumption that workers with a certain level of education are homogeneous, which is clearly false. Functional literacy is a cognitive skill that plays a key role in the process of matching workers to jobs, as shown in Table 3.5.

Data in the rows in Table 3.5 show clearly that functional literacy of workers with a given education increases as the occupational tier increases.[8] Thus, those with a university education working in occupations where most had less than a university education had lower functional literacy than university-educated working in university-level jobs. In the table we include standard errors so that readers can make calculations to prove to themselves that most of the difference in functional literacy scores between cells are statistically significant. Such evidence points toward the unfortunate conclusion that the university-educated in high-school jobs pursued them because they had lower cognitive skills than other university-educated workers and, moreover, could not obtain jobs in occupations commensurate with their formal education.

The low functional literacy of many university graduates represents a serious indictment against the standards of the U.S. higher educational system. We must, however, not be hasty in making sweeping generalizations, because of the possibility that a certain amount of reverse causation may be present. That is, sometimes functional literacy may be partly the result of on-the-job learning. If this is true, then to a certain extent chance factors such as the initial job obtained after completion of formal education can play a role in this relation between occupation, education, and functional literacy. In part, functional literacy is also a result of attitudes and motivation which, of course, also have an impact on the type of employment chosen.

Some Conclusions

From this brief discussion using data on 500 occupations we can draw the following four important conclusions:

8 The conclusions of this discussion can be more exactly established by means of a regression

    • An increasing share of university-educated workers are taking jobs where the average educational level has been much lower. In some cases this may represent a technological upgrading of the occupation; in most cases, however, it appears that other factors are at work in this process of downward occupational mobility.

    • From 1971 through 1987 a rising share of male and female university-educated workers of all ages took such high-school jobs. The largest increase occurred in the 1970s and corresponded, at least in the early 1970s, with the surge of university graduates onto the job market and the declining wage premium of a university degree. Nevertheless, the rising share of university-educated workers taking high-school jobs continued up to 1987, albeit at a decreasing rate. Between 1987 and 1995, however, the percentage of university-educated men and women in high-school jobs decreased slightly among younger workers, but continued to increase for older workers, especially older men.

    • Those university-educated experiencing downward occupational mobility have considerably lower functional literacy on the average than other university graduates.

We argue in Chapters 5 and 6 that the considerable increase in wages of the university-educated who are pursuing jobs in tier 4 occupations reflects a shortage of university-educated workers with the functional literacy that corresponds with such academic credentials. That is, once functional literacy is taken into account, there is no contradiction between a shortage (and rising real wages) of highly-skilled university graduates, the relatively stagnant wages of university graduates in tier 4 jobs that do not require high functional literacy, and an increasing number of university-graduates taking high-school jobs. We must, however, defer detailed discussion of the wage issue until more aspects of the employment picture have been brought into focus.

Special Topics

In this section we wish to deal with two other important questions. How are general skill requirements (not just for functional literacy requirements)

---

analysis in which the variable to be explained is the literacy score of the individual. One such exercise indicated that, within a typical occupation, each additional year of education of a worker in that occupation meant that his or her functional literacy score was about four points higher.

changing for jobs with different educational intensities and how does the changing industrial structure affect this situation? And how can our results be reconciled with the common observation that we are suffering from a scarcity, rather than an excess, of qualified workers?

Changes in Skill Requirements for Jobs in Different Educational Tiers

Formal education is only one of the characteristics of workers sought by employers, and it is useful to look at a variety of other skills as well. We present some relevant data in Table 3.6 which represent structural shifts, since we are holding the skill ratings for the various occupations constant over the period and are looking at averages for different tiers where the educational intensity is measured at the end points.

The data on skills reveal few surprises as we move from those occupations of workers with the lowest educational intensity (tier 1) to those occupations of workers with the highest educational intensity (tier 4). With few exceptions, analytical skills, data skills, people skills, specific vocational training, and the various functional literacy scores increase, while physical demands decrease. Motor skills (which increase between tiers 1 and 2) appear anomalous.

Although it may seem surprising that many of the cognitive skills required for occupations in particular educational tiers decrease between 1971–72 and 1994–95, the explanation is quite simple. The occupations included in the various tiers are different during these two periods. For 1994–95 the occupations included in tiers 3 and 4 include many occupations with lower skills which had, in 1971–72, been classified in a tier with a lower educational intensity, so that the average scores of these jobs were diluted. By way of contrast, tiers 1 and 2 lost many of their "higher level" occupations, so their average skill levels are lower as well. As a result, the average skill levels in each occupational tier declined at the same time that the average skill levels for the labor force as a whole increased due to shifts in the occupational distribution. The same phenomenon is also observable in the functional literacy scores.

The Alleged Shortage of Qualified Workers

We present a picture of downward occupational mobility where American workers have more education than is needed. As noted above, this

Table 3.6 Structural Shifts of Skill Characteristics of the Four Educational Tiers

Ratings: 0 = low; 10 = high

Occupational tiers	1971–72 education intensity and occupational distribution				1994–95 education intensity and occupational distribution			
	1	2	3	4	1	2	3	4
Department of Labor skill ratings								
Factor-analysis based scales								
Analytic skills (substantive complexity)	2.11	3.57	5.24	7.33	1.19	2.15	4.33	6.91
Motor skills	5.25	5.44	4.92	4.10	4.37	5.14	4.98	4.26
Physical demands	3.61	2.85	0.65	0.62	5.81	3.23	1.70	0.67
Data skills	1.74	4.72	6.17	7.78	1.37	1.87	5.32	7.37
People skills	0.82	1.87	2.86	5.66	0.62	0.67	2.45	4.68
Specific vocational training	3.66	4.99	6.00	7.78	2.94	3.69	5.44	7.39
Strength required	5.01	3.93	1.63	1.69	5.63	5.06	2.73	1.80
Weighted average scores								
Functional literacy								
Prose scale	261	284	311	339	256	257	296	334
Document scale	260	284	308	332	257	257	294	327
Quantitative scale	266	289	312	339	265	260	299	334
Average of three scales	262	286	310	337	259	258	296	332

Notes: These calculations only reveal structural changes. The skill ratings for a single year are weighted by the prime-age labor force in 1971–72 and also 1994–95. The skill ratings come from Roos and Treiman (1980) and have been rescaled. The functional literacy data come from the National Adult Literacy Survey.

contradicts the complaint voiced by many executives of large U.S. enterprises about the shortage of workers having the basic skills needed to fill vacancies in their enterprises.[9]

We can, of course, dismiss the complaint by noting that if there were a real shortage of such skilled workers, their real wages should be rising. As we show in Chapter 5, only the wages of university-educated in tier 4 jobs have been rising over the last quarter-century, while in all other tiers wages have either remained stationary or have declined. We might also dismiss such complaints by enterprise executives on grounds of excessive vagueness. In many cases it is difficult to determine whether their judgements are based on the entire labor force, or on workers in particular age/gender/ethnic cohorts. The meaning of "basic skills" is also unclear: Are they referring to what we call functional literacy, or are they referring to specific work skills?

Assuming, however, that these business executives are addressing a problem of the entire labor force, it is worthwhile to ask how our results and these views might be reconciled. At this point, however, let us rule out three plausible reasons that are not supported by the available empirical evidence:

a. The shortage of educated workers does not appear to be due to declining educational standards. As shown in Chapter 2, functional literacy is not lower in the more recent age cohorts than in older cohorts. The standard errors of the regressions reported in Table 3.2 also show that the variations of functional literacy are not much different in the various age cohorts.

b. The shift in industrial and occupational mix has led to an increase in the required functional literacy scores of four to five points, and it can be argued that this might underlie some of the shortage. More specifically, using Table A3.3 in the Appendix, we can calculate the shift in industrial and occupational mix causing this increase in the required functional literacy scores. Nevertheless, supply considerations must be taken into account. Using the regressions explaining the literacy scores, we can simulate the change in the functional literacy scores for the prime-age population with data on the changing gender/race/educational mix. These calculations indicate that changes in the population mix are more than adequate to account for the four to five point increases in functional literacy scores, so this compositional factor does not seem to underlie the shortage discussed earlier.

c. The shortage also does not appear to be due to an increase in the level of skills necessary to carry out a given lower-level occupation. This topic receives considerable attention in our previous discussion.

---

9 A typical example can be found in "(More) Help Wanted," *Business Week,* December 2, 1996, p. 8.

Three possible factors may reconcile our views with those of the American business executives:

a. American companies may be unable to obtain workers with sufficient basic skills as a result of other types of structural unemployment. For instance, unemployed workers with the necessary skills may be living in one region, while the place of employment is located in another region. This Spacial phenomenon, in turn, may be the cause of their complaints.

b. American companies may not be offering wages sufficiently high to attract workers with the necessary skills. If, for instance, they make the mistaken judgment that a certain skill should be mastered by a person with a high-school education and, in actuality, that job cannot be performed by a person with such skills, then they may have problems finding suitable people to fill the jobs for the low wages they are offering.

c. American companies may not be looking for the skills that we discuss in this chapter. For instance, the skills of concern to executives may have nothing to do with education or functional literacy *per se*, but with certain social behavior such as punctuality, motivation for hard work, or the ability to interact well with co-workers. We discuss these issues in greater detail in Chapter 8.

Unfortunately, we could not find any survey information focusing specifically on the alleged shortage of workers with basic skills (which locations? which industries? what wages offered?). Lacking such data we can only speculate about this matter. Given the size of the nationwide samples used to derive our results, we stand by our conclusions until solid information about this alleged shortage of workers having basic skills is available.

Summary and Conclusions

This analysis of several massive data sets lead to some important conclusions about the prime-age labor force that can be summarized as follows:

• *Change in skill and educational requirements.* Taking into account transformation of the occupational mix caused by changes in technology and in the structure of production, the demands for work skills, education, and functional literacy have slowly increased over the past quarter century.

• *More rapid change in actual educational levels.* The actual educational levels of the prime-age labor force or population have increased faster than the demand for educated workers. This conclusion does not appear biased by a general increase in the required educational level of all occupations, as shown by our analysis of wage differentials and education changes in specific occupations. This increasing gap between actual and necessary educational levels is consistent with a screening or signaling model of employment, where employers pay more attention to formal educational credentials than to the actual skills of the workers.

• *More rapid increases in low-education jobs than the number of the less-educated population.* The number of jobs requiring relatively low levels of education increased faster than the actual number of prime-age workers with a high-school diploma or less.

• *A displacement (or bumping) effect.* Often workers with particular educational credentials are taking jobs where the average level of education of the workers is much lower. For university graduates, the average functional literacy of these downwardly mobile workers is considerably lower than university graduates as a whole. Indeed, there appears to be a shortage of university graduates with a functional literacy corresponding to what employers seek. We explore this matter further in Chapter 5.

As we later show, many of these downwardly mobile workers displace other workers. And these displaced workers, in turn, enter other occupations where the average level of education is even lower. In the next chapter we explore in greater detail the mechanism underlying this bumping effect and how unskilled workers are pushed entirely out of the labor force.

CHAPTER 4

Labor Force Displacement Mechanisms

In Chapter 3 we introduce the concept of "education intensity" and use this idea to group detailed occupations into four broad categories designated as "tiers." This approach allows us to discuss some important changes in the demand side of the labor market. In particular, we show that over the last quarter-century, jobs requiring relatively little education have increased faster than the number of less-educated prime-age workers while, at the same time, jobs requiring more education have increased more slowly than the number of more-educated prime-age workers.

Given these growing imbalances in supply and demand, labor markets must somehow adjust. Some wage adjustment has occurred, but not all of it is in the "correct" direction. More specifically, by applying a simple textbook supply and demand model of the labor markets, we would predict wages falling in more-educated jobs and rising in less-educated ones. In fact, as we discuss in detail in Chapters 5 and 6, average wages have fallen in less-educated jobs and have stayed approximately the same in more-educated jobs, while wage variance has increased. This is more consistent with excess labor supply for the less-educated jobs, rather than the excess labor demand we demonstrate in Chapter 3. What is happening?

Our interpretation of the data is that there is strong downward wage stickiness for jobs in education-intensive occupations. This stickiness is perhaps due to efficiency wages. That is, firms are reluctant to lower wages too much, thereby risking increases in turnover and shirking, as well as reduced morale. Such changes would lower average productivity, from the firm's view. If this decrease in average productivity is larger than the decrease in average wages, the firm will reduce its profits if it lowers wages. Wage stickiness may also have something to do with implicit contracts favoring senior workers over junior ones, by allowing labor demand to vary more easily along the quantity dimension than the wage dimension.

Regardless of the cause of wage stickiness, the result is that a growing excess supply leads to real or potential joblessness more than wage reductions. When those facing joblessness are well-educated, they can react to joblessness by applying for jobs in less education-intensive occupations. This in turn increases labor supply in the next lower tier of occupations, and the process repeats itself down to the bottom of the occupational ladder, where those facing joblessness have no alternative employment possibilities.

In Chapter 3 we use the results of the National Adult Literacy Survey to show that workers who are displaced from one tier and subsequently employed in a lower one have, on average, lower functional literacy than the workers in their original tier who were not displaced. This suggests that cognitive skills do play a role in both the hiring and turnover process when there is an excess supply of workers available with adequate formal education.

Other displacement mechanisms are also functioning, which arise from head-to-head competition of workers with similar levels of both formal education and functional literacy. In this chapter, we focus particularly on the displacement of men by women. We show that the fraction of employed women with jobs in more education-intensive occupations has grown significantly. Since the fraction of employed men in such positions has decreased, this represents a type of displacement. Firms may encourage such displacement for a variety of reasons including gender differences in productivity, affirmative action laws, or because women are paid lower wages than men.

Other kinds of head-to-head competition can also be specified. For instance, it can be argued that the alleged fall of discriminatory barriers against African-Americans enable such workers to compete more successfully against whites for jobs commensurate with their educational qualifications. We present some contrary evidence below.

In this chapter we sort out the relative importance of these mechanisms by means of a decomposition analysis of the changes in employment and joblessness which have occurred over the last quarter-century. In the first section, we cross-classify the prime-age population by gender, race, level of formal education, labor force participation, and occupation tier. We compare the results for 1995 to those for 1971. We also use the "multivariate Theil decomposition" technique to show what fraction of the changes can be explained by the simultaneous trends in these five variables. These are called "aggregate changes." The remaining changes that cannot be explained by the trends, we refer to as "structural changes." These structural changes offer insight into the displacement process.

In this middle section we explore the structural changes and the patterns of job displacement from a macro-viewpoint. We show that replacement of men by women is the major type of job displacement mechanism. The final section looks at these mechanisms from a more microeconomic standpoint and explores the who, how, when, and why of job displacement.[1]

---

1 The processes we identify are consistent, in many ways, with the job-competition model developed by Lester Thurow (1975).

Decomposition Into Aggregate and
Structural Changes

In any decomposition analysis the goal is to separate a total change into several discrete components, each of which can be linked to a particular set of economic factors. In this way it is possible to measure both the effects and importance of various causal factors.

The sequential method we use below allows us to decompose the total change into two broad components, and then to decompose both of these components into two or three sub-components. In the first step of the decomposition analysis we separate the effects of "aggregate changes," or those caused by broad trends in demographics, education attainment, labor force participation rates, and occupation structure. After interpreting these, we turn to the "structural changes," that is, the remaining effects after the aggregate changes are taken into account.

The Impact of Trends in Demographics, Employment Status and Occupation Tiers

We start by dividing the population under consideration into 80 sub-categories. The primary focus is on four subgroups of the prime working-age population: white males, black males, white females, and black females; other races are omitted from the analysis. These four groups are cross-classified by four education levels: high-school dropouts, those with just a high-school diploma, those with some university training, and those with a university degree. Finally, we cross-classify these 16 groups into five employment status/occupation tier groups.[2] This particular grouping allows us to identify the changes caused by simultaneous trends in population, race, gender, education, employment status, and occupation structure. In Table 4.1 we present the number of prime working-age people in each of these 80 subcategories for both 1971 and 1995.

What underlying changes occurred in the distribution of people across these 80 subcategories during the quarter-century ending in 1995? This is basically a problem of comparing two tables (or two matrices). Since the 1995

---

2 The four occupation categories are based on the groupings of education-intensiveness, which are discussed in Chapter 2. (In this grouping, tier 1 occupations are associated with the lowest average levels of education, while tier 4 occupations are associated with the highest levels of education). The fifth group consists of the non-employed or jobless. We define education–intensiveness in terms of the 1971–72 rankings.

population under consideration is 163 percent of the 1971 population, one simple method is to scale up the 1971 matrix by this amount and to compare the results with the 1995 matrix, an exercise carried out in Appendix 4.1. This comparison clearly shows that growth was not spread out uniformly across the 80 subcategories. For example, the number of white female college graduates working in tier 4 occupations in 1995 are almost three million larger than the scaled-up table suggests. Yet at the other extreme, the white, male, high-school dropouts working in tier 2 occupations in 1995 are more than two million less than suggested by the scaled-up table. Overall, this comparison shows that prime-age workers in 1995 acquired more education than formerly, were less likely to be jobless, and more likely to be in education-intensive occupations.

To move beyond such simple observations, we utilize a well-established multi-variate method for decomposing each of the labor market changes over this quarter-century period into two components. This method, first developed by Theil (1977) and Theil and Ghosh (1980), was originally used to analyze production and employment data disaggregated by industry and region. Theil's decomposition technique, as it has become known, makes use of a standard quantitative method from input-output analysis, namely the biproportional matrix (or RAS) technique, which was originally developed by Richard Stone (1961, 1962) for updating input-output matrices.[3]

The basic idea is to examine the change that has occurred in each individual term in the table over the period and determine what fraction can be best explained by proportional changes in the entire row or column, and what fraction seems unique to this term. In practice, this involves multiplying every term in the original table by three factors: one for the change in the total prime-age population (the population multiplier which is the same for all terms in the

---

3 In its original context, the RAS technique is used to extrapolate the most likely details of a current input-output matrix when only the row and column totals are known. It requires that a completely known input-output matrix be available for some previous year.

Theil shows how to use this technique with two completely known matrices to summarize and decompose the differences between the matrices. He uses this technique to determine what fraction of the overall changes in his data to attribute to shifts in production and employment across industries, and what fraction to attribute to shifts in production and employment across regions. In doing this, he focuses on what we call the aggregate changes, and provides no analysis of what we call the structural changes.

Theil and Ghosh refer to the structural changes as "region-industry interaction terms." In other words, changes which are unique to a particular region-industry cell in the table and cannot be explained by the simple sum or product of the appropriate region effect and industry effect. This interpretation is entirely consistent with ours. However, for their particular application, they implicitly suggest that these interaction (or structural change) terms are not of great interest. In our application, we argue that these terms capture some of the most important behavioral and institutional changes occurring in the U.S. economy.

Table 4.1: *Distribution of the Prime Working-Age Population by Employment Status and Occupation Tier Versus Gender, Race, and Education (in thousands of persons)*

Panel A: 1971 prime-age population

Highest educational level	Jobless	Occupational tiers				Total
		Tier 1	Tier 2	Tier 3	Tier 4	
White male, high-school dropout	861.	3316.	2194.	841.	34.	7246.
Black male, high-school dropout	257.	918.	269.	67.	2.	1513.
White female, high-school dropout	4622.	1385.	1074.	540.	24.	7645.
Black female, high-school dropout	899.	589.	154.	79.	7.	1728.
White male, high-school diploma	552.	2367.	3423.	3043.	305.	9691.
Black male, high-school diploma	83.	376.	209.	120.	17.	806.
White female, high-school diploma	6971.	862.	1597.	3488.	155.	13072.
Black female, high-school diploma	414.	255.	231.	230.	7.	1137.
White male, some university	269.	344.	742.	1850.	421.	3626.
Black male, some university	22.	48.	63.	73.	8.	213.
White female, some university	1807.	74.	248.	1169.	152.	3450.
Black female, some university	83.	14.	46.	107.	24.	275.
White male, university degree	209.	52.	219.	1722.	2716.	4918.
Black male, university degree	13.	6.	13.	46.	72.	150.
White female, university degree	1225.	22.	60.	42.	1079.	2877.
Black female, university degree	25.	2.	2.	25.	113.	167.
Total	18313.	10630.	10544.	13891.	5136.	58514.

Panel B: 1995 prime-age population

Highest educational level	Jobless	Occupational tier				Total
		Tier 1	Tier 2	Tier 3	Tier 4	
White male, high-school dropout	1227.	2260.	1039.	269.	22.	4817.
Black male, high-school dropout	421.	306.	125.	32.	0.	884.
White female, high-school dropout	2168.	991.	647.	397.	34.	4238.
Black female, high-school dropout	623.	226.	167.	57.	8.	1082.
White male, high-school graduate	1584.	4583.	4073.	2988.	156.	13383.
Black male, high-school graduate	428.	947.	508.	342.	20.	2245.
White female, high-school graduate	3920.	1537.	2731.	5239.	495.	13923.
Black female, high-school graduate	947.	440.	515.	596.	75.	2573.
White male, some university	986.	2074.	2912.	4225.	730.	10927.
Black male, some university	224.	385.	446.	404.	60.	1519.
White female, some university	2975.	518.	1823.	6368.	844.	12529.
Black female, some university	483.	143.	422.	967.	102.	2116.
White male, university degree	610.	436.	867.	5362.	5031.	12306.
Black male, university degree	106.	73.	104.	343.	307.	932.
White female, university degree	1881.	126.	416.	4139 .	4469.	11031.
Black female, university degree	107.	11.	60.	450.	363.	990.
Total	18690.	15055.	16854.	32179.	12718.	95496.

Notes: All data come from the March Current Population Surveys and authors' calculations.

table); one for the change in the total number of people in that particular gender/race/education group (the demographic-education multiplier, which is the same for any two terms in same row); and one for the change in the total number of people in that particular employment status/occupation tier (the employment-occupation multiplier, which is the same for any two terms in the same column). Thus the individual multiplier – which is the product of the three multipliers – is different for every term in the table.

These three factors, or "multipliers," as they are usually called, are chosen simultaneously. They are used to produce a new table with a distribution of numbers across the rows and columns which is "similar" to the 1971 table but which has identical row and column totals as in 1995. We choose the multipliers so the numbers within the derived table are as close as possible to the distribution of numbers in the 1971 table, yet still consistent with the changes in the size of the labor force, gender and racial composition, levels of education, and distribution of occupations among occupation tiers.[4] We refer to this new table as the hypothetical 1995 table, and it shows what the prime-age population would have looked like if the detailed structure of the labor force (the relative sizes of the cells) stayed as close as possible to their 1971 levels, while the aggregate groups (the row and column totals) changed to their 1995 level to reflect the overall changers in population, education, race/ethnicity and occupation occurring during the period.

To derive this hypothetical 1995 table, we start with the actual 1971 table. We then use the RAS iterative techniques to "scale up" the individual terms in this table so they add up to the 1995 row and column totals. The RAS technique does this in such a way that the distribution of the terms across the

---

4   There are many different but reasonable ways to define the "closeness" of two tables of numbers. Most of them involve defining: (a) a way of measuring the distance between any pair of identically-placed terms across the two tables; and (b) a way of calculating overall distance by averaging across the measures for each pair of terms. In our method the distance between any two terms in identical positions within the two tables is just the difference between the natural logs of the two terms. Overall distance is then defined as the weighted arithmetic mean of these pairwise distances, where the weights are proportional to the size of the terms in one of the two tables.
Mathematically, this can be written as:

$$ \text{ID} = \sum_{i=1}^{M} \sum_{j=1}^{N} b_{ij} \log \left(\frac{b_{ij}}{a_{ij}} \right) \quad , $$

where ID stands for "information distance," A and B are the two matrices (or tables), with dimensions m x n (m rows and n columns), and a_{ij} and b_{ij} are individual terms within matrices A and B respectively. The two tables are then "close" to each other if ID is small.

scaled up table is as close as possible to the distribution across the actual 1971 table. In more technical language, the RAS technique finds the table that is "closest" to the 1971 table in the sense of minimizing the "information distance," but which has row and column totals equal to the 1995 matrix.[5] Panel A of Table 4.2 shows the set of multipliers and the hypothetical 1995 matrix we derived by applying the Theil technique to the tables in Table 4.1. Three sets of multipliers must be noted: there is one "proportional multiplier," shown in the bottom right-hand corner; there are 16 "row multipliers," shown in the last column; and there are five "column multipliers," shown in the bottom row.[6] The population multiplier, which is 63 percent, accounts for the overall increase in the prime-age population. The other two sets of multipliers deal only with relative size effects, so some must be greater than one, while others must be less than one.

The demographics-education multipliers show that, given the column changes, there has been a decrease in the relative number of all high-school dropouts and all white high-school graduates. All other demographic-education groups have increased in relative size. However, some have increased much more than others. For instance, the relative number of blacks with more than a high-school education has increased by more than a factor of four. The relative number of white females with some university education or a university degree has increased by a factor of about three, while the relative number of white males with more than a high-school education has increased by a factor of only 1.84. It is clear that every demographic group has increased its average level of education, but this has occurred most dramatically among black males and black females. White females increased their average level of education somewhat less, but still much more than white males.

---

5 Bacharach (1970, pp. 83-5) and Theil (1977) both use concepts from Information Theory to show that the RAS estimate minimizes the "expected information" of the message transforming the original matrix into the estimated matrix, subject to the row and column constraints. Mathematically, the RAS technique minimizes the information distance, which is defined in formula 1 in the previous footnote. Bacharach (pp. 79-82) also shows that the RAS estimate is an approximation to the matrix which minimizes the chi-square distance between the original matrix and the estimated matrix, subject to the row and column constraints. In particular, it is the closest approximation which guarantees that all terms are non-negative (assuming that all terms in the original matrices are non-negative.

6 It is these row and column multipliers that Theil and Ghosh use to decompose their changes into region versus industry effects. In our application, it is tempting to think of the row multipliers as labor supply effects and the column multipliers as labor demand effects. However, this would be misleading. The simultaneous row and column effects explain the movement from an initial set of market equilibrium points to a final set. Thus, they incorporate the shifts in both labor supply and labor demand. There is not enough information to "identify" the supply and demand effects separately.

Table 4.2: *The Hypothetical 1995 Matrix and the Derived "Aggregate" Changes*

Panel A: Hypothetical 1995 matrix and multipliers

Highest educational level	Jobless	Occupational tiers				Total	Row multipliers
		Tier 1	Tier 2	Tier 3	Tier 4		
White male, high school dropout	289.	2543.	1454.	518.	14.	4817.	(0.36)
Black male, high school dropout	75.	616.	156.	36.	1.	884.	(0.32)
White female, high school dropout	1790.	1228.	823.	384.	12.	4238.	(0.42)
Black female, high school dropout	359.	539.	122.	58.	4.	1082.	(0.43)
White male, high school diploma	395.	3875.	4842.	4002.	268.	13383.	(0.78)
Black male, high school diploma	117.	1209.	581.	309.	30.	2245.	(1.53)
White female, high school diploma	5188.	1469.	2351.	4773.	142.	13923.	(0.81)
Black female, high school diploma	564.	796.	624.	576.	12.	2573.	(1.48)
White male, some university	456.	1335.	2489.	5769.	877.	10927.	(1.84)
Black male, some university	84.	418.	472.	509.	35.	1519.	(4.13)
White female, some university	4715.	439.	1280.	5607.	487.	12529.	(2.84)
Black female, some university	405.	159.	444.	962.	147.	2116.	(5.30)
White male, university degree	354.	201.	734.	5361.	5655.	12306.	(1.84)
Black male, university degree	55.	57.	103.	350.	367.	932.	(4.51)
White female, university degree	3730.	151.	360.	2752.	4038.	11031.	(3.31)
Black female, university degree	113.	19.	18.	211.	629.	990.	(4.94)
Total	18690.	15055.	16854.	32179.	12718.	95496.	
(Column multipliers)	(0.56)	(1.29)	(1.12)	(1.04)	(0.69)		(1.63)

Panel B: *"Aggregate" changes between 1971 and 1995*

Highest educational level	Jobless	Occupational tiers Tier 1	Tier 2	Tier 3	Tier 4	Total
White male, high school dropout	-573.	-773.	-740.	-323.	-20.	-2429.
Black male, high school dropout	-181.	-302.	-113.	-31.	-2.	-628.
White female, high school dropout	-2831.	-157.	-251.	-155.	-13.	-3407.
Black female, high school dropout	-540.	-50.	-32.	-21.	-4.	-647.
White male, high school diploma	-157.	1508.	1419.	959.	-37.	3693.
Black male, high school diploma	33.	833.	372.	189.	13.	1440.
White female, high school diploma	-1783.	607.	754.	1286.	-13.	851.
Black female, high school diploma	150.	541.	393.	346.	5.	1436.
White male, some university	187.	991.	1747.	3919.	457.	7301.
Black male, some university	62.	370.	410.	436.	28.	1305.
White female, some university	2908.	365.	1032.	4438.	335.	9079.
Black female, some university	322.	145.	398.	854.	122.	1841.
White male, university degree	145.	149.	515.	3639.	2939.	7388.
Black male, university degree	42.	51.	90.	304.	295.	783.
White female, university degree	2505.	129.	301.	2261.	2959.	8154.
Black female, university degree	88.	17.	16.	186.	517.	824.
Total	377.	4425.	6310.	18288	7582.	36982.

Note: All data come from the March Current Population Surveys and authors' calculations.

The employment-occupation multipliers show that, given the row changes, there has been a decrease in the relative number of jobless, and with jobs in tier 4 (highest education) occupations. The largest increase has been in the relative number of people with jobs in tier 1 (lowest education) occupations, with smaller increases in tier 2 and tier 3 occupations. The column multiplier for joblessness of 0.56 reflects the dramatic increase in labor force participation over this quarter-century period. In 1971, 18.3 million of the 58.5 million prime working-age persons were jobless. In 1995, 18.7 million of the 95.5 million prime working-age persons were jobless. This represents a 37 percent decrease in the fraction of prime working-age persons without employment

The employment-occupation multipliers need to be interpreted carefully. It is important to remember that the demographics-education multipliers and employment-occupation multipliers are derived simultaneously. In the tables we present, it is useful to think of the employment-occupation multipliers as modifying the much larger changes occurring in demographics and education levels. With average levels of education of all demographic groups increasing so dramatically, if the employment-occupation multipliers were all equal to one (i.e., no change in relative size), there would have been an enormous increase in the number of people with jobs in tier 3 and tier 4 occupations.

Among those employed and having a university degree in 1971, 94 percent had jobs in the education-intensive occupations (tiers 3 and 4). If this were still true in 1995, when a much larger fraction of the population had college degrees (211 percent more), the increase in tier 3 and tier 4 occupations would be almost 200 percent (= 94 percent x 211 percent). The actual number of people in tier 3 and tier 4 occupations did increase significantly, by 136 percent in fact, but not by 200 percent. The column multipliers indicate, therefore, that the fraction of people in each demographic/education group who have jobs in tier 4 occupations is 31 percent smaller than in 1971. In the same way we determine that the fraction in tier 3 occupations is 4 percent higher, the fraction in tier 2 occupations is 12 percent higher, and the fraction in tier 1 occupations is 29 percent higher. This result reinforces our previous finding about downward occupational mobility discussed in detail in Chapters 2 and 3: namely, a particular level of education no longer guarantees a job in as high an occupation tier as was true in the past.

Overall, these results show that there have been large aggregate changes in the U.S. labor market over the last quarter-century. Our decomposition of these aggregate changes shows that they have been driven by large changes in population size, educational attainment, and employment status, as well as smaller changes in demographics and occupation tier structure.

The Distinction Between Aggregate and
Structural Components

For each cell we calculate the product of the three relevant multipliers and then multiply the 1971 number by this result to calculate the hypothetical 1995 matrix, which is shown in Panel A of Table 4.2. This table represents our prediction of the labor market status of all of the different subgroups in 1995, given the changes in population, gender, educational attainment, employment status, and occupation tier. In this hypothetical table the individual rows and columns add up to the corresponding 1995 totals, but the numbers within the matrix are different.

The aggregate changes can then be determined by taking the difference between the *hypothetical* 1995 table (Panel A of Table 4.2) and the *actual* 1971 table (Panel A of Table 4.1). Thus, for example, the number of black females with some college education employed in tier 3 occupations was 107 thousand in 1971. In the hypothetical table for 1995, the similar value is 962 thousand. The aggregate change is 855 thousand (= 962 thousand − 107 thousand). We show the aggregate change terms for all of the subcategories in Panel B of Table 4.2. These numbers represent what the changes in the U.S. labor market would have been over the last quarter-century if the *only* forces of change were simultaneous trends in demographics, education attainment, labor market outcomes, and occupation structure.

We define as "structural changes" those changes which cannot be explained by these various multipliers. The absolute size of these structural changes can be determined by the difference between the *actual* 1995 table (Panel B of Table 4.1) and the *hypothetical* 1995 table (Panel A of Table 4.2).[7] For example, the number of black females with some college education employed in tier 3 occupations was 967 thousand in 1995. In the hypothetical table for 1995, the similar value is 962 thousand. The structural change is 5 thousand (= 967 thousand − 962 thousand).[8] Almost all of the change in this category is an aggregate change. In Panel B of Table 4.2 and in Panel C of Table 4.3, we decompose the total changes between 1971 and 1995 into aggregate and structural components for all 80 subcategories.

---

7 Alternatively, these structural changes can be determined by taking the difference between the actual changes (Panel B minus Panel A of Table 4.1) and the aggregate changes (Panel B of Table 4.3). Thus, for example, the actual change in the number of black females with some college education employed in tier 3 occupations was 859 thousand persons. The aggregate change was 854 thousand persons. Thus the structural change was five thousand persons (=859-854).

8 Notice that the structural change (=5 thousand) and the aggregate change (=855 thousand) necessarily add up to be equal to the actual change (=860 thousand).

Since the aggregate and structural changes represent very different economic phenomena, it is important to understand their relative sizes in this application. Using Theil's measure of informational distance (shown in footnote 4) we can calculate that the information distance between the hypothetical 1995 and actual 1971 matrices is 0.270. Also, the informational distance between the actual 1995 and actual 1971 matrices is .342. Thus 78.8 percent (= .270 / .342) of the total changes are explained by the hypothetical matrix.

Explaining almost 80 percent of the total changes in the labor market over this quarter-century year period is a very successful result. In our example for black females with some college education employed in tier 3 occupations, more than 99 percent (= 962 / 967) of the total change is explained by these simultaneous trends. Unfortunately, the hypothetical table does not explain all of the changes equally well. In particular, for some of the changes we are most interested in, namely the non-employment of less-educated men and the employment of more-educated white women, the hypothetical table works poorly.

Two specific examples of the poor predictive value of the hypothetical matrix deserve attention. According to the numbers in Table 4.2 the hypothetical matrix predicts that joblessness of white male high-school dropouts should have been 289, a decrease of 573. In actuality (Table 4.1), it increased by 366. To explain why the actual rates of non-employment have increased, we must consider structural changes that are large enough to overcome and reverse the push of the aggregate changes.

At the same time, the hypothetical matrix predicts that joblessness of white females with some university training or a university degree should have increased by 5.4 million. In actuality, it increased by only 1.8 million. As we will see in the next section, this structural decrease in non-employment among educated white females is linked with the structural increase in non-employment among less-educated males.

A Closer Look at the Structural Component

In this section we focus on the structural changes, or "job displacement," that have occurred and cannot be explained by trends in population, gender, race/ethnicity, educational attainment, employment status, and occupational tier. We first analyze the net displacement flows from one job tier to the next in the various race/gender/education groups. We then decompose the structural change into two subcomponents to develop further insights into the displacement process.

Evidence from the Structural Change Matrix

To acquire some insight into these unexplained changes, we need to look carefully at the structural change matrix in Panel C of Table 4.3. If a number in a particular cell is positive, it indicates that the number of people in that category grew more than can be explained by the aggregate factors described above. A negative number means the opposite. It is also a property of these residuals that each row and each column must sum to zero. Thus, if one group is over-represented in one row or column, other groups within the same row or column must be under-represented by the same amount. These structural change numbers represent shifts in the underlying labor force structure between 1971 and 1995 that cannot be explained using information about changes in the column and row totals (i.e., the aggregate changes).

Before looking at all of the detail in the full matrix, it is useful to look first at some more aggregated forms of this matrix of structural changes. In Panel A of Table 4.3 we combine the structural changes into four demographic groups, cross-classified by the four occupational groups (and non-employment). This exercise allows us to see some crucial clues. In column 1, the number of jobless white females decreased by almost 4.5 million persons while the number of jobless white males, black males, and black females increased by a corresponding amount. In columns 3, 4, and 5 the number of white females with jobs in tier 2, 3, and 4 occupations increased dramatically while the number of white and black males in these occupation decreased. The number of white males, in row 1, with jobs in tier 2, 3, and 4 occupations decreased while the number in tier 1 occupations and non-employment increased. For black males, in row 2, the results are similar except that their numbers decreased in all four occupation categories, and increased only in joblessness.

These results provide very strong evidence that white females entering the labor force displaced both white males and black males – not just from jobs in tier 2, 3, and 4 occupations but also from employment in general. These results are also consistent with the hypothesis that these displaced males moved a step or two down the job ladder and, in turn, displaced other males in that occupation. This displacement ultimately left many more males either jobless or in tier 1 occupations.

In Panel B of Table 4.3, we divide people into four groups with different levels of education, cross-classified into non-employment or one of the four occupation tiers. The results in columns 1 through 4 show very clearly that people with more education displaced people with less education. The fact that only positive numbers are below the diagonal in columns 2 through 4, and

Table 4.3: *Structural Changes in the Distribution of the Prime Working-Age Population Between 1971 and 1995 (in thousands of persons)*

Panel A: *"Structural" changes by race and gender*

	Jobless	Occupational tiers Tier 1	Tier 2	Tier 3	Tier 4	Total
White males, total	2913.	1398.	-629.	-2808.	-874.	0.
Black males, total	848.	-590.	-129.	-82.	-47.	0.
White females, total	-4479.	-115.	802.	2627.	1165.	0.
Black females, total	718.	-693.	-44.	263.	-244.	0.
Total	0.	0.	0.	0.	0.	0.

Panel B: *"Structural" changes by education*

Highest education level	Jobless	Occupational tiers Tier 1	Tier 2	Tier 3	Tier 4	Total
Total, high school dropouts	1927.	-1143.	-576.	-241.	33.	0.
Total, high school diploma	615.	158.	-572.	-494.	293.	0.
Total, some university	-992.	768.	919.	-885.	190.	0.
Total, university degree	-1550.	217.	229.	1620.	-516.	0.
Total	0.	0.	0.	0.	0.	0.

Panel C: "Structural changes" by race, gender, and education

Highest education level	Jobless	Occupational tiers Tier 1	Tier 2	Tier 3	Tier 4	Total
White male, high school dropout	939.	-283.	-415.	-249.	8.	0.
Black male, high school dropout	346.	-310.	-31.	-4.	-1.	0.
White female, high school dropout	378.	-237.	-176.	13.	22.	0.
Black female, high school dropout	264.	-313.	46.	-1.	4.	0.
White male, high school diploma	1189.	708.	-770.	-1014.	-113.	0.
Black male, high school diploma	311.	-262.	-73.	34.	-10.	0.
White female, high school diploma	-1268.	68.	380.	466.	354.	0.
Black female, high school diploma	383.	-356.	-109.	20.	63.	0.
White male, some university	530.	738.	424.	-1545.	-147.	0.
Black male, some university	140.	-33.	-26.	-105.	25.	0.
White female, some university	-1740.	79.	543.	761.	357.	0.
Black female, some university	78.	-16.	-22.	5.	-45.	0.
White male, university degree	255.	235.	132.	1.	-623.	0.
Black male, university degree	51.	15.	1.	-7.	-60.	0.
White female, university degree	-1849.	-25.	55.	1387.	431.	0.
Black female, university degree	-7.	-8.	41.	239.	-266.	0.
Total	0.	0.	0.	0.	0.	0.

Notes: A positive number indicates that the number of people in the particular cell increased more than our prediction from the aggregative factors described above. All data come from the March Current Population Surveys and authors' calculations.

only negative numbers are above it is consistent with the idea that more-educated people are displacing less-educated people, who move into either lower-level occupations or join the ranks of the jobless. The one strong exception to his pattern, however, appears in column 5, the tier 4 occupations. In the occupations associated with the highest average levels of education, we see less-educated persons displacing those with university degrees. To explain this, we need to add more details in Section C of this chapter.

Panel C of Table 4.3 shows the full range of details we used for our analysis. A look at the numbers for persons with some university training or a university degree and jobs in tier 4 occupations suggests that two different changes are occurring simultaneously. The most striking change is the displacement of white males with college degrees by white females, some of whom do not have a college degree. There are at least four possible explanations for this type of displacement: gender productivity differences, gender wage differences, affirmative action policies, and educational downgrading.

The first two possible explanations relate directly to profit maximization motives. If a firm can replace a current worker with one who is more productive and/or willing to work for lower pay, then most firms will do so. On the productivity side, it is sometimes argued that many of the most "talented" women in previous generations chose to work at home rather than for pay. Now, as such women enter the work force for the first time, some are more productive – even without a college degree – than some of the less productive men with college degrees. Some firms choose to maximize profits and replace these men with these women. On the wage side, most recent studies of wages across gender conclude that there is still some subtle wage discrimination against women in some firms and in some jobs. Among firms that are in a position to discriminate in this way, some will choose to do the profitable thing and replace men with women. We are unable to test the productivity explanation directly, but in Section C of this chapter we do find bits and pieces of evidence supporting it. In Chapter 6, we present strong empirical support for the wage explanation.

The other two possible explanations are more institutional. The first is that affirmative action policies and/or changed attitudes of men in positions of power have caused some firms to actively recruit and hire women that they would have ignored in the past. This is also hard to test, but there is some empirical evidence to support this proposition.[9] The last possible explanation is that firms may be "downgrading" the necessary educational level of some jobs in tier 4 occupations. We look at certain aspects of this possibility in the next section of this chapter and find some evidence to support this idea.

---

9 According to Badgett and Hartman (1995): "At the broadest level, measures of activity related to both Title VII and the federal contract compliance programs are consistently correlated with labor market outcomes (e.g., wage, employment, occupational status, and quits), after removing the effect of other labor market influences. In most cases, these effects are consis-

Another striking change shown in Panel C of Table 4.3 occurs among those persons with some university training, or a university degree, and jobs in tier 4 occupations: A large number of black females with a college degree have been displaced from jobs in tier 4 occupations, a phenomenon that is difficult to explain. Part of this change may represent a decline in the average productivity of black women with a college degree. Along these lines, it is possible that in 1971, the small proportion of black prime-age women who had a college degree were an unusually talented and/or hard-working group. Discrimination in education had made it difficult for any black woman to obtain a college degree, so perhaps the small group that succeeded was very exceptional. By 1995, with a much larger proportion of black females earning a college degree, the average levels of ability and effort within this group would be lower. Another aspect of this change may represent occupational barriers within tier 4 jobs that make it difficult for black women to enter some faster-growing sub-occupations. We examine this second possibility in section C of this chapter and find some evidence to support it.

Continuing to look at Panel C of Table 4.3, one additional important detail deserves comment. Although the movement of women with high-school diplomas or more into the labor force was the main source of displacement, women high-school dropouts were affected in approximately the same way as men. They were bumped down from tier 2 occupations into tier 1 occupations or into joblessness. Thus, not only men, but also women with low levels of education were being displaced as the effect of the new, more-educated female entrants rippled through the labor force.

Further Decomposition of the Structural Component

In this section, we analyze the structural change so as to clarify the mechanisms underlying the various displacement patterns identified above. More specifically, we further decompose the structural changes into what we call the "proportional employment component" and the "occupation shifting component." This decomposition can be done separately for each gender-race-education row in our table.

Proportional employment changes represent the additional amount (beyond the hypothetical level) that each employment cell must change to explain the

tent with the policies' intended outcomes..." A more popular treatment with similar conclusions is by Bergmann (1996). We must note, however, that these are controversial matters and considerable contrary evidence also exists.

structural change in total employment for that row.[10] Proportional employment changes are determined by taking the percent difference between the actual 1995 and hypothetical 1995 value of total employment in a row,[11] and applying this percent to each employment cell in that row of the hypothetical 1995 matrix. For example, since actual employment in 1995 for white women with a high-school diploma is at a level 14.5 percent above what the aggregate changes predict, then the proportional employment change for each of the employment tier cells in this row is 14.5 percent of the predicted level for that cell. Of course, since the actual structural change for white women with a high-school diploma in tier 2 occupations is equal to 16.2 percent of the predicted level, there is still a residual.

We call these remaining residuals the "occupation shifting changes." These are simply the differences between the structural changes and the proportional employment changes. It is useful to think of the proportional employment changes as accounting for differences in total employment in each row, while the occupation shifting changes account for differences in relative employment across the occupation tiers within each row.[12]

In Appendix Table A4.2 we show the results of this further decomposition of the structural change numbers from Panel C of Table 4.3. From this exercise, several patterns are clear:

(a) White women with a high-school diploma or more entered into employment, especially in more education-intensive occupations (tiers 2, 3, and 4). In doing so, they displaced males of all education levels as well as black females with less than a university degree and white females with less than a high-school diploma. As these groups were displaced, some became jobless, while others moved down to jobs in less education-intensive occupations (tiers 1 and 2) and displaced males as well as females with low levels of education. This process continued, until many people who previously held jobs in tier 1 occupations were bumped into joblessness.

(b) The pattern across white males of different education levels is remarkably consistent. White males were flowing both out of employment entirely and down the job ladder. For white males with a high-school diploma or more, the occupation shifting changes were large enough relative to the proportional employment changes, resulting in an increase in the total number of white males in the tier 1 occupations. In other words, the number of people

---

10   When these changes are added to the hypothetical 1995 matrix, it generates the closest matrix to the actual 1995 matrix which is 100 percent consistent with all 16 of the actual non-employment numbers in 1995.

11   As a percentage of the hypothetical 1995 value of total employment.

12   The mathematical details of this further decomposition are explained in Appendix 4.3.

bumped down into tier 1 occupations from above was greater than the number who left tier 1 occupations to become jobless. For those with some university training or a university degree, this pattern was also true for tier 2 occupations. This suggests increased "crowding" of white males into the bottom tier occupations, which is consistent with the decline in real wages occurring in the bottom occupation categories over the last 25 years.

(c) The pattern of structural changes across white females is more complex. Only those with less than a high-school diploma show a net decline in employment. All other white women experience a net increase in employment. Among those with a high-school diploma and/or some university education, there was a more than proportionate movement into tier 2 and tier 4 occupations, and a less than proportionate movement into tier 3 occupations. Since wages increase with occupation tier, this bifurcation suggests increased variance in earnings among these moderately educated white women. This result is consistent with the many studies of wage variations showing an increase in earnings inequality within most groups of persons with similar personal characteristics.

Interestingly, however, the variance in earnings among employed white females with a university degree is likely to be compressed as they were moving much less than proportionately into tier 2 and tier 4 occupations, and much more than proportionately into tier 3 occupations. One possible explanation for this is that as the number of white females getting university degrees has increased, the average quality or productivity of this group has declined. The rapid growth of this cohort in relation to the number of job openings in tier 4 precludes the possibility of matching the fraction of educated women who obtained employment in these occupations.

(d) The pattern for black males and for black females is similar across both high-school dropouts and those with just a high-school diploma. All four of these demographic-education groups reveal a net flow out of employment originating disproportionately from occupations with lower education-intensiveness (tiers 1 and 2). As with some other changes, these would tend to increase income dispersion within each of these demographic groups. For black males with some university training or a university degree, the pattern is similar to that for white males at the same educational levels. That is, there was a net flow out of employment which pulled disproportionately from the higher tier occupations (those with greater education-intensiveness). For black females with some university training there was a small net flow out of employment combined with some movement toward tier 3 occupations. Black females with a university degree reveal very little movement in or out of employment. Nevertheless, there was a large structural movement out of tier 4 occupations and into tier 3 occupations, which we will discuss further below.

Before turning to a more microeconomic examination of displacement mechanisms, it is useful to note that wage evidence also supports the interpretations that we have offered. We discuss such evidence in considerable detail in Chapters 5 and 6.

Who, How, When, and Why

Some of the important details of the displacement process now need to be examined more closely. In this discussion we focus on such key questions as who bumped whom, how did it happen, when did it take place, and why did it occur.

Who Bumped Whom?

How important has head-to-head competition been in this displacement process? Or, to rephrase the question within the framework of this analysis, were most of the displaced or "bumped" workers replaced by someone with a similar level of education? The numbers in Appendix Table A4.2 can be used to answer this question. For example, in the tier 3 occupations, 4897 thousand persons were displaced. Of those doing the bumping, 2200 thousand had a university degree. Of those being bumped, only 579 thousand had a university degree. If we make the assumption that the entering persons with the most education displaced the exiting persons with the most education, and so on, we can then calculate how many people were displaced by those with levels of education similar to their own.

We summarize these estimates in a convenient form in Panel A of Table 4.4 for all four tiers. In the less education-intensive occupations – tiers 1, 2, and 3 – the majority of the bumping involves people with more education displacing those with less education. In tier 3, for instance, 4897 people were bumped. In 2294 (46.8 percent) of these cases, the person entering and the person exiting had the same level of education. In the other 2603 thousand (53.2 percent) bumping cases, the person entering had more education than the person exiting. The number of people being bumped by those with higher education ranges from 80 percent for the tier 1 occupations to 53 percent for the tier 3 occupations. In tiers 1, 2, and 3, all of the remaining cases involve people with identical levels of education. Although educational upgrading occurred in all three of these tiers, it was much larger in the bottom level (tier 1) jobs than others.

The results for jobs in the most education-intensive occupations (tier 4) are quite different. While 60 percent of the displacement involved people with

Table 4.4: *Some Relevant Data on the Who of Structural Changes*

Panel A: Type of displacement process by occupation tiers (number of cases in thousands)

	Lower education replaces higher education	Those with a given education replace those of similar education	Higher education replaces lower education	Total	Percent of total displacement
Tier 4 occupations	745	1126	0	1871	13.5%
Tier 3 occupations	0	2294	2603	4897	35.3%
Tier 2 occupations.	0	2444	1951	4395	31.6%
Tier 1 occupations	0	455	2272	2727	19.6%
Total	745	6319	6826	13890	
percent	5.4%	45.5%	49.1%		100%

Panel B: Tier 4 occupations with the largest increases in the number of workers with some university, but not a university degree

Rank	Occupation Title	Occupation number	Increase (in thousands)
1.	Computer systems analysts and scientists	64	192
2.	Accountants and auditors	23	142
3.	Managers, medicine and health	15	130
4.	Financial officers, not accountants, auditors, underwriters	25	63
5.	Teachers, prekindergarten and kindergarten	155	59
6.	Securities and financial services salespersons	255	58
7.	Social workers	174	49
8.	Administrators, education and related fields	14	43
9.	Personnel and labor relations managers	8	31
10.	Clergy	176	28
	Total Increase for all ten occupation		795
	Total Increase for all tier 4 occupations		1134

Notes: All data come from the March Current Population Surveys and from the authors' calculations.

similar levels of education, the other 40 percent involved people with less education bumping those with more education. This result is surprising and requires further exploration. For each of the 100 or so detailed occupations comprising tier 4, we calculate the net change in the number of employed workers with some university training, but no university degree. We then examine the 10 detailed tier 4 occupations with the largest increases in this value, which are listed in Panel B of Table 4.4. Collectively, they accounted for 70 percent of the total increase in workers with some university education, but no university degree, in tier 4 jobs.

Compared to many other detailed occupations within tier 4, most of the 10 in Panel B have somewhat nebulous definitions. An "accountant" or a "financial officer" may be a professional with an advanced degree or a person with less than a university degree who has developed some bookkeeping skills and has been given significant responsibilities. A "computer systems analyst" may be someone with an advanced degree in computer science or a hacker with less than a university degree with some programming skills. These results are consistent with the view that educational "downgrading" is occurring in some jobs in tier 4. This may represent an attempt by employers to cut costs by using lower-paid workers as substitutes for higher-paid workers.

These results for the four tiers suggest that we should observe significant increases in the average education levels for tier 1, 2, and 3 occupations, with the largest increase in tier 1 occupations. For tier 4 occupations, two effects are at work. First, we would expect the average level of education to increase less because it already approached the highest limit. Second, the effect of the structural changes was to reduce the average level of education. However, the underlying increase in the acquisition of education captured in the aggregate changes will push average education levels in all occupations higher. Thus the education level in tier 4 can still increase, but by much less than in the other tiers. In Chapter 3, Table 4.4 we show that the average education level has increased dramatically in tier 1 occupations, and by a large amount in tier 2 and tier 3 occupations. At the same time in tier 4 occupations, average education has increased by only a small amount, just as we would expect.

How Did It Happen?

Did the women replacing men literally take their jobs away by filling existing positions? Or did they just fill a more than proportionate number of the new jobs created over this quarter-century? For an answer, we calculate the growth of employment between 1971 and 1995 for each of the 500 detailed

Table 4.5: *Some Relevant Data on the How and When of Structural Change*

Panel A: *Representation of women in occupations grouped by growth rates*

Occupational group names	Total growth 1971–95	Percent female in 1971	Percent female in 1995	Change in female representation
W	More than 190%	40.5%	53.4%	12.9
X	68% to 190%	34.1	45.5	11.4
Y	0% to 67%	35.6	41.5	5.9
Z	Less than 0%	37.0	39.0	2.0

Panel B: *Relative size of the aggregate and structural changes over three subperiods*

Time period	Total change	Aggregate change	Structural change
1971 to 1979	.077	.060 (78.5%)	.017 (21.5%)
1979 to 1987	.032	.020 (62.3)	.012 (37.7)
1987 to 1995	.032	.028 (86.6)	.004 (13.4)
1971 to 1995	.342	.270 (78.8)	.072 (21.2)

Notes: All data come from the March Current Population Surveys and authors' calculations. Groups W, X, Y and Z contain roughly equal numbers of occupations, ranked according to the growth in the number of jobs. All data come from Current Population Surveys.

occupations. In Panel A of Table 4.5 we then group the occupations into four roughly equal-sized categories based on these growth rates (these are not the same as our four occupation tiers). Employment in the occupations in group Z actually decreased over this period. The occupations in group W increased their employment by more than 190 percent. The occupations in groups X and Y fell in between. Finally, for each group of occupations, we calculate the fraction of female workers in both 1971 and 1995.

In every category, women increased their representation. In the shrinking and slowest-growing job groups, their representation increased by 2.0 and 5.9 percentage points respectively. In the two fastest-growing job groups, however, their representation increased by 11.4 and 12.9 percentage points respectively. This implies that women are moving into new and growing occupations at a much faster rate than men. Clearly, considerable displacement involved women filling a more than proportionate number of the new jobs. Thus it is clear that a significant share of the displacement occurred in this indirect manner, rather than directly replacing men in their current positions.[13]

When Did It Happen?

It is useful now to consider next the timing of these structural changes. Using data from the March 1979 and March 1987 CPS, we calculate matrices similar to those in Tables 4.1 through 4.4 for the three 8-year subperiods that make up our quarter-century of data. We then use Theil's measure of information distance to calculate the total magnitude of the changes occurring over each subperiod, as well as the fraction of the changes which were aggregate and structural. These results are in Panel B of Table 4.5.

We must emphasize that the changes in the three subperiods do not add up to the total change over the entire period. This should be expected since the measure of distance or change is very non-linear. Despite this non-linearity, however, the measures of change for each of the three subperiods are directly comparable. The total change was clearly largest during the 1971 to 1979 subperiod. It was more than twice as large as the change in either of the two later periods. The structural change, on the other hand, has been a little more spread out over time. About half of the total structural change occurred during 1971 to 1979, and an additional 3/8 occurred during 1979 to 1987. Very little structural change occurred after 1987, a result found in a quite different way in our discussion of the data in Table 3-4.

These results over time are also consistent with the fact that both the women's labor force participation rate and the fraction of young persons attending university first began to increase sharply in the late 1960s. Both numbers continued to climb dramatically in the 1970s and only gradually began to slow in the 1980s.

Why Did It Happen?

Although the pattern and timing of job flows and displacements are now clear, we still do not have an explanation for why employers implemented these changes. Were the replacement people more productive than those

---

13 Women might directly take away the jobs of men in those occupations where the number of men absolutely declined, a situation occurring in the Group Z jobs. Since the absolute number of women in this group also declined, this evidence cannot be used to show that direct displacement occurred.

they displaced, even in the relatively rare cases when they had less education? Or were they working for lower wages than those they displaced? Or was there some type of screening or signaling occurring that helped firms keep their recruiting and hiring costs down? Finally, did job discrimination also play a role?

As shown in the previous chapter, some people doing the bumping have a higher level of cognitive skills (and presumably greater productivity) than those they are replacing. As we have also previously noted, women with a high-school diploma or less have higher functional literacy than men with the same education. As we show in Chapter 6, in tier 1 and 2 occupations, women are actually moving into higher wage positions. In particular, some women entering the work force with higher than average levels of cognitive skills may be displacing men with lower than average levels of cognitive skills, given their education and their occupation. It has also been conjectured that some displacement may occur because women have different attitudes toward work than men, particularly in low education-intensity occupations; unfortunately, we have little concrete evidence of this productivity differential.

It is also probable that some bumping occurs due to wage differentials. In Chapter 5 we look in detail at data on average hourly wages, disaggregating the numbers by race and gender as well as educational level and occupation. A clear message from the analysis in this chapter is that, when holding functional literacy, education and occupation tier constant, white males earned considerably more per hour than white females, black males, or black females. In Chapter 6 we show that this is of particular importance in education-intensive occupations – tier 3 and 4 jobs.

The structural changes showing a displacement of black women with a university degree from the most education-intensive occupations (tier 4) raises another issue, namely occupational discrimination. To examine this possibility, we calculated the percentage change in employment between 1971–72 and 1994–95 for each of the 100 or so detailed occupations in tier 4. We also calculated the percentage of workers in each tier 4 detailed occupation who are black women with university degrees. In 1971, 78 percent of these black women were in just two detailed occupations: "teachers, elementary school" and "teachers, secondary school." Over the quarter-century, total employment in these two occupations increased by only 91 percent and 20 percent respectively, while total employment in all tier 4 occupations increased by 148 percent.

At the same time, among the 10 detailed tier 4 occupations showing the fastest percentage growth, total representation of black women with university degrees was just 1.80 percent in 1995, while their representation in all tier 4 jobs was 2.85 percent. The only large (more than 200,000 workers), fast-growing (more than a 260 percent increase) tier 4 occupations with an over-representation of black university-educated women in 1995 were "teachers, special education" and "social workers."

These facts suggest that black women with university degrees have had difficulty in moving out of the two slow-growing "traditional" occupations to the faster growing tier 4 occupations. It is also noteworthy that the two fastest-growing occupations in which black women have had success are primarily in the public sector. These facts suggest that either discrimination, or, perhaps, the lack of an aggressive approach by many employers to attract minorities, may have influenced the structural changes in the employment of black university-educated women.

Summary and Conclusions

In this chapter we present a large range of data and analysis showing the existence of an important labor market phenomenon which has received relatively little attention by economists. This is the displacement of men by women, which occurred in the U.S. labor market over the last quarter-century, but particularly between 1971 and 1987. We identify a market mechanism in which women with a high-school diploma or more, who previously chose to remain out of the labor force, have entered the workforce. They have displaced men with similar or slightly lower levels of education, but who are at the low end of the productivity distribution within their education group. These men, in turn, moved down to slightly lower-paying jobs and displaced other less-educated men (and eventually women too), and so on. The cascade effect continued until the least educated men and women were either crowded into the lowest-paying occupations (with lower pay than ever due to the crowding) or were bumped into unemployment, or out of the labor force. Furthermore, most of the displacement occurred by women filling new jobs, rather than directly displacing men. This indirect displacement is, of course, much less dramatic than a direct displacement where the male workforce of a particular enterprise is suddenly replaced by women.

This analysis does not tell us why the fraction of prime-age women who were employed increased so much over this quarter-century. On the labor supply side, this rise in labor force participation certainly had something to do with changing attitudes towards women – especially married women – pursuing more education and working outside the home. On the labor demand side, this had something to do with the shift in demand away from manufacturing, where women workers were a small minority, toward services, where women workers were more common.

Some argue that the increasing entry of women in the labor force may also have had something to do with the "baby-boom" generation. In 1971, the first of the baby-boom generation entered prime-age. By 1995, all of the baby-boomers were prime-age. This helps to explain the large increase in the prime-age population over this period. However, our analysis suggests that it was not just the increase in prime-age population that drove the structural changes documented here. It may be that the early baby-boomers were the first generation to have new ideas about women's education and work – which was a critical factor – but their sheer number was not a critical factor.

Since all of these changes occurred gradually over the late 1960s and 1970s it is difficult to sort out their relative importance. However, our analysis shows that the convergence of these forces had its most important impact in initiating and sustaining the displacement process we have outlined here.

At various points throughout this and previous chapters focusing on employment, we refer to evidence from wage changes in order to support our arguments. It is now time to turn directly to this set of arguments to complete our picture of the changing U.S. labor market.

CHAPTER 5

Wage Levels

In previous chapters of this book, we focus on employment and joblessness – the quantity side of the labor market. Along the way, we develop and find support for several controversial hypotheses about changes in the U.S. labor market over the last quarter-century. So far, our themes focus on the rising joblessness of prime-age males, the displacement mechanisms, and the growing importance of cognitive skills as a determinant of employment. In this chapter and the next, we turn our attention to the price side of the labor market – average wages and their distribution across individuals. In doing so, we look for corroborating evidence to support our previous hypotheses. We also hope to gain some new insights into the causal mechanisms underlying these changes in the labor market.

At the aggregate level, three well-documented wage trends have been occurring in the U.S. over the quarter-century between 1970 and 1995. First of all, real wages of most major groups in the labor force stagnated or fell. In fact, for prime-age men, we will show that only those with a university degree and employment in a tier 4 occupation managed to increase their wages. Secondly, the rate of return to a college degree increased. However, we will show that this "fact" is not as clear once we introduce a measure of cognitive skills into the analysis. Finally, wage inequality increased both between and within most groups. In this chapter we present evidence on the first two issues; in Chapter 6 we examine changes in wage inequality.

In the first section we outline the basic trends in wage levels. We then present preliminary evidence showing the positive link between cognitive skills, as measured by NALS scores, and wages. We also discuss how the considerable discrepancy between male and female wages accelerates the displacement effect, and how the displacement of workers from tiers 3 and 4 has increased competition for jobs in tiers 1 and 2 so that, as a result, real wages have fallen. After presenting this perspective of the overall wage structure, we can then begin to look at the determinants of wages to isolate the particular importance of cognitive skills.

In the following section we analyze the determinants of wages at a single point in time showing, for instance, that cognitive skills have a considerable payoff, independent of education. We then examine the separate impacts on wages of an individual's education and cognitive skills versus the average education and skill characteristics of the detailed occupation in which they are employed. In this exercise we find that the average characteristics of a worker's occupation is the more important determinant of wages. We also discover an important anomaly in the three less education-intensive tiers of occupations. Women have very little representation in those detailed occupations with modest average levels of education but high average levels of cognitive skills.

In the third section we examine whether the rate of return to cognitive skills has increased. We use data on changes in median wages of occupations over time to show that occupations employing workers with high functional literacy have experienced the highest wage increases. This suggests that the rate of return to cognitive skills has increased. Also, by means of an analysis of regression residuals, we show that real wage increases were least in occupations exhibiting little real educational upgrading or real upskilling and increased most in some occupations where real upskilling had occurred.

In the final section we examine two special topics. The first is a brief examination of the methods used to combine our information on determinants of employment probabilities and of median wages to derive estimates for expected wages. The second is an exploration of some implications of wage behavior over time that are based on the Blanchflower-Oswald proposition linking unemployment and wages.

Trends in the Level of Real Hourly Wages

Two questions need answers: What are the most relevant facts about wage trends? And how do the impacts of the displacement effect and supply/demand situation for cognitive skills influence these wage trends?

The Key Trends

We focus on median wages because average wages are unduly influenced by a small and non-representative group of workers in various occupation/education groups earning extra-high wages. We also deal only with wages and not total compensation. That is, we do not take into account various types of benefits such as employer contributions to health and pension plans because, unfortunately, the databases used in this study do not supply such information.

As shown in Table 5.1, wage trends of real median hourly wages for men and women have been quite different (we present comparable data for 1978 and 1986 in Appendix 5.1). Several features of the data deserve attention.

For men between 1970 and 1994, real median hourly wages stagnated or

Table 5.1: *Median Hourly Real Wages of Prime-Age Workers, 1970 and 1994*

Occupational tier (defined by average education of practitioners in 1971)

Highest educational attainment	Tier 1 10.5 years or less	Tier 2 10.6 to 12.0 years	Tier 3 12.1 to 14.5 years	Tier 4 14.6 years or more	All occupational tiers
Panel A: Men, 1970 median hourly wages (1994 prices)					
High-school dropout	$10.71	$12.42	$12.92	$14.03	$11.56
High-school diploma or equivalent	12.90	14.26	15.58	17.82	14.28
Some university or trade/vocational school	13.12	14.92	16.23	17.84	15.74
One or more university degrees	13.00	14.00	19.63	19.98	19.39
Total	11.78	13.72	16.08	19.32	14.31
Part B: Men, 1994 median hourly wages (1994 prices)					
High-school dropout	7.21	8.82	10.13		7.70
High-school diploma or equivalent	9.89	11.32	12.64	15.56	11.05
Some university or trade/vocational school	10.40	12.61	14.39	16.68	12.91
One or more university degrees	10.02	12.31	18.08	20.16	18.02
Total	9.23	11.53	15.13	19.23	12.60

Panel C: Women, 1970 median hourly wages (1994 prices)

High-school dropout	6.10	6.15	7.41	7.80	6.31
High-school diploma or equivalent	6.28	7.14	9.06	9.41	7.97
Some university or trade/vocational school	6.14	7.39	10.04	9.95	9.27
One or more university degrees	6.58	7.76	12.14	13.16	12.50
Total	6.17	6.82	9.22	12.30	7.91

Part D: Women, 1994 median hourly wages (1994 prices)

High-school dropout	5.67	5.61	7.40	8.61	5.79
High-school diploma or equivalent	6.40	6.66	9.61	9.90	8.00
Some university or trade/vocational school	6.87	7.50	10.56	11.08	9.61
One of more university degrees	6.58	7.28	14.42	15.17	14.41
Total	6.24	6.73	10.85	14.15	9.61

Notes: The wage data represent total wage income divided by the number of hours worked and deflated by the personal consumption price index in the GDP accounts. These medians take into account the weight of each sample point. The data come from various years of the Current Population Survey. In Appendix Note 5.2 we describe how these wage data are estimated from the CPS. Subsequent to the calculations for this table, real wages changed relatively little for men in all educational groups and occupational tiers between 1994 and 1998. For all women real wages increased about 2.5 percent between 1994 and 1998; real wages slightly declined, however, for high-school dropouts and tier 1 occupations.

fell for all aggregate groups defined either by education or by occupation alone. The wage spread for workers in occupations commensurate with their education (the northwest-southeast diagonal of the table) increased considerably, especially at both ends of the wage distribution. Looking at specific education/occupational tier cells in the table, real median wages rose only for those with university degrees who were employed in the most education-intensive (tier 4) occupations. The relative fall in real wages was greatest among the less-educated and in the lowest occupational tiers. The data also show that those workers experiencing downward occupational mobility experienced a special decline in real hourly wages which influenced wages for their entire educational group. For instance, although university graduates in tier 4 occupations experienced increased real median wages, such wages fell for male university graduates as a whole because the median was lowered by those in tier 2 and 3 occupations.

For women between 1970 and 1994, the pattern of wage changes was much different. Real hourly wages actually fell only for high-school dropouts in low tier jobs and for those with a high-school diploma in tier 2 jobs. For all other groups wages either stagnated or rose. In most cases this represented a narrowing – but not closing – of the wage gap between men and women. Similar to men, real hourly wages increased most among the most-educated or those occupying tier 4 jobs. The highest increase was among the university-educated in jobs commensurate with their education.

The Impact of Cognitive Skills on Wages

In Table 5.2 we present the median weekly wages of men and women with various levels of education and cognitive skills. The four classes of NALS scores contain roughly the same number of people. Again, it is not surprising that average weekly wages generally rise with increases in both the NALS (functional literacy) score and education. The combined effect of the two factors is considerable.

Several possible mechanisms link wages to cognitive skills.[1] (a) If job performance is related to cognitive skills and if wages are related to performance,

1   Thee various studies linking cognitive skills and wages differ between each other and with our study in the handling of endogenous relations among the explanatory variables. For instance, we calculate an ordinary least squares regression that includes schooling as an explanatory variable, a procedure similar to that of O'Neill (1990) and Murnane *et al.* (1995). By way of contrast, Neal and Johnson (1996) omit schooling from most of their regressions because schooling opportunities may differ for whites and blacks, and they wish to focus particularly on white-black wage differences. Maxwell (1994) tries to circumvent this problem with an instrumental variable approach by calculating a special regression to predict schooling and

Table 5.2: *Median Weekly Wages of Full-Time, Prime-Age Workers by Education and Functional Literacy Score in 1992*

NALS scores	0-271	272-305	306-338	339-500	All workers
Highest level of education					
Men					
High-school dropout	$ 343	$ 329	$ —	$ —	$ 343
GED (high-school equivalent)	312	530	615	—	482
High-school diploma	420	500	500	600	480
Trade/vocational school	523	500	580	600	550
Some university	489	500	600	650	550
B.A. or B.S.	480	625	700	770	750
Graduate degree	—	930	1000	1038	1000
Total	400	500	600	769	550
Women					
High-school dropout	250	251	—		255
GED (high-school equivalent)	300	250	—	—	300
High-school diploma	283	314	360	352	312
Trade/vocational school	300	400	390	380	350
Some university	320	00	403	450	400
B.A. or B.S.	408	500	545	600	550
Graduate degree	—	500	625	750	658
Total	300	355	450	550	390

Notes: The sample includes only full-time workers with a positive weekly wage. The dashes indicate cells with less than 25 workers. The wage data represent the previous week's wage of the respondents and these medians take into account the weight of each sample point. The data come from the National Adult Literacy Study.

then wages and cognitive skills are correlated. By including a measure of cognitive skills (NALS scores) in the wage equation we have, in essence, an expanded human capital model of wage determination. (b) Occupational mobility also plays a role. As we show in Chapter 2, workers with a given education but with lower functional literacy than others with the same education

then using predicted schooling, rather than actual schooling, as an explanatory variable for wages. Such a procedure has, however, little impact on the relationship between cognitive skills and wages, which is our chief concern. Moreover, we find it difficult to imagine explanatory variables influencing schooling that also do not have an independent impact on cognitive skills and wages.

are much more likely to experience downward occupational mobility. The reverse is true for those experiencing upward mobility. Although the average wages received by these workers with occupational mobility lie between the average for their job tier and the job tier corresponding to their education, this mechanism results in a positive correlation between cognitive skills and wages when all other factors are held constant. (c) If an occupation is being upskilled, then only those with higher cognitive skills who can master the new productive techniques earn higher wages.

Wage Levels and the Displacement Effect

As argued in the previous chapter, a key mechanism underlying the displacement effect is the replacement of male by female workers. In this process the difference in wages of prime-age men and women shown in the previous tables is particularly important. It should be clear that the wage differences between men and women with the same level of education and functional literacy provide employers with a considerable incentive to replace the former with the latter. Such a process is, of course, easier when the occupation is expanding so that the replacement can be carried out by differential hiring, rather than by direct replacement. As we show in Chapter 4, this has been occurring. Our later empirical analysis also suggests that wage undercutting by women has been of greater importance in the more education-intensive (tier 3 and 4) occupations, than in tiers 1 and 2.[2]

The movement of the workforce induced by the displacement effect has several effects on wages. Certainly the entry of workers into lower occupational tiers, either from a higher occupation tier or from the new female entrants into the labor force, lowers wages. However, there is enough wage stickiness to keep the market from fully absorbing the excess supply of labor. As a result, some of the less productive workers look for a job in a still lower tier occupation. This partially reverses the original increase in labor supply, but not enough to restore wages or employment to their original levels.

The displacement effect means that the occupation tier requiring the least amount of education has become increasingly crowded. Newcomers, as well as long-time workers in this tier face the unpleasant alternative either of accepting lower real wages or being forced out of employment. To the extent workers in the lowest occupational tier are displaced by workers with more education, they have no place to go but out of the labor force, a key reason for the rise in joblessness of the less-educated.

---

2 For tier 1 and 2 occupations, an alternative mechanism involving differential productivity rates is more significant, as we point out below and in the next chapter.

An offsetting demand effect, however, also occurs because the supply of workers with relatively little formal education is declining faster than the number of jobs, a phenomenon discussed in Chapter 3. The rising joblessness and the falling wages among the less-educated shows, however, that the supply effect outweighs the demand effect.

This kind of mechanism does not explain, however, why the wages of university graduates in tier 4 occupations have risen, especially since the supply of workers with the corresponding educational credentials has risen faster than the number of jobs. We discuss this phenomenon later in this chapter when we examine the economic returns to cognitive skills, independent of education.

Determinants of Wages at a Single Point in Time

The two tables presented in Section A show positive relations between education, occupation tier, cognitive skills, and wages. To make these relations more precise, we need to move to a regression analysis which focuses on the determinants of wages. This can be done in a straightforward fashion for a single point in time with the use of the individual level data from the National Adult Literacy Study. To avoid unnecessary statistical noise, we focus only on wages of full-time workers.[3] Following convention, we use the log of this wage as the dependent variable and look separately at the wages of men and women.

Our wage equation includes not only the standard demographic variables but also a set of dummy variables for the occupational tier, that is, the education-intensiveness of the occupation.[4] This procedure requires a brief explanation. We conjecture that the relative level of education typical of individuals in the various occupations influences the wage rates of those in that occupation, regardless of their own level of education. That is, a person with a given degree of education who is in an occupation where most have a higher level of education may earn more than a similarly educated person who is in an occupation where most have a lower level education. Three possible explana-

3 For part-time workers there are some non-linearities in the wage function that divert our attention from the major theses of this study. We limit our sample further because some full-time workers earned little in the week for which the wage information was collected, either because of illness, short-hours, or temporary layoff. In our calculations, therefore, we include only those workers earning at least $120 a week.

4 Neal and Johnson (1994) reject the inclusion of occupation variables, arguing that racial factors might influence the choice of occupation. We show below that this is, indeed, the case, but that such an interrelation can be handled within the framework of our analysis.

tions for this phenomenon revolve, respectively, around unmeasured productivity effects, higher productivity associated with greater capital, and norms of fairness.[5]

• Some aspects of a worker's productivity might not be reflected in the data at our disposal. For instance, workers with an education less than typical in their particular occupation might have special abilities or more appropriate work attitudes than most of those with the same education and cognitive skills. For such reasons they might obtain jobs in occupations with a higher education-intensity and receive correspondingly higher wages. Similarly, workers with an education more than typical in their particular occupations might end up with such jobs because they have fewer productive traits than other workers with the same education and cognitive skills. Thus they receive lower wages than we would predict.

• More education-intensive occupations might provide workers with more capital resources than less education-intensive occupations. In some education-intensive occupations, workers with less education than the norm can "do the work" of that occupation. Those workers fortunate enough to be hired for such positions can take advantage of the greater capital resources to become more productive than similar workers in less education-intensive occupations.

• Norms of fairness might also play a role. More specifically, those with less education than is typical in their particular occupation might receive higher wages than workers with the same education and cognitive skills in less education-intensive occupations on grounds of equity. That is, employers and fellow workers may feel that fairness requires roughly similar pay for all workers within a well-defined occupation. This is especially true if the worker's actual productivity is hard to measure, a job feature of increasing importance in the service sector or of jobs requiring considerable education.

---

5 Our approach might be considered as a weighted combination of certain institutional approaches toward wage determination (such as John Dunlop's (1957) hypothesis about wage contours and the dual labor-market hypothesis) and the efficiency wage theory because arguments from both approaches can be used for our formulation as well. For instance, occupations differ in the degree to which employers believe that those in these occupations are interchangeable. For jobs requiring little education, employers often have little incentive to pay higher than market wages to retain workers since they believe that they can easily find replacements if some workers leave. Further, additional education for many of these jobs may have little payoff in higher productivity. For jobs requiring a great deal of education, replacement is more difficult and employers are often willing to pay wages higher than the going rate to discourage workers from quitting and/or shirking. This means that a worker in these occupations receives a higher wage than workers with the same education and cognitive skills who are in lower education-intensive occupations. Moreover, this wage gap should increase as the education-intensiveness of the occupation increases, a prediction tested (and confirmed) in Table 5.3.

Of course, both the second and third explanations leave unanswered the question of why a worker with less than the typical level of education would be initially hired for such a position. The answer might revolve around factors such as innate abilities or skills, work attitudes, personality, special connections between the employer and employee, random factors such as being at the right place at the right time, and "mistakes" in hiring due to difficulties of assessing the potential productivity of new hires.

Aside from the gender, race/ethnicity, education, and location variables included in other regressions, we also add three other less common variables in our wage equation that deserve brief comment. The first is a variable indicating whether the person is foreign-born, but prediction of the sign is difficult because counteracting forces are at work. If more energetic and ambitious people emigrate to the United States, then we would expect their wages to be higher, other things being equal. But their wages might be lower if they are burdened by poor English. At least for men, the energy factor seems stronger than the language factor. The second is a set of dummy variables dividing the labor force into 21 different industries because special factors within each industry influence wages. We omit presentation of these calculated coefficients of the industry variables because they are not relevant for this discussion. The third variable is for age, which is a crude proxy for work experience.

The regression calculations presented in Table 5.3 explain between 37 and 40 percent of the variance in the log of weekly wages. The results also seem reasonable in the light of the previous discussion.

Holding all other factors constant, weekly wages are positively and significantly related to cognitive skills. More specifically, if the average score of the three literacy scales increases one standard deviation, men's weekly wages increase 9.0 percent, and women's weekly wages increase 10.0 percent. (These and other estimates reported below are calculated from the estimated parameter values given in Table 5.3, converting the derived logarithms to absolute amounts.)

Similar to the regressions reported to explain employment, these calculated coefficients for cognitive skills are influenced by offsetting biases. Because some data on other skills required for carrying out particular occupations are available (for instance, physical strength, "people skills," and analytical skills), we can investigate the upward bias caused by the correlation of cognitive skills with these other skills influencing wages.[6] From these experiments it appears that the calculated coefficients for cognitive skills

6 We used skill evaluations from the *Dictionary of Occupational Titles*, as condensed into the

Table 5.3: *Regression to Explain Weekly Wages of Full-Time Prime-Age Workers in 1992*

	Calculated regression coefficients				
Dependent variable = natural log of weekly wages	Men Regression coefficient	Standard error		Women Regression coefficient	Standard error
Independent variables					
Intercept	+5.298*	0.080		+4.928*	0.101
Functional literacy score (original units)	+.00171*	0.00021		+.00207*	0.00021
Highest educational level: High-school diploma is the basis of comparison					
High-school dropout	-0.0520	0.0305		-0.0266	0.0287
GED (high-school equivalency)	-0.0189	0.0428		+0.0173	0.0388
Trade/vocational school	+0.0740*	0.0341		+0.0791*	0.0306
Some university	+0.0818*	0.0231		+0.1095*	0.0207
B.A./B.S. degree	+0.2049*	0.0271		+0.3161*	0.0252
At least one graduate degree	+0.4525*	0.0358		+0.5022*	0.0345
Race/ethnicity variables: White, non-Hispanic is the basis of comparison					
Black, non-Hispanic	-0.120*	0.030		+0.0538*	0.0238
Hispanic	-0.136*	0.033		+0.0353	0.0305
Other races/ethnicities	-0.283*	0.049		-0.0274	0.0446
Place of birth (foreign-born = 1; native-born = 0)	+0.0567	0.0344		-0.0389	0.0316

Occupation groups by level of educational-intensiveness in 1971-72. Tier 2 occupations (10.6 years to 12.0 years) is the basis of comparison

Tier 4 occupations: More than 14.5 years	+0.263*	0.032	+0.234*	.030
Tier 3 occupations: 12.1 to 14.5 years	+0.146*	0.022	+0.139*	.022
Tier 1 occupations 0 - 10.5 years	-0.084*	0.022	-0.020	.028
Region of residence: Northeast is basis of comparison				
South	-0.0728*	0.0220	-0.1025*	0.0207
Mid-West	-0.0387	0.0236	-0.0814*	0.0228
West	+0.0358	0.0238	+0.0337	0.0233
Live in metropolitan area (yes = 1; no = 0)	+0.148*	0.019	+0.199*	0.018
Age: 25.29 is basis of comparison				
Age 30-34	+0.147*	0.023	+0.0935*	0.0221
Age 35.39	+0.262*	0.023	+0.0994*	0.0213
Age 40-44	+0.276*	0.025	+0.1351*	0.0224
Age 45.49	+0.352	0.025	+0.1848*	0.0240
Inclusion of dummy variables for 21 industries	Yes		Yes	
Adjusted coefficient of determination (R^2)	.3713		.4022	
Size of sample:	3962		3386	

Notes: Asterisks designate statistical significance at the .05 level. The data cover only full-time workers earning more than $120 a week. In this sample the (weighted) average weekly wage for men is $711 and for women is $473. Some of the dummy variables representing various industries are statistically significant; most are not. The data come from the National Adult Literacy Survey.

have an upward bias of about 20 percent of their value. But because of random errors in both the wage data and the measurement of functional literacy, the calculated coefficients in Table 5.3 also have an additional bias of an unknown size.

As expected, wages increase with the level of education, particularly after high-school, when other factors influencing wages are held constant. If the regressions are recalculated omitting NALS scores, the coefficients for education are generally larger. This magnification of the impact of education arises because of the positive correlation between education and cognitive skills, a matter discussed in greater detail below. It is interesting that workers holding a GED who are able to obtain work receive wages that are not statistically different from those with a regular high-school diploma.

What about the role of gender? Our particular specification of wage equations allows the impact of every independent variable to differ for men and women. But how does gender itself affect wages? One way to summarize the role of gender is by taking the average characteristics of the entire sample – men and women combined – and substituting these into both the male and the female wage equations. This exercise shows that a woman with the average demographic characteristics and NALS scores of the population receives wages about 26 percent lower than a man with the same characteristics and scores. The size of this wage gap might decrease if data on actual work experience were available. However, the wage gap is unlikely to disappear completely.[7]

Various studies show quite different impacts of race/ethnicity variables on wages and we find that this impact varies by gender.[8] For men, ethnicity plays a statistically significant role. Black-non-Hispanics, Hispanics, and those of other races receive respectively 11.3 percent, 11.7 percent, and 24.6 percent

census occupational categories by Roos and Treiman. In Appendix Note 5.3 we discuss these matters in greater detail.

7   Years of work experience plays an important role in explaining differences in male and female wages. Our proxy variable for work experience, namely age, obviously does not work as well for women as for men. Nevertheless, these differences in wages for men and women are roughly the same in all four occupational tiers when age is held constant. Such a result suggests that a more accurate measure for work experience than our age variable would not greatly change this conclusion.

8   We discuss the impact of the race/ethnicity variable in much greater detail in Pryor and Schaffer (1998).

Various studies differ on whether race has a statistically significant impact on wages when other factors such as the level of cognitive skills are held constant. For instance, Neal and Johnson (1996) find that for men, blacks have significantly lower wages than whites, but for women the race variable has no impact, at least when the Armed Forces Qualification Test (AFQT) scores are included in the regression. Murnane et al (1995) report mixed results for men – in one of their two regressions the dummy variable indicating the person is an African-American lower wages than white-non-Hispanic men when other factors influencing wages are held constant. According to data presented in Appendix 5.4, these differences appear to have decreased over the quarter-century starting in 1970. For women, by way of contrast, our calculations in Table 5.3 show that black-non-Hispanics receive 5.5 percent higher wages than white women. For both Hispanics and those of other races, the wages are not significantly different from white-non-Hispanic women.

For men the inclusion of the variables for the occupational tiers reduces the difference in wages between whites and blacks. This means that part of the difference in wages between these men is because black men with a given education are more likely to be in less education-intensive occupations than otherwise identical white men. For women, on the other hand, this effect does not occur.

The inclusion of occupation tiers has a statistically significant impact in almost all cases. More specifically, for people with a given education and cognitive skills, wages are positively related to the education-intensiveness of their occupation, all other factors remaining the same. For example, as a prime-age male worker moves up from a tier 1 to a tier 2 occupation, their wage increases 8.1 percent; from tier 2 to tier 3, an additional 15.7 percent; and from tier 3 to tier 4, 14.4 percent. For women the wage increases are respectively 2.0 percent, 14.9 percent, and 11.5 percent. These effects occur although all other attributes of the mobile workers, including their level of education, remain unchanged. If these workers also increase their level of education, while moving into more education-intensive occupations, their wages will increase at an even faster rate. This is because both the level of education of the individual workers and the education-intensiveness of their occupation make independent and positive contribution to their wage rate.

The calculated coefficients for foreign-born workers are not statistically significant. As noted above, two counteracting causal factors are at work. The

has no significant impact on wages when scores of a mathematics test are held constant. For women, their result showing that African-American women receive higher wages is the same as ours in Table 5.3. O'Neill (1990) finds that less-educated black males have lower wages than whites, but not more-educated blacks, other factors held constant. In a more complex analysis of wage differences of men, Maxwell (1994) also finds a significantly lower wage for blacks when he holds constant the AFQT test results. In reviewing these studies and our own results, the differential impact of the race variable between men and women stands out. Studies by Wilson (1996) and Holzer (1996) suggest employers perceive that less-educated black men carry attitudes toward work and take orders from superiors quite differently than less-educated black women. Whether these perceptions are accurate or not, they can result in a difference in the impact of the race variable.

roles of the other causal variables in the regressions are relatively self-explanatory and are not germane to this discussion.[9]

Changes in Wages Over Time with Special Attention to the Returns to Cognitive Skills

As we argue below, the demand for university-educated workers is bifurcated. For university-educated workers with cognitive skills above the average university level, demand has been growing faster than supply. For university-educated workers with cognitive skills at or below the average university level, demand has been growing slower than supply. As a result, wages have increased for those with relatively high cognitive skills. At the same time, downward occupational mobility has occurred for those with relatively low cognitive skills as they are forced to take high-school jobs. Thus skill-biased technical change has played a role in the changing wage structure, but in a way quite different than is usually argued.

Our primary hypothesis here is that the rate of return to cognitive skills within the most education-intensive (tier 4) occupations has increased. In order to test this hypothesis directly, we need data on labor market variables and cognitive skills at two different points in time. In this respect, we encounter some problems.

Many studies have looked at changes in the rate of return to education (rather than cognitive skills) over time. Our data from the Current Population Survey are well-suited for such an exercise. In Appendix 5.4, we use the results from a wage equation estimated from CPS data to calculate the percentage wage gap between high-school dropouts and university graduates at different points in time. These results show that, for instance, between 1970 and 1994, the considerable percentage gap in weekly wages between high-school dropouts and university graduates widened about 6.7 percentage points for men and 17.3 percent for women, all other causal factors remaining constant.

Unfortunately, these regressions or others that are presented in the economic literature do not include cognitive skills. As a result, it is difficult to

9 The location variables suggest that weekly wages of workers in both the South and Mid-West are significantly lower than in the Northeast. On the other hand, wages in the Northeast and West are not statistically different. Wages of those living in metropolitan areas are also significantly higher, for reasons that have received extensive comment elsewhere. As we would expect, weekly wages are also a positive and significant function of age, at least for those in the prime-working ages. This reflects, of course, the impact both of experience and of the time necessary to match people with occupations in a different tier.

determine what really underlies these differences over time: changes in the returns to education *per se*, changes in the returns to cognitive skills alone, or some combination of both. It is also unfortunate that comparable data on cognitive skills of the workforce are available for only a few years so that most people trying to isolate their changing role as a determinant of wages have been forced to use samples separated by only a few years . In most cases these studies also focus primarily on workers 26 years or younger. In this discussion we use a different approach.

The major reason for trying to determine if the rate of return to cognitive skills has increased is to resolve the problem of why wages of university-educated workers are rising when there appears to be an apparent oversupply of such workers. Our explanation divides university-educated workers into two distinct groups based on their cognitive skills. Those with high skills experience increasing wages while those with lower skills experience falling wages and/or displacement to a job in a lower tier. The wage increases of the former outweigh the wage decreases of the latter, so that the average wage for all university graduates has risen. This argument has several steps and it is useful to start at the beginning.

The First Step: A More Complex Cross-Section View

To gain more insight into the relative impact of cognitive skills and education, we tried a more complex version of the wage regression on individuals from Table 5.3. For this extended version, we include each individual's years of education and NALS score as well as the average years of education and the average NALS score in their detailed occupation. This allows us to separate the effects on wages of an individual's level of cognitive skills and education from the effects of their detailed occupation's characteristics. Although the sample is somewhat smaller, since we eliminate all occupations where our sample has less than three people, the results are quite illuminating and are presented in Table 5.4.

The total results for the samples of all men and all women can be interpreted in a relatively straightforward fashion. First of all, for men, the total rate of return to education and cognitive skills is similar. For women, the total rate of return to education is 50 percent higher than the rate of return to cognitive skills. Secondly, for both genders, the education and cognitive skills characteristics of an individual's detailed occupation are more important determinants of their wage than are their own levels of education and cognitive skills. This means, for example, that an individual can gain more of an increase in wages by moving to a job one standard deviation up the occupation ladder

Table 5.4: *Impact on Wages in Each Occupation of an Individual's Cognitive Skills and Education*

| | Impact on wages of one standard deviation change | | | | | |
| | Education | | NALS score | | Adjusted R² | Size of sample |
	Average in occupation	Individual's education	Average in occupation	Individual's NALS score		
Men: Total	10.2*%	9.3*%	12.1*%	5.5*%	.3989	3767
Tier 4	-	17.6*	26.3*	6.1*	.2856	655
Tiers 1-3	10.0*	9.1*	12.8*	5.1*	.3498	3112
Women: Total	13.0*	9.9*	8.7*	6.7*	.4313	3303
Tier 4	-	18.2*	24.2*	10.0*	.3416	604
Tiers 1-3	31.5*	8.2*	-1.5	6.2*	.4103	2698

Notes: The underlying data are the same as in Table 5 3. Race/ethnicity, place of birth, region of residence, metropolitan area residence, age, and industry are held constant. The asterisks denote statistical significance at the .05 level. For occupations, we multiply the regression coefficient by the standard deviation for occupations; for individuals, we use the weighted standard deviation by individuals. Because the variance for occupations is not great, it is omitted from the regressions. Because the variance for the variable designating average education of tier 4 occupations is not great, it is omitted from the regressions.

(based on either education or cognitive skills) than by staying in the same occupation and moving one standard deviation up the education or cognitive skills ladder.

In looking at the importance of education and cognitive skills by job tiers, a problem arises with the most education-intensive (tier 4) occupations (those requiring at least 14.5 years of education) since there is not much variation in the average education for the different occupations. Therefore, we have omitted the variable for the average level of education. For both men and women in these tier 4 occupations, the results are similar. For both genders, the average cognitive skills for the occupation as a whole are much more important wage determinants than a person's individual cognitive skills are. This indicates that the tier 4 labor market places a much greater premium on the average cognitive skills of an individual's detailed occupation than on the differential cognitive skills of individuals within that detailed occupation.

For occupation tiers 1 through 3 where the average level of education is lower, the wage determinants for men appear roughly the same as for the entire sample of men. All four variables play a role in wage determination and, moreover, group characteristics appear somewhat more important than individual characteristics.

For women, however, the determinants of wages for occupation tiers 1 through 3 are more difficult to interpret. They suggest that the average education within the occupation is really the key determinant of their wages and that all other factors – the average cognitive skills of those in the occupation or the woman's own education or cognitive skills – are of secondary importance. Indeed, the average cognitive skills within these less-skilled jobs appear to have no impact on their wages. In exploring this phenomenon more closely we found that those occupations with relatively low education but high cognitive skills are primarily male dominated, for instance, jewelers, telephone line workers, and mechanical control repairers. Whether barriers to entry for women exist in these occupations is unclear, but the implication is clear: There is not much opportunity for a woman with a job in tiers 1, 2, or 3 to benefit from moving to a detailed occupation with similar levels of education but higher average cognitive skill levels. The only way for a woman within these three bottom tiers to make significant wage progress, is to move to an occupation with similar cognitive skill levels but higher average years of education.

The separation of barriers to entry, education, and cognitive skills at this level of disaggregation requires considerable future research and, at this point, all we can say is that the wage market for women seems to work in an asymmetric fashion: For jobs in education-intensive occupations, if a woman has high cognitive skills and enters an occupation where others have such skills, she receives a considerable wage premium; for other types of jobs, she does not.

Previous Studies of Time-Series

Is the economic payoff to cognitive skills increasing over time? In order to address this question clearly, it is necessary for us to make a distinction between two types of upskilling. Technical change over time can lead to the upskilling of an entire occupation, so that all workers in the occupations have higher cognitive or other skills. This "general upskilling" implies that there may be considerable turnover in the occupation as those with higher skills replace those with lower skills, and that the median wage in the occupation rises. By way of contrast, technical change might lead to a situation where only those with high cognitive skills within an occupation receive higher wages, while the remaining wages are unaffected or even decrease. For instance, highly-skilled surgeons may see their salaries soaring over time, while average surgeons may experience no change in income. This "segmented upskilling" implies not just that turnover in the occupation might be low but also that both the median wage and the median cognitive skills in the occupation as a whole might not greatly change.[10]

Recent studies focusing on the question include those by Bishop (1991), Blackburn and Neumark (1993), Ferguson (1993), and Murnane, Willett, and Levy (1995). All four use longitudinal data and explore the determinants of wages for relatively young workers (in most cases, below 26 years of age). Although they use somewhat different measures of cognitive skills, all focus primarily on traditional academic skills. Further, all deal with relatively short time intervals of eight years or less.[11]

Conclusions drawn from the four cited studies are mixed. The first two find little change in the economic return to cognitive skills over the short time periods under consideration. The last two find considerable change. More specifically, for Murnane, Willett, and Levy, the economic return of an increase of one standard deviation in cognitive skills increased from 3 percent to 6 percent

---

10 The average wage in that occupation also might not greatly change if, at the same time that wages for the most-skilled were rising, wages for the least-skilled were falling.

11 A study by Autor, Katz, and Krueger (1997) shows that use of computers, which presumably requires higher-than-average cognitive skills in any given occupation, is concentrated among those with the most education and, moreover, is associated with a wage premium that has increased over time. They estimate such an increase to be roughly 3 percentage points between 1984 and 1993. Their cross-section approach is, however, controversial. DiNardo and Pischke (1997) show that inclusion of occupational data considerably lowers the wage premium for computer usage. They also argue that the computer use variable can be a proxy for hidden variables influencing wages, so that such cross-section regressions yield biased results.

for men and from 8 percent to 11 percent for women between 1978 and 1986.[12] For Ferguson (1993), the economic return of a similar increase changes from 8 percent to 35 percent between 1980–82 and 1986–88. For the sake of comparison, our calculations with the NALS scores (Table 5.2) for a single point in time show that in 1992, an increase of one standard deviation in our measure of cognitive skills led to an increase of about 9 to 10 percent in wages.

None of these four studies, however, separates the impact of returns to education or cognitive skills *per se* and to moving to a different occupation. Such occupational shifts are a particularly important phenomenon for younger workers, upon whom all four studies focus. By way of contrast, our sample deals with those from 25 up to 50, who presumably experience fewer occupational shifts.

The Major Temporal Supply and Demand Issues

Instead of trying to measure directly the changing economic returns to cognitive skills, an alternate approach would look at the relative changes in the supply of, and demand for, such skills. This raises problems, however, because of difficulties of quantification and because we have a measure of cognitive skills for only one year.

On the supply side, average test scores by level of education have been quite stable over the years for many (but not all) of the various standardized tests. For instance, in tests administered in the nationwide National Assessment of Education (reported in various editions of *Statistical Abstract),* the scores of primary and secondary school pupils reveal few marked changes over the last few decades. Our own regression analysis in Chapter 2 (Table 2.2) shows little difference in NALS scores by age group at a single point in time (1992) when education is held constant.

At first sight these results suggest that the supply of those with a high-level education and high cognitive skills is increasing at roughly the same rate as the growth in the number of university graduates. It seems more likely, however,

---

12 These are approximations calculated by multiplying the standard deviation of the measure of cognitive ability by the coefficient of the measure in the regression linking cognitive ability and other determinants of the logarithm of wages. For Murnane, Willett, and Levy (1995) we draw data from Tables 2, 3, and 4. For Ferguson (1993) we draw data from Tables 2 and 4, using the regressions including family background variables. Since he uses the decile rankings on a scale from one through 10, we use the standard deviation of such a ranking. We should add that the dramatic changes in the returns to cognitive abilities in such a short time interval seem counter-intuitive, although we have no particular objections to his statistical methods.

that those with really high cognitive skills are increasing somewhat more slowly than the number of university graduates since universities attempt to skim off those with the potentially highest cognitive skills before dipping into a pool of students with less potential. Nevertheless, for the labor force as a whole, as the average level of education increases, the average level of cognitive skills increases as well since formal education and cognitive skills are correlated.

On the demand side, two factors play crucial roles: real educational upgrading and real upskilling. At the level of our 500 detailed occupations, we did some qualitative analysis to try to see the relation between the attributes of a detailed occupation and the likelihood that it was experiencing real educational upgrading or real upskilling. This qualitative look at the data revealed one particular pattern: the higher the average education level of a detailed occupation, the higher the likelihood that workers are undergoing real upskilling. In other words, the necessary cognitive skills of those occupations characterized by more education are changing more rapidly than other occupations.

It seems important, therefore, to test systematically two propositions: First, the demand for cognitive skills has increased faster than the supply of educated workers with high cognitive skills. Second, the demand for university-educated workers with average cognitive skills has increased more slowly than the number of jobs requiring this level of education.

Although the two hypotheses may seem counter-intuitive, the crucial fact is that education and cognitive skills are to some degree correlated, but also have independent impacts on wages and employment. For instance, the work of chemical technicians appears to require more cognitive skills now than 25 years ago. The average years of formal education of chemical technicians increased only about half a year between 1971–71 and 1994–95, which is lower than the average occupation. However, actual wages climbed considerably faster than predicted. This suggests that upskilling over and above the changing educational requirement may have occurred.

Both of the two hypotheses rely crucially on the distinction between upskilling and educational upgrading. Both are related to the commonly believed proposition that more-educated workers are more flexible and more capable of acquiring new skills. Both are also consistent with the finding of Chinhui Juhn and Kevin Murphy[13] that the relative demand for highly-skilled workers, in contrast to moderately-skilled workers, increased dramatically in the 1960s. This version of the skill-biased technical change hypothesis, how-

13 Juhn and Murphy (1995).

ever, is quite different from the general view which argues that such change results primarily in a decline in low-skilled jobs and an increase in high-skilled jobs.

If the two hypotheses are true, they suggest that at the upper end of the occupational ladder, the key to the wage paradox lies in the fact that education and cognitive skills are only imperfectly correlated. If the distribution of cognitive skills among university graduates has remained relatively constant, then clearly the demand for cognitive skills at a very high level can increase faster than their number, even while the demand for *all* university graduates is increasing at a much slower rate. If variations in cognitive skills of university graduates are increasing (as we suspect to be the case), then we can expect an even greater divergence between the demand for university graduates in general and those with high cognitive skills.[14]

A Regression Experiment

With these ideas in mind, we can now begin the empirical analysis. In particular, we need to develop a more precise way of determining what has happened to the rate of return to cognitive skills over the last quarter-century. In this analysis, however, we can only focus on what is happening on an occupational level since we lack longitudinal data on cognitive skills of individuals, even though we can create such data for occupations.

If the CPS data included functional literacy scores, then we could simply calculate separate cross-section wage equations across individuals for 1971–72 and 1994–95. By then comparing the coefficients on the functional literacy scores, we could measure the change in returns to cognitive skills across individuals. Unfortunately, this is not possible because the CPS data include no test scores.

Alternatively, if we had NALS test scores on individuals from two different years near the beginning and end of our time period, we could use these to determine the average score in each detailed occupation. We could then combine these with wage, education, and other data on each detailed occupation derived from the CPS and calculate separate cross-section wage regressions across detailed occupations for 1971–72 and 1994–95. By comparing the coef-

14 This might be argued by reference to the increasing share of high-school graduates who are going to universities. This could mean that the universities are enrolling more students with less ability. Looking at the variances of NALS scores for university graduates of different age groups, we could find no evidence to support this conjecture.

ficients on the functional literacy scores, we could measure the change in the rate of return to cognitive skills across occupations. Unfortunately, we have NALS test scores for only one year, 1992.

Nevertheless, we can still use the available data to get an approximate measure of the change in the return to cognitive skills across occupations. Our measure will be biased, but we argue below that the bias is not likely to be very great. We must, however, also take account of the distinction noted above of "general upskilling" and "segmented upskilling." In sum, statistical difficulties abound.

We have to be crafty. A useful starting point for the analysis of wages by occupation is a pair of wage equations similar to that used in Table 5.3.The dependent variable is the natural log of the median wage in each occupation in each year. The independent variables include the mean years of education in the occupation, the mean functional literacy test scores in the occupation[15], as well as other important characteristics of each occupation such as the share of women, non-white, part-time, and part-year (seasonal) workers. Because of the nature of the data available to us, the specification of our regression experiment is crucial and, as a result, it is necessary to be very explicit about what we are doing. The two wage equations can be written as:

1) $\ln W_i 95 = \alpha'_0 + \alpha'_1 C_i 95 + \alpha'_2 X_i\, 95$
2) $\ln W_i 71 = \alpha_0 + \alpha_1 C_i 71 + \alpha_2 X_i\, 71$,

where W_i = median wage in occupation i
   C_i = cognitive skills in occupation i
   X_i = all other determinants of wages in occupation i
   and 71 and 95 designate 1971 and 1995

Next we calculate an equation for the change in wages over time and across occupations, allowing for all the independent variables and their parameters to change over time, namely equation (1) minus (2).

3) $\Delta \ln W_i = (\alpha'_0 - \alpha_0) + (\alpha'_1 C_i 95 - \alpha_1 C_i\, 71) + (\alpha'_2 X_i\, 95 - \alpha_2 X_i\, 71)$

By adding and subtracting appropriate 1995 terms to each of the expressions within the parentheses, we then derive:

---

15 Unfortunately, the NALS sample did not contain workers in a number of the smaller occupations, so that our sample covers less than the full occupational range. Since we calculate regressions weighted by the number of people in the various occupations, this should not make much difference.

4) $\Delta \ln W_i = \Delta \alpha_o + [(\Delta \alpha_1) C_i 95 + \alpha_1 (\Delta C_i)] + [(\Delta \alpha_2) X_i 95 + \alpha_2 (\Delta X_i)]$

The $(\Delta \alpha) C_i$ 95 term corresponds to changes in the rate of return to the average cognitive skills of an occupation, while the $\alpha_1 (\Delta C_i)$ term corresponds to general upskilling of an occupation. We have data on all the necessary C's and X's except for Δ C. That is, we only have functional literacy data for the endpoint of our sample, so we cannot calculate the change in average test scores within each occupation. If we omit this term in our regression, then all the other estimated coefficients will be biased. However, if the change in average test scores within most occupations is small, then this bias will also be small; indeed, if Δ C is equal to zero for all occupations, then there is no bias.

In Table 5.5 we run the regression in equation (4) with all terms except α_1 (ΔC).[16] The explanatory variables explain more than half of the variance in the median log wage differences – a strong result for this type of regression. The estimated coefficients show that education and age have a positive and growing impact on wages. Moreover, the larger the fraction of each occupation consisting of women, non-whites, part-time workers, and self-employed, the lower the median wage in that occupation. However, the negative wage impact of women, non-whites, part-time workers, and self-employed workers has declined over the quarter-century.

The negative value of the intercept means that the constant term in the wage regressions for each year decreased significantly over time. This means that for occupations with many young workers with minimal education, the average wage has decreased. Occupations with a higher average age and level of education have, by way of contrast, experienced significantly higher wages. In this sense the rates of return to education and experience have increased across occupations.

The coefficient on the average NALS score is significant at the 10 percent, but not the 5 percent level. It is positive, indicating that the rate of return to cognitive skills is increasing. Taking into account that the standard deviation of the NALS for this sample arranged by occupations is 24.97, we can convert the regression coefficient into standard deviation units so that it becomes .0194. This indicates that an occupation with a one standard deviation higher NALS score will experience a 1.94 percentage point greater increase in its median wage between 1971–72 and 1994–95. Seen from a different angle, the wage gap between occupations with lower average cognitive skills and those

16 The sample has one extreme value of wage increases, namely for physicians (occupation group 84). Since this occupation has certain atypical elements, we omitted it from the regression, although it is included in the calculation of the residuals.

Table 5.5: *Determinants of the Change in the Real Hourly Wages of Prime-Age Workers by Occupations*

For regression: Dependent variable is change in the logarithms of median real hourly wages of occupation between 1971–72 and 1994–95

	Calculated coefficient	Standard error
Intercept of regression	- 0.6669**	0.2546

Variable	Interpretation of coefficient	Calculated coefficient	Standard error
Δ education	Impact of education 1971–72,	+ 0.0335**	0.0128
Education, 1994–95	Change in impact of education	+ 0.0149*	0.0089
Δ age	Impact of age, 1971–72	+ 0.0149**	0.0050
Age, 1994–95	Change in impact of age	+ 0.00398	0.00598
Δ share of women	Impact of share of women, 1971–72	- 0.3131**	0.0601
Share of women, 1994–95	Change in impact of share of women	+ 0.0910**	0.0326
Δ share of non-whites	Impact of share of non-whites, 1971–72	- 0.4384**	0.0922
Share of non-whites, 1994–95	Change in impact of share of non-whites	+ 0.0618	0.1052
Δ share of part-time workers	Impact of part-time workers, 1971–72	- 1.1182**	0.1105
Share of part-time workers, 1994–94	Change in impact of part-time workers	+ 0.3190**	0.0882
Δ share of part-year workers	Impact of part-year workers, 1971–72	+ 0.0267	0.1011

Share of part-year workers, 1994–95	Change in impact of part-year workers	− 0.3184**	0.0860
Δ share of self-employed workers	Impact of self-employed workers, 1971–72	− 0.7771**	0.0996
Share of self-employed workers, 1994–95	Change in impact of self-employed workers	+ 0.0522	0.0503
Average NALS score, 1992	Change in impact of cognitive skills	+0.00078*	0.00045
Coefficient of determination (adjusted)		.5723	
Size of sample		426	

Notes: The occupations used in the OLS regression are weighted by the average number of workers in the various occupation in 1971–72 and 1994–95. The change in the median hourly wage is measured in 1994 prices. Non-whites include African-Americans and "other races." For the regression we use all occupations for which we have both a NALS score and the appropriate data from the CPS. A double asterisks denotes statistical significance at the .05 level; a single asterisk, statistical significance at the .10 level. This regression excludes occupation group 84 (physicians), which was an extreme outlier. We discuss the interpretations of the coefficient in the text.

Sources: Data on the median hourly wage and the level of education come from the Current Population Survey. The data from the National Adult Literacy Study (NALS) came from a data diskette supplied by the National Center for Educational Statistics, U.S. Department of Education. Data were not available for all occupations.

with higher average cognitive skills has been growing at a steady, albeit modest rate, even after controlling for many other factors influencing wages. This increase in returns to average cognitive skills within an occupation is particularly important because of our results in the previous table showing that the average NALS score in an occupation was the most important wage determinant.

It is important to remember that these may be biased estimates due to the omission of the α_1 (ΔC_i) term. When this consideration is combined with the t-statistic of only 1.74 on the NALS score coefficient, it is clear that these results provide only modest support for the hypothesis that the rate of return to cognitive skills across occupations has been increasing and that segmented upskilling has been occurring. Nevertheless, the exercise is useful to tell us whether our approach leads at least to the expected signs of the calculated coefficients, which it does.

Additional insight into the importance of cognitive skills and the specific impact of upskilling can be seen by examining the prediction errors of the regression. These error terms should include the effect of the missing term for changes in the level of cognitive skills as well as any occupation- specific differences in the impact of all of the other variables. Occupations with wages much higher than predicted have either experienced an increase in the level of cognitive skills within their occupation (which we cannot directly measure), or an idiosyncratic effect from one of the other variables. Occupations with wages lower than predicted may have experienced a decrease in the level of cognitive skills.

We carry out this exercise of prediction errors in Table 5.6. To reduce statistical noise and to focus only on the most familiar occupations, we look only at those 178 occupations where the number of workers was 100,000 or more in both 1971–72 and 1994–95 (a procedure also used in Chapters 3 and 6). Nevertheless, different cut-off lines do not affect our major conclusions.

Turning first to a comparison of the extremes with each other, it is clear that the average years of education are considerably lower (12.7 years versus 14.0 years) in those occupations where the wage changes were much lower than predicted (Part A), than in those occupations where the wage changes were higher than predicted (Part B). This is important. It suggests that general upskilling, consistent with a large positive residual, has occurred more frequently in detailed occupations with higher average levels of education, as we have previously conjectured.

Examining those occupations where the wage changes were much lower than predicted (Part A), we find few surprises. It is difficult to imagine that most featured any real upskilling or real educational upgrading, although three possible exceptions must be noted: (primary and secondary) teachers not elsewhere classified, airplane pilots and navigators, and mechanical engineers.

The teachers include many without a college education such as (unskilled) teachers' aids. Pilots and navigators appear on the list possibly as the result of changes within the industry accompanying deregulation and the increasing competition between airlines which has put considerable downward pressure on high wages of workers. Mechanical engineers remain a puzzle although it must be noted that many in this group lack college degrees and may have relatively routine jobs.

In Part B the results are more challenging to explain. For at least three of the occupations (physicians, dentists, pharmacists), the large positive residuals may be due to the enormous increase in the demand for health care in the U.S., combined with an upskilling in the first two occupations. For another five (chemists, chemical technicians, lawyers, securities and financial services sales occupations, and possibly precision inspectors), the large positive residuals are probably due to general upskilling. For others in the list, we believe that the higher than expected wages are due to forces other than upskilling. Some of the prediction errors might be traced to effective labor union pressures over the period in four occupations (electric power installers, telephone installers, mail carriers, and firefighting occupations). Stenographers have experienced a considerable increase in part-time and self-employed workers and it is possible that median hourly wages did not fall as predicted, even while total wages did (i.e., the changing penalty to part-time workers was less than in other detailed occupations). The remaining two occupations in the list (property and marketing managers) both experienced dramatic increases in the share of women which were not accompanied by the predicted fall in average wages. This suggests that in these occupations, at least, the principal of equal pay for men and women appears to have taken hold, in contrast to other occupations.

The results drawn from Tables 5.5 and 5.6 provide evidence consistent with the hypothesis that wage changes in various occupations are related to both the level and the change in functional literacy scores when all other factors are held constant. Most of the detailed occupations that have experienced upskilling due to technical change also have relatively high average levels of education. However, some occupations with high average levels of education have experienced no upskilling – presumably due to very little technical change. Similarly, there is relatively little evidence to support the claim that many lower tier occupations are experiencing real upskilling or any direct effects of technical change. Finally, the rate of return to the average cognitive skills across occupations appears to have increased in the quarter-century between the early 1970s and the mid 1990s in the U.S.

It is important to stress that our purpose of these statistical exercises is to establish a credible case for an alternative approach to changes in wage dif-

Table 5.6: *Largest Prediction Errors of Wage Changes of Prime-Age Workers, 1971–72 to 1994–95*

Occupation code	Median hourly wages		Average years of education		Occupation
	Actual change	Prediction error	71–72	94–95	
Part A. Wage changes less than predicted					
226	-11.60	-5.48	14.13	15.35	Airplane pilots and navigators
266	-3.75	-3.57	12.24	13.45	Sales workers, furniture and home furnishings
195	-3.34	-3.49	14.98	15.58	Editors and reporters
159	-0.78	-3.29	14.24	14.89	Teachers, n.e.c.
197	-4.87	-2.90	14.30	15.51	Public relation specialists
155	-2.38	-2.83	14.69	14.73	Prekindergarten and kindergarten teachers
57	-2.54	-2.55	14.97	15.69	Mechanical engineers
186	-2.67	-2.39	13.87	14.84	Musicians and composers
719	-2.22	-1.97	10.29	11.88	Molding and casting machine operators
585	-5.44	-1.90	11.02	12.42	Plumbers, pipefitters, steamfitters
268	-2.24	-1.82	12.31	13.35	Sales workers, hardware, builder supplies
348	-1.24	-1.70	11.93	12.86	Telephone operators
877	-3.24	-1.69	10.86	12.10	Stock handlers and baggers
364	-3.51	-1.63	11.28	12.53	Traffic, shipping, receiving clerks
853	-5.19	-1.62	9.90	11.95	Excavating and loading machine operators
Unweighted average	-3.67	-2.59	12.73	13.81	

Part B. Wage changes higher than predicted

84	+30.16	+27.86	17.45	17.95	Physicians, medical and osteopathic
85	+ 2.49	+ 8.32	17.84	18.00	Dentists
96	+ 5.35	+ 5.39	16.33	16.52	Pharmacists
577	+ 0.91	+ 4.09	11.50	12.66	Electric power installers and repairers
314	+ 0.74	+ 3.78	12.53	13.69	Stenographers
18	+ 3.49	+ 3.45	12.38	13.98	Managers of property and real estate
529	+ 1.45	+ 3.27	12.19	13.05	Telephone installers
73	+ 1.36	+ 3.22	15.94	16.50	Chemists except biochemists
224	+ 0.35	+ 3.22	13.01	13.67	Chemical technicians
689	+ 0.43	+ 3.08	11.34	12.73	Precision inspectors, testers, and graders
178	+ 5.20	+ 3.02	17.60	17.95	Lawyers
355	+ 0.74	+ 2.86	12.10	13.35	Mail carriers, postal service
255	- 1.39	+ 2.81	15.02	15.59	Securities and financial services sales occupations
417	+ 2.08	+ 2.79	11.90	13.82	Firefighting occupations
13	+ 1.90	+ 2.75	13.44	15.24	Managers: marketing, advertising, and public relations
Unweighted average	+ 3.68	+ 5.36	14.04	14.98	

Notes: These are calculated from the regression residuals from Table 5.3. The wages for both years are in 1994 prices. The prediction errors are the actual wage change divided by the regression residual minus one.

ferentials. Because of the nature of the data available to us, we have not definitively proven our case. We have, however, tried to establish plausibility and to suggest that changes in wage differentials are not just due to foreign trade and to some skill-biased technical change, but to some simple micro changes in the supply and demand for particular skills.

Two Special Topics

We end this discussion of the level of wages by considering two related topics with some important policy implications. The first is the manner in which the various separate functional literacy, employment, and wage effects are combined. The second is the relation between wages and the unemployment rate.

Combination Effects

Throughout this book we have taken pains to separate the various causal forces and, when examining a particular variable, to hold all other factors constant. Although the real world does not work this way, it is possible to combine our results in a number of different ways to determine what happens when several variables are changing simultaneously. We carry out this exercise in considerable detail elsewhere (Pryor and Schaffer, 1998). The purpose of this discussion is simply to illustrate some of the different possibilities of analysis.

In this chapter we examine the determinants of hourly wages and in Chapter 2 we carry out the same task for employment. Expected wages are simply the product of these two factors. For instance, if the weekly wage for a person with a given set of characteristics is $400 and if the chances of employment for this same person are 90 percent, then the expected wage is $360.

We can easily make such a calculation of expected wages from our regression results. Other things being equal, for example, a man with a university degree can expect to obtain a weekly wage 23.8 percent higher than a similar man who has only a high-school diploma. For women, the corresponding estimate is 42.0 percent. For both men and women, the wage differences between people with different education are the most important factor in this calculation of expected wages.

Since education influences cognitive skills and the latter variable has an impact on both employment possibilities and wages, this indirect effect should also be taken into account. This calculation can be easily carried out by combining our results on the impact of education on cognitive skills and the employment and wage regressions. Between men with a university degree and a high-school diploma, the expected weekly wage difference now becomes 36.9 percent; for women, 60.1 percent. In short, cognitive skills magnify the impact of education on economic outcomes, a phenomenon we also discuss earlier.

Such an approach allows us to take more complicated combination effects into account. An analysis of the impact of race on expected wages provides an interesting example for such an exercise. Looking just at the direct impact of race (we refer in this discussion only to the non-Hispanic, prime-age population), black men have an expected weekly earnings 14.4 percent below whites, other things remaining equal. For women, the corresponding estimate is 4.9 percent above. However, as pointed out in Chapter 2, blacks have lower NALS scores than whites. Further, blacks have a lower level of education than whites so this compositional effect must be taken into account as well. And as noted above, education has an impact on cognitive skills as well. When these three effects are taken into account, the expected earnings of black men are 27.5 percent below those of white men; for women, the corresponding estimate is 15.0 percent below. We must also note that other combination and composition effects must be taken into account before we can fully explain the difference in expected wages between the two racial groups.

Wages and Unemployment Rates

Our analysis in this book focuses primarily on total joblessness. It is useful, however, to give brief attention to one type of joblessness, namely unemployment, which includes those who are actively looking for work, but without success.

According to some neoclassical economists, if real wages fall, unemployment rates should fall at the same time for two reasons. First, employers are willing to hire more workers at the lower wage. Second, some unemployed workers would leave the labor force because going wages would be too low to provide them an incentive for employment. Thus low and/or falling wages should be directly related to the unemployment rate.

In a recent book David G. Blanchflower and Andrew J. Oswald (1994) argue this point quite differently, namely that low wages should be related to high unemployment. Among their many arguments, two seem particularly cogent: Groups with high unemployment rates have a lack of bargaining power in the labor market. Further, employers do not need to pay them additional wages to reduce their labor turnover (an efficiency wage argument). In short, they argue from unemployment rates to wages, rather than the reverse.

They also provide a massive amount of evidence – primarily cross-sectional – to show that their hypothesized relation is empirically valid. The evidence in Charts 5.1 and 5.2 on unemployment rates of men and women with different levels of education provides more insight into the problem. The charts show for both men and women that not only do the less-educated have higher unemployment, but their unemployment rates have risen faster than those of the more-educated. As noted previously, the wages of the less-educated are also falling in relation to those with more education. In other

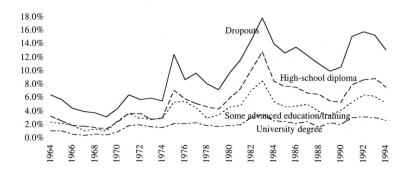

Chart 5.1: Prime-age male unemployment rates by highest level of education

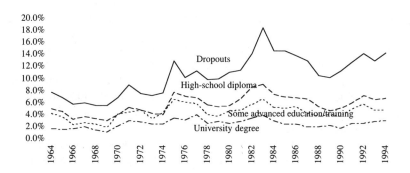

Chart 5.2: Prime-age female unemployment rates by highest level of education

Note: For each year the data come from the Current Population Survey for March. The denominator is the total counted labor force in that respective educational group. Subsequent to the calculations for Charts 5.1 and 5.2, the percentage of unemployment for prime-age men and women fell respectively 1.6 and 2.1 percentage points between March 1994 and March 1999. Nevertheless, the unemployment rate among prime-age high-school dropouts was still 6.9 and 4.2 percent and, as noted in Chapter 1, the jobless rate was considerably higher.

words, at least among the less-educated, falling wages and rising unemployment are associated over time.

Various types of institutional factors, for instance minimum wage laws, union pressure, and inchoate notions of "fair wages" for particular occupations, may retard this fall, so that wages for a particular occupation may not reach their equilibrium where the quantity of labor demanded and the quantity supplied are the same. As long as the impact of the displacement effect is not offset sufficiently by a rising demand for such labor, such a disequilibrium can persist for a long time.

Meanwhile, many of those workers who have fruitlessly looked for work drop out of the labor force, only to be replaced by workers from higher educational tiers who are looking for jobs in that occupational tier. As long as the displacement mechanism continues to operate at the same rate – an issue discussed in the last chapter – we can expect the real wages of the less-educated to continue to fall slowly.

Summary and Conclusions

Over the quarter-century period from 1970 to 1995, median real hourly wages of various groups of less-educated prime-age workers (especially men) either fell or stagnated, even while the number of jobs requiring few educational credentials increased faster than the number of those with a high-school diploma or less. At the same time real median hourly wages rose for those with university education, particularly those in highly education-intensive (tier 4) occupations. This occurred even while the number of jobs increased more slowly than the number with high educational credentials.

By calculating a wage regression across all individuals, we can isolate the various causal factors underlying wage differences more exactly. In addition to the usual determinants of wages such as education, race/ethnicity, age, and industry, we also find that wages are directly related to cognitive skills when education is held constant.

By combining the results from our regressions predicting median wages and probabilities of employment, we can also calculate expected real wages. This allows us not only to show the direct effects of both education and cognitive skills, but the indirect impact of education on cognitive skills. Similarly, we can examine not just the direct effects of race/ethnicity, but indirect and compositional effects as well.

We also provide some support for the Blanchflower-Oswald hypothesis that unemployment and declining real wages occur together. Their evidence was based primarily on a number of cases at a single point in time. We obtain similar results when looking at trends in unemployment and wages.

The key part of this discussion in this chapter is determination of the impact of technical change on wages. We base our empirical analysis on three hypotheses: (1) The demand for high cognitive skills due to upskilling has increased faster than those possessing such skills. (2) The jobs for other university graduates have increased more slowly than the number of such graduates. (3) Downward occupational mobility has occurred, which has increased competition for jobs requiring less education. Such a model implies that the returns to cognitive skills have increased, when all other factors such as education are held constant.

We carry out the empirical analysis in terms of the average wages by occupations. Given the nature of the data our results are not conclusive but they are, nevertheless, consistent with the model. We do find a positive impact of cognitive skills on the change in wages by occupation and, based on an analysis of prediction errors, find that those occupations that have been upskilled have experienced higher wage increases.

In sum, skill-biased technical change has resulted in a faster increase in demand for workers with high cognitive skills than the increase in supply. It is these university graduates who are experiencing an increase in real wages. For the other university graduates, by way of contrast, the supply is greater than the demand. As a result, their wages are stagnating and downward occupational mobility is occurring. At the bottom end of the occupational ladder the displacement effect has resulted in considerable downward occupational mobility and this, in turn, has more than offset the ostensible demand surplus of workers in lower occupational tiers. As a result, wages in these lower tiers are falling and an increasing number of workers are becoming jobless.

Although differences in wage levels between groups of people, defined in terms of their education and occupational tier, are increasing, this is not the end of the story. As noted by many, changes in differences in wages within particular groups account for most of the increasing inequality of wages. We directly address this and other issues of wage inequality in the next chapter.

CHAPTER 6

The Distribution of Hourly Wages

In the previous chapter we focus on a series of issues relating to the average level of wages in various subgroups of the labor force. A key finding is that over the last quarter-century, a growing excess *supply* has occurred throughout much of the U.S. labor market and that a growing excess *demand* has appeared primarily in the market for university graduates with relatively high cognitive skills.

In that discussion we touch on several issues involving the wage distribution and show three important trends underlying the growing gap in average wages between those with and without a university degree. (1) The growing wage gap is driven primarily by the substantial reduction in wages for those with less than a university degree, rather than an increase in wages of those with a university degree. (2) The real wages for the university-educated increased only because a minority of workers – those in the upper one-third of the wage distribution – experienced considerable increases in real wages over this period. (3) Some of what others are interpreting as an increased rate of return to education is in fact an increased rate of return to cognitive skills independent of education.

We now turn our attention more directly to the distribution of wages of workers both within and across occupations. A large amount of previous research by economists has convinced most observers that wage inequality has increased significantly over the last quarter-century, not just for the U.S. population as a whole but also within most subgroups of the population. However, most of these results are based on just one or two summary measures of the wage distribution as a whole.

In this chapter we approach the problem of how and why the wage distribution has changed in a broader fashion and obtain three clear results: (1) The overall wage distribution has changed in complex ways, becoming less equal at the upper end and slightly more equal at the bottom end, even while the wage distribution within most low-skilled occupations is widening; (2) The causes of changes in the wage distribution vary for the different occupation tiers; and (3) Technical change has a direct impact on workers in the most education-intensive occupations (tier 4), but it affects all other workers indirectly through the displacement process it generates.

A very large literature has appeared in the last decade attempting to explain the widening of the wage distribution, and economists have developed a standard list of possible causes.[1] These include many of the factors used to analyze employment changes, such as technical change increasingly biased toward those with greater skills; increased international trade with developing nations; and increased legal and illegal immigration of less-skilled workers. Other factors advanced to explain this increasing wage inequality include significant declines in union membership and bargaining power, a considerable reduction in the real value of the federally-mandated minimum wage, a shift in labor market institutions toward "winner-take-all" style wage setting, a slowdown in the growth rate of skilled workers, and increased labor force participation by women with relatively high levels of education. No agreement has been reached on which of these causes is most important.

While all of these factors may have contributed to the increased dispersion of wages, we believe that four causes explain the largest part of the wage distribution changes: entry of women into the labor force; a variant of the technical change argument; the increasing importance of winner-take-all wage setting; and the large-scale growth in the health care and legal services industries. Each of these deserves brief comment.

We explore the theme of increased labor force participation by women in previous chapters. Their entry into the labor force, combined with downward occupational mobility of men with lower cognitive skills, has increased competition for jobs in the lower occupational tiers. It has also increased the range of educational groups competing for these low-tier jobs, thus affecting the range of wages offered to workers in the individual occupations.

As previously noted, our story about technical change is much different than others. We focus on the increasing demand for those with relatively high levels of cognitive skills in occupations requiring considerable education. Large increases in the supply of highly-educated persons can be attributed to increased enrollment rates in universities and also the increased participation of women with at least some college education. The fast-growing demand for high functional literacy, combined with high education, has resulted in an excess demand for workers with both attributes and at the same time, an excess supply of university educated workers with lower levels of functional literacy. As a result, wage dispersion increases in these high-education occupations (both tails of the wage distribution grow larger), and some workers at the low end decide to look for a job in alternative occupations, which have not been previously asso-

---

1 Levy and Murnane (1992) have written a broad and comprehensive summary of the literature. Other surveys include those by Bound and Johnson (1992, 1995), Bradbury *et al.* (1996), Brauer and Hickok (1995), Burtless (1995), Freeman (1996), Karoly (1993), Katz and Murphy (1992), and Kodrzycki (1996).

ciated with such a high level of education. Thus, inequalities at the top half of the wage distribution increase. It is less clear what will happen to wage inequality in the lower tier occupations. One goal of the empirical analysis is to determine how the displacement process works at each level.

Our analysis of winner-take-all labor markets is based on a generalization of some of the ideas proposed by Robert H. Frank and Philip J. Cook (1995) in their important and controversial book. They define winner-take-all labor markets as those in which: (a) reward is determined more by relative performance than absolute performance; (b) rewards are concentrated among a few people; and (c) small differences in talent or effort may give rise to enormous differences in earnings. One of the main implications of winner-take-all style labor markets is a wage distribution with a very long, thin right tail (as shown in Chart 6.1). In our analysis, we show that winner-take-all wage setting mechanisms appear to be growing in importance. At least four separate mechanisms are involved:

• In some occupations, people with special skills can earn extra-high wages if they can exercise these abilities by managing vast assets. For instance, as Frank and Cook argue, highly capable business persons charged with running billion-dollar corporations can make more total profits and also a higher profit rate for their stockholders than their identical twins running million dollar corporations, since these greater assets allow them to exercise more market power. As a result, they can expect to receive higher compensation, even though they work the same number of hours. Similarly, capable lawyers handling lawsuits involving $100 million can expect to earn more than those handling lawsuits involving $1000, even though they are equally skillful and have an equal degree of aggressiveness.[2]

• In some occupations where information about the quality of work carried out by different individuals is difficult to obtain, a herd behavior may result among consumers.[3] If, for instance, one physician becomes "known" as a particularly good heart surgeon, because of one well-publicized successful operation, many patients may be willing to pay a substantial premium to have this doctor perform heart surgery rather than "take a risk" with a less well-known surgeon. As a result, the popular surgeon's fees may be much higher than others. This can happen even when the popular surgeon is no more skill-

---

2 Norman Lebrecht (1997) analyzes the dismal impact of a winner-take-all style of wage setting for conductors and concert stars in the classical music industry. In the field of academic economics, an example is Columbia University's offer of $300,000 (plus a subsidized apartment, job for spouse, and private-school placement of a child) to a Harvard University economics professor. Examples of the star system can be found in many other professions as well.

3 We borrow this terminology and the general idea from the finance literature on "herding." For some recent examples of this literature, see Devenow and Welch (1996), Gale (1996), Kortian (1995), Orlean (1995), and Shiller (1995).

ful than many other surgeons. In a similar way, some artists can be publicized by a gallery and can prosper, while those of equal talent may starve.

• In other occupations special niches may open such as psychologists specialized in recovering allegedly lost memories. These niches are difficult to enter, but they offer extra high wages. The growth of self-employment at the high end of the wage distribution is an indicator of such high-wage niches; at the bottom end of the wage distribution, however, self-employment may indicate that people are unable to obtain a full-time job and are making-do with lower earnings. Similar arguments can be made about part-time work.

• Finally, in some occupations tournament-style incentives are becoming more important. This occurs when it is difficult to monitor the absolute productivity of individual workers, but it is less difficult to measure relative productivity. The pay schedule is then based on relative productivity rankings, with the most productive worker getting paid substantially more than the second-most productive worker, who is paid more than the third-most productive worker, and so on. In this situation, many workers will choose to work hard to increase the probability of getting relatively high pay. Lazear and Rosen (1981) first introduced tournament theory, and their ideas have resulted in a considerable literature.[4]

In addition to these mechanisms operating within the labor markets for individual occupations, another cause of the changes in wage inequality can be traced to two particular industries (rather than occupations). In both the health care industry and the legal services industry, unique factors have resulted in average wages for everyone with a college degree or more increasing significantly faster than for similar workers in other industries. In the health care industry, indirect payment schemes (through public or private health insurance) abound, weakening the link between price and quantity demanded. In addition, technology is changing rapidly, government regulation is relatively strong, and the American Medical Association sometimes acts like a profit-maximizing cartel. This combination of factors has lead to a rapid increase in the demand for health care workers, a relatively small increase in labor supply, and thus a sharp increase in their real wages. Similar features appear to pervade the legal services industry.

These four causal forces are the main ingredients of the analysis in this chapter. Before we plunge in, however, we need to discuss several technical issues.

---

4 Lazear (1995) has an excellent general survey of this literature. Frank and Cook (1995, p. 146) actually exclude this last case from their discussion, focusing only "on instances in which tournament pay schemes are a natural feature of the market structure, not an artifact imposed for the sake of stimulating extra effort."

Defining and Measuring Wage Inequality

To establish the most important facts about the wage distribution and its changes over the 1970–1994 period, it is necessary to define both our measure of individual wages as well as our methods for summarizing an entire distribution of wages. Although we try to leave most detailed methodological discussions in this book for the appendices, in this case some discussion is necessary because the results we obtain are so closely related to the analytic methods.

For individual wages, we use retrospective data from the March Current Population Survey on total yearly earnings, weeks worked, and usual hours worked during the previous calendar year to calculate the mean hourly wage rate of each individual in the sample. For workers whose yearly earnings are top-coded (lumped into a single category above a certain amount), we use the information on the distribution of yearly earnings within their detailed occupation to estimate the most likely value of their earnings. As with most of the previous analysis in this book, we focus on the prime working-age population, that is, those between 25 and 50.

A key step in analyzing changes in the wage distribution involves deciding what measures to use to summarize an entire distribution. Many authors rely heavily on one or two summary statistics when discussing the wage distribution and wage inequality. If hourly wages are distributed according to a log normal distribution over all relevant subgroups, as often assumed, then knowledge of the mean and variance for each subgroup is sufficient to describe and thoroughly compare these distributions. In fact, under these simple conditions, a complete description of the distribution requires only some measure of central tendency (the mean, median, or mode) and some measure of dispersion (the variance, the 10th to 90th percentile gap, the coefficient of variation, or even the Gini coefficient). Unfortunately our analysis, as well as some previous work in the field, suggests that the log-normal assumption is frequently unjustified so focusing strictly on one or two statistics to measure inequality can sometimes result in an erroneous interpretation. For instance, we show later in this chapter that changes in the upper half of the wage distribution are quite different from those in the lower half.

Graphical methods lie at the opposite extreme from such statistical analyses. These involve estimating and drawing complete graphs of both the actual wage distribution and counterfactual wage distributions for various subgroups of the populations.[5] Such techniques (sometimes called "kernal density estimation" or "conditional weighted density estimation") present the maximum

---

5   These methods are thoroughly developed in the wage distribution context by DiNardo, Fortin and Lemiex (1996). Valetta (1997) presents a less technical explanation and application of these techniques.

amount of detail and can be very useful for discovering important anomalies that are not apparent using the summary statistic approach. As with all detailed approaches, however, these can sometimes obscure the big picture.

We believe that no single type of analysis can capture all of the important phenomena involved in the complex changes in the wage distribution. Thus, in the analysis below, we use elements of both the summary statistic approach and simple versions of the graphing approach.[6] On the summary statistic side, we use two different families of statistics.

The first is the percentile range family. This includes, for example, the wage gap between the 10th percentile wage and the 90th percentile wage, or the wage gap between the 10th and 50th percentile wages, or between the 50th and 90th percentile wages. These statistics have two advantages in the wage distribution context: they are relatively easy to understand and measure (in dollars per hour), and they can easily be used to identify where in the wage distribution the changes are occuring. If the entire wage distribution shifts, the difference between wages in the 10th and 90th percentiles does not change and, for this reason, we consider the percentile range as an absolute measure of inequality. If, on the other hand, each wage is doubled, then obviously the range of wages between two specified percentiles changes.

The second type of statistic we use is the Generalized Entropy (GE) family of inequality measures. These measures are more difficult to understand, but they have a number of desirable properties that other measures lack. All members of this widely-used family of inequality indices are defined in the following way:

$$1) \quad E_\alpha = \left(\frac{1}{\alpha^2 - \alpha} \right) \left[\left(\frac{1}{N} \sum_{i=1}^{N} \left(\frac{w_i}{\mu} \right)^\alpha \right) - 1 \right] \text{ for } \alpha < 2, \, \alpha \neq 1, \, \alpha \neq 0,$$

where E_α is the generalized entropy index calculated with a specified value of α, α is an arbitrary constant and is discussed below, N is the size of the sample, w_i is the wage of the ith respondent, and μ is the average wage. For $\alpha = 1$ or 0, this index is undefined. However, for these two cases, we substitute the value of the index in the limit as α approaches 1 or 0. These limits are well-defined in terms of functions of logarithms.[7] Although this formula appears

---

6   Some advanced graphical methods can be used to quantify more of our results, particularly conditional weighted density estimations.

7   These formulae are:

$$E_1 = \frac{1}{N} \sum_{i=1}^{N} \left[\left(\frac{w_i}{\mu} \right) \log \left(\frac{w_i}{\mu} \right) \right] \text{ for } \alpha = 1$$

$$E_0 = \frac{1}{N} \sum_{i=1}^{N} \left[\log \left(\frac{\mu}{w_i} \right) \right] \quad \text{for } \alpha = 0$$

daunting, the results lend themselves to a relatively straightforward interpretation. We therefore do not need to spend much time analyzing the mathematical properties of this measure, which have been widely discussed elsewhere.

The inequality measures in the GE family are measures of dispersion, ranging from 0 to some large number. This can be seen by looking at the ratio of a given wage to the mean. If all of the wage observations are close to the mean, then this ratio will be close to 1 for most observations. When N of these ratios are taken to the α power (α not equal to 0) and added together, the sum will be close to N in value. Dividing this by N and then subtracting 1 gives a number close to zero. On the other hand, if the wage observations are widely dispersed, then the ratio of a given wage to the mean will frequently be a positive fraction close to zero, or a positive number much larger than 1. These ratios will add up to a number larger than N, with the actual size depending entirely on the distribution of wages above and below the mean.

In contrast to the percentile range family, the members of the GE family are relative measures (rather than absolute measures) of inequality or dispersion. This means that if the entire distribution is scaled up or down proportionately (e.g., each wage is doubled) then all of the GE values will remain the same. This property is referred to as "mean-independence."

This family of inequality measures has several attractive properties which have led to its popularity among economists. First of all, if the value of α is selected to be less than 2, the Generalized Entropy family includes all indices which simultaneously satisfy properties like symmetry, mean-independence, the strong principle of transfers, and additive decomposability.[8] The last property is particularly relevant to our analysis of the sources of inequality and of changes in inequality because it allows for overall inequality to be decomposed into within subgroup inequality and between subgroup inequality for any relevant subgroups.

8 Symmetry (or anonymity) requires that the inequality measure depend only upon the shape of the distribution, and not upon what person is at which position. Thus, if two persons switch positions in the wage distribution, the inequality measure must be unchanged. All familiar inequality measures have this property.

  Mean independence requires that if all wages are scaled up or down proportionately, the measure of inequality must not change. The percentile range family does not have this property. However, any member of the percentile range family divided by the median wage is mean independent. In our analysis, we utilize the advantages of having one set of absolute inequality measures (the percentile range family) and one set of relative, or mean independent, inequality measures (the GE family).

  The principle of transfers requires that any distribution that can be reached by an income transfer from a higher to a lower income group must have less inequality than the original distribution. The strong principle of transfers requires this condition plus the size of the effect to be independent of all other persons' wages. An inequality measure without these properties

Second, the parameter α, which defines each member of the family, can be assigned an economic interpretation. This allows α to be set at a level which is most appropriate for a particular problem, or most consistent with a particular set of values or beliefs. For values of α close to positive 2, the index gives approximately the same weight to all regions of the wage distribution. As α becomes smaller and eventually becomes negative, more and more weight is given to the lower end of the wage distribution. As α approaches negative infinity, the index becomes very "Rawlsian," in the sense of putting all of the weight on the bottom position in the wage distribution.

Third, several familiar inequality measures are members of the GE family and these are specified in Table 6.1.

Changes in the Overall Hourly Wage Distribution

The primary purpose of the exercises in this discussion is to show that changes in the top and bottom halves of the wage distribution are quite different and that these differences reveal some important clues about the underlying causal mechanisms.

Table 6.1 presents some results for five different members of the GE family and for two different sets of years (1970–71 and 1993–94).[9] For the top four members of the GE family in the table we see that wage inequality increased significantly over this quarter-century. For $\alpha = +2$, which gives equal weights to all sections of the wage distribution, the increase is very large. However, for increasingly smaller values of α, which give relatively more weight to the lower end of the wage distribution, the change in inequality becomes smaller. For $\alpha = -2$, which gives very little weight to high wages, wage inequality appears to have decreased.

cannot be used to establish a unique ranking, by inequality, of all possible distributions. Several familiar inequality measures, including the widely-used Gini Coefficient, fail to have this property.

Additive decomposability requires that the aggregate inequality measure can be decomposed into various subgroup inequality measures, as well as a between-subgroup inequality measure, which will sum to the original inequality measure. In addition, the between-subgroup inequality measure must depend only on the mean value of the wage in each subgroup. Very few inequality measures outside of the GE family have this property.

For a more detailed explanation of all of these properties, see Jenkins (1991).

9   Throughout this chapter we use combined data from 1970 and 1971 for the beginning of the period, which are calculated from data of the March 1971 and 1972 Current Population Survey. Similarly, we use combined data for 1993 and 1994, for the end of the period, which are calculated from data of the March 1994 and 1995 Current Population Survey. This procedure allows us to increase our sample size enough to allow a more reliable estimation of wage inequality within most detailed (three-digit) occupations.

Table 6.1: *Changes in the Generalized Entropy Measure of the Inequality of Hourly Wage of Employed Prime-Age Workers*

Value of α	Equivalent measure	1970–71	1993–94	Difference
+2.0	(1/2) coefficient of variation squared	0.422	0.815	0.393
+1.0	Theil entropy measure	0.245	0.369	0.124
+0.0	Mean log deviation	0.252	0.312	0.060
-1.0		0.428	0.447	0.019
-2.0		1.343	1.227	-0.116

Notes: The data come from the Current Population Surveys of March 1971, 1972, 1994, and 1995. By March 1999 the Theil entropy measure had decreased to 0.341, which represents a reversal of about 20 percent of the large increase in wage inequality between 1970 and 1994.

In sum, any conclusions drawn about overall wage inequality trends depend on the weight placed on the lower end of the wage distribution. The simplest interpretation of these results is that inequality is increasing significantly in the upper end of the wage distribution and is decreasing moderately at the lower end. In other words, the most dramatic changes are occurring in the upper end of the overall wage distribution, which is thickening and/or lengthening; while smaller changes are occurring in the lower tail, which is thinning and/or compressing. Such results also suggest that we need to use relatively high values of α if we want to focus on the increasing inequality in the upper tail of the wage distribution. Therefore, for much of our remaining analysis we use the Theil entropy measure, which is the GE measure where α = +1.

The results in Table 6.1 are also consistent with more complex changes in the wage distribution, so further investigation is necessary. In Chart 6.1 we present a graph of the distribution of real hourly wages for 1970–71 and 1993–94 in 1994 prices. Since the graph is in constant prices, it should be clear that the central tendency (however defined) of the real wage distribution has not changed much over this long time period. In fact, the median wage remained virtually unchanged (decreased by $0.44 per hour), while the mode decreased by about $1.50 an hour and the mean increased by more than $1.25 an hour. This is due to the fact that the middle part of the distribution shifted leftward, while the right tail thickened and stretched much further to the right. Thus, the biggest concentration of employed prime-age workers earned less per hour in 1993–94 than in 1970–71, but those in the top decile or two earned much more per hour than previously.

Another important aspect of the overall wage distributions is seen more clearly in Graphs A6.1 and A6.2 in the appendices. These are drawn with a logarithmic scale on the wage axis and allow us to see some of the details of the lower tail (Chart A6.1) and of the upper tail (Chart A6.2) which are obscured in Chart 6.1. In particular, it is clear from the two appendix charts

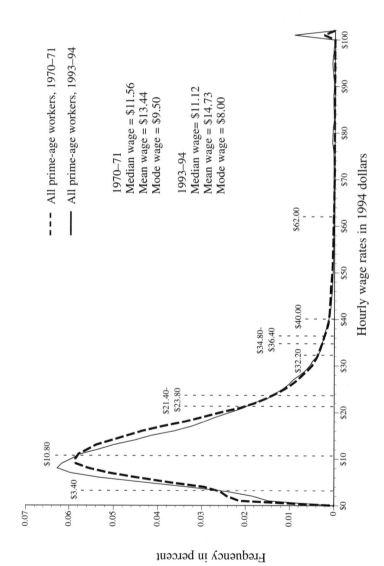

Chart 6.1 Overall wage distribution, prime-age workers

Legend:
- - - All prime-age workers, 1970–71
——— All prime-age workers, 1993–94

1970–71
Median wage = $11.56
Mean wage = $13.44
Mode wage = $9.50

1993–94
Median wage= $11.12
Mean wage = $14.73
Mode wage = $8.00

Y-axis: Frequency in percent (0, 0.01, 0.02, 0.03, 0.04, 0.05, 0.06, 0.07)

X-axis: Hourly wage rates in 1994 dollars ($0, $10, $20, $30, $40, $50, $60, $70, $80, $90, $100)

Data labels: $3.40, $10.80, $21.40–$23.80, $32.20, $34.80–$36.40, $40.00, $62.00

that the two distribution curves cross each other seven times. A smaller fraction of workers earned less than \$3.40 an hour in 1993–94 than in 1970–71, and this is what the GE measure with α = -2 points out to us. However, a smaller fraction also earned between \$10.80 and \$21.40 an hour, between \$32.20 and \$34.80 an hour, and also between \$40.00 and \$62.00. On the other hand, a much larger fraction of workers earned more than \$62.00 an hour in the later years. This multiple crossing of frequency distributions causes the various single-number inequality measures to yield such different results. Some parts of the wage distribution are becoming more equal and other parts are becoming less equal. No single number measuring inequality can capture this complexity.

The frequency distributions in Chart 6.1 and in the appendices are plotted for all prime-age persons of any race who worked at least one hour for pay. If the overall frequency distribution is plotted for workers of all ages, or for just full-time, full-year workers, or for just white workers, or for any combination of these, the results are very similar. In all of these cases, the more recent frequency distribution crosses the older one several times, the mode of the distribution shifts left, the lower tail compresses, and the upper tail expands significantly.

Changes in Hourly Wage Inequality by Looking at Subgroups

The next step is to take advantage of the property of the GE inequality measure that allows us easily to decompose the inequality measure into components. In this way we can determine the contribution to wage inequality of changes between and within various subgroups which, in turn, allows us to identify the sources of the changes in wage inequality.

Changes Within and Between Subgroups

Table 6.2 presents the relevant results from an exercise using the Theil entropy measure (the GE index with α = 1). Overall wage inequality increased from .245 to .369. Each line of the table corresponds to a different way of dividing the population into subgroups. For each year we distinguish the relative importance of inequality between and within these subgroups, where the two numbers add up to total inequality. For example, line 2 divides the prime-age employed population into men and women and shows how much is due to wage inequalities within the subgroup (that is, within-gender inequality) and how much is due to inequality between the subgroups (that is,

Table 6.2: Decomposition of Changes in the Theil Entropy Measure of Wage Inequality by Gender, Race, Education, and Occupation of Prime-Age Worker

	1970–71 Total inequality	Between-group inequality	Within-group inequality	1994–95 Total inequality	Between-group inequality	Within-group inequality	Change in total inequality	Change in between-group inequality	Change in within-group inequality
Line									
1 1 group	0.245	0.000	0.245	0.369	0.000	0.369	+0.124	0.000	+0.124
2 2 groups by gender	0.245	0.037	0.208	0.369	0.013	0.356	+0.124	-0.024	+0.148
3 3 groups by race	0.245	0.005	0.240	0.369	0.003	0.366	+0.124	-0.002	+0.126
4 4 groups by education	0.245	0.029	0.216	0.369	0.053	0.316	+0.124	+0.024	+0.100
5 4 groups by occupational tier	0.245	0.022	0.223	0.369	0.040	0.329	+0.124	+0.018	+0.106
6 6 groups by gender/race	0.245	0.041	0.204	0.369	0.015	0.354	+0.124	-0.026	+0.015
7 9 groups by gender/education	0.245	0.062	0.183	0.369	0.066	0.303	+0.124	-0.004	+0.120
8 8 groups by gender/tier	0.245	0.062	0.183	0.369	0.061	0.308	+0.124	-0.001	+0.125
9 12 groups by race/education	0.245	0.031	0.214	0.369	0.055	0.314	+0.124	+0.024	+0.100
10 12 groups by race/tier	0.245	0.024	0.221	0.369	0.041	0.328	+0.124	+0.017	+0.107
11 16 groups by education/tier	0.245	0.033	0.212	0.369	0.060	0.309	+0.124	+0.027	+0.097

12	24 groups by gender/ race/education	0.245	0.064	0.181	0.369	0.068	0.301	+0.124	+0.004	+0.120
13	24 groups by gender/ race/tier	0.245	0.063	0.182	0.369	0.063	0.306	+0.124	+0.000	+0.124
14	32 groups by gender/ education/tier	0.245	0.068	0.177	0.369	0.078	0.291	+0.124	+0.010	+0.114
15	48 groups by race/ education/tier	0.245	0.035	0.210	0.369	0.062	0.307	+0.124	+0.027	+0.097
16	96 groups by gender/ race/education/tier	0.245	0.069	0.176	0.369	0.079	0.290	+0.124	+0.010	+0.114

Notes: Total inequality is the sum of between–subgroup and within-subgroup inequality. The meaning of the indices is explained in the text. The numbers are based on calculations using the March CPS surveys from 1971, 1972, 1994, and 1995.

between men and women). In 1970–71 most of the wage inequality (.208/245 = 85 percent) was due to inequality within genders. By 1993–94 even more of the wage inequality (.356/.369 = 96 percent) was due to this inequality within genders. Thus, between 1970–71 and 1993–94, between-gender inequality fell by .024 (that is, the male-female wage gap narrowed),[10] while within-gender inequality increased by .148.

Similar results hold for a decomposition into three race/ethnicity groups (white, black, and other races). Virtually none of the wage inequality in 1970–71 or in 1993–94 (or the change in wage inequality between the two years) can be explained by wage inequality between races.[11] The decompositions by education and by occupation tier are somewhat more informative. Changes in between- education group inequality (that is, the inequality arising from different average wages of people with different levels of education) can explain 19 percent (= .024/.124) of the increase in total inequality. Changes in between-occupation-tier group inequality (that is, between average wages of people in the four occupation tiers) can explain 15 percent (=.018/.124) of the increase in total inequality. Changes in education and tier combined (data line 11 in Table 6.2) can explain 22 percent (=.027/.124) of the increase in total inequality. This last result is consistent with the increase in returns to both education and to cognitive abilities that we document earlier.

One of the main goals of this type of decomposition analysis is to identify subgroups where changes in the inequality between the subgroups (the "explained" part of the change) is large compared to the changes of inequality within subgroups (the "unexplained" part of the changes). In this regard we have failed, because this type of analysis cannot explain much of the increased wage inequality. Indeed, in none of the cases in Table 6.2 is the change of between-subgroup inequality greater than 22 percent of the size of the total changes in wage inequality. It is striking that even when the prime-age employed population is divided into 96 groups by gender, race, education, and occupation tier (the last line in Table 6.2), less than 10 percent (.010 out of .124) of the increase in overall wage inequality can be attributed to changes of inequality between subgroups.

These results, we might add, are consistent with most previous work in this area. Most of these studies find that very little of the increased wage inequality can be explained by easily-measured characteristics of the working popu-

---

10 The results reported in this sentence imply that, at the aggregate level, the changing differences between male and female wages have reduced inequality. This is consistent with the recent findings of Juhn and Murphy (1997). We show below, however, that these results do not always remain the same at a more disaggregate level.

11 This result might differ, however, if we extended our sample of prime-age workers to include both younger and older workers.

lation. Instead, most of the increased wage inequality is attributed to changes in inequality within well-defined groups. Nevertheless, the immense detail of our data set and the variety of inequality measures we examine allows us to go beyond the type of decomposition in Table 6.2 and to identify one type of between-subgroup inequality which has increased significantly. The relevant data are in Table 6.3.

The first line presents data for the division of all workers aggregated into four occupation tiers (similar to line 5 in Table 6.2). Only 14 percent (.018/.125) of the change in inequality is explained by changes in the inequality between tiers. The second line shows the results of the same calculation when workers are divided into approximately 500 detailed occupations, a unique type of calculation for which data has not hitherto been available. Even with this immense detail, only 29 percent (.037/.126) of the change in inequality is explained by the changes of inequality between detailed occupations, which is lower than expected.

Some interesting differences do appear in the last four lines of Table 6.3, which show the inequality of wages in each occupational tier separately, The degree of wage inequality increases as we move from the least-education intensive occupations (tier 1) to the most-educational occupations (tier 4). Moreover, for the bottom three tiers, the changes in wages between the detailed occupations making up the tier explain very little of the increase in what inequality within the tier. By way of contrast, for tier 4 occupations, 58 percent of the change in inequality is explained by changes in inequality between detailed occupations. This phenomenon is obscured in line 2, which incldues the entire sample, because the bottom three tiers behave so differently than tier 4. We need to investigate this matter in greater detail.

Tier 4 Occupations: Changes Between
Detailed Occupations

As a group, tier 4 occupations have experienced the largest increase in total inequality (.142). As previously noted, almost 60 percent of this increase is explained by an increase in inequality between the 100 or so detailed occupations comprising this tier. That is, the greater part of the changes in Table 6.3 are due to an increase in the gap between the median wages of occupations in the low-wage end of tier 4, such as pre-kindergarten and kindergarten teachers, clergy, and social workers, and the median wages paid to occupations at the high-wage end of tier 4 such as physicians, dentists, and lawyers. The other 40 percent of this increase is explained by an increase in inequality within some of the detailed occupations.

Table 6.3: Changes in Wage Inequality Within and Between Occupational Tiers and Detailed Occupations of Prime-Age Workers

Line	Main group		1970–71			1994–95			Change in total inequality	Change in between subgroup inequality	Change in within-subgroup inequality
			Total inequality	Between-subgroup inequality	Within-subgroup inequality	Total inequality	Between-subgroup inequality	Within-subgroup inequality			
1.	All workers	4 occupational tiers	0.243	0.022	0.221	0.368	0.040	0.329	+0.125	+0.018	+0.108
2.	All workers	400+ detailed occupations	0.243	0.073	0.170	0.369	0.110	0.259	+0.126	+0.037	+0.089
3.	Workers in tier 1 occupations (least education)	100+ detailed occupations	0.185	0.049	0.136	0.275	0.042	0.233	+0.090	-0.007	+0.097
4.	Workers in tier 2	100 + detailed occupations	0.197	0.057	0.140	0.302	0.047	0.255	+0.105	-0.010	+0.115

5.	Workers in tier 3 occupations	100 + detailed occupations	0.241	0.043	0.198	0.321	0.047	0.274	+0.080	+0.004	+0.076
6.	Workers in tier 4 occupations (most education)	100 + detailed occupations	0.253	0.064	0.189	0.395	0.147	0.248	+0.142	+0.083	+0.059

Notes: Total inequality is the sum of between-subgroup and within-subgroup inequality. The meaning of the indices is explained in the text. The numbers are based on calculations using the March CPS surveys from 1971, 1972, 1994, and 1995.

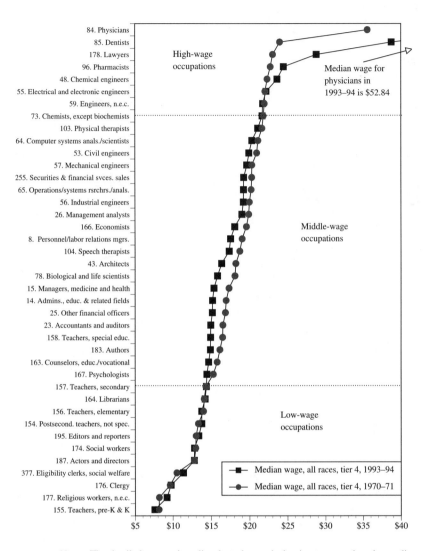

84. Physicians
85. Dentists
178. Lawyers
96. Pharmacists
48. Chemical engineers
55. Electrical and electronic engineers
59. Engineers, n.e.c.
73. Chemists, except biochemists
103. Physical therapists
64. Computer systems anals./scientists
53. Civil engineers
57. Mechanical engineers
255. Securities & financial svces. sales
65. Operations/systems rsrchrs./anals.
56. Industrial engineers
26. Management analysts
166. Economists
8. Personnel/labor relations mgrs.
104. Speech therapists
43. Architects
78. Biological and life scientists
15. Managers, medicine and health
14. Admins., educ. & related fields
25. Other financial officers
23. Accountants and auditors
158. Teachers, special educ.
183. Authors
163. Counselors, educ./vocational
167. Psychologists
157. Teachers, secondary
164. Librarians
156. Teachers, elementary
154. Postsecond. teachers, not spec.
195. Editors and reporters
174. Social workers
187. Actors and directors
377. Eligibility clerks, social welfare
176. Clergy
177. Religious workers, n.e.c.
155. Teachers, pre-K & K

High-wage occupations

Median wage for physicians in 1993–94 is $52.84

Middle-wage occupations

Low-wage occupations

■— Median wage, all races, tier 4, 1993–94
●— Median wage, all races, tier 4, 1970–71

$5 $10 $15 $20 $25 $30 $35 $40

Notes: The detailed occupations listed on the vertical axis correspond to the median wages in 1993–94. They do not correspond to the median wages in 1970–71. The data come from the March Current Population Survey for the various years.

Chart 6.2: Comparison of median wage distribution across detailed occupations in tier 4: 1970–71 vs. 1993–94

Chart 6.2 suggests some possibilities about what is driving this increase in wage dispersion across the tier 4 occupations. It shows median wage data on the 40 largest detailed occupations in tier 4. (These include all occupations with more than 100,000 workers in both 1970–71 and 1993–94). The detailed occupations are listed from bottom to top based on their median wage in 1993–94. The black line with squares shows the value of the median wage for each detailed occupation in 1993–94. Thus, pre-kindergarten and kindergarten teachers earned the least, about $7.60 an hour, while physicians earned the most, about $52.84 per hour.

The grey line with circles represents the median wages for the same 40 detailed occupations in 1970–71 showing how the wage distribution between occupations has changed. These are also listed from bottom to top based on their median wage, but in 1970–71, rather than in 1993–94. This means, of course, that the (1993–94) occupation names do not necessarily match the 1970–71 numbers.

For instance, in 1993–94 the four highest-paid occupations were physicians ($52.84), dentists ($38.75), lawyers ($28.79), and pharmacists ($24.45). In 1970–71 the four highest-paid occupations were dentists ($35.60), electrical and electronic engineers ($23.00), lawyers ($22.70), and physicians ($22.30). In Chart 6.2, therefore, the square above "physicians" shows the median wage of physicians in 1993–94 (the highest paid tier 4 occupation in those years). The circle, however, shows the median wage of dentists in 1970–71 (the highest paid tier 4 occupation in those years). The implication of such a comparison is that the highest-paid tier 4 occupation in 1993–94 earned 48 percent more ($52.84 versus $35.60) than the highest-paid tier 4 occupation in 1970–71. This represents an enormous increase.

With this in mind, Chart 6.2 can be used to illustrate wage distribution changes occurring across tier 4 occupations over the last quarter-century. Median wages in the bottom 10 or so occupations showed little change. In the next 20 or so occupations, median wages decreased slightly. Finally, in the four most highly paid occupations, median wages increased dramatically. These results show that there has been a general reduction or stagnation in median wages in all but a few of the tier 4 occupations. At the same time, the top 4 occupations reveal a remarkable increase in median wages. Thus, we need to explain why wages increased so dramatically in the most highly paid occupations and why they decreased or stagnated in many of the remaining occupations.

Table 6.4 provides insight into forces underlying wage increases among occupations in the upper tail. The table shows the 10 occupations with the largest changes in hourly wages between 1970–71 and 1993–94. Panel A shows that the top seven are physicians, pharmacists, lawyers, physical therapists, special education teachers, speech therapists, and dentists. It should

Table 6.4: *Some Characteristics of the Largest Detailed Occupations in Tier 4*

Panel A: Occupations with the largest increase in the median hourly wage of prime-age workers between 1970–71 and 1993–94

Rank	Occupation code	Occupation title	Change in median hourly wage
1	84	Physicians	+$30.53
2	96	Pharmacists	+ 6.25
3	178	Lawyers	+ 6.06
4	103	Physical therapists	+ 4.55
5	158	Teachers, special education	+ 4.42
6	104	Speech therapists	+ 3.28
7	85	Dentists	+ 3.18
8	73	Chemists, except biochemists	+ 2.06
9	176	Clergy	+ 1.59
10	177	Religious workers, n.e.c.	+ 1.01

Panel B: Occupations with the highest NALS scores of prime-age workers in 1992

Rank	Occupation code	Occupation title	Average NALS score
1	104	Speech therapists	366
2	164	Librarians	359
3	26	Management analysts	358
4	178	Lawyers	356
5	55	Electrical and electronic engineers	355
6	195	Editors and reporters	355
7	187	Actors and directors	353
8	85	Dentists	353
9	43	Architects	350
10	64	Computer systems analysts and scientists	350

Panel C: Occupations with the largest increase in hourly wage inequality of prime-age workers between 1970–71 and 1993–94

Rank	Occupation code	Occupation title	Changes in hourly wage inequality (Theil entropy index, $a = 1$)
1	187	Actors and directors	+0.519
2	174	Social workers	+0.320
3	183	Authors	+0.281
4	255	Securities & financial services sale services	+0.270
5	65	Operations & systems researchers, analysts	+0.197
6	166	Economists	+0.154
7	26	Management analysts	+0.139
8	25	Other financial officers	+0.131
9	78	Biological and life scientists	+0.115
10	23	Accountants and auditors	+0.093

Notes: The data come from the Current Population Surveys of March 1971. 1972, 1994, and 1995, and the National Adult Literacy Survey of 1992.

come as no surprise that all but one of these occupations (lawyers) is related to the health care industry. This is undoubtedly related to the widely discussed increase in total spending on health care over the last quarter-century. Our results suggest that this spending increase is due in part to increased hourly wages for workers in many health care occupations.

More germane to our study, these results also suggest that a significant part of the increase in between-occupation wage inequality in tier 4 is due to increasing wages in the health care occupations (plus lawyers). The wage increases probably have more to do with the special nature of the health care and legal services markets than with any more general trend. Both of these markets have experienced rapid increases in demand over the last quarter-century. In addition, many of the health care occupations have had strong supply-side constraints in place – for example, limits on the enrollment size of medical schools in the United States – which have contributed to the increased excess demand.

One final aspect of the occupations with increasing wages should be noted. In the previous chapter we present evidence that the return to cognitive skills has increased across occupations. Can the enormous relative wage increases in the health care and legal occupations be explained by the unusually high cognitive abilities required by those occupations? For the 40 large tier 4 occupations in Chart 6.2 we calculated the average NALS scores and ranked the occupations from the highest average scores to the lowest. The highest scores, listed in Panel B of Table 6.4, are for speech therapists, librarians, and management analysts. Of the health care occupations other than speech therapists, only dentists ranked in the ten highest scores. Physicians ranked only 15th out of 40. Thus it does not seem that unusually high cognitive abilities among the health care occupations explain their wage increases (with the possible exception of speech therapists). On the other hand, lawyers had the 4th highest NALS scores, so perhaps part of their wage increase is due to an increase in the return to the (cognitive) skills required to navigate an ever more complex and changing legal system.[12]

The other part of the puzzle involves explaining why median wages have fallen across the majority of highly education-intensive occupations, especially in the middle part of the tier 4 wage distribution. We believe that much of this is caused by women displacing men in this occupational tier. In particular, women displace men in these middle-wage tier 4 occupations by accepting

---

12 These results do not support the notion that there has been no increase in the rate of return to cognitive skills. We show in Chapter 5 that, over the entire sample of occupations, those occupations with higher average NALS scores have been more likely to experience large increases in wage rates, other things being equal. The results in Table 6.4 simply indicate that something other than high NALS scores was responsible for the large wage increases in most of the health care occupations.

Table 6.5: *Determinants of the Fraction of Prime-Age Female Workers in Tier 4 Occupations*

Dependent variable:
The fraction of prime-age female workers in each tier 4 occupation in 1994

	Coefficient	Standard error	t Statistic
Constant	+0.338	.0917	+3.68
Fraction of prime-age females in each occupation in 1971	+0.765	.0601	+12.71
Average over time of the median real wage gap prime-age workers in each occupation	-.0106	.00450	-2.36
Average over time of the median real wage gap between men and women in each occupation	+0.0253	.00542	+4.67
Sample size	90		
Adjusted R^2	.8170		

Notes: The regressions are weighted OLS regressions, with weights as the average number of workers in each occupation. Only 90 of the 99 occupations in tier 4 are included. We eliminated five occupations because of lack of data for both years. We dropped another four with the highest median wages because, as discussed in the text, these labor markets exhibit different behavior than the middle- and low-wage occupations in tier 4.The averages are based on 1971 and 1994 data. The data underlying these calculations come from the March CPS samples of 1971, 1972, 1994, and 1995.

lower wages than men. These ideas can be tested in a straightforward fashion in a regression analysis by looking at the following simple hypothesis. Within the most education intensive occupations, women are disproportionately entering those occupations which either have a low median wage for all workers, or which have a middle level median wage across all workers but a significantly lower wage for women than for men.

To implement these ideas in Table 6.5, we look at the fraction of prime-age female workers for each tier 4 occupation in 1993–94 as a function of the fraction of such workers in 1970–71, the average value over time (from the 1970–71 and 1995–95 values) of the median wage in each occupation, and the average value over time of the male-female wage gap in each occupation. Our hypothesis suggests that the average median wage should have a negative impact on fraction female in 1993–94, holding initial fraction female and average wage gap constant. On the other hand, the average male-female wage gap should have a positive impact on fraction female in 1993–94, holding initial fraction female and average median wage constant.

Two problems arise in setting up this calculation. Although there are a total of 99 detailed occupations in tier 4, we have data for both years on only 94 of these to include in the regression. Furthermore, as we discuss in greater detail below, the labor market for the most highly paid occupations paying more than $30 an hour (namely physicians, dentists, lawyers, and pharmacists) operates rather differently from the labor market for the other occupations. As a result, we felt it important to drop these occupations from the calculations as well, leaving a total of 90 occupations on which to perform the statistical tests.

The results in Table 6.5 provide strong support for our hypotheses.[13] The statistical fit of the regression is very good with an R^2 of 0.8170. All the estimated parameters have the expected signs and are significant at the 1 percent level. The estimated coefficient on the average (over time) male-female wage gap variable is 0.025, which indicates that if a particular occupation has an average wage gap which is one dollar larger than for an otherwise identical occupation, then that occupation will experience a 2.5 percentage point greater increase in the fraction of its jobs held by women. This tells us exactly what we would expect: The greater the male-female wage gap in an occupation, the more likely it is that firms will hire women instead of men.

The estimated coefficient on the average (over time) median wage is −0.011. This indicates that if a particular occupation has an average median wage which is one dollar larger than for an otherwise identical occupation, then that occupation will experience a 1.1 percentage point *smaller* increase in the fraction of its jobs held by women. This result can be interpreted in two conflicting ways. Either a *greater* median wage in an occupation makes it less likely that firms will hire women instead of men or that a *lower* median wage indicates a particular occupation is more likely to attract (or to be taken by) women than men. We can, of course, combine these results from the regression coefficients to perform some interesting thought experiments to gain insight into relative magnitudes when both factors are operating simultaneously.[14]

---

13 These statistical results are also very robust. For instance, we calculated regressions in which, instead of the average values (over time) of the median wage and the male-female wage gap, we used the 1971–70 values or, alternatively, the 1993–94 values. In all of these cases, the estimated coefficients were identical in sign and similar in magnitude.

14 For instance, if an occupation initially consists of 75 percent men and 25 percent women with each group earning, on average, $10 per hour, and if the average female wage then drops to $9 per hour, this will cause a 2.531 percentage point increase in the fraction female (due to the increased wage gap) plus a 0.275 percentage point increase (due to the lower median wage), for a net increase of 2.806 percentage points. On the other hand, if the average male wage increases to $11 per hour, this will cause a 2.531 percentage point increase in the fraction female (due to the increased wage gap) plus a 0.825 percentage point decrease (due to the higher median wage), for a net increase of only 1.706 percentage points. As this example

These regression results confirm our displacement argument that women are entering education-intensive occupations where the majority of workers have been men and where average wages fall within in the middle of the wage distribution. However, these women are receiving wages significantly lower than men. In almost all of the 20 or so occupations in the middle wage range (shown in Chart 6.2), women are displacing men and female wages are lower than male wages (that is, there is a positive male-female wage gap). From the labor demand point of view, women are replacing men by accepting lower wages, a phenomenon that also explains why median wages in these occupations are falling.

Why hasn't this phenomenon pulled down wages of occupations at the upper end of tier 4 as well? Part of the answer, shown in Table 6.6, is that women have made only small inroads into the two highest paid occupations – physicians and dentists – even though the male-female wage gap is enormous. For instance, between 1970–71 and 1993–94, the percentage of women only increased 9 and 15 percentage points respectively. Clearly, a large wage gap does not necessarily lead to an expansion in the share of female workers if other factors are impeding the entry of women.[15] Women have had more success at becoming lawyers and pharmacists, the third and fourth highest-paying occupations. The wage gap is moderately large for lawyers, so the entry of women may have slowed the increase of wages in this occupation. The wage gap is nonexistent for pharmacists, so the entry of women would not have affected their median wage. The percentage of women had increased respectively 21 and 27 percentage points.

In sum, tier 4 has the largest increase in wage inequality and 60 percent of this can be explained by an increase in inequality between the 100 or so detailed occupations in the tier. This inequality between occupations is driven by two factors: a large increase in median wages of a few of the most highly-paid occupations plus a modest decline in median wages in most of the middle-wage occupations. The former is explained by persistent excess demand conditions in the markets for workers in health occupations and for lawyers. The latter is explained by the entry of women with high NALS scores into many of the middle-wage occupations, frequently at wages lower than those of the men they displace.

shows occupations with a growing male-female wage gap driven primarily by a decrease in women's wages will increase their fraction female more than similar occupations in which the gap is driven by an increase in men's wages.

In these calculations, we assume the average and median values of wages to be identical for each group. This is a valid assumption if wages are symmetrically distributed around the average.

15 Inclusion of the four highest paid occupations in the regression from Table 6.5 completely changes the results, seemingly indicating that the average male-female wage gap has no significant effect on the fraction female. This is largely because of the extreme male-female wage gap for physicians, combined with a relatively low fraction female in 1993–94.

Table 6.6: *Major Occupations in Tier 4 With the Highest Median Wages in 1993–94*

| Net displacement | | Occupation | | Median wage 1993–94 | | Fraction of female workers 1970–71 | | Male-female wage gap 1993–94 | |
Rank	Value	Code	Title	Rank from lowest to highest	Value	Rank from highest to lowest	Value	Rank from highest to lowest	Value
28	11%	84	Physicians	40	$52.84	24	14%	1	$72.00
27	15	85	Dentists	39	38.75	39	1	2	25.22
21	23	178	Lawyers	38	28.79	32	5	14	3.03
15	28	96	Pharmacists	37	24.45	22	20	33	- 0.14

Notes: The ranks are in terms of the entire 40 largest tier 4 occupations. The data on median wages include all members in that occupation. The median wages for women are much lower and the median wages for men are much higher than this overall median, so that the gap in the median wages between men and women can be much larger than the overall median wage. The sources are the same as Table 6.5.

*Tier 4 Occupations: Changes Within
Detailed Occupations*

If about 60 percent of the increased wage inequality among the tier 4 occupations can be explained by changes in inequality between occupations, this still leaves 40 percent to be explained by increases in inequality within occupations. What is driving this increase in wage dispersion within many of the tier 4 detailed occupations? We believe three factors contribute to this:

• As documented in Chapter 5, the increase in the rate of return to cognitive skills within occupational tiers and educational groups has played a role. Within many of the detailed occupations in tier 4, those with high NALS scores are earning significantly higher wages than those with lower scores.

• The increased importance of winner-take-all wage setting has influenced wage increases in Tier 4. To see this, we calculated the change in the Theil entropy index (GE index with $\alpha = 1$) for each of the 40 large occupations in tier 4 (enumerated in Chart 6.2) and list the top 10 according to largest increases in wage inequality in Panel C of Table 6.4. Three of the top four occupations – actors and directors, authors, and securities and financial service sale occupations – are well-known for their winner-take-all style wage determination. That is, for every actor, director, or author who becomes nationally known and earns millions of dollars per year, there are hundreds of similar talent whose wages are inadequate to live on. This is one of the defining characteristics of winner-take-all wage determination.

The range of wages is a little less extreme for securities and financial services sales workers, but the pattern is similar. A small number of such workers earn, through commissions and bonuses, more than a million dollars per year. This translates into a wage rate of more than $250 an hour, even if they work 80 hours per week. A much larger number earn between $30,000 and $100,000 per year, which translates into an hourly wage rate between $10 and $50 an hour. To a lesser degree, this is also true of all but one of the remaining eight occupations with the largest increases in wage inequality: operations and systems researchers and analysts, economists, management analysts, and other financial officers. The one significant and inexplicable exception to this pattern is social workers, who experienced the second largest increase in wage inequality.

• Finally, the process by which women are displacing men in tier 4 occupations plays an important role as well. Just as the entry of women has helped to increase between-occupation inequality within tier 4 by reducing the median wage of the middle-wage occupations, it has also helped to increase within-occupation inequality of the same occupations. Chart 6.3 shows wage histograms for all prime-age workers in tier 4 occupations, broken down by gender and by year. (We carried out similar calculations for just whites so as to obtain a more homogeneous sample, but the conclusions were the same.) The wage distributions in Chart 6.3 are for all tier 4 occupations combined. Most of the detailed occupations in the middle-wage range, however, have qualitatively similar wage distributions, a fact that we will use in our interpretation of the chart.

In both sets of years, the wage distributions for women are to the left of those for men. Both the mean and the median wage for women are lower than those for men. Both the mean and the median wage for women are lower than those for men as well. In addition, the low-wage tails of the wage distribution of women are slightly more compressed than those of men, while the high-pressed than those of men. Most strikingly, women have a much lower probability than men of earning an hourly wage three or more times greater than the median wage.

Changes over time reveal more important clues. We see that the wage distribution for women has flattened in the middle and thickened on the high-wage tail, while the distribution for men has flattened in the middle and shifted left, with the high-wage tail stretching further toward the highest wages. The overall impression from Chart 6.3 is that, within a typical middle wage tier 4 occupation, women are expanding from the lower-middle to the middle of the wage distribution, while men are moving away from the middle and the upper-middle into either end of the wage distribution. As men move into the upper tail of the wage distribution, this increases wage variation (variance) of the upper half of the distribution. This effect reinforces the impact of the increase in the rate of return to cognitive skills, as well as the increased importance of winner-take-all wage setting. As men move into the lower tail, this increases the variance of the lower half of the distribution as well.

*Lower Tier Occupations: The Roles of Gender
and Education*

In this section we take a somewhat less extensive look at the wage inequality changes in tiers 1, 2, and 3. The patterns in tier 3 are roughly similar to those in tier 4 and have the same explanation, so we need say little about them. The patterns in tier 1 and 2, by way of contrast, are quite different from those in tiers 3 and 4, but they are similar to each other. Therefore, we combine much of our discussion of these two tiers.

Outside of the tier 4 occupations, the increases in wage inequality are primarily generated by increases of wage inequality within the subgroups identified in Table 6.3. The smallest overall increase in wage inequality is in the tier 3 occupations, which had an increase in the Theil Entropy index of +.080

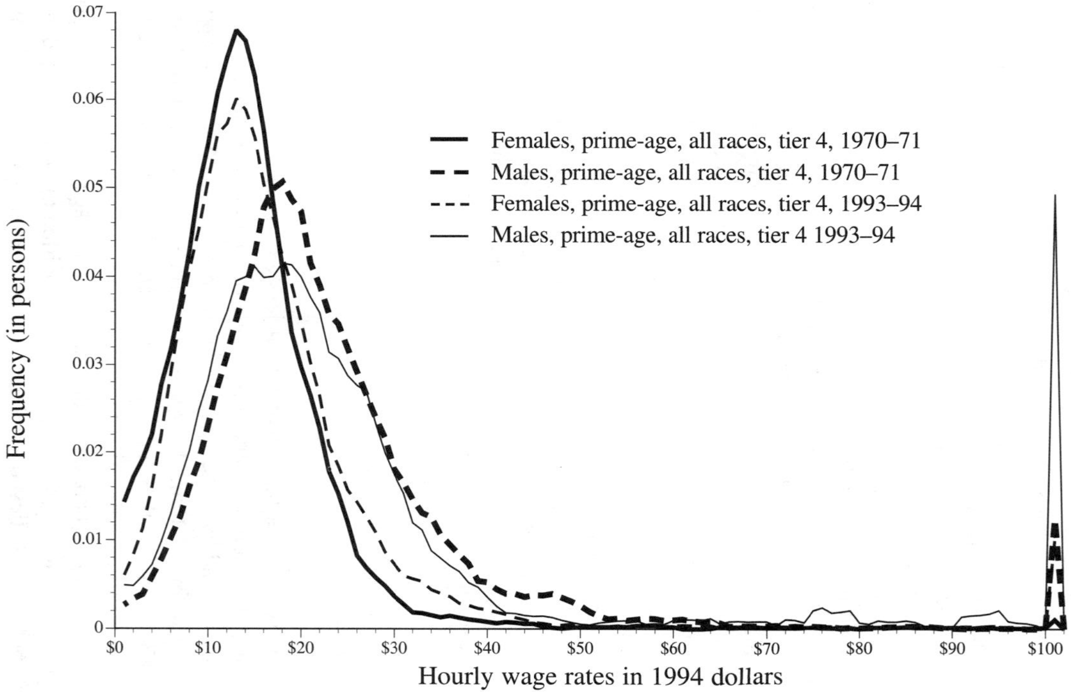
0.07
0.06
0.05
0.04
0.03
0.02
0.01
0
Frequency (in persons)
Females, prime-age, all races, tier 4, 1970–71
Males, prime-age, all races, tier 4, 1970–71
Females, prime-age, all races, tier 4, 1993–94
Males, prime-age, all races, tier 4 1993–94
$0
$10
$20
$30
$40
$50
$60
$70
$80
$90
$100
Hourly wage rates in 1994 dollars

Chart 6.3: Male and female wage changes in tier 4 occupations

(versus +.142 in tier 4). Of this increase, about 95 percent (=.076/.080) was due to changes in inequality within the 100 or so detailed occupations comprising tier 3. Examination of the details of tier 3 suggests that the forces causing these within occupation increases are similar to those causing within occupation increases in tier 4.

More specifically, the increase in the rate of return to cognitive skills accounts for some of the increased wage dispersion within detailed tier 3 occupations. The increased importance of winner-take-all wage setting also contributes, although not as much as in the tier 4 occupations. Finally, the displacement process operates as it does with the tier 4 occupations except that now not only women, but also men displaced from tier 4 occupations move into the middle of the wage distribution in the typical detailed tier 3 occupation and push other workers to the two tails of the wage distribution or down to jobs in tier 2 occupations.

As shown in Table 6.3, the overall increase in wage inequality in the first three occupation tiers are roughly the same. Nevertheless, tiers 1 and 2 manifest a small reduction in between-subgroup inequality within these two tiers, so that the average increase in inequality within the detailed occupations comprising these two tiers is slightly larger than the overall increase.

Whereas the wage distributions in tiers 3 and 4 flattened out and expanded in both the upper and lower tails, the distributions in tiers 1 and 2 flattened out and expanded mainly in the lower tail. Thus, neither increased returns to cognitive skills nor increased importance of winner-take-all wage setting can explain this phenomenon. That is, the changes in wage inequality within tier 1 and tier 2 have very different explanations than those for tier 3 or tier 4.

Two standard explanations for the wage distribution changes in tiers 3 and 4 are offered in the literature: (1) The real level of the federal minimum wage declined over this quarter-century, making it possible for firms to pay lower real wages to the least productive workers in lower tier occupations; and (2) The degree of unionization also declined, weakening the wage-compression that has occurred under the banner of worker solidarity in collective bargaining. We do not have the data to test directly the validity of either of these explanations, but we believe they both contribute something to the increased inequality within occupations. We also believe, however, that the displacement process begun in tiers 3 and 4 generates two additional forces which contribute significantly to the increased within-subgroup wage inequality in tiers 1 and 2.

The first causal influence is gender and the pattern of displacement of men by women. Chart 6.4 shows the special pattern in tier 1 occupations. Whereas in the tier 3 and 4 occupations, women are moving into the middle of the wage distribution, in the tier 1 and 2 occupations women are moving into the top of the wage distribution. Chart 6.4 presents the wage distribution for tier 1 (men and women combined), as well as what we call the "net displacement" curve. At each hourly wage rate the net displacement curve shows whether the representation of women obtaining that wage rate increased or decreased between 1970–71 and 1993–94.

Chart 6.4 shows that the representation of women within tier 1 declined dramatically for all wages below about $12.00 per hour, declined modestly for wages between $12.00 and $15.00 per hour, and increased modestly for wages above $15.00 per hour. This suggests that women are moving into the highest-paying jobs in tier 1 and displacing men downward. This pattern is quite similar for tier 2, where the representation of women declines for all wages below $12.00 per hour and increases for all wages above this level.

What gives women the ability to move into the highest paying jobs in tiers 1 and 2 when they seem unable to do so in tiers 3 and 4? As documented in Chapter 2, among those persons competing for jobs in tier 1 and 2 occupations, women have higher average NALS scores in the non-quantitative parts of the test. Since many of the fastest-growing occupations in tiers 1 and 2 require clerical-type reading and writing skills, this gives women an advantage. In addition, women competing for jobs in tier 1 and 2 occupations have, on the average, completed more years of education than the men.

The second causal force underlying the increasing wage inequality within most of the detailed occupations in tiers 1 and 2 also has to do with the displacement process, and may be quantitatively more important. One of the main implications of this displacement process is that jobs in tiers 1 and 2, which were filled primarily by persons with a high-school diploma or less in 1970–71, are being sought in 1993–94 by large numbers of persons with some university or even a university degree who are unable to find jobs in the higher tier occupations. This means that the variance in education levels among workers within any particular tier 1 or tier 2 occupation is greater in 1993–94 than in 1970–71. Whether due to a positive relation between productivity (actual or perceived) and education within any particular detailed occupation, or whether due to norms of fairness, this trend has led to a greater variance in wages.

The most obvious way to show this is to calculate the change in the variance of education (measured in years completed) for workers in each of the detailed occupations in tiers 1 and 2. If our hypothesis is correct, a significant majority of these occupations should have experienced an increase in this variance. Surprisingly, the variance in education has declined for most of these occupations. An alternative measure, the average absolute deviation from the median (AADM), which is less sensitive to extreme values, yields approximately the same result. Is this inconsistent with our hypothesis?

Closer examination of the education numbers suggests a novel explanation. In the CPS survey, workers are asked to indicate how many years of schooling they have completed, from 0 to 18. In the March 1971 and 1972 samples,

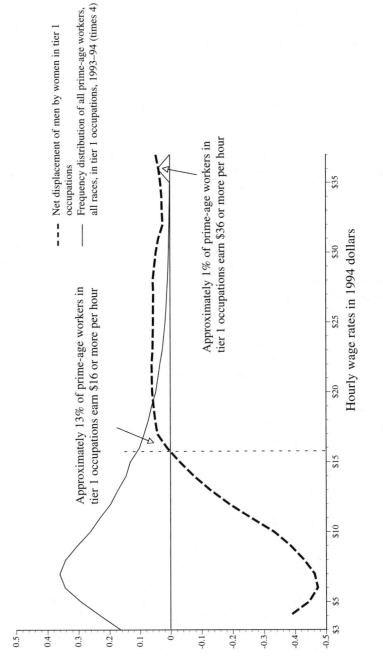

Net displacement of men by women in tier 1 occupations

Approximately 13% of prime-age workers in tier 1 occupations earn $16 or more per hour

Approximately 1% of prime-age workers in tier 1 occupations earn $36 or more per hour

- - - Net displacement of men by women in tier 1 occupations
—— Frequency distribution of all prime-age workers, all races, in tier 1 occupations, 1993–94 (times 4)

Hourly wage rates in 1994 dollars

Chart 6.4: Net displacement of men by women in tier 1 occupations

the variance in the years of education among those with less than a high-school diploma was large, with significant numbers of workers indicating that they had three, five, or seven years of education. However, in the March 1994 and 1995 samples, the variance in the years of education among those with less than a high-school diploma was much smaller, with very few workers indicating that they had less than nine years of education.

Whether this trend is due to an actual change in enforcement of required education, or whether it is due to reporting differences between the two sets of years, the net result is to make the lower tail of the wage distribution for most tier 1 and 2 occupations much smaller in 1993–94 than in 1970–71. Arguably, much of this variance beneath 11 years of education is irrelevant to wage setting. Most firms hiring people with less than a high-school diploma make their own judgements about applicants' abilities to do the necessary job rather than relying on whether 10 versus 8 years of schooling were completed. Thus, wages are unlikely to correlate well with years of education completed among workers with less than a high-school diploma.

In order to evade this difficulty, we looked at the average absolute deviation from the median (AADM) of just the top half of the education distribution in each detailed tier 1 and 2 occupation in 1970–71 and compared it to the similar number for 1993–94. In doing so, we found strong support for our hypothesis that the high end of the educational spread in various low-skilled occupations is increasing. Of the 120 tier 1 occupations, about 65 percent (=78/120) experienced an increase in the AADM of the top half of the education distribution. Of the 143 tier 2 occupations, about 77 percent (=110/143) experienced an increase in the AADM of the top half of the education distribution. We interpret this to mean that the "relevant variation" in education levels has increased in a significant majority of the detailed occupations in tiers 1 and 2, and this has contributed to an increase in the variance of wages within each detailed occupation.

Summary and Conclusions

Changes in the distribution of wages are difficult to analyze because different causal forces are affecting different parts of the distribution. At an aggregate level, wage inequality has increased at the high end of the wage distribution and slightly decreased at the low end. At a more detailed level, however, wage inequality has increased among almost all subgroups of the work force including those at the lower end of the wage distribution.

In the tier 4 (highest education) occupations, about 60 percent of the increased wage inequality can be explained by increased inequality between detailed occupations. The most important causes for this phenomena are increased excess demand for lawyers and health care workers, and the entry of women with high cognitive skills into middle-wage Tier 4 occupations at wages lower than those of the men they displace. The other 40 percent can be explained by increased inequality within detailed occupations. The three most important causes for this phenomena are: the increase in the rate of return to cognitive skills within occupations; the increased importance of winner-take-all wage setting within certain tier 4 occupations; and the entry of women into the middle of the wage distribution within most detailed occupations and the resulting displacement of men toward the tails of the distribution.

The increased wage inequality within the bottom three tiers is caused almost entirely by increased inequality within detailed occupations. In the tier 3 occupations, this is explained by the same three forces as in tier 4. For the tier 1 (lowest education) and tier 2 occupations, however, the explanations are quite different and two factors are of primary importance. First, women are displacing men in the higher wage jobs in part, as we argued in previous chapters, because their cognitive skills at this educational level are somewhat higher. Second, men in these lower tier occupations who are not leaving the labor force are crowding into the jobs at the lower end of the wage distribution and pulling the lower tail further to the left.

At the same time, the displacement process across the four tiers has brought people with more education into occupations where the level of education was traditionally lower. In a considerable majority of these lower tier occupations, we found that the distribution of education has expanded significantly at the upper end. This, in turn, has undoubtedly expanded the upper tail of the wage distribution within these detailed occupations.

The analysis of the wage distribution completes our major argument about the changing nature of the U.S. labor market. We now must confront and refute some of the alternative explanation to the phenomena we have been discussing. These are the tasks for the next two chapters.

CHAPTER 7

Five Misleading Theories About Joblessness

In the previous six chapters we present a detailed explanation for the changes that have been occurring in the U.S. economy over the last quarter-century. Our analysis has some similarities with other, more standard explanations in that it emphasizes technological change and an increased rate of return to cognitive skills as two of the important forces behind the other changes. It differs, however, from alternative explanations by placing more significance on the combination of exogenous shifts in labor supply (for instance, educated women choosing to enter the workforce) plus downward "stickiness" in wages. It also differs by suggesting that the increase in the rate of return to a college degree is not as unambiguously large as other studies have suggested.

Throughout the previous chapters, we show that our explanation "fits the facts" closely. It is possible, however, that other explanations explain these patterns just as well, or perhaps even better. In this chapter and in Chapter 8 we examine most of the major alternative explanations and show that they all have difficulty explaining some of the key empirical results.

The five most popular theories explaining the falling employment rates of less-educated males focus on: (a) technological change; (b) structural changes in production and productivity; (c) imports from low-wage nations; (d) immigration; and (e) spatial mismatch of people and jobs. Although all five have some merit, in this chapter we argue that they play only minor causal roles in determination of employment rate changes. In the next chapter we focus on subjective and institutional factors that some have also used to explain labor market changes.

The technology theory deals with both the rate and type of such changes and has three separate strands.

(1) Technological change in the last quarter-century has had a bias toward increasing the relative demand for more-skilled-labor, resulting in a decline of jobs that can be filled by those with little education. We argue in previous chapters that the job structure is shifting toward those occupations requiring more education and skills, and that the demand for more-skilled

labor has increased faster than supply, a position also buttressed by considerable empirical analysis in the economic literature.[1] But this simple approach toward technological change says nothing about the number of workers with few skills or low educational qualifications. As we show empirically and at great length in Chapter 3, low-skilled jobs have increased faster than the number of poorly-qualified workers to fill them. Using less detailed data, others such as David Howell (1997) reach similar conclusions. Since this strand of the technology argument has received extensive discussion in previous chapters, we turn to other threads of the argument for this discussion.

(2) A rising level of technology has contributed to increasing turbulence in the labor market. This alleged fact means that over time, shifts in the structure of employment, occupations, and output have increased; and this change, in turn, leads to greater frictional and structural unemployment. As shown in the discussion below, this strand of the technology theory proves to be as weak as the first.

(3) The general rate of job disappearance in individual factories and individual jobs has accelerated because of greater downsizing. Unfortunately, the evidence on this question is mixed and, even if true, cannot account for the large changes in employment rates among less-educated workers documented in Chapter 1.

The production and productivity theory attributes the falling demand for low-skilled labor to changes in the structures of production and productivity. Allegedly, these changes have skewed production toward those sectors requiring more-educated workers. Deindustrialization – the shift from manufacturing to services – is supposed to be a major culprit in this process. We show empirically, however, that this approach does not explain a very large part of the actual shifts in the educational structure of the labor force.

The foreign trade theory rests on the argument that low-wage developing nations have a comparative advantage in exporting those goods requiring few labor skills or little capital per worker. The importion of these goods into the United States has led to a decline in production of those branches of industry

---

1 For instance, Berman, Bound and Griliches (1993) show quite carefully the impact of skill-biased technical change on the manufacturing labor force in the U.S. Berman, Machin, and Bound (1996) also argue convincingly that such trends are worldwide. In quite a different way, Howell and Wolff (1991) and Pryor (1996, pp. 53, 192) demonstrate how the occupational structure for the economy has shifted towards those occupations requiring more education and skills. But, as noted in the text, it is a nonsequitur to blame domestic unemployment on such trends, at least not until labor force supply effects are also taken into account. As we demonstrate in Chapters 4 and 5, skill-biased technical change does have an important impact on the labor market, but mostly among the most-educated workers.

which employ low-skill U.S. workers or are labor-intensive. We show through both regression and shift-share analyses that foreign trade accounts for little of the rising joblessness of the less-educated.

The immigration argument focuses on the degree to which foreign-born workers displace less-educated native workers. Again we show that the available evidence does not offer much support for this conjecture.

Finally, the spatial mismatch theory argues that the rise in joblessness of less-educated males has occurred because manufacturing and other jobs have relocated to the suburbs, while those with the requisite educational credentials live in the cities. Because of lack of access to such jobs, or information about them, these workers lose employment as jobs are relocated out of the city. There is some evidence for this theory, but it cannot explain the major part of the fall in male employment rates.

Technology and Turbulence as a Cause for Changes in Employment Rates

According to this theory, accelerating technological change has led to greater turbulence in the job market. This is a situation where both unemployment and unfilled job vacancies grow because of increased problems in matching job-seekers and positions. Due to technological change, the industrial and occupational structures of the labor force are allegedly changing more rapidly than in previous decades, so many workers are losing their jobs. Due to the uneven spread of these new technologies, labor market turbulence can also occur even if the industrial and occupational structures remain the same. This is because the same industries and occupations can be increasing in one area and decreasing in another.

Two serious objections must be raised immediately against these strands of the technology argument:

First, readily available evidence about technological change in the United States, for instance, measures of labor or total factor productivity, do not support any argument about accelerated technical change. Indeed, most signs point in the opposite direction. For instance, in a comparison of 29 industrial nations between 1950 and 1988, the United States revealed the greatest deceleration of growth of GDP per economically active (Pryor, 1994). Looking at a more exact measure of labor productivity, namely GDP per equivalent full-time worker, we find that the growth of labor productivity was significantly higher between 1950 and 1970 than in the period between 1970 and 1994. Focusing on just the latter period, by way of contrast, we could find relatively little change in the rate of growth of total facor productivity.[2] Of course, over time the measurement of labor productivity becomes increasingly more difficult as the share of services rises, since the measurement of the output of services raises severe problems. Nevertheless, up to now no one has been able to demonstrate in a convincing fashion that technological change has accelerated in the post World War II period, and this is the key component underlying the turbulence argument.

Second, public opinion pollsters find little perception among American workers that their job security has decreased. More specifically, from 1972 to the mid 1990s, survey data show no noticeable increase in the percentage of workers fearing they might be fired.[3] By way of contrast, job security is becoming more important to workers in their choice of employment, which suggests they have less optimism about obtain ing similar employment if they lose their job. For less-educated prime-age male workers, this worry may also stem from their overall rising rate of joblessness.

This technology argument can also be recast in terms of the level of technology, rather than the acceleration of technological change. Rather than pursuing this dubious conjecture at greater length, the key issues can be more quickly resolved by examining empirical evidence on two questions: Are the structures of employment – geographical, occupational, or industrial – chang-

---

2 For these exercises we calculated quadratic trends for productivity. For the period 1970 through 1994 we also estimated a Cobb-Douglas type production function with a quadratic trend. From this regression we derive a growth rate of total factor productivity of 2.12 percent in 1971 and 2.02 percent in 1994.

The GDP data come from *Survey of Current Business* (SCB) 76, January and February 1996, Table 2. The data on net fixed reproducible tangible wealth are from SCB 74, August 1994, p. 62. Data on GDP and full-time equivalent workers are from U.S. Department of Commerce, Bureau of Economic Analysis (1986, 1992/3) plus various issues of *Survey of Current Business*.

3 Public opinion data collected by the Inter-university Consortium for Political and Social Research (ICPSR) reveals no marked trends between 1972 and the mid-1990s in the answers to the question: "How likely is it that you will lose your job."(www.icpsr.umich.edu/gss/code book/joblose.htm). In contrast, over the same period there was a noticeable increase in the percentage of respondents who felt that "no danger of being fired" was important to them in their choice of jobs (www.icpsr.umich.edu/gss/codebook/jobsec.htm). Such seemingly contradictory results suggest that although perceptions of actual job loss did not greatly change, people worried more about the consequences stemming from joblessness if it actually occurred to them, perhaps because of their perceptions about the changing nature of the job market.

ing more rapidly in later years than in former years? And has job destruction at the plant level increased?

Labor Market Turbulence From a Structural Perspective [4]

In recent years David Lilien has revived interest in examining the effects of labor market turbulence to explore unemployment over the business cycle.[5] Since there is no evidence of an increasing severity of the business cycle in the post World War II era, we cannot rest our analysis of rising long-term unemployment on such short-run considerations and, instead, must turn to a long-term comparison of structural changes of employment.

The analysis begins with various time series of the structure of employment on an occupational, industrial, or geographical basis. A "turbulence index" is calculated, which indicates the percentage of the labor force in an earlier year that must be transferred to achieve the employment structure in the later year.[6] Assume, for instance, a situation where there are only two occupations (or industries or geographical areas) and the labor force is evenly divided between them in the first year. Suppose also that in the second year one-quarter are in the first occupation and three-quarters are in the second occupations. This indicates that 25 percent of the labor force must be transferred from the first

4   Our discussion in this section draws heavily upon the analysis in Pryor (1996, Chapter 3).

5   Lilien's (1982) thesis is controversial and several recent studies have approached the problem from quite different perspectives, for instance Davis and Haltiwanger (1992) or Parker (1992). The turbulence thesis (sometimes called the "mismatch hypothesis," although this term is a misnomer) has also received considerable criticism. Some like Johnson and Layard (1986) focus on the statistical problems arising from the reduced form of equation used to test the idea; others such as many of the authors in Padoa-Schioppa (1991) do not find the relationship between turbulence and unemployment for other countries that Lilien and Parker show for the United States.

6   More specifically, the following formula is used: $T_t = .5 \Sigma_i \mid s_{i,t} - s_{i,t-1} \mid$,

where T is turbulence, s is the share under examination, i is the particular group (geographical, industrial, or occupational), and t is the year. The turbulence statistic holds the degree of unemployment for the economy as a whole constant, and measures the share of the labor force that must be changed from one place, industry, or occupation to another in order to maintain this assumption. Turbulence in the short-run is measured every year and in the long-run, every 10 years.

In the economic literature some such as Abraham (1991) have raised objections about such a statistic, especially because it focuses on actual employment shares rather than desired employment shares. Although other, less intuitive measures are used, experiments with these measures reveal roughly the same trends over the long-run as reported in the table.

Table 7.1: *Trends in Labor Market Turbulence, Mid 1950s Through 1990*

Variable	Average index value	Average annual rate of change of index value
Geographical: Short-run (48 states)	.007	No significant trend
Geographical: Long-run (48 states)	.050	No significant trend
Industrial: Short-run (66 industries)	.014	-1.1%
Industrial: Long-run (66 industries)	.086	No significant trend
Occupational: Short-run (12 groups)	.010	No significant trend
Occupational: Long-run (12 groups)	.058	-1.8%
Occupational: Long-run (census data, 380 - 480 groups)	.136	No apparent trend

Notes: We discuss the method of calculation in the text. Only those trends that appear statistically significant at the 0.05 level are included in the table; the trend values are calculated by fitting an exponential curve to the data by an ordinary least-squares technique.

The annual (short-run) series run from 1954 through 1990 and are adjusted to achieve comparability after the definitional changes in the early 1980s. For the series indicating ten-year periods (long run), such changes were calculated for the years only starting 1958 or 1959. This procedure avoids problems of comparing changes with employment structure during or immediately after World War II.

This table comes from Pryor (1996), p. 66.

occupation to the second occupation. The comparisons can be made from one year to the next (short-term comparisons) or from one decade to the next (long-term comparisons). Trends are then calculated to determine the direction of change in the turbulence index.

These calculations in Table 7.1 lead to a simple conclusion: Labor market turbulence along all dimensions and measures has *not* increased and, in certain cases, has decreased instead. Although this turbulence in the U.S. economy appears considerable, an increasing rate of turbulence does not appear to underlie the trends in employment rates that we are investigating.

Labor Market Turbulence From the Perspective of Job Destruction

A different way of looking at labor market turbulence is to examine the annual rates of job creation and destruction at the level of individual productive establishments, as measured by the total change in jobs occuring within these individual productive units. Job destruction can occur because of

Table 7.2: *Gross Rates of Job Creation and Destruction in the Manufacturing Sector*

Panel A: Job destruction and creation by year

Year	Annual job flow (turnover) rates		Year	Annual job flow (turnover) rates	
	Job destruction	Job creation		Job destruction	Job creation
1973	6.1%	11.9%	1984	7.6%	13.3%
1974	9.3	9.0	1985	11.1	7.9
1975	16.5	6.2	1986	12.1	7.9
1976	9.4	11.2	1987	10.1	8.4
1977	8.6	11.0	1988	8.3	8.3
1978	7.3	10.9	1989	7.9	9.5
1979	7.0	10.3	1990	9.4	7.8
1980	9.1	8.0	1991	12.1	6.7
1981	11.4	6.3	1992	10.7	7.2
1982	14.5	6.8	1993	9.6	8.5
1983	15.6	8.8			

Panel B: Job Destruction and Creation by Exposure to Foreign Trade, 1973 to 1986

B-1. Arranged by Import Ratio (Imports as a percentage of imports plus output), four-digit level

Quintiles	Job destruction	Job creation
Very low (0.0 to 0.8 percent)	10.1%	8.9%
Moderately low (0.8 to 3.3 percent)	10.2	9.6
Average (3.3 to 6.8 percent)	10.0	9.4
Moderately high (6.8 to 13.1 percent)	9.5	8.8
Very high (over 13.1 percent)	12.2	9.4

B-2. Arranged by Export Ratio (Exports as a percentage of output), four-digit level

Very low (0.0 to 1.3 percent)	10.9%	9.5%
Moderately low (1.3 to 3.1 percent)	10.9	9.3
Average (3.1 to 5.8 percent)	9.7	9.0
Moderately high (5.8 to 12.5 percent)	10.1	9.0
Very high (over 12.5 percent)	10.2	9.2

Notes: The data come from panel data and are presented by Davis, Haltiwanger, and Schuh (1996), pp. p. 19. 48; and from Haltiwanger's anonymous FTP file (haltiwan.econ.umd.edu). A comparison of these data with job turnover data from labor force surveys is found in Haltiwanger (1997).

substitution of capital for labor, loss of sales, downsizing to reduce costs, or a variety of other reasons. Recently Davis, Haltiwanger, and Schuh (1996) have developed such a series for the manufacturing sector. Although the manufacturing sector employs only about one-sixth of the labor force, most attention on job turnover focuses on this sector because of its vulnerability to import competition. In Part A of Table 7.2 we present some of these results. From these data conclusions can be drawn immediately.

First, over the course of a year, nearly about one-fifth of all manufacturing jobs are either destroyed or created. This high fluidity in the distribution of job opportunities across locations in the U.S. is not unique among industrialized nations, and others have rates that are as high or higher.[7]

Second, neither job creation nor job destruction rates reveal any statistically significant trends. Variations from year to year are so great over the 21 year period that a simple linear trend explains less than 1 percent of the variation of job destruction and less than 15 percent of job creation. Despite the high turbulence in the labor market of the manufacturing sector, the increase in joblessness over the years is not explained by any rise in job destruction

Labor Market Turbulence From the Perspective of Changes in Job Tenure

The empirical arguments in the previous two sub-sections contradict the common notion that job tenure has been decreasing because of an increase in corporate downsizing, a phenomenon receiving attention on a frequent basis in the popular press. Although anecdotes abound, the systematic empirical evidence on changes in job retention rates is quite contradictory. Several of the most important problems can be quickly listed:

a. The basic data which cover all industries are not satisfactory. If respondents are asked about job tenure (How long have you worked with your present employer?), panel data show considerable inconsistencies if results from two different periods are compared (Brown and Light, 1992). If, on the other hand, questions are asked about job change (Have you changed employers during the previous 12 months?), other types of problems of interpretation arise, particularly with respect to whether the change was temporary or permanent.

b. Different databases yield different results.[8] For most of these, the time period under examination is relatively short, so long-term trends are dif-

---

7 Davis, Haltiwanger, and Schuh (1996, p. 21) provide some useful international data.
8 Three recent studies drawing upon the Panel Study of Income Dynamics (Hamermesh, 1989;

ficult to discern. Moreover, one database (the Panel Study of Income dynamics) allows analysis only of job stability of men. A recent survey of the results from different databases by Henry Farber (1997, pp. 57-70) concludes that job stability did not generally decrease during the 1979–91 period, although the distribution of long-term jobs has shifted and, in periods of economic slack, job loss has increased for some groups. The high rate of job loss in the 1993–95 period has yet to be fully explained, especially since the greatest increase in the category of job loss occurs for reasons that are not specified by the displaced workers.[9] Because of the booming economy, however, the percentage of displaced workers who have obtained other employment has risen during the same period.

c. A variety of technical issues bedevil the analysis of job turnover. These include the handling of business cycle effects when comparisons are made between two dates, the treatment of non-responses in the survey, changes in the wording of key questions over time so that difficult adjustments must be made, selecting the most relevant groups of workers for the comparisons, rounding and heaping errors by respondents, and weighting of the responses.

Although the various studies disagree about whether overall job stability has decreased or remained the same, some agreement emerges with regard to relative job stability of subgroups. For instance, all of the studies see greater job instability among the less-educated than the more-educated. Most, but not all, show that these job retention rates decreased relatively more for the former than the latter, although the differences in these trends vary. All studies dealing with both men and women find job stability greater among the former than the latter, but they obtain mixed results about differences in trends of job stability of the two groups. All show that initially blacks had higher job retention rates than whites, but job retention rates of blacks decreased relatively more than whites.

In brief, this type of evidence on job stability is sufficiently mixed that we cannot draw any firm conclusions about overall trends. For greater certainty,

Marcotte, 1995; Rose 1995) show declining job stability. On the other hand, most but not all of the five recent studies drawing upon data from the Current Population Survey of various years (Farber, 1993, 1995, and 1996; Diebold, Neumark, and Polsky 1994, Swinnerton and Wial, 1995; and Gardiner, 1995) conclude that job retention rates have not markedly changed over time. Some of the technical issues involved in these estimates are aired in an exchange of views by Diebold, Neumark, and Polsky (1996) and Swinnerton and Wial (1996). The latter study also presents new data for the 1979–91 period.

9 Katherine Abraham (1997) presents some unpublished BLS evidence that because of the way in which the question about job displacement was worded, most of those claiming to be displaced for "other reasons" left their jobs for personal reasons and, therefore, should not be counted as displaced. Following this approach, job displacement decreased slightly, at least among males in the 1993–95 period, rather than rising.

Table 7.3: *Hypothetical Changes in Production, Productivity, and Employment of All Employed Workers with Different Levels of Education, 1971–1991*

Assumption about education of government workers	High-school dropouts	High-school diploma	Some university or trade/vocational school	University degree	Total
Assumption 1	+35.6%	+48.3%	+58.4%	+57.4%	+47.3%
Assumption 2	+35.6	+46.8	+56.9	+67.6	+47.3
Actual changes					
Assumption 1	-55.5	-8.0	+45.7	+115.9	+47.3
Assumption 2	-50.8	+5.5	+65.6	+37.3	+47.3

Hypothetical case: Total labor productivity (unadjusted for education) and production in each industry reflect actual changes. The educational structure of the labor force in each industrial branch, however, is held constant.

Notes: In this table the labor force includes all full- and part-time employed workers. The calculations are made with 59 branches of production corresponding roughly to the two-digit level of disaggregation. Due to problems in combining two databases, we must carry out the analysis using two different sets of assumptions about the education of government workers. The first assumption presupposes a higher level of education of these workers than the second assumption; the two assumptions bracket the high and low estimates.

The underlying data for the GDP and labor force by sector of origin come from U.S. Department of Commerce, Bureau of Economic Analysis (1992) and a data diskette of gross product by industry (USDOC, BEA, NIWD (BE-51), released August 21, 1996. Workers with various levels of education at different sectors of the economy come from the Current Population Survey data tapes for March 1991. Because the Census Bureau and the BEA define industries somewhat differently, we calculated percentages of the labor force with different educational qualifications from the CPS data and applied these to the BEA data. Unfortunately, for the government sector the labor force estimates from the two sectors are quite different because the Census Bureau excludes the military and classifies workers by the industry in which they work, while the BEA excludes workers in government facilities (such as elementary-school teachers) and aggregates them with other government workers.

It is, therefore, necessary to make new estimates of the distribution of workers by education in the government sector ("more-educated government workers") by adding to the government sector a number of services in which workers in government facilities seem to predominate and then recalculating the percentage of workers with various levels of education. Due to our treatment of the military sector our two estimates bracket the actual situation.

studies must be made using the same statistical methods on the two major databases and on both the job tenure and the job displacement data. Until then, it is impossible to sort out what conclusions are due to the choice of the database, the question analyzed, or the statistical methods employed.

Nevertheless, for the sake of argument, suppose that job mobility has increased over the last two decades by 20 percent. What difference would this make? Certainly frictional unemployment would be higher, but this type of unemployment constitutes a relatively small share of total joblessness. This type of process would not greatly affect structural unemployment. Moreover, it seems unlikely that this type of process would have much impact on the number of those dropping completely out of the labor force. In short, any such increasing job mobility should only explain a very small share of the large changes in employment rates of less-educated males.

In sum, the data on the supply and demand for workers with different levels of education, which we discuss in detail in Chapter 3, provide no support for the argument that skill-biased technical change underlies the increasing joblessness of less-educated workers. The data on labor market turbulence and on job destruction also offer no support to the argument. The evidence on changes in job tenure rates is mixed, but even if decreasing job tenure has occurred, its impact on employment rates should be small. Moreover, the public opinion data mentioned reveal no upward trend over time of workers fearing that they will lose their jobs.

Changes in the Structure of Production and Productivity as a Cause of Changing Employment Rates

Pundits in the daily press sometimes argue that the structure of the U.S. economy is moving away from those branches of production or industries employing large shares of less-skilled workers. A more sophisticated version of the same argument is that average labor productivity is increasing fastest in those industries employing large shares of less-skilled workers. In either case such structural changes reduce the demand for less-skilled workers.

We can quickly dispose of this idea by a simple thought-experiment/simulation by asking the following question: What would have happened to the employment of less-skilled workers if production and average labor productivity had changed as they did between 1971 and 1991, but the percentage share of employment of workers with different educational qualifications had remained the same in each branch of production? This counterfactual is then compared with what actually occurred for the purpose of isolating those changes in employment affected by alterations in the structure of production and productivity and those caused by educational upgrading of the labor force in each industry.

For this purpose we combine two databases. One contains data on the total production and on the number of full-time and part-time workers by 59 (two-digit) branches of production covering the entire economy. The other has data on the distribution of workers by level of education in each of these industries.[10]

The results in Table 7.3 show clearly that neither changes in the structure of production nor the differential changes in labor productivity were responsible for most of the change in the number of workers with different educational requirements. For instance, the number of jobs that could be filled by workers who did not have a high-school diploma would have *increased* 35.6 percent in the counterfactual case. Since this is 11.7 percentage points below the average increase in the employed labor force (which is 47.3 percent), the differential production and productivity changes had a small effect.

Nevertheless, the actual number of these less-educated workers *decreased* somewhere between 50.8 and 55.5 percent in the same period (an area of uncertainty generated by the two assumptions used to estimate the education of governmental workers). These results have two interpretations. Biased technical change could have occurred in each branch of the economy leading to an overall upgrading of the educational level of the labor. But we discount this argument about the biased technical change in the discussion in previous chapters. Or we can conclude that this upgrading of the educational requirements of the labor force was driven primarily by forces on the labor supply side. More particularly, young entrants into the labor force had obtained more education than actually required by the changes in production and productivity. In neither of these cases, however, does the change in the structure of production

10 The educational distribution of the employed workforce comes from the Current Population Survey, which includes many public employees in the various functional categories. For instance, public-school teachers are included under education, rather than the government sector. These data also exclude military personnel. Data on the GDP by sector of origin come from the Bureau of Economic Analysis of the U.S. Department of Commerce, which separates all public production into a separate category. Thus, public-school teachers are included in the government sector. For the low-education estimate of the government sector, we used the CPS estimate; for the high-education estimate, we added to the CPS government sector a number of services where the percentage of workers actually working for the government is quite high.

We describe how we handle these differences in the footnote to the table. It is important to note that the results are not very sensitive to the two sets of assumptions. Thus, our overall conclusions are not greatly influenced by our estimation techniques, particularly regarding less-skilled workers.

or the differential changes in overall labor productivity have much impact on the employment of workers with different educational qualifications

Some might object that this empirical demonstration is carried out at too great a level of aggregation. Later in the chapter we carry out a similar exercise with more disaggregated data for the manufacturing sector alone and obtain the same results (see Table 7.5). Separating the effects of a change in the production pattern and the differential changes in productivity in Table 7.3 provides little additional information.

In sum, differential production and productivity effects explain very little of the actual fall in the number of less-educated employed workers. This means that such loudly-touted factors as deindustrialization have not played an important causal role in the changing employment rates, particularly among unskilled males.

Foreign Trade as a Cause of Changing Employment Rates

The long-established Heckscher-Ohlin theory of the comparative advantage tells us that nations export those goods embodying a country's abundant (and therefore relatively less expensive) factor of production, and import those goods embodying a country's least abundant (and therefore relatively more expensive) factors of production. The U.S. has a relative scarcity of less-skilled workers, especially in comparison to the developing nations, and a relative abundance of capital (buildings and equipment) and more-skilled workers. Such factor proportions should be reflected in the structure of U.S. trade – and they are.

Some, however, have extended this simple idea to argue that foreign trade has played an important role in the rising rate of joblessness of less-skilled U.S. workers since the 1970s. This rests on two arguments:

First, the relative importance of foreign trade in the U.S. economy, as measured by the ratio of trade to the gross domestic product, has roughly doubled since 1970.[11] In the manufacturing sector the importance of foreign trade has increased even faster. For instance, as a ratio of GDP originating in manu-

---

11   For instance, in the period from 1950 to 1970 imports as a share of GDP edged up from about 4.3 percent in the early 1950s to 5.4 percent in 1970. By 1980, however, this ratio has risen to 10.6 percent where it remained roughly constant until 1990 when it began to rise to close to 12 percent by 1994. These data come from national accounts tables published by the U.S. Department of Commerce, Bureau of Economic Analysis (1992, 1993) and are updated with data from various issues of the Survey of Current Business. Data on trade in various sectors as a percentage of GDP originating in these sectors are in Pryor (1996), p. 189.

facturing, merchandise imports (excluding petroleum) more than doubled. According to the conventional wisdom, the increasing penetration of trade into the U.S. economy in general and the manufacturing sector in particular means that economic shocks from abroad have a greater impact on the U.S. economy than before, and that these shocks should result in increased unemployment. In the fall of 1997 and the spring of 1998, the popular press was full of dire predictions about the consequence of the falling value of various currencies in Southeast Asia.

Nevertheless, at first glance it seems unlikely that foreign trade should have a significant impact on the employment of unskilled U.S. workers. For instance, imports from non-OPEC low-wage nations amount to less than two percent of the GDP.[12] Most quantitative attempts to measure the impact of imports from low wage nations on domestic wages do not show a very significant impact.[13]

Second, the balance of goods and services fell from an average of +0.3 percent of the GDP in the 1950s and 1960s to -0.3 percent in the 1970s and -1.5 percent in the subsequent 15 years. This suggests that aggregate demand for domestically-produced goods has fallen, which means, in turn, that there is less demand for domestic labor. This reduced demand, however, does not have a significant impact on unskilled workers, because many of the imports are high-tech goods produced primarily by skilled-labor.

But rather than spend our time in theoretical disputation, we can address the matter directly by empirically investigating the actual impact of foreign trade. Such an attempt is related to the exercise carried out in Table 7.3, but it focuses attention primarily on changes in domestic production induced by trade and is carried out on a more disaggregated level.

More specifically, in this discussion, we look for answers to the following two questions: Is labor market turbulence greater in those industries with higher foreign trade exposure (where the ratio of imports or exports to domestic production is high)? And do the data on the changing structure of domestic production caused by the impact of foreign trade reveal a significant displacement of less-educated American workers?

12 By low-wage nations we include all Latin American nations plus all non-OPEC nations in Africa and Asia except Israel, Japan, and South Africa. In 1994 such imports amounted to 1.8 percent of the GDP or, using as the denominator just the GDP originating from the manufacturing, agricultural, and mining sectors of the economy, 9.0 percent. The data for this calculation come from Survey of Current Business 76, Numbers 7 and 8, and U.S. Department of Commerce, Bureau of the Census (1996).

13 Burtless (1995) reviews many of the available studies. The recent estimates by Borjas, Freeman, and Katz (1997, Table 18) also show a relatively small impact on wages of net imports from developing nations.

Foreign Trade and Job Destruction

If foreign trade *per se* results in greater unemployment, then we would expect that job destruction in particular industries would be directly related to foreign trade exposure of the industry. The data in Part B of Table 7.2, however, do not reveal any such systematic relationship. Job destruction in the quintile of industries with the highest import penetration is slightly higher than the average. Nevertheless, there is no systematic relationship between job destruction and import exposure when the other quintiles are also considered. Moreover, when the industries are ranked according to export exposure, there is little difference in job destruction or creation by quintiles. As Davis, Haltiwanger, and Schuh (1996, p. 49), creators of this data set, conclude: "On balance, the evidence is highly unfavorable to the view that international trade exposure systematically reduces job security." The data also show that industries with very high import penetration exhibit greater gross job flows (job destruction and creation), most probably because their workers are relatively untrained with few skills specific to the industry, and not because these branches experience greater shocks due to foreign competition.

Long-Term Changes in Net Exports in Low-Skill Intensive Industries

In this section we investigate import penetration occurring in those branches of manufacturing that are less-skilled-labor intensive. Evidence of a direct correlation would provide strong support for the view that import penetration has played a major role in the rising joblessness of less-skilled workers. The initial year for the comparison is 1971, two years before the first oil shock; and the end year is 1991, a roughly comparable year in terms of the business cycle. Comparable data on trade, production, and the characteristics of industrial branches are available to make this two-decade analysis.

As noted above, data in Chapter 3 show a faster growth of jobs requiring relatively low educational credentials than the available prime-age population with just a high-school degree or less. Although this single result casts grave doubt on the foreign trade hypotheses, it is also necessary to attack the problem from other standpoints as well.

In these statistical experiments the variable to be explained is the change of net exports (exports–imports) to domestic consumption (domestic shipments + imports–exports) of the various product branches. The explanatory variables reflect the initial state of each production branch and changes in the structure of production over time. In particular we focus on the general labor intensity of production as measured by the labor/capital ratio, and the relative importance of unskilled workers. This allows us to isolate the particular impact of trade on unskilled-labor – in contrast to all labor. We measure unskilled-labor by two variables: the percentage of workers in each industry with a high-school education or less (available only on a three-digit basis), and by the share of production workers in the total labor force. We also experimented with another measure, the average wage, but since doing so resulted in the same conclusions found with the other two measures, we do not report these results.

According to the hypothesis under examination, the initial level of unskilled-labor-intensity of the industry should be direct related to changes in import penetration. To rephrase the argument in terms of our variables, this unskilled-labor variable in the initial year should be inversely related to changes in the ratio of net exports to domestic consumption. Moreover, the change over time of the unskilled-labor variables in the various industries should also reveal such an inverse relationship. Our approach to this hypothesis assumes that the ranking of industries characterized by skilled or unskilled-labor is roughly the same in the U.S. and its trading partners, or, more technically, that factor reversals are relatively unimportant.

It would be desirable, of course, to hold both domestic and foreign productivity changes constant in these experiments. Unfortunately, data on foreign productivity changes are not available and data on changes in domestic total factor productivity changes alone add little to the explanatory power of the regressions. Moreover, the calculated coefficients of this variable are the wrong sign and are usually not statistically significant.

We look only at the direct unskilled-labor intensities, labor/capital ratios, total and factor productivity growth rates of the various industries, rather than using an input-output table to take both direct and indirect labor phenomena into account. On this topic Feenstra and Hanson (1996-a, 1996-b) contend that focusing solely on the skills directly embodied in various domestically produced goods misses the impact of increased outsourcing abroad (either from their own factories or from foreign companies). This trend, which was particularly important in the 1979–90 period, allows a firm to focus its domestic efforts only on skilled-labor-intensive parts of their production and to import unskilled-labor-intensive inputs, thus staving off import penetration. From this we can infer that import penetration should be inversely related to upskilling. More specifically, those industries that have upskilled, either by changing their production methods or by outsourcing unskilled-labor-intensive parts of their production process, have experienced less import penetration than other industries. In Table 7.4 we specifically test this hypothesis and find no empirical evidence to suggest that this effect is statistically signifi-

Table 7.4: *The Impact of Skill Intensity of Production on the Change in Net Exports*

	Two-digit industrial classification		Three-digit industrial classification		Four-digit industrial classification
Constant	-0.1482 (0.2184)	-0.0844 (0.1741)	+0.0893 (0.0991)	+0.0716 (0.0809)	+0.1051 (0.1595)
Low-skilled workers, 1971					
Percent of less-educated workers	+0.1925 (0.2498)	—	-0.0413 (0.1123)	—	—
Percent of production workers	—	+0.1457 (0.2400)	—	-0.0276 (0.1037)	-0.1734 (0.2089)
Average annual change of low-skilled workers, 1971–91					
Percent of less-educated workers	-2.947 (6.453)	—	+0.2294 (1.4580)	—	—
Percent of production workers	—	-3.971 (8.872)	—	-2.626 (2.870)	+2.939 (4.460)
Labor/Capital Ratio in 1971	-2.151* (0.671)	-2.310* (0.531)	-2.280* (0.377)	-2.278* (0.376)	-0.6563 (0.3740)
Average annual change, 1971–91	+0.1775 (2.5100)	-0.1983 (1.7682)	+0.0125 (0.8064)	+0.2034 (0.8168)	-2.226* (1.102)
Coefficient of determination (R^2)	.5969	.5917	.3975	.4055	.0173
Sample size	20	20	71	71	449

Notes: Standard errors are reported in parentheses below the estimated regression coefficients; an asterisk designates statistical significance at the .05 level. Because of controversy about measurement, we omit SIC 357 (office, accounting, computing equipment) and SIC 3573 (computing equipment). The trade data come from Feenstra (1996, 1997); the industrial data, from the Bartelsman-Gray (1996) database; and the education data from the Current Population Survey, adjusted for consistency to the SIC classification used for the trade and production data.

cant.[14] Moreover, when we examine the entire structure of industry in a quite different way in Table 7.5, we also find no such effect.[15] Our approach also allows us to calculate the regressions at different levels of aggregation of the industry and trade data, a procedure providing a number of useful insights.[16]

The results of the calculations reported in Table 7.4 can be summarized quickly. Most importantly, the coefficients for the variables representing the relative importance of unskilled workers in the industry are not statistically significant in any of the five regressions. It is also noteworthy that when the labor/capital variables are dropped and the regressions recalculated, the same negative results occur. Part of the explanation of such results lies in the fact that at higher levels of aggregation the variation in the share of the less-educated workers is relatively low. For instance, in the 71 industries under consideration at a three-digit level, the coefficient of variation (the ratio of the standard deviation to the mean) of this ratio is only 12.4 percent. Roughly the same results are obtained when the average wage in the industry, and the average annual change in these wages, are used as proxies for the skill variables. Calculating weighted regressions with the value of shipments as the weights leads to the same general conclusions.

The calculated coefficients for the labor/capital variable are statistically significant. In other words, U.S. net exports increased relatively more in those industries more characterized by low labor intensity, or where the labor intensity is falling relatively faster. To look at the results from a different perspective, import penetration has had the most adverse effect on those industries with labor-intensive production methods, while the skill-mix within individual industries seems relatively unimportant.

14 Feenstra and Hanson (1996-a, 1996-b) also focus their econometric attention solely on imports. We also take exports into account and deal with changes of net exports (exports minus imports) to production, rather than import penetration alone.

15 Another problem arises when we try to interpret changes in total (direct and indirect) requirements of skilled and unskilled labor. This is most clearly seen when we compare direct and indirect requirements of one good for a dollar's worth of production of another good over a period of more than a decade and a half. The changes have been enormous and, combined with the important shifts in the structure of imports, we have a problem interpreting the relevant regression coefficients. That is, we don't know what are the key causal forces: they could be either changes in production methods in the industry under examination, in the domestic industries supplying the inputs, or in the outsourcing abroad. If we focus just on requirements of skilled and unskilled-labor, then the causal relation is clear and the impact of outsourcing abroad is detected by directly examining net import penetration of those products used as inputs in the production of other goods.

16 Since the regressions cover the entire universe of U.S. manufacturing production, it is not necessary to use tests of statistical significance if we could be completely certain of the accuracy of the data. Given the uncertainties of the data, however, we have chosen to accept the results only if the calculated coefficients meet the test of statistical significance at the .05 level.

Thus, the factor proportion argument seems to have validity, but only regarding aggregate labor and capital, and not different subcategories of labor. Differential unemployment of unskilled workers could occur as second-round effects, of course, but only if the unemployed high-skilled workers started competing for the jobs previously held by the low-skilled workers. The regression experiments provide no direct evidence to support the proposition that the U.S. net exports have shifted away from unskilled-labor-intensive industries. Some indirect evidence, however, also merits examination.

Although such empirical evidence seems powerful, several obvious objections to this procedure can be raised. The results in Table 7.4 do not take into account the fact that actual or potential import competition might result in downward pressure on domestic prices and wages in unskilled-labor-intensive branches of industry, even if there is no increase in import penetration. Elsewhere (Pryor, 1998) we carry out a more extensive exercise to explore such defensive measures and find little evidence for such a phenomenon. We also find that domestic prices of unskilled-labor-intensive products have not risen as fast as other prices. Nevertheless, this seems to arise from domestic causes that we discuss in Chapters 5 and 6.

These regression results also do not take into account defensive measures adopted by unskilled-labor-intensive industries to prevent import penetration. For instance, producers might upgrade the skill levels of their labor force, substitute capital for unskilled-labor, or outsource unskilled-labor-intensive segments of production. Adding both the average annual change in the labor/capital ratio and the change in labor-skill variables as independent variables does not, however, alter any of the conclusions drawn from Table 7.4. That is, they add little explanatory power, their calculated coefficients are not statistically significant, and they do not lead to greatly different coefficients of the other variables. We carry out a more direct empirical investigation of this phenomenon elsewhere (Pryor, 1998). In this statistical exercise we also find no evidence of such defensive measures against actual or potential import competition occurring in manufacturing branches characterized by a high share of unskilled workers.

Finally, the regressions shown in Table 7.4 say nothing about the problem of the impact of non-competing imports, which Adrian Wood (1994, 1995) has so strongly emphasized. He argues that imported goods are quite different from domestically-produced goods, in that the former represent that end of the product line produced by low-skilled workers, such as standardized textiles. He claims, by way of contrast, that domestic producers manufacture the much more skill-intensive specialty textiles. Such a division of labor results in shifts in demand occurring in the U.S. away from less-educated toward more-educated workers. Using a different type of statistical analysis, we show elsewhere (Pryor, 1998) that such a phenomenon does not seem important. Two aspects of our regression results in Table 7.4, however, are relevant to this problem.

First, the degree of explanatory power (as measured by the coefficient of determination) of these regressions decreases as the degree of disaggregation increases. At higher levels of aggregation, other causal variables influencing changes in net exports appear correlated with factors we are examining. As we disaggregate to focus more closely on the actual goods being traded, however, these correlations become less important. This works against the non-competing import hypothesis, at least in as far as these imports are particularly important in unskilled-labor-intensive branches of manufacturing. Our regression results suggest that this type of causal analysis would have almost no explanatory value on the most potentially disaggregated level.

Second, as the data become increasingly disaggregated, the causal relation between unskilled-labor-intensity and net exports (measured by the calculated coefficient for the unskilled-labor variable) becomes increasingly inverse. Since the hypothesis predicts that import penetration is greater in more unskilled-labor-intensive branches of production, such a result supports the hypothesis under investigation. In so far as non-competing imports on the low end can be isolated through increasing disaggregation of the industry category, these calculations also provide evidence for Adrian Wood's conjecture about non-competing imports. Nevertheless, the overall explanatory power of the regression at the highest level of disaggregation is very low and, as a result, the relative skill level explains very little of the changing pattern of net exports.

It is, of course, difficult to examine directly the relevant evidence for Wood's hypothesis because it requires highly detailed data that are not available. Nevertheless, the indirect empirical evidence from other studies roughly supports our own conclusions that this phenomenon is not a major determinant for the rising rate of joblessness, especially among less-educated prime-age males.[17]

In sum, the regression experiments provide little direct evidence to support the proposition that the U.S. trade pattern has shifted away from those unskilled-labor-intensive industries. Foreign trade has not had a major causal impact on the employment rates of unskilled U.S. workers.

An Alternate Approach

Although regression analyses provide insight into causation, they do not easily allow us to guage the number of unskilled workers who have been

---

17   Such empirical and theoretical evidence is reviewed by Pryor (1998).

Table 7.5: *Hypothetical Changes in Trade, Production, and Employment of Manufacturing Workers With Different Levels of Education*

Part A: Aggregative analysis for changes in manufacturing, 1971–1991

	Percentage change
Actual change in domestic shipments of manufactured goods	+102.6%
Actual change in manufacturing labor force	-4.5
Hypothetical change in manufacturing labor force if domestic shipments had increased at the same rate as consumption of manufactured goods	-3.3

Part B: Changes in Manufacturing Employment by Level of Education, 1971–1991

Structure of consumption	Share and structure of foreign trade	Labor force structure defined by highest education received by worker	Highest level of formal education				Total
			High-school dropouts	High-school diploma	Some university or trade vocational school	University degree	
Hypothetical changes							
Changed	Constant	Constant	-20.6%	+8.0%	+59.2%	+66.0%	+6.1%
Constant	*Changed*	Constant	-4.9	-3.3	-2.7	-1.9	-3.8
Constant	Constant	*Changed*	-54.5	+13.3	+63.6	+92.7	-3.3
Actual changes			-57.1	+10.6	+66.3	+101.6	-4.5

Notes: The trade and manufacturing shipments by three-digit SIC classification come from Feenstra (1996,1997). Data about prices, employment, and other aspects of the same industries come from Bartelsman and Gray (1996). For this discussion we assume that the change in shipments represents the change in production for the 20-year interval.

The data on educational levels of workers come from the March Current Population Surveys for the respective years. Since the Census Bureau uses a somewhat different industrial nomenclature than the BEA, for each industry we applied the percentage distribution of workers by educational group derived from the Census data to the BEA data on employment, the same procedure used for Table 7.3.

displaced by trade or by other possible causes such as a change in the pattern of domestic consumption. It is simplest to approach this problem by first looking at the changes occurring in trade and production and then comparing the current situation with a series of counterfactuals. We can then investigate the relative impact of external and internal factors affecting the displacement of unskilled workers.

A simple shift-share analysis similar to that carried out in Table 7.3 provides us with the clearest view of the changes occurring between 1971 and 1991. The object of the exercise is to determine what part of the changes in employment of workers with various education levels can be traced to changes in the pattern of consumption, the share of trade, and the employment of differently-skilled workers within specific industries. Our method of analysis requires construction of a series of counterfactuals where these factors remain constant and then comparing the results with actual changes in employment of workers with different levels of education.[18]

Part A of Table 7.5 shows that although manufacturing production has more than doubled between 1971 and 1991, employment declined 4.5 percent. This was mostly due, of course, to the dramatic increase in labor productivity. If the share of exports and imports had remained the same so that production would have grown as fast as domestic consumption (shipments + imports − exports), then the manufacturing labor force would have declined only 3.3 percent. The 1.2 percentage point difference is due to the increased imbalance of trade in manufacturing during the two years under examination.

In Part B we use disaggregated data and simulate three scenarios. In the first statistical experiment, we allow the structure of consumption to change as

18 Essentially this is the same approach as that followed by Sachs and Shatz (1994). They, however, use a 51 sector input-output table to determine both the direct and indirect amounts of workers at different skill levels affected by trade. If we understand their argument, they would argue that if the net imports of electric pumps increase, the workers in the domestic industries making the metal, motors, and measuring gauges used by the pump manufacturer should be taken into account in determining the impact of trade. In the same case our approach takes account of any decline in employment in the metal-working, motor, and instrument industries in terms of what is happening to total production in these separate industries. In other words, in our counterfactual we assume that the consumption pattern (domestic usage in each industry, but not necessarily final consumption) in 1991 was the same as in 1971. In their counterfactual they seem to assume that the final consumption pattern in 1990 was the same as in 1978 and, moreover, that inter-industry relations remained the same. Our counterfactual allows for changes and can take into account that a multinational might ship U.S. instruments to its foreign electric pump factory for those pumps that were exported to the United States. They also conclude that imports did have an impact on low-skilled U.S. workers, in contrast to our own conclusions which indicate a much less important role of imports. Our study and theirs also differ with regard to time period and to several less crucial aspects of the calculations.

it did between 1971 and 1991. However, in all 77 manufacturing industries we hold constant the share of exports and imports and also the shares of workers with different educational qualifications for each industry. In the second experiment we allow foreign trade to change as it did between 1971 and 1991, while holding the other two variables constant. In the third experiment, we allow the upgrading of the education of workers to change as it did in each industry between 1971 and 1991, while holding constant the two variables reflecting the structure of consumption and of foreign trade.

To explain the changing composition of employment of workers with different educational credentials, the general changes in the educational levels of workers alone account for almost all of the actual changes shown in the final line of the table. The trade effect tells us little about this composition effect, and the changes in the consumption structure seem to reinforce the general upgrading of the educational level of the manufacturing workforce, rather than serving as a major explanatory variable.

The trade effect (driven by the negative trade balance) seems to explain the overall 4.5 percent fall in manufacturing employment better than the other factors. Without knowing the degree to which skilled workers can substitute for unskilled workers, it is difficult to determine the overall employment impact of such educational shifts of the workers on theoretical grounds. The statistical experiment in Part B suggests that the change in education of workers in each industry led to an overall decline which reinforces the trade balance effect. The changing composition of consumption works in the opposite direction as the actual change. The similarity between the overall employment effect of the change in education in Part B, and the hypothetical change in the manufacturing labor force calculated in Part A, occurs by chance.

This kind of statistical exercise leads to several conclusions. First, foreign trade is not a major cause of the decline in employment of less-educated workers, a conclusion supporting the results from Table 7.4 which approach the problem from a different angle. Second, the general upgrading of the educational credentials of the manufacturing workers is much more important in explaining the shift in the average educational levels of these workers than shifts in the structure of consumption. Third, although the decline of overall manufacturing employment appears linked to the surplus of imports over exports, it does not follow that closing the trade gap will reduce the decline in manufacturing employment since, at the same time, consumers may choose to buy fewer manufactured goods and to save more.

In short, any great sucking sound of a trade-induced outflow of U.S. jobs to points abroad seems faint indeed except, perhaps, to certain U.S. politicians. We have to look elsewhere to explain the rising joblessness of less-educated prime-age American males.

Immigration as a Cause of Falling Employment Rates of Less-Skilled Males

Although it is commonly argued in the popular press that immigrants have "taken away" the jobs of native-born workers, the view among many specialists is much different. For instance, a recent survey by the National Research Council of the National Academy of Sciences (Smith and Edmonston, 1997) bluntly states: "The evidence leads us to conclude that immigration has only a small adverse impact on the wage and employment opportunities of competing native-born groups. This effect appears not to be concentrated in the local areas where immigrants live; much of it is probably dispersed across the United States as competing native workers migrate out of the areas to which immigrants move." This is an important conclusion because a considerable share of immigrants – both legal and illegal – number among the less-educated. Allegedly, these immigrants replace less-educated native-born workers, who become jobless.

In this section we look briefly at three issues. How many immigrants are in the labor force? How would this affect our previous conclusions? How large is the employment effect of these immigrants on native workers?

The Relative Importance of Immigrant Workers

According to U.S. Census data from 1970, 1980, and 1990, the percentages of foreign-born in the total labor force were 5.2 percent, 6.7 percent, and 9.2 percent respectively.[19] These data include not just legal immigrants, but many undocumented (illegal) immigrants as well. For instance, Borjas, Freeman and Lang (1991) estimate roughly 60 percent of undocumented Mexican immigrants were included in the 1980 census. In another calculation Abowd and Freeman (1991) focus on undocumented immigrants not enumerated in the Census, estimating that they would only raise the percentage of the foreign-born in the 1980 labor force from 6.7 to 7.3 percent.

In Table 7.6 we look at employed persons by age, gender, education, and immigrant status for both 1979 and 1995. Part A includes legal immigrants and those undocumented immigrants who were enumerated in the *Current Popu-*

---

19   These Census data come from Abowd and Freeman (1991), Table 3 and U.S. Department of Commerce, Census Bureau (1993-c), Table 4.

lation Survey.[20] In both years immigrants clearly constituted a significant percentage of the labor force lacking a high-school diploma. In 1979, 13.8 percent of this group consisted of immigrants, and by 1995 the number grew to 37.5 percent. For the other educational groups, immigrants amounted to less than eight percent in 1979 and to less than 12 percent in 1995.

In Part B we recalculate these percentages and include a rough estimate of unenumerated and undocumented immigrants. This raises the share of immigrants among dropouts by about one-ninth, but the increase is considerably less for the other categories of workers. The inclusion of these unenumerated and undocumented workers into the calculations does not, we must emphasize, dramatically change the orders of magnitude involved in the analysis of the impact of immigration.

The data in Table 7.6 seem consistent with the hypothesis that less-educated immigrants are replacing less-educated native-born workers. However, this ignores the demand side of the labor market. It is possible, and we think it likely, that although these changes on the supply side of male dropouts were great, increased demand for less-educated workers may have counter-balanced any such supply effects. These issues require us to turn to some direct empirical studies.

The Impact of Immigration on Employment Rates

The empirical literature on the employment impact of immigration is large and growing.[21] Of crucial importance to our empirical analysis, the Current Population Survey data include the vast majority of all immigrant workers, even those with little education. Thus, our major conclusions in this book do not change because we have consciously focused our analysis on the entire labor force, not just on native workers.[22]

For the analysis of the impact of immigration, the key facts are those which we analyze in considerable detail in Chapter 3 and which concern the relative

20 In our analyses of the data from the Current Population Survey we are handicapped for early years because a variable indicating place-of-birth is not included. For this reason we can only calculate the table using 1979 data. Thus we are looking at a period when the jobless rates for native-born, prime-age male high-school dropouts and those with just a high-school diploma rose from 16.9 to 34.0 percent and from 7.2 to 12.8 percent respectively.

21 See especially the summary oby smith and Edmundston (1997). We present a brief overview of some major studies in Apendix 7.1.

22 The data on workers born in the U.S. would show the same results as we derived in Chapter 3, namely unskilled jobs increasing faster than the number of unskilled workers.

Table 7.6: *Share of Immigrants in the Employed Labor Force, 1979 and 1995*

Highest educational level

	1979				1995			
	All workers		Prime-age workers		All workers		Prime-age workers	
	Men	Women	Men	Women	Men	Women	Men	Women

Part A: Immigrants as percent of employed workers as enumerated in the Current Population Survey

High-school dropouts	9.4%	9.4%	13.8%	12.9%	27.1%	18.3%	37.5%	27.0%
High-school diploma	4.2	4.5	4.2	4.9	7.9	6.8	8.2	7.2
Some university or trade/ vocational schools	4.8	5.1	5.1	6.0	6.8	6.7	7.0	6.6
University degree	6.7	7.0	6.6	7.8	10.2	8.5	11.0	8.4
Total	6.1	6.0	6.6	6.7	10.9	8.5	11.7	8.8

Part B: Immigrants as percent of employed workers including estimates of unenumerated and undocumented immigrants

High-school dropouts	10.6	10.4	15.6	14.4	29.7	20.6	40.6	30.0
High-school diploma	4.6	4.7	4.7	5.2	8.5	7.1	8.8	7.6
Some university or trade/ vocational schools	5.3	5.4	5.6	6.3	7.4	7.0	7.5	6.9
University degree	7.1	7.3	6.9	8.1	10.7	8.9	11.4	8.7
Total	6.7	6.4	7.3	7.2	11.9	9.1	12.6	9.4

Notes: We base this table on the assumption that the total undocumented immigrants in 1979 and 1995 numbered 2.0 and 4.5 million respectively. The first is an estimate by Warren and Passel (1989); the second is the average of official estimates for 1994 (U.S. Department of Commerce, Bureau of the Census (annual, 1996), p. 12) and 1996 (*New York Times*, February 8, 1997, p. 9). Of those undocumented and employed immigrants, we assume that 60 percent were enumerated in the Current Population Survey, a datum estimated for undocumented Mexican workers by Borjas, Freeman, and Lang (1991).

We use percentages derived from the Current Population Survey data for non-citizen immigrants for March 1979 and March 1995 as the starting point for estimating the non-enumerated immigrants according to the categories of the table. We adjusted these ratios, however, because it seems likely that the unrecorded and undocumented immigrants had a somewhat higher percentage of men, percentage of employed people, and percentage in the prime- working ages than the enumerated non-citizen as a whole. In addition, it seems likely that a greater share of these unenumerated immigrants had less education as well.

Although our estimates for undocumented and non-enumerated immigrants in the labor force are rough, they allow us to gain some idea of the relevant orders of magnitudes.

supply and demand of workers with various educational levels. As we have already mentioned, the number of workers with a high-school education or less have increased at a slower rate than the number of jobs that do not require many skills or educational qualifications. Low-skilled immigrants, therefore, are not displacing low-skilled native workers from their jobs because there are enough for both groups, assuming that workers with higher education do not compete for the same jobs. If we consider unenumerated low-skilled workers, then we must add not just these workers to the total low-skilled workers, but the jobs they are occupying to the number of low-skilled jobs. Thus, the conclusion still stands.

To look at the matter in a different way, between 1979 and 1994 the jobless rate for native males without a high-school diploma rose much faster than the similar rate of increase of less-educated immigrant males.[23] By way of contrast, the share of immigrants among prime age males with just a high-school diploma was relatively low and yet, according to the data presented in Chapter 1, the jobless rate for this group also increased dramatically. So the rising joblessness among males with less than a high-school education appears to have been caused by something else.

One other facet of the problem concerns unemployment rates. Any direct replacement of native-born workers by immigrants who are willing to work for lower wages suggests that unemployment rates between the two groups would also be different. This does not, however, prove to be the case. More specifically, unemployment rates as a percentage of the relevant population are not greatly different among native-born and immigrant males; indeed, for women, they are lower for the native-born.

The image of native-born workers being displaced by immigrants is vivid but misleading. Many less-educated native-born prime-age persons have been displaced from their jobs because of the mechanisms described in Chapters 3 and 4. At the same time, immigration of less-educated persons has increased. Nevertheless, the causal relation between immigration and joblessness is weak because of the impact of these other factors influencing the labor market of less-educated workers.

Spatial Mismatch: People in the Cities, Jobs in the Suburbs

Spatial mismatch occurs when jobs are found in one location, while workers live in other locations. The mismatch can occur on a regional basis –

---

23 More specifically, for those without a high-school education, the percentage of the

the new jobs are in the South, while those without employment live in the Northeast. Little evidence supports the importance of this regional phenomenon, as shown in the regressions presented in Appendix 1.3.

The mismatch can also occur at a local level. Over the last few decades jobs have been moving steadily from the cities to the suburbs. Factories have relocated to suburban areas to have more room to expand and, at the same time to pay lower taxes; services have moved to suburban areas to meet the needs of customers who have also moved out of the cities. Such a movement of population and jobs is embodied in the title of William Julius Wilson's (1996) recent book about inner-city Chicago: *When Work Disappears*. The debate has been joined by those analyzing the spatial distribution of poverty. They show, for instance, that although a majority of the poor do not live in the inner city or in high-poverty urban areas, over the last few decades an increasing concentration of the poor live in these areas. A key question is whether race, education, or space is the determining element in the increase in jobless rates in the central cities.[24]

For a theory of job mismatch to tell us anything about employment, we must supplement it with a theory of job mobility. For instance, if population mobility keeps up with the changing geographical pattern of new jobs, then no permanent job mismatch should occur. Similarly, if those living in the city find net wages (wages minus transportation costs) sufficiently high, they may commute to new jobs opening up in the suburbs, at least if suitable public transportation is available.

Research on these various issues raises some difficult problems and direct approaches provide insights, but few solid answers. For instance, the readily available data on residential mobility do not prove very helpful.[25] Further,

---

prime-age men without employment is 34.0 percent for the native-born, and only 17.7 percent for immigrants. For women, the corresponding percentages are 50.0 percent and 59.1 percent. For those with just a high-school diploma, by way of contrast, joblessness rates are lower for both prime-age native-born men and women than immigrants. Such differences have some important sociological implications

24 Three recent survey articles summarizing the literature are by Jencks and Mayer (1990), Holzer (1991) and Kain (1992). Recently Paul A. Jargowsky (1997) has made an important contribution to this literature, although his major focus was on poverty, rather than employment per se. In this section we carry out the analysis in a simple fashion. In the regression analysis presented in Appendix 1.3, we hold a variety of factors influencing poverty constant when we analyze the impact of the spatial variables. The conslusions reached there are the same as in this discussion.

25 On a state or regional level, it does not appear that residential mobility has greatly changed. For instance, census data tell us that the percentage of people more than four years old who are living in the same county during the last five years has not changed greatly between 1950 and 1990. Moreover, the percentage of the population born in the state in which they are currently residing also has not greatly changed over this period. Using data from the U.S. cen-

most empirical analyses of job mismatch have focused on the situation occurring at a single period in time, but with mixed results. For instance, Hughes (1989) shows that the spread of concentrated areas of the poor within central cities is a function, not of deindustrialization *per se*, but of the deconcentration of manufacturing. This occurs when urban factories relocate to the suburbs, or out of the metropolitan area. By way of contrast Jargowsky (1997, p. 99) finds little difference in the distribution of employment by industries of those living in high-poverty areas in cities and of those living in the entire metropolitan area. Commuting-time studies show little difference between those living in poverty areas in cities and in other parts of the metropolitan area.[26] Many central city residents rely more heavily on public transportation than suburbanites and the deterioration of the transportation infrastructure (particularly in cities in the Northeast) has affected their ability to reach jobs located out of the city.

We wish to investigate a more dynamic question: To what degree has *changing* job mismatch contributed to *changing* rates of joblessness? As we show in the analysis below, residence location affects the jobless rate at a single point in time. Nevertheless, it appears that *changing* job mismatch has played only a secondary role in the changing jobless rates of the population as a whole. These results are of considerable relevance to the discussion of joblessness of certain subgroups. Some argue, for instance, that the job mismatch problem for African-Americans is severe and worsening because of their difficulties in obtaining affordable suburban housing.

We present our key empirical evidence in Table 7.7, which contains data on prime-age persons by gender, race, education, employment status, and whether or not they live in the "central city" of a Metropolitan Statistical Area (MSA). Note that the "inner-city" constitutes only a part of the central city of the MSA.[27] For each of the four prime-age demographic groups – all men, all women, black men, and black women – we first show jobless rates, and then show what fraction of the total jobless population in a specific demographic group resides in central cities.

sus, we tried to correlate population mobility between U.S. states of the less-educated with differences in wages, but the experiments were not very successful. This suggests that wage differences, at least among the less-educated population, are not an important determinant of mobility.

26   These data come from Jargowsky (1997), p. 196. Studies focusing more specifically on commuting patterns, for instance Kasarda (1995), p. 255, provide many insights but such data tell us little about the wages net of transportation expenses, which seem to us to be the key variable.

27   For example, the entire city of Philadelphia is the "central city" of the Philadelphia, Pennsylvania—Trenton, New Jersey—Wilmington, Deleware Metropolitan Statistical Area. Only certain neighborhoods within the city of Philadelphia, however, are "inner city" in the sense of having a dense population with high poverty rates. We would prefer to use data on whether individuals lived in an "inner city" neighborhood, but the CPS data does not contain enough information to perform such an analysis.

Table 7.7: *Jobless Rates of the Prime-Age Population in Central Cities, 1971 and 1995*[a]

Highest level of formal education	High-school dropout	High-school diploma	Some advanced education	University degree	Total
Part A: Prime-age men living in central cities					
Jobless rate, 1971	15.5%	8.0%	10.6%	7.2%	10.7%
Jobless rate, 1995	32.6	18.2	11.7	7.5	15.8
Predicted 1995 jobless rate[b]	34.8	16.6	15.3	9.9	15.9
Actual minus predicted 1995 rate	-2.1	+1.5	-3.7	-2.4	-0.1
Share of total male jobless, 1971	35.1	32.9	39.4	45.3	36.1
Share of total male jobless, 1995	41.7	36.3	32.0	38.7	37.3
Part B: Prime-age women living in central cities					
Jobless rate, 1971	59.4	47.4	44.7	35.1	49.8
Jobless rate, 1995	57.4	34.8	25.9	15.8	31.3
Predicted 1995 jobless rate[b]	50.0	24.7	19.4	14.2	23.8
Actual minus predicted 1995 rate	+7.4	+10.1	+6.5	+1.6	+7.5
Share of total female jobless, 1971	31.1	23.5	25.0	26.1	26.5
Share of total female jobless, 1995	44.7	31.7	29.7	26.2	33.2
Part C: Prime-age black men living in central cities					
Jobless rate, 1971	18.6	12.5	9.1	13.1	15.3
Jobless rate, 1995	52.6	20.8	15.8	10.7	23.0
Predicted 1995 jobless rate[b]	50.8	32.4	9.0	62.0	23.9
Actual minus predicted 1995 rate	+1.7	-11.6	+6.8	-51.2	-0.9

Table 7.7. (cont.)

Highest level of formal education	High-school dropout	High-school diploma	Some advanced education	University degree	Total
Share of total black male jobless, 1971	58.2	76.9	61.7	88.2	63.6
Share of total black male jobless, 1995	61.7	58.9	59.2	48.5	59.0
Part D: Prime-age black women living in central cities					
Jobless rate, 1971	53.5	36.7	30.0	18.0	43.2
Jobless rate, 1995	64.3	41.4	26.0	10.6	36.2
Predicted 1995 jobless rate[b]	51.8	31.4	18.3	18.5	26.9
Actual minus predicted 1995 rate	+12.5	+10.1	+7.7	-8.0	+9.3
Share of total black female jobless, 1971	56.6	64.8	70.3	70.3	60.0
Share of total black female jobless, 1995	64.5	64.4	63.9	50.8	63.6

Notes: a. The central city refers to the core city of the Metropolitan Statistical Area, (MSA) and is discussed in the text. The shares of joblessness are calculated in terms of the entire United States population in the relevant demographic category, for instance, all men or all black men.

b. For calculating the "predicted joblessness," we assume that the joblessness rates in the central cities should increase at the same rate as those calculated for the suburbs and the non-metropolitan areas.

The data come from the March 1971 and March 1995 tapes of the Current Population Survey. For 1995 about 15 percent of the population was not allocated by residence in the central city, the suburbs, or out of the MSAs for reasons of data confidentiality. Therefore, we allocated the population and the non-employed classified simply as living in the MSA according to the proportions of the population and non-employed who were classified according to their central city or suburb residence. We also classified those whose residence was not specified at all according to the proportions of the specified population in the central city, suburbs, and non-MSA.

Parts A and B demonstrate that joblessness in the central cities of metropolitan statistical areas constitute roughly somewhat more than a third of total joblessness, although this varied somewhat by educational group. Overall, the fraction of the jobless prime-age population living in central cities grew by about one percentage point for men and seven percentage points for women. Since employment is the single most important determinant of income for most persons, it should come as no surprise that, between the early 1970s and 1993, the share of all individuals below the poverty line who lived in central cities grew from roughly one-third to 43 percent (Blank, 1997: 29).

Parts C and D show, by way of contrast, that over 60 percent of jobless prime-age African-Americans live in central cities. Between 1971 and 1995, such concentration fell somewhat for men, while it rose among women.

Data presented in Chapter 1 show that jobless rates rose among men, particularly among the less-educated. Similar results occurred among men in the central city. Depending upon the highest level of education, the jobless rates increased slightly more or slightly less than what we would predict. We use jobless rates of similarly educated groups in the suburbs and non-metropolitan areas as the basis of these predictions. For men, the relative (but not absolute) impact of spatial mismatch over the quarter-century period does not appear to have changed greatly.

For women in the central cities, the situation is somewhat different. As for all women, jobless rates have fallen. This decline, particularly among the less-educated, was less than the jobless rate for women in the suburbs and non-metropolitan areas. Among those with a high-school education or less, spatial mismatch may have played a role in the employment changes.

For African-American males, jobless rates are considerably higher than for the male population as a whole. Nevertheless, the relative (but not absolute) impact of spatial mismatch over the period does not seem to have greatly *changed*. Indeed, for those with a high-school diploma or a college degree, jobless rates increased considerably less than predicted. For African-American women, the picture is roughly the same as for women as a whole, namely that spatial mismatch seems to have played a secondary role in the *changing* jobless rates.

In sum our evidence presented in Table 7.7 suggests that spacial mismatch has not played a major role in the *changing* employment rates. This, of course, is the phenomenon we have focused upon in previous chapters.

Summary and Conclusions

Changing technology, the changing structure of production, increasing foreign trade, immigration, and spatial job mismatch undoubtedly cause some changes in jobless rates. Nevertheless, the evidence presented in this chapter suggests that their impacts are neither systematic nor very important. We must look toward other causes.

In the economic literature there is no dearth of other explanations for the long-run rising rate of joblessness, particularly among less-educated males. These include the impact of the minimum wage, increased incentives for unemployment or joblessness arising from the welfare system, higher costs of job search, rising indirect costs of labor such as increased difficulties in firing workers, and changes in the work ethic. The evidence that any of these factors play an important role in the long-term rising rates of joblessness among men ranges from shaky to unbelievable.[28] We explore some of these subjective and institutional factors in greater detail in the next chapter to tie up the loose ends of our argument.

---

28   These various theories are discussed at much greater length in Pryor (1996), Chapter 3. This study, however, makes certain assertions about the impact of technology which are refuted by the evidence in this book

CHAPTER 8

Notes on Subjective and
Institutional Factors

This is the second of our two chapters addressing alternative explanations for labor market changes over the last quarter-century. In our analysis in the first six chapters we examine explanations based on a variety of "objective" and quantifiable variables such functional literacy, education, race/ethnicity, age, and occupation; and in the previous chapter we explore the impact of such "objective" variables as imports, immigration, location, technological change, and structural changes in production. To complete this analysis it is necessary to examine the role of several "subjective factors" and "institutional factors" believed to play important roles in the labor market.

The impact of these subjective and institutional factors is easiest to study in the employment process. Subjective factors influencing employment include work attitudes and other soft-skills affecting the way workers interact with others, as well as employer preconceptions about these skills. Institutional factors influencing employment are those practices and policies that shape the functioning of the labor market.

Of course, some influences on the labor market have both an objective and subjective component. For instance, the gender and race/ethnicity variables included in the list of objective variables also have some important subjective and institutional implications.

We turn first to subjective factors influencing employment at a single point in time. This leads us to consideration of certain such factors that change over time. Finally, we survey briefly some institutional factors that affect our results.

Subjective Factors Influencing Employment at a
Single Point in Time

A large social science literature focuses on work attitudes influencing employment. For instance, some such as Elijah Anderson (1990) argue that certain attitudes needed for young, less-educated black males to survive in their ghetto neighborhoods – a tough demeanor; a distrust of everyone, especially those in authority, an unwillingness to look anyone straight in the eye; a scorn of bourgeois values – are hardly the characteristics that help them either obtain employment or make them good employees.

The impacts of such perceived attitudes by these potential labor force participants are unfortunate. William Julius Wilson (1996) and Harry J. Holzer (1995) show that many white *and* black employers have a deep distrust of less-educated black males from poor neighborhoods. We wish to stress that although racial prejudice may certainly be involved, certain objective factors also play a role. Relevant to these concerns, economists such as Richard J. Murnane and Frank Levy (1997, Chapter 2) provide evidence that in addition to certain skill requirements, employers are increasingly looking for soft-skills and appropriate work attitudes. For example, they note that in the late 1960s, U.S. auto makers such as Ford were willing to hire "any warm body" as entry-level workers. By way of contrast, in the late 1980s at the Honda factory in Marysville, Ohio, employment personnel looked at the ability of entry-level workers to communicate with others, take responsibility, and exhibit flexibility and a willingness to help others.

Actual Employment Criteria

At this point two questions immediately arise. How typical are such anecdotes about employment criteria? What type of entry-level workers are sought by employers? Some answers can be obtained from a recent survey by the U.S. Census Bureau, which was part of a broader project on the educational quality of the workforce. The Bureau asked several thousand employers to rate the importance of specific hard and soft-skills of entry-level workers looking for work.[1] The results reported in Table 8.1 are illuminating.

These data suggest that two soft-skills, namely general attitudes and communication skills, are the most important hiring criteria in the middle 1990s, a result appearing to confirm the approach of Murnane and Levy. These criteria are, however, the two most subjective criteria of the list of 11 and it is certainly possible they might provide merely a convenient excuse for not hiring someone who was unsatisfactory on other grounds. Although we provide certain evidence for the occurrence of credentialism in Chapter 3, we must also note that, according to these data, the years of schooling rank seventh in importance on the list. Teacher recommendations and grades scored even lower.

---

1 The concept of "entry-level work" is not well defined since there seems to be an educational cut-off point. That is, we do not speak of entry-level physicians. Very roughly, these entry-level jobs seem to correspond to those that we classify as tier 1 or 2 occupations.

Table 8.1: *Important Factors in the Hiring of Front-Line Workers*

Question posed to employers: When you consider hiring a new non-supervisory or production worker (front-line worker), how important are the following in your decision to hire. Please use a scale from 1 to 5 where 5 is very important and 1 is not important or not considered:

		Mean scores	Standard deviations
1.	Applicant's attitude	4.62	0.69
2.	Applicant's communication skills	4.23	0.93
3.	Previous work experience of applicant	3.96	1.09
4.	Recommendations from coworkers	3.42	1.14
5.	Previous employer's recommendation	3.37	1.25
6.	Industry-based credentials (certifying applicant's skills)	3.17	1.36
7.	Years of completed schooling	2.88	1.17
8.	Scores received in any test administered as part of the interview	2.54	1.50
9.	Academic performance (grades) of applicant	2.48	1.08
10.	Reputation of applicant's school	2.41	1.27
11.	Teacher recommendations	2.07	1.19

Notes: These results come from the Educational Quality of the Workforce study carried out in 1994. The employers responding to the questionnaire used their own criteria for the five-point rankings. The Census Bureau sampled establishments with 20 employees or more, but omitted public sector employers, nonprofit institutions, and corporate headquarters. Moreover, it over-sampled establishments in the manufacturing sector and establishments with more than 100 employees. For this table various replies number from 2858 to 2897, depending on the question. These results represent weighted averages and standard deviations, with the weights representing sampling probabilities.

These data come from Economic Quality of the Workforce database, which are found on the web at: www.irhe.upenn.edu/~shapiro/. We would like to thank Daniel Shapiro for his assistance in using this database.

The Real Meaning of Employment Criteria

How can we interpret these results in light of the importance assigned to education in the previous chapters? Moreover, to the extent that high turnover is costly to the firm, why aren't such educational criteria used as a screening device to avoid hiring less-qualified workers? We can approach the problems from two perspectives which we label the "naive" and the "cynical" approaches.

According to the naive approach, we can infer from the table that employers do not believe that information on schooling, grades, and teachers' evaluations of potential employees have much validity. Zemsky, Shapiro *et al.*

(1996) argue this inference is inaccurate. They analyze these data in detail to show that firms using grades, teacher recommendations, and the reputation of an applicant's school to screen job applicants have significantly less job turnover.

From a more discerning use of the naive approach we can also infer that such data on education do not tell the employer about the soft-skills they believe are actually more important in the current workplace. For instance, Peter Cappelli (1993) takes this interpretation one step further to argue that much of the alleged "skills gap" (the alleged gap between skills needed by employers and skills of potential employees) is really about work attitudes. Drawing from a number of surveys by private-sector organizations, he finds that "character," "self-discipline," and "dedication and discipline in work habits" ranked as the most important criteria for selecting entry-level workers. Such an argument about the relative unimportance of the alleged skills gap is, of course, in line with our analysis about downward occupational mobility and the overeducation of the labor force that is documented in previous chapters.

According to the cynical approach, employers "just say" they are interested in attitudes and communications skills. In reality, these serve as masks for other criteria, which the employers might not want to reveal. For instance, Roy Marshall (1994) provides evidence that only a tiny fraction of American companies are moving away from the traditional production methods toward those placing great emphasis on soft-skills. Moss and Tilly (1995) find employers claiming that requirements for soft-skills (defined in terms of work motivation and interaction skills) have been rising over the last decade. Nevertheless, employers in their sample also perceived black men as lacking in these soft-skills, a result the authors attributed to prejudice, a misreading of cultural differences, and reality. Kirschman, Moss and Tilly (1995) note that heavier reliance on less formal, more subjective methods of screening (such as pre-employment interviews) and less reliance on formal methods such as tests are associated with reduced black employment.

One way to pierce this verbal veil is to determine whether the weight employers place on these two criteria is related to more basic factors including race and education. More specifically, using the relative importance employers place on a particular hiring criterion as the variable to be explained in ordinary least squares regressions, we then select a wide number of characteristics of their labor force as explanatory variables that "really" underlie this criterion.

Based on the results of such regressions, shown in Appendix Table A8.1, those productive establishments placing the greatest weight on work attitudes are significantly more likely to have their workers represented by a union, to have greater job rotation, to have fewer inexperienced workers, and to have lower wages. Such criterion is also more likely to be used in hiring in retail trade, hotels, and business services. Most of these results make intuitive sense.

Moreover, such establishments are also more likely to have a higher percentage of women and a lower percentage of minorities in their labor force. The latter results are consistent with the cynical view toward employers' stated hiring critiera. Nevertheless we cannot be completly sure because we have no way to ascertain objectively the work attitudes of these groups. This is a crucial issue for public policy – and for future research.

One last feature of this regression experiment deserves comment: Regardless of the number of variables we add to the regression, we cannot explain more than 3.3 percent (that is, the adjusted R^2 = .0325) of the variation in the importance placed on the work attitudes variable.[2] In addition, although the variable reflecting the percentage of women is statistically significant, the variable reflecting the percentage of minority workers is not and the latter only explains 0.1 percent of the variation in the scores of the attitude variable. From these results we conclude that the cynical view toward these employment criteria receives only weak support.

A similar statistical experiment with communications skills yields slightly different results. Those establishments placing a high weight on this criterion are likely to have a smaller percentage of production workers in their workforce, more-educated production workers, a higher percentage of non-managerial staff participating in decisions, a higher ratio of employees to supervisors, fewer inexperienced workers, and lower wages. Moreover, establishments in retail trade, banking, insurance, and hotels are more likely to attach greater importance to this criterion in their hiring practices. Again, most of these results match our intuitive expectations. Like work attitudes, this criterion is positively related to the share of women and negatively related to the share of minorities in the labor force. This time, however, both calculated regression coefficients are statistically significant.

Our statistical experiment explains more of the variation in the weight given to communication skills than to the weight given to work attitudes. Nevertheless, at best we can only explain about one-sixth (adjusted R^2 = .1609) of the variation of this variable. The race variable alone explains only 0.8 percent of the variation of the weight placed on communication skills. Still, this offers some support for the cynical view about stated employment criteria.

In concluding our look at these experiments to explain the stated criteria for hiring, we must add that the direction of causality between the weights firms give to various employment criteria, the composition of the workforce they employ, and the nature of the jobs they provide is unclear. The regressions just discussed assume that the employment criteria are a function of workforce composition and the nature of the jobs. We tried two additional experiments (reported in Appendix Table A8.2) in which we reversed this assumption about

2 Some of the results of these regression experiments are presented in Appendix 8.1.

causality. More specifically, we used the percentage of women and minority workers as the variable to be explained and used all eleven employment criteria as the explanatory variables. In both cases, the degree of explanatory power was less than three percent and no additional implications are apparent.

Formal Education Criteria in Hiring

At this point we face a disturbing contradiction. On the one hand, our analysis of the displacement effect, especially in Chapters 3 and 4, strongly implies that in hiring workers, employers use years of education as a screening device. On the other hand, the analysis of employer criteria for hiring, shown in Table 8.1, suggests "work attitudes" and "communication skills" are the most important hiring criteria and that actual years of education of production workers plays only a secondary role in the hiring process. How do we reconcile these results?

One possibility is that years of education is a primary determinant of both work attitudes and communications skills. Although employers verbally emphasize the latter criteria, they are indirectly using an education criterion. It is likely that this partially explains our apparently contradictory results.

Another possibility is a peculiar type of selection bias. The crucial clue comes from the variable identifying education of the front-line workers, which shows little variation. More specifically, in the sample of 2904 employers, the coefficient of variation (the standard deviation divided by the mean) is only about 13 percent. When the data are aggregated into 20 productive sectors, the coefficient of variation is only about four percent. This relative similarity in the number of years of formal education of these production workers suggests that employers never hired workers with fewer than a specific number of years of education. Although employers claimed that years of education was relatively unimportant in hiring decisions, this apparently applied only for potential employees with more years of schooling than the cutoff limit. As a result, we cannot easily isolate the actual role of education in the hiring process from this data set, or the importance of education as an underlying cause of attitudes and communication skills.

A third possible resolution of this contradiction between the importance of education in the hiring process (as discussed in previous chapters) and the unimportance of education shown in Table 8.1 requires a look at the people involved in the process. A professional human resources manager suggested to us that many people hiring front-line workers do not really know what they are doing. That is, supervisors who do such hiring came into their position by virtue of their technical, rather than supervisory, skills. They simply do not know which hard data (such as academic performance, grades, and recommendations) serve as better predictors for successful employment, so they are forced to rely on "gut instinct." Thus, their focus on soft-skills of the candidates is a fancy way of expressing their intuitive interpersonal reactions to the job candidate. This could explain the result of Zemsky, *et al.* (1996) which found that those employers who approach personnel decisions with more professionalism, and who rely more on academic screens have reduced job turnover and other costs associated with more subjective methods of evaluating job candidates.

Alternative interpretations of these kinds of data can also be offered. For instance, the use of such "hard" data may mean that the workers who are hired are also treated better and, as a result, are less inclined to quit. The inverse correlation between education and the turnover rate may also simply reflect a random employment process with more-educated workers performing their jobs better and, therefore, reducing the probability of being fired. Given such ambiguities, the information we can extract from surveys on employer attitudes and employment results is limited.

Subjective Factors Influencing Employment Over Time

Have employers always placed great weight on applicants' attitudes in the hiring process, or has this particular criterion increased in importance as the work ethic has declined? This is a difficult question because few standardized surveys have been carried out over a quarter-century or more to determine the relative changes in the work ethic of employees.

Relying on our memory to answer this question is unreliable because of "nostalgia bias." For instance, over a half-century ago an Italian sociologist, Andriano Tilgher (1930, p. 140) laconically noted: "Every country resounds to the lament that the work-fever does not burn in the younger generation." In more recent times, denunciation of the decline of the work ethic in America is a telltale sign of "serious" social analysis. In a survey of production managers (Pryor, 1983), a vast majority of the respondents reported that over a twenty-year period absenteeism had soared, while attention to quality and hard work had declined. Government statistics, however, show no rise in absenteeism over the same period!

We must be cautious, however. The concept of the work ethic has many dimensions and is difficult to pin down.[3] Nevertheless, some evidence about

---

3   Two studies illustrating the dimensions of the concept and the pitfalls in measuring it are: Buchholz (1978) and Morrow (1993).

the broadest meaning of the phrase are available, both in terms of public opinion data and more objective criteria, and they also provide little support for the conjecture that the work ethic is declining.

From 1973 to the present, for instance, the National Opinion Research Center (NORC) has asked its respondents whether hard work or luck is the most important for "getting ahead." Over this entire period about two-thirds have responded that hard work is the most critical. Indeed, in the early 1990s the responses are higher than in the middle 1970s.[4] The Roper Poll has asked how satisfied people are with their work, and from 1973 through 1992, about 85 percent claimed they were satisfied.[5] In 1992, 82 percent of those queried said they felt loyal to their work organization, 84 percent said people usually notice when a job is done well, 89 percent were proud to be working for their employer, and 76 percent found their values and those of their work organization similar. NORC surveys also revealed little change in job satisfaction between 1973 and 1990.

Unfortunately, attitudes expressed to survey-takers may not be the best indicators of underlying feelings. One more objective indicator is the rate of work absenteeism and, contrary to common belief (as well as the beliefs of the production managers noted above), from 1957 to the present, no upward trends can be found. Indeed, from the mid 1980s to the present, the rate of absenteeism declined markedly.[6] Similarly, no long-term upward trends in voluntary quits, at least between 1950 and 1981 in the manufacturing sector, can be found. On the other hand, retirement rates at a given age show a steady increase, although the U.S. still has one of the highest employment rates of people over 65 of any industrialized nation (Lipset 1988).

In the period since 1970 the work ethic, at least in a general sense, does not seem to be declining in the United States, although its content may be changing. Nevertheless, employers who need to fill a particular job with a particular person still need to be selective since certain indicators of a commitment to work vary considerably among the population. For instance, preference of work over leisure appears proportional to age and, as we might suspect, is lowest among the young. In particular, those from 18 to 29 manifest three-quarters as much preference for work as those between 45 and 59 (Lipset, 1988). Those believing that the work ethic has declined may be confusing differences in the work ethic of those in different age groups with changes over time.

4 Data for most of the period can be found in: Anon (1992). We obtained data from the NORC for the entire period and would like to thank Thomas Smith for his assistance.

5 These 1992 data come from ibid, as do the data cited in the next sentence. Other data on job satisfaction over the years can be located at the website of the Institute for Social Research, University of Michigan, General Social Survey, www.icpsr.umich.edu/gss/trend/satjob.htm. The NORC results come from (Anon, 1990).

6 The data sources for this and the following sentence are in Pryor (1996), pp. 72-3.

If we are correct that the work ethic has not greatly changed, then it is quite likely that the work attitudes variable has been a key criterion used by employers in years past. This could arise simply because employers have been using this criterion to screen out those subgroups in the population who are not fully committed to hard work, even though the overall work ethic has not changed.

By way of contrast, it seems likely that the emphasis on communications skills is relatively recent. In part we base this judgement on the changing nature of the work place. In particular, some productive establishments have moved away from Taylorism – mass production, highly standardized work, and a centralized structure of authority in the workplace – and toward a more flexible system where workers are given more responsibility in structuring their work and solving particular work problems. Moreover, managers of many more enterprises are talking about introducing such production systems. In part, we also base this judgment on the structural upgrading of the occupational mix, as well as the real educational upgrading and upskilling of certain occupations, particularly in the more education-intensive occupations in tiers 3 and 4.

A Brief Survey of Some Institutional Factors Influencing Employment and Wages

Aside from subjective factors, certain institutional factors can also influence employment, particularly in the public sector. We begin this brief discussion by noting several particular policies such as income taxes and unemployment compensation and then move to several ways in which the government influences labor market institutions. We then turn to several ways in which private sector institutions also influence employment.

Income tax rates can influence the supply of labor, although several counteracting forces are at work. The lowering of tax rates can encourage people to reduce their leisure and work more because the additional consumption of an extra hour of work has increased (the substitution effect). On the other hand, the additional real income to an individual that arises from lower taxes might encourage more leisure (the income effect). So the net effect is far from clear. In a recent survey Nada Eissa (1996) notes: "Essentially all research shows that male participation and hours of work do not respond to changes in after-tax wages." By way of contrast, Eissa's studies and those of others suggest that female supply of labor is influenced by changes in tax rates. Given the problems in separating the impact of the tax changes in the 1980s and early 1990s with the general trend toward increasing employment rates for women, particularly those with relatively more education, we do not believe that the last word on the relation between tax rates and labor force participation of women has yet been uttered.

Some such as Murray Weidenbaum (1994) also argue that the structure of taxes can also influence the demand for labor. For instance, various govern-ment mandates on employers raise the cost of labor. To the extent that their long-run impact cannot be passed on to employees or consumers, the quantity of labor demanded falls. To us, however, it seems more likely that the long-run impacts can be passed on, so the labor demand effects of such measures are small.

Obviously unemployment insurance offers workers without jobs an alter-native source of income that can discourage them from seeking employment. We must emphasize, however, that in the years between 1970–74 and 1990–94, the real value of the average weekly unemployment benefits fell slightly. At the same time, because average real wages fell more, such benefits rose as a percentage of the average weekly wage in the private sector from 41.6 percent to 47.4 percent. In terms of the average weekly wage of the less-educated, this "earnings replacement rate" rose even more.[7] Some economet-ric evidence, for instance, Baumol and Wolff (1996), suggests that the rising replacement ratio has encouraged those eligible for such payments to extend their period of unemployment. Nevertheless, simple arithmetic suggests that this would not constitute a significant share of the overall rate of joblessness among the less-educated.[8] The impact on employment of other types of social welfare payments is a matter of great controversy, although some clarity will be gained when sufficient data are available to evaluate the employment effects of the 1994 revisions of the federal welfare law.

At a much different level of analysis, the public sector has a decisive impact on the transportation infrastructure and the provision of public transportation. These, in turn, affect the ability of potential workers living in the inner city to work in jobs in the suburbs where businesses are relocating. As argued in the previous chapter, although the spatial mismatch of jobs and people explains a certain portion of the lack of employment of those in the central city, it does not appear to have played a major role in the *changing* employment rates.

Public policy also has an an important impact on the functioning of gov-ernmental agencies participating in the labor market. These measures include providing information about available jobs, assisting the non-employed to obtain these jobs, and training for those who lack the necessary hard- or soft-

---

7   These data come from U.S. Council of Economic Advisors (annual, 1997), Tables B-3, B-43, and B-45. Because the wages of the less-educated fell as a percentage of the median wage (Chapter 5), the replacement rate for this group rose faster than for workers with the average education.

8   This can be seen by a simple numerical example. In 1995 9.2 percent of the population who were prime-age male dropouts were unemployed. In this year the average length of unem-ployment was 16 weeks, so that if each person extended his unemployment by two weeks, this would raise the unemployment rate 1.2 percentage points. This would constitute only a small part of the overall non-employment rate of 28.7 percent for this group.

skills needed for the available jobs. Of the various training and other programs designed to increase employment among the less-educated, job placement programs have proven among the most successful, at least as measured in terms of cost effectiveness. We discuss these programs in greater detail later in the next chapter. It should be clear, however, that there are some obvious limits to the degree to which such programs can reduce joblessness.

Private sector institutions, particularly with regard to the selection and training of workers, also influence employment rates. As noted above, reliance on hard data, rather than subjective evaluations and sole attention to soft-skills, improves job retention and reduces turnover, which is a major factor underlying frictional unemployment (the unemployment occurring when jobs are unfilled, even when unemployed workers with the requisite skills are available to be hired).

Other institutional and public policy barriers that have some impact on employment can be easily specified. Nevertheless, we have been focusing on the factors underlying the *changing* employment rates during the last quarter-century. In this regard we have been unable to find any convincing links between these or other changing institutional factors, and the dramatic changes in employment discussed in previous chapters.

Finally, we must note the impact of the minimum wage on both employment and wages. Although the exact effect on employment, particularly among low-productivity workers, is controversial,[9] its impact on wages is clearer. Since 1970 the real value of the minimum wage has fallen about five percent in real terms. Because median real wages of men in tier 1 and 2 occupations fell considerably more, this federally-mandated minimum provided a floor that acted to compress wages in these occupational tiers, a phenomenon discussed in considerable detail in Chapter 6. The 1996 increase in the minimum wage will accentuate this tendency.

A Very Brief Conclusion

Without doubt, the subjective and institutional factors we have surveyed have some influence on labor market outcomes. We find no reason to believe, however, that they are the major factors influencing the changing behavior of the labor market or that their influence would change our conclusions drawn in previous chapters.

---

9 We refer specifically to the controversy engendered by a recent study by David Card and Alan B. Krueger (1995).

Final Observations

In the previous eight chapters we present our explanation for the major trends in the U.S. labor market over the last quarter-century. In particular, we focus on explaining four critical and interrelated trends in employment and wages. Along the way, we cover considerable territory and, therefore, it is useful to provide a perspective by briefly restating our entire argument. We must then try to answer several broad and important questions: Will joblessness, particularly among prime-age males, continue to rise? Will other labor market trends of the past quarter-century continue into the future? And what measures are available to the government to ameliorate some of the adverse effects of the trends we document?

A Summary of the Analysis

The framework for our labor market analysis is a model of four distinct labor markets defined by occupation. The tier 4 labor market consists of the market for all the jobs in occupations with the highest levels of education intensity. The tier 1 labor market consists of the market for all the jobs in occupations with the lowest levels of education intensity. The tier 3 and tier 2 labor markets fall in between.

Within each labor market, we assume that supply and demand determine employment and wages, subject to a considerable degree of wage stickiness. This wage stickiness is generated by various "efficiency wage" type situations in which individual firms decide that the advantages of lowering wages (for instance, lower salary costs) are outweighed by the disadvantages (for instance, lower morale, higher turnover, more shirking).

In this type of framework, excess supply in the tier 4 labor market is not quickly eliminated by falling wages. Instead some people with the education and the aspiration to obtain a tier 4 job are unable to do so. As a result, they are forced to look for a job in a lower tier occupation. As they do so, this creates excess supply in the lower tier markets which is only partly eliminated

216

by wage declines. At the end of the process, some potential workers are left jobless. In the long-run, perhaps, wages may decrease enough to absorb this excess supply, or labor demand may increase, or labor supply may decrease. However, in the short-run, some individuals are displaced completely from the labor market while others are displaced into labor market tiers lower than the one matching their educational levels and aspirations.

Table 9.1 summarizes the major strands of our empirical argument. Among men, employment rates have fallen over the past quarter-century, especially among those with less education. Employment rates for women have risen, but least among those with less education. Although the number of jobs requiring more education has risen considerably faster than the number with lower educational requirements, the number of educated workers has risen even faster. Moreover, women have filled a disproportionate number of these jobs. These two circumstances have initiated a chain reaction of job displacements. More specifically, university-educated women have replaced men with a similar education, but with lower cognitive abilities than others with the same education. Those displaced have taken jobs previously held by workers with less education who, in turn, have displaced those with even lower cognitive skills. Many of the least-educated workers have been knocked completely out of the labor force.

Although the number of jobs that can be fulfilled by those with just a high-school education or less is increasing faster than the number of prime-age workers with the corresponding educational credentials, real wages in these jobs have stagnated or fallen. In other words, excess demand for workers in the lower tier labor markets seems to result in a decrease in wages. This is due to the fact that the pool of workers competing for such jobs has been augmented by those with more than the requisite education who are displaced from jobs commensurate with their education, the same mechanism that has led to a rise in joblessness among the less-educated. In addition, the greater dispersion in education levels among those working in low-level jobs has increased wage inequality within most of these occupations.

Although the jobs that can be fulfilled only by those with a university education have increased more slowly than the number of prime-age workers with the requisite educational credentials, average real wages in these jobs have risen. In other words, a situation with excess supply of workers in the highest tier labor market seems to result in an increase in average wages. This is due to a technology – and institution – driven segregation of the tier 4 labor market into two sectors which we might call tiers 4-A and 4-B.

Tier 4-A consists of most professionals in the health care and legal service industries, as well as workers with particularly high cognitive skills in some of the other education-intensive occupations. Increased demand for health and

Table 9.1: *A Summary of the Major Arguments Made in This Book*

Observable changes in the U.S. economy over the last quarter-century
1.   Increased joblessness of poorly educated prime-age males (Chapter 1)
2.   Downward occupational mobility, e.g., increased number of college graduates taking "high-school" jobs (Chapter 2)
3.   Increased rate of return to a college education (Chapter 5)
4.   Increased wage inequality throughout the labor market (Chapter 6)

Exogenous causes of these changes
 1. *Causal factors of primary importance:*
   A. Increased labor force participation rate of women with at least a high-school diploma (Chapters 1, 4)
   B. Skill-biased technological change: Increased demand for workers in tier 4 occupations who also have high cognitive skills (Chapter 5)
   C. Increased average level of education of the population (Chapters 2, 3)

 2. *Causal factors of secondary importance:*
   A. Expansion of demand for professionals in health care and legal occupations (Chapter 6)
   B. Increased winner-take-all wage setting in tier 4 occupations (Chapter 6)
   C. Lower real minimum wage (not discussed in detail)
   D. Decreased union participation and bargaining power (not discussed in detail)
   E. Pool of high-school dropouts has increasingly lower average abilities as more able members obtain more education (not discussed in detail)

 3. *Causal factors of little importance*
   A. General technical change
      i. Especially in low-skilled occupation (Chapters 3, 7)
      ii. As a cause of turbulence in the labor market (Chapter 7)
   B. Changes in the structure of production and productivity (Chapter 7)
   C. Increased imports, especially from developing nations (Chapter 7)
   D. Increased immigration, especially with low levels of education (Chapter 7)
   E. Increased geographical mismatch between jobs (in suburbs) and workers (in cities) (Chapter 7)
   F. Subjective factors (Chapter 8)

legal services, plus the peculiar instituions of these sectors, have increased the demand for well-educated workers in these industries. In many other industries skill-biased tehcnical change has increased the demand for workers with high cognitive skills and a university degree faster than the supply. Average real wages in tier 4-A have increased considerably over the last quarter-century.

Tier 4-B consists of university graduates with average or below-average cognitive skills who are not in the health care or legal services industries. Given the large-scale entry of women with a university degree into the workforce, this group has seen their wages stagnate or decrease slightly. Wage stickiness prevents these wages from decreasing dramatically, but also it ensures that some of these workers are unable to obtain any job in the tier 4 labor market. These workers either opt for a lower-paying job in the tier 3 or tier 2 labor markets or they leave the labor force completely.

Average wages for all college graduates increase only because occupational tier 4-A has experienced such large wage increases. Median wages for all prime-age men with a university degree have actually decreased (see Table 5.1). This segregation of the tier 4 labor market into two sectors also helps to explain the relatively large increase in wage inequality across workers with a university degree.

While providing the evidence for these propositions, we also show that other explanations for the changing employment rates do not play a major role. More specifically, the falling employment rates of the less-educated cannot be tied in a major way to general technological change, increased turbulence in the labor market, the increasing importance of imports, rising numbers of immigrants, or increasing geographical mismatch between jobs and workers.

Two last questions remain: First, are the changes in the labor market that we have analyzed going to continue? The most pessimistic answers are offered by those economists who have raised the possibility of a new stagnation of employment and production in advanced capitalist societies. We need to explore, however, whether the causal forces influencing the labor market in the last quarter-century will remain as important. Second, if the current employment and wage trends continue, what general policy options are open to alleviate some of the major problems?

Is Rising Joblessness Inevitable in the U.S.A.?

The stagnation hypothesis – that advanced capitalist economies must inevitably experience long-term unemployment – is making a comeback in recent years.[1] This time around, however, the justification of the stagnation hypothesis lies not just in a deficiency of aggregate demand or automation that displaces workers but in structural changes in the economy. For reasons outlined below, we remain unpersuaded by these claims. Nevertheless, it is important to look briefly at these arguments.

Economists have advanced many different reasons why unemployment or joblessness might occur. Stagnationists argue that some of these reasons are becoming more important over time. The traditional stagnation argument generally starts from demand side considerations: As our wants allegedly become satisfied with rising per capita income, aggregate demand will not rise as fast as our production potential, and the unemployment rate rises. Given the fact

---

1 An extreme form of the argument is by Rifkin (1995).

that consumption is rising faster than income, this argument appears to have been abandoned. Thus, stagnationists have focused attention instead on certain supply side factors and policy considerations, particularly those related to the impact of increasing world economic integration ("globalization") and the effects of automation.

According to John Eatwell (1996-b), for instance, the post-Bretton Woods trading and payments system has been unable "to deal with international trading imbalances other than by deflation and growing unemployment in weaker countries – a deflationary impulse that has proved contagious." This is exacerbated by the deregulation of global markets and the huge increase in short-term capital flows, driven especially by currency speculation. The economic consequences include wild currency rate fluctuations and much greater exchange rate risks to domestic producers and traders. Among other things such risks discourage investment, which in turn limits the growth of employment.

To reduce these risks, government policy-makers must place greater emphasis on the maintenance of market credibility, especially those associated with deflationary policies. In short, central banks have increasingly elevated financial stability over employment as policy priorities.

Alice Amsden (1996) raises other considerations associated with globalization. With the fall of barriers to international trade, the ratio of imports to total domestic production has been rising in most nations. As a result, governments are less capable of using fiscal policy to reduce unemployment because a larger share of any domestic fiscal stimulus leaks into the international economy, rather than raising employment at home. This is exacerbated by the convergence of technological capabilities throughout the world, signifying the loss of U.S. technological hegemony. Among other things this updating of Raymond Vernon's argument about the product cycle means that competing products are being produced in many different countries, so substitution of domestic by foreign products is easier.

She also argues that the increased global competition gives greater incentives for labor-saving process innovations. When the U.S. had technological dominance in the world, such increased productivity led to greater exports and domestic employment. In recent years, however, such downsizing measures are increasingly necessary merely to meet foreign competition and maintain sales in domestic markets, resulting in no additional employment.

Finally, the global technological convergence, abetted by multinational firms, means that the product cycle is shortened and production innovations in one country are rapidly copied in other countries. Such increased competition lowers the rate of return to innovation, which leads to less investment and lower employment increases.

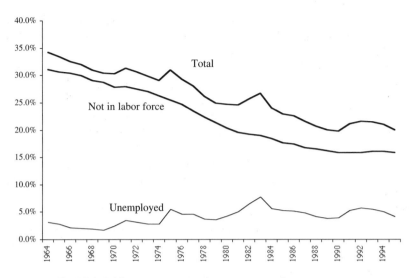

Chart 9.1: Joblessness among prime-age men and women

Although we do not wish to enter these arguments in detail, three general comments are in order. First, the endpoint of globalization is not in sight and U.S. integration into the world economy, at least as measured by the rising rate of imports to the GDP, shows no sign of abatement. Second, it seems indisputable that increasing globalization is placing increasing constraints on the efficacy of monetary and fiscal policy. This is occurring for the same reason that fiscal and monetary policy by state and local governments is seldom an effective way to reduce unemployment.[2] Finally, some risks associated with increasing integration into the world economy, for instance, exchange rate fluctuations, can be insured against through the futures market and other institutions.

The key argument against the stagnationists is empirical. The data in Chart 9.1 show a declining rate of joblessness over the 31-year period from 1964 through 1995. Although the percentage of the unemployed prime-age workers has risen, the percentage of those who are totally out of the workforce has plummeted. This fall is primarily due to the entry of women into the labor

2 For fiscal policy we are speaking of employment effects other than on the first round. Clearly a government can put unemployed workers to work by borrowing and paying them to do something, but the second round effects for a highly open economy such as a city or a region are seldom very significant.

force, which has more than offset the withdrawal of prime-age men. That is, overall labor market absorption has been high, even though the employment situation for particular subgroups such as less- educated prime-age males has deteriorated markedly. We might add that our investigations in Chapter 7 also show that not much of the change in the U.S. employment rate can be explained by the nation's increasing involvement in international trade.

To digress briefly from the path of our narrative, we looked fleetingly at the problem of how to measure the "tightness" of the labor market to explore certain facets of the stagnationist arguments. Throughout this book, we have been examining the rate of joblessness, and yet in most discussions the unemployment rate is generally considered the preferred measure of labor market problems. The issue is particularly acute for those trying to estimate the relation between tightness of the labor market and inflation (the Phillips curve). A typical equation relates price increases (for instance, of the GDP deflator) to some measure of price expectations (such as last year's increase in the GDP deflator), some measure of price increases coming from the outside world (such as the increase in crude material prices), and some measure of labor market tightness such as the unemployment rate for the economy as a whole.

This standard approach does not, however, explain the simultaneous decrease in unemployment and inflation that occurred in the mid 1990s. If we instead use the jobless rate among prime-age males as a measure of labor market tightness, the calculation yields a much better statistical fit. This is because the jobless rate decreased only slightly during the 1990s, so that according to this measure the labor market tightness did not markedly increase.[3]

Will Employment and Wage Trends of the Last Quarter-Century Continue in the Future?

This brief exploration of the stagnation hypothesis leads us to a more important question, namely whether the trends we have chronicled in the last 25 years are bound to continue. We approach this issue by asking a more tractable question: Does the period from 1970 through 1995 exhibit sufficiently unique features that they cannot be expected to recur in the future? Table 9.1 suggests that the three primary sources of these trends are the

---

3 More specifically, for the period 1987 through 1997 the coefficient of determination when using the unemployment rate measure is .7854 and is .8931 when using the jobless rate for prime- age males. For the period 1980 through 1997, the jobless rate still provides a superior fit, although the difference is much less. The coefficients of determination are respectively .9496 and .9599. The data for this calculation come from the national income and product accounts, the producer price index of the Bureau of Labor Statistics, and our calculations

increased labor force participation of women, a particular type of technological change, and the increased average level of education. We will briefly examine each of these.

Increased Labor Force Participation of Women

The increased labor force participation of women over the last quarter-century has led to a labor absorption problem: the large increases in labor demand have not kept up with the even larger increases in labor supply. Will this continue? To answer this it is useful to examine certain key indicators for the entire period from 1950 to the present to show that the problem of labor absorption during this period was particularly acute.

From the data presented in Table 9.2, we can draw two quick conclusions. First, the decade of the 1970s featured the fastest growth in population of potential workers. This is, of course, the result of the baby-boom generation reaching the legal minimum age for employment, and indicates a serious problem of labor force absorption. The prime working-age population reached its peak growth in the decade of the 1980s. Second, the faster growth of the employed labor force indicates a rising labor force participation ratio. This, of course, is the result of the rapid influx of women into the labor force, and it exacerbates the labor-force-absorption problem.

In certain respects these conditions are not likely to be repeated in the foreseeable future. In the quarter-century from 1995 to 2020, the U.S. Census Bureau (1996) projects that the population (middle series) from 16 through 64 will grow at average annual rates of 0.7 percent, an estimate that includes the "baby-boom echo." This, of course, is significantly lower than the average annual rate of 1.4 percent that this population grew between 1970 and 1995, fueled primarily by the post-World War II baby boom.

Furthermore, the rapid increase in the employment rate of women is unlikely to be repeated. As shown in Table 9-2, the growth of average employment rates of women in the prime working-ages began to decelerate in 1980-84, when it rose 7.3 percentage points over the previous five years. By the first half of the 1990s, the prime-age female employment rate increased only 2.4 percentage points over the previous five years.

Several counteracting factors can be mentioned. Women have increasingly more education which is associated with higher levels of labor force participation. Moreover, as long as the average wages of women are less than those of men, employers have an economic incentive to substitute female for male employees. These, however, do not seem strong enough to offset public opin-

of the jobless rate (only for the month of March) from the Current Population Survey.

Table 9.2: *Indicators of the Growth of Population, Labor, Capital, and Investment*

Indicator	Average annual growth rates				
	1950-1960	1960-1970	1970-1980	1980-1990	1990-1995
Civilian non-institutional population, 16–64	0.8%	1.5%	2.0%	1.1%	0.9%
Employed civilian labor force	1.1	1.9	2.1	2.0	1.0
Gross reproducible tangible wealth	3.3	3.6	3.4	2.9	2.6
Net reproducible tangible wealth	3.8	4.0	3.2	2.6	2.1
	Annual averages				
	1950-1959	1960-1969	1970-1979	1980-1989	1990-1995
Ratio: total gross investment to GDP	23.0%	20.4%	20.7%	20.5%	17.3%
Ratio: total net investment to GDP	14.2	12.4	11.0	9.1	7.0
Share of total investment in government sector	28.9	25.6	17.6	17.3	18.9
Share of total investment by foreigners	-0.6	-3.0	-1.3	8.3	6.8
Federal government deficit as a share of total investment	-0.8	-1.9	9.6	16.2	18.8
	1970-1974	1975-1979	1980-1984	1985-1989	1990-1994
Employment rates: Prime-age males	92.5%	90.0%	87.6%	88.7%	87.2%
Employment rates: Prime-age females	48.7	55.5	62.8	68.8	71.1

Notes: The gross capital stock and investment data include investment in both the private and public sectors.

Sources: The population and labor force data come from Council of Economic Advisors (annual, 1997), Tables B-32 to B-34. The wealth data come from: U.S. Department of Commerce, Bureau of Economic Analysis (monthly, 8/1994), p. 62, supplemented by data for 1994 supplied by the Bureau of Economic Analysis and our own estimates for 1995. The national accounts data come from Council of Economic Advisors (annual, 1997), Tables B-1, B-24, B-30, and B-34, supplemented by U.S. Department of Commerce, Bureau of Economic Analysis (1992, 1993), Tables 1-1, 3-2, and 5-1 plus our own estimate of depreciation of the government capital stock from 1950 through 1959. The data on employment of prime working-age workers come from the CPS.

ion results presented by Wattenberg (1991) indicating that the percentage of all women wanting to stay home has stopped falling. We believe it is likely that the percentage of women in the labor force will grow very slowly, or even level off in the next few years.

Skill-Biased Technical Change

It is much more difficult to predict trends in technological change. We have identified that the two most important implications of recent technological change are a large increased demand for individual workers in high-education occupations who also have high cognitive skills, plus a smaller increased demand for occupations in higher-education tiers. What type of technological change is behind this? We have no specialized data or knowledge in this area, but we do believe that much of the technological change that has affected labor demand can be attributed to the computer/electronic/communications/information systems revolution which began about a quarter-century ago.

Are the major changes caused by this revolution finished? Certainly there are incremental technological improvements occurring in these areas constantly. There also continue to be major changes every few years. The conversion of the command-line driven Internet into the World Wide Web (WWW), filled with millions of graphically intense "home pages" is perhaps the most recent example. In just three or four years, the WWW has dramatically changed the way that many economic transactions are handled, both within and between firms. Although it is hard to envision what the next big change will be, we are unlikely to see an end to such changes in the near future.

One constraining factor on technological growth deserves mention. In so far as new technology is embodied in new capital investment, it is necessary to consider capital accumulation. Table 9.2 shows that over the last quarter-century, capital was rising at a faster rate than labor, so that the capital/labor ratio was increasing. Nevertheless, the rate of increase of this ratio was much slower than in the first two decades of the post-World War II era. In recent years, the growth of the capital stock has declined as the ratio of investment to GDP has fallen. Although part of this was due to a fall in the share of investment carried out by various levels of government, the table shows that a major share was due to a fall in domestic savings. Indeed, the growth of the capital stock would have been even slower if foreigners had not increased their assets in the United States. If the savings rate continues to fall, the importance of the skill-biased technical change may lessen, other factors remaining the same.

Rising Average Education

Finally, what can be said about trends in average levels of education? In Chart 2.1 in Chapter 2 we present some relevant evidence. The fraction of the population completing at least some schooling beyond the high-school diploma has increased over the entire quarter-century. However, the rate of increase has slowed in recent years.

As the costs of most types of post-secondary education (including public) continue to grow much faster than average earnings, this deceleration may continue. On the other hand, our analysis throughout this book strongly supports the notion that obtaining a college degree will increase a person's expected lifetime income considerably more now than 25 years ago. This increases the incentive to acquire more education. It is likely, though, that the budget constraint issue will dominate for most of the population, at least barring massive new governmental subsidies to post-secondary education. This, in turn, will lead to a continued slowdown in the increase in average education, and perhaps a leveling-off of average years of education in the near future.

Summary

So how do we pull these predictions together? The shards of evidence presented above suggest that the displacement of men by women will be less strong in the future as the percentage of women in the labor force levels off. As a result, the impact of their disproportionate employment in jobs requiring more education will not be as great in the coming years as in the period from 1970 through 1995. Also, as the increase in the average level of education slows down, the downward occupational mobility generated by this will also level off. These considerations lead us to give even less credence to the pessimistic employment predictions of the stagnationists, even while we remain gloomy about trends in the distribution of wages.

The one highly unpredictable element is technological change. If it continues in its current direction, the demand for workers with both high education and high cognitive skills will continue to grow, as will wage inequality. If technological change, which is difficult to predict, diverges from its current trend, anything is possible.

Some General Policy Implications

This is not a book on labor market policies. Nevertheless, our arguments have some important implications, mostly negative, about the likely success of a wide range of public policies aimed at reducing the joblessness of less-educated prime-age workers and/or decreasing wage inequality. In this section we briefly describe the likely impact on joblessness, the wage level, and wage inequality of a number of widely discussed policies. For the sake of expositional clarity, we divide these polices into groups according to their focus on workers in low-wage or high-wage jobs (or all jobs) and to their direct impact on the supply or the demand side of the labor market, or on institutions involving both supply and demand.

Policies Targeted at Low-Wage Workers and the Jobless

It is useful to distinguish policies focusing on the supply and demand sides of the labor market with those dealing with overall market functioning.

Supply-side policies: Policies concerned with low-wage jobs and the supply side of the labor market usually focus on increasing human capital or establishing greater incentives for people to choose to work. The human capital policies, in turn, can target persons either before or after they first enter the workforce.

Several programs under discussion focus on improving the human capital of U.S. workers before they enter the workforce, either by increasing their years of formal schooling or by improving the content of their education. For instance, at the primary and secondary levels of education these include proposals to restructure the educational system by using vouchers, or the Murnane-Levy (1997) proposals to increase the effectiveness of education by teaching the "new basic skills." In 1997, at the university level, these proposed policies include plans by both the President and the Congress to give certain tax incentives for university study. The biggest weakness of such programs is the difficulty in improving the quality of education, especially in low-income urban neighborhoods, without improving many other characteristics of life there.

The alternative approach is to target human capital programs at jobless workers who are no longer in school. Unfortunately, the benefit/cost ratios of many such programs designed to improve the education and/or skills of less-educated workers have been low. Indeed, some economists have argued that such a focus on low-skilled workers is not the most effective way of spending scarce educational resources (Heckman, Roselius, and Smith, 1994). Although the Job Training Partnership Act (JTPA) led to modest wage gains for adult women that were higher than the costs of the program, for adult men and for youth, the program did not seem to have any significant impact on the income of the participants (Orr *et al.*, 1995). Economists have also studied the benefits and costs of other job training programs, but their economic payoffs seem modest at best.[4]

This category of labor supply policies also includes proposals to cut back on unemployment insurance benefits, welfare payments, or Medicaid to increase incentives to work (actually, to decrease disincentives to work). These

---

4 Recent studies of the benefit/costs of job training programs include those of : Friedlander and Burtless (1994); Grubb (1996), Heckman, Lochner, Smith and Taber (1997), and Kodrzycki (1997).

are, of course, harsher policies than those enhancing human capital. Discussion of such approaches usually hinge on the question about whether joblessness is voluntary or involuntary.

Policies aimed at changing work incentives also include raising the real value of the minimum wage. This is just a positive incentive version of reducing unemployment insurance benefits, welfare payments, or Medicaid. As such, it also creates an incentive for low-wage workers to choose to work, while also potentially increasing their economic well-being. Of course, the welfare increase only occurs if they can acquire a job at the new higher minimum wage. Unfortunately, an increased minimum wage may cause a reduction in the quantity of labor demanded.

From our viewpoint in this book, the major problem with all of these labor supply policies is that they may not lead to any net increase in employment. Instead, such policies may just lead to new types of displacement as those who are lucky enough to benefit from a human capital enhancing program or unlucky enough to be cut off from a welfare-type program, will be in a better position, and try harder, to take a job away from another relatively low-wage worker. If this happens, net employment will be unchanged. The wage rate paid may increase because the new worker is more productive than the old worker, or decrease, because the number of persons competing for the job is greater. Thus, wage inequality can either narrow or widen.

This problem of displacement is a serious one. The employment equations (Table 2.4) suggest that those obtaining additional education will increase their probability of employment. For instance, a GED does increase employment rates. We need to take into account, however, the fallacy of composition: what is true for a single individual may not necessary be true for an entire group which, in this case, is the entire cohort of those with the same education. For instance, if education among the less-educated is upgraded, without changing the number of jobs available, only the educational mix of the unemployed will change. In addition, those who still have not obtained higher educational credentials may end up with highter rates of joblessness.

We do not mean to imply that such education policies should be abandoned, because such policies achieve other social goals. In particular, decreasing the number of less-educated workers and increasing the number of more-educated workers can have one useful long-run outcome. It would result in a reduction in the relative price (or wage) of more-educated workers and therefore encourage producers to adopt more advanced methods to take advantage of the lower cost of such skilled workers. This, in turn, would help in the long-run to maintain the nation's position as a technological leader. But such policies would not, in and of themselves, create new jobs in the short-term.

Demand-side policies: Policies targeting less-educated, low-wage workers and the jobless from the demand side include wage or employment subsidies that reduce the hourly costs to employers of hiring less-educated workers. These might lead to an increase in the employment of the least-educated, and, although a small amount of displacement might occur, it would certainly be less than with policies enhancing human capital. This would not necessarily lead to a change in wage inequality, but it would lead to a decrease in income inequality as more of the less-educated are employed.

On the negative side, such subsidized workers could be stigmatized, increasing the reluctance of employers to hire them. Results of experiments of certain wage-subsidy programs have been mixed, although not all parameters of such policies have been thoroughly explored. Recently, Edmund Phelps (1997) has made a strong case for employment subsidies, arguing that besides the obvious direct benefits to recipients, the indirect positive benefits greatly outweigh the indirect negative impacts.

Market-functioning policies: Market functioning policies facilitate the matching of less-educated workers to jobs by either direct or indirect methods. The former include programs that are specifically aimed at helping individual low-income persons find employment. In this regard it is important to note that programs to help workers find jobs have had a higher payoff to the individuals involved than the job training programs. Unfortunately, Uchitell (1997) shows that helping welfare recipients obtain jobs often means that the working poor who hold these jobs find themselves unemployed. Thus, federal mandates for job creation for one group of the less-educated workers can take away employment from another group - the displacement problem again.

A similar conclusion would apply to any attempts to reduce the amount of "credentialism" in the hiring process. For instance, some have argued that weakening anti-discrimination laws would make employers more willing to test workers for both hard and soft skills without having to worry as much about lawsuits claiming that the tests have little to do with the direct requirements of particular jobs. Such a measure might alter the mix of workers that a typical firm hires. Those with the least education would certainly have a better chance of being offered a job if "credentials" were not the primary hiring determinant. Nevertheless, such a change would not necessarily lead to an increase in the total number of jobs available.

Additional indirect programs matching less-educated workers to positions requiring few skills include those requiring employers to list all job openings at a central employment registry. By consolidating the dissemination of information about job openings, both information costs to job seekers and unfilled job-openings would be reduced.[5] Improved public transportation would also help central city dwellers reach jobs in the suburbs.

5 Of course, it is possible that greater employment of the less-educated could come at the

Policies Targeted at Medium- or High-Wage Workers

The policies discussed so far are all aimed at the jobless and those in low-wage jobs. Yet our analysis suggests that the cause of their employment problems lie in a different part of the labor market. Are there any policies which deal more directly with the source of the problem? We again divide these policies according to the same criteria as used above.

Supply-side policies: One intriguing supply-side policy has received considerable discussion in Europe, namely work sharing and/or work spreading. For instance, in some of the middle and high-wage occupations, each worker could work fewer hours per week (at approximately the same hourly wage rate) and more total workers could be hired. Within our model, this would lead to less downward occupational mobility and would alleviate some of the excess labor supply in the low-wage jobs. This would decrease joblessness among the less-educated and also raise wages. It would probably result in a decrease in wage inequality as the lowest wages move a little closer to the middle of the overall wage distribution.

Such policies would, of course, have an impact on average weekly working hours which slowly declined in the U.S. until 1990, when they began to level off (Bureau of the Census, annual, 1995, Table 666). Certainly, measures could be taken to encourage enterprises to begin cutting back further on the hours worked by existing workers, and to begin hiring new workers as substitutes.

These policies have two major difficulties. Unfortunately, many kinds of work require high fixed costs for new workers – recruiting, training, benefits, and logistics – so that this solution is often costly. Moreover, policies leading to the reduction of work hours means lower weekly earnings and many families may not willingly accept such a situation.

An alternative supply-side approach would be to increase the cognitive skills of many of the low- and middle-level college graduates. They could then take advantage of the excess demand for these skills, receive a high wage, reduce downward occupational mobility, and alleviate some of the excess labor supply in the low-wage occupations. Unfortunately, there are no widely-accepted ideas as to how to accomplish this proposal.

Demand-side polices: Demand-side policies targeting medium- and high-wage jobs have received little discussion and it is difficult to think of any that would be politically feasible. Given this consideration, it is ironic that our analysis suggests that the most direct way to remedy the increased joblessness

expense of more-educated workers, who are now holding these jobs and who could be more readily replaced. In this case, such a program might also lead to a reduction in wages in these low-skill jobs because of the increased competition. Of course, replacement might not occur if employers preferred to hire workers with more educational credentials than those necessary for the job.

and lower wages among less-educated persons is to increase the demand for college graduates with average or below-average cognitive skills. The most obvious way to do this is through wage or employment subsidies to firms that hire such college graduates. This would keep average and below-average college graduates from competing for jobs in tier 3 and tier 2 occupations and thus prevent the displacement mechanism from occurring. Of course this would require a method for distinguishing which types of jobs and/or college graduates would be eligible for the subsidy – a very difficult task. However, the biggest obstacle to this type of program would be the perception that the people with the most education – and therefore the best chance of economic success – are receiving a subsidy which less-educated persons are not.

A slightly more realistic demand-side policy – which would help reduce wage inequality but not joblessness – would be salary caps. In the U.S., the only well-known examples of such salary caps are for various types of government workers but, of course, they could also be imposed on private sector firms in the same way as the minimum wage mandate. Much recent public discussion has focused on the possibility of imposing salary caps on CEOs - perhaps defined as some fixed multiple of the average non-executive wage within their company. There have been some grass-root attempts by workers and shareholders to get CEOs to accept a "voluntary" salary cap as evidence of commitment to everyone involved with the firm. It should not be surprising, however, that no prominent CEOs have accepted such an agreement.

Market-functioning policies: Market functioning policies focusing on the labor market for medium- and high-wage jobs in order to decrease joblessness or reduce wage inequality have received little public attention. While it is doubtful that any feasible policy could reduce joblessness at this level, wage inequality can be accomplished with progressive income, earnings, or consumption taxes. In the U.S. we currently have a progressive income tax, although it is less progressive today than at any time since the 1950s. This is the most direct type of policy to reduce wage inequality, but it does nothing to improve the problems of joblessness and low-wages among less-educated workers.

Policies Targeted at the Entire Labor Force

A more direct solution to the problems of joblessness and wage inequality lies with economy-wide programs to accelerate the job creation process, regardless of educational credentials required in these new job openings. Since the absorption problem of less-educated workers will be less acute in the coming quarter-century than in the last 25 years, problems of job creation by public policy are more tractable than in the recent past. We must note, of course, that job creation in the U.S. over the period under examination has been higher than almost any industrialized country in the world, an achievement driven partly by a faster growth of the labor force. But U.S. labor force participation rates have also been among the highest in the OECD.[6] Nevertheless, the rising jobless rates among less-educated males in the U.S. suggests that even more should be done.

Such job creation policies are easier to prescribe on a general level than to design the particulars. In the short-run, such policies could involve some combination of expansionary fiscal and monetary policies. In the long-run, such policies could focus on increasing savings and investment so that the capital stock grows. The latter would typically lead to some increase in the demand for labor (capital widening). In some cases an increasing capital stock could just increase the productivity of existing workers (capital deepening) and lead to higher wages but no increase in employment.

A major difficulty with such policies is that the short-run requirements often conflict with the long-run requirements, and the long-run requirements are difficult to implement. If strongly expansionary fiscal policies are combined with moderately restrictive monetary polices, as was done through much of the 1980s, this leads to short-term job creation plus high interest rates. However, the high interest rates discourage investment which is necessary for the long-run goal of increasing the capital stock. Thus, an alternative short-run strategy might involve strongly expansionary monetary policy with mildly contractionary fiscal policy. With this combination, the private savings formerly used to finance the government deficit would be diverted to the private sector. Interest rates would fall initially, which would encourage more investment. The obvious problem is that such policies, unless carefully administered, might unleash inflationary forces which, in turn, would eventually result in increased interest rates and reduced investment.

What if we ignore short-run job creation and focus strictly on long-run results? Unfortunately, we are not sure how to increase savings and investment in the long-run. Considerable debate currently centers around the issue of whether the savings incentives offered by the U.S. government (such as IRAs or 401(k) plans) have actually led to an increase in savings. We believe that they probably haven't been very effective, as evidenced by the general decline in the personal savings rate in the last several decades. The appropriate data on the issue, however, are fiendishly difficult to interpret.[7]

---

6   OECD (1996), p 196. Of the 24 nations with labor force participation data from 1973 through 1995, the increase in the U.S. was fourth highest. Only Iceland, Netherlands, and New Zealand were higher.

7   A useful summary of the current state of the debate is found in the exchange between Hubbard and Skinner (1996), Poterba, Venti, and Wise (1996), and Engen, Gale, and Scholz (1996).

Although additional saving might result in lower interest rates, a related question is whether this would lead, in turn, to more domestic investment, instead of flowing abroad. Some such as Bayoumi (1990) argue that although governmental policy may influence savings and investment at a single point in time, savings and investment are correlated over time primarily because of disturbances to the economy as a whole. This means that attempts to increase domestic investment financed by domestic savings have little long-term impact

Of course, it is also possible that direct job creation policies, for instance, investment incentive programs such as reduction of the capital gains tax on new investment or, for that matter, tax incentives tied directly to job creation, might be more effective than saving incentives. But enormous controversy exists over the cost effectiveness of such measures that have been tried in the past. Still on the micro-level, a restructuring of capital markets to increase the quality of information available to potential lenders might reduce their lending risks and increase aggregate investment. Unfortunately, specification of the most effective investment incentive program to encourage job creation would take us light years away from the major theme of this book and, therefore, must be left for others.

One simple policy truth must be stressed. Simply increasing the demand for workers by the creation of new jobs would not be enough. Such policies would also have to be combined with other programs to match workers with jobs. In addition, effective methods of determining the actual skills of individual workers so that employers would not need to rely on formal educational credentials alone, would have to be combined with changes in labor market institutions so that better information about available jobs is available.

Final Words

Our analysis also has one last important policy message. Until the problems of obtaining more employment for less-educated men and reducing wage inequality are viewed in terms of the entire labor market, the key parameters for policy success remain hidden. Of course, the unprecedented boom in the last decade of the century did lead to a fall in unemployment and narrowing of wage differentials in the late 1990s. Nevertheless, by the beginning of the new millennium the jobless rate was still at a very high level and the level of wage inequality was much higher than a quarter of a century before. Although macro-economic success can reduce the magnitude of these problems, the basic labor market difficulties still remain.

These problems must be viewed broadly in order to judge the real impact of programs designed to help a particular segment of the labor force. It is our hope that this study provides such a perspective to the joblessness and low-wage problems that have had a devastating effect on so many lives.

Appendix Notes

Chapter 1

Note 1.1: The Current Population Survey Data

The basic data for this book come from the Current Population Survey (CPS) for March of each year. We obtained 32 years of March CPS data (March 1964 through March 1995) from the Inter-University Consortium for Political and Social Research (ICPSR). In describing these annual data we borrow freely from descriptions published in ICPSR (1996).

The CPS is a household sample survey conducted monthly by the Census Bureau to provide estimates of the population as a whole and of various subgroups in the population. In addition to demographic characteristics such as age, sex, race, marital status, and household relationships, the CPS also provides data on employment status, occupation, and industry of persons 14 years of age and older. Data on labor force activity are provided for the week prior to the survey. The universe for the surveys is the civilian noninstitutionalized population of the United States living in households, from which a national probability sample of about 120,000 persons is selected.

The March survey, often called the Annual Demographic Survey, includes all of the usual monthly labor force data, plus detailed supplementary data on every adult's work experiences during the previous calendar year. The annual data include weeks worked, usual hours worked per week, and total earnings of each individual.

The data available for the earlier years are much sparser than for recent years. The samples are smaller – usually about 60,000 persons. The number of questions asked is also much smaller – perhaps only one-third as many as in recent years. Many of the quantity variables in these earlier surveys are "coded" into categories, rather than listed directly. For example, in the first 12 years of this series, the information for "usual work hours worked per week last year" is not listed as a number of hours from 0 to 88, as in the newer surveys, but a data code of 0, 1, or 2, indicating whether the person typically worked 0 hours, 1 to 34 hours, or more than 35 hours per week last year.

Some problems about the consistency over time also arise. The most infamous example, which we work very hard to circumvent (see Appendix 3.1), is the significant change in the classification system for occupations introduced between the March 1982 and the March 1983 surveys. This change has limited much economic analysis of the last quarter-century by making it difficult to compare economic data by occupations before and after this 1982–83 change. Fortunately, we gained access to computer programs written at the Census Bureau which allow us to impute for each individual in any of the older samples their likely occupation classification in the newer system, given their classification in the older system as well as such characteristics as their gender, race, age, education level, class of job, industry of job, average hours worked per week, average weeks worked per year, and earnings.

Note 1.2: Unemployment and Labor Force Non-Participation of the Prime-Age Population

Table A1.1 presents unemployment rates of the prime-age population (as a percent of the cohort) for different levels of education. Generally speaking, the table reveals the expected inverse

234

Table A1.1: *Unemployment of the Prime Working-Age Population as a Percent of the Total Cohort*

Highest level of education	White males	Black males	Other males	White females	Black females	Other females	Total
March 1964							
High-school dropout	5.6%	9.3%	*	2.8%	5.2%	*	4.6%
High-school diploma	2.8	10.7	*	2.0	5.3	*	2.6
Some university	2.1	*	*	1.4	6.6	*	2.0
University degree	1.0	*	*	1.0	*	*	1.0
Total	3.5	9.1	1.7	2.1	5.1	*	3.2 (4.6)
March 1971							
High-school dropout	5.9	6.3	11.8	3.7	5.5	7.3	5.0%
High-school diploma	3.5	4.4	*	2.5	4.4	1.3	3.0
Some university	3.4	3.2	*	2.4	1.3	*	2.9
University degree	1.8	*	*	1.6	4.5	3.9	1.8
Total	3.9	5.1	6.0	2.7	4.7	3.7	3.4 (4.8)
March 1979							
High-school dropout	6.2	8.0	6.1	4.4	7.0	2.1	5.6
High-school diploma	3.7	8.9	3.2	3.1	6.0	4.5	3.0
Some university	3.0	7.1	*	2.2	5.2	5.3	2.9
University degree	1.5	4.9	4.0	2.1	3.5	1.2	1.8
Total	3.4	7.9	3.4	3.0	6.0	3.1	3.4 (4.6)

Table A1.1 *(cont.)*

March 1990							
High-school dropout	8.0	14.3	6.7	4.9	10.4	5.8	7.5
High-school diploma	4.7	7.9	4.5	3.2	7.0	5.5	4.4
Some university	3.4	7.4	6.0	2.7	4.8	2.5	3.4
University degree	2.0	1.9	2.9	1.4	2.1	2.2	1.8
Total	4.1	8.2	4.4	2.9	6.5	3.9	3.9
							(4.7)
March 1994							
High-school dropout	10.4	12.1	11.9	6.4	10.8	7.2	9.0
High-school diploma	6.3	10.6	7.7	4.0	9.9	7.1	6.0
Some university	4.5	8.1	7.0	3.4	6.4	4.3	4.4
University degree	2.5	3.8	2.9	2.1	5.1	3.7	2.6
Total	5.2	9.1	8.4	3.6	8.3	5.3	5.0
							(6.0)

Notes: University degrees include advanced degrees as well. "Other" includes native American and Asians. The sample sizes of the some of the cells are too small to reflect accurately the true situation and, therefore, these are marked with an asterisk. In parentheses are the unemployment rates conventionally defined (with economically active as the denominator). The data come from the Current Population Survey discussed in Appendix 1.1.

relations between level of education and unemployment, measured as percent of the total cohort at a single point in time. The same results hold when the unemployment rate is measured more conventionally as a percentage of the economically active.

Over time, however, unemployment rates rose more in an absolute sense for the less-educated than for the more-educated. For instance, between 1971 and 1990 the unemployment rate of high-school drop-outs rose from 5.0 to 7.5 percent, while for those with only a high-school education, it rose from 3.0 to 4.4 percent. At the same time, the unemployment rate of those with at least one college degree remained roughly the same and only increased slightly for those with some higher education.

Roughly the same pattern is observable for men and women of each race separately. In comparing white and black men or white and black women, however, it is readily apparent that the relative changes in unemployment at low levels of education had a greater impact on blacks than whites. The relatively level rate of unemployment for the entire labor force from the mid 1970s through 1994 seems to be the result of two offsetting effects: the decline in the share of the less-educated population and their rising level of unemployment. Whether this level overall long-term unemployment rate will continue in the future can be decided by a simple simulation model that takes into account these factors, an exercise carried out below.

Data on non-participation in the labor force are presented in Table A1.2. Among the prime working-age population, such non-participation can come about for several reasons: job seekers can drop out of the labor force for personal reasons such as their attitudes toward work or the desire to devote more time to their families; the job search may prove too discouraging to continue; or the job seeker may be in poor health and unable to work. The latter reason does not appear of major importance for those in the prime working-ages. The time-series behavior is, however, quite different since the percentage of non-participants increased dramatically for men, while it decreased for women, particularly whites. Moreover, there was a remarkable convergence in non-participation rates of white and black women. For men, however, the story appears more complicated since the percentage point difference remained roughly the same, while the differences were widening among poorly-educated men and narrowing among men with more education.

The percentage of male non-participants in the labor force falls over time and generally falls as the level of education rises. The remarkable entry of white women, particularly those with relatively more education, completely masks what is happening among men when the data are grouped.

Note 1.3: Determinants of Employment in 1971 and 1994

To get a better picture of the effect of education on employment, while holding other factors constant, we use the data on individuals from the March 1971 and March 1994 CPS to calculate some logit regressions. These allow us to determine the probabilities of employment for men and women with different educational credentials while holding other factors constant, so that these probabilities differ somewhat from actual employment rates. The logit technique is necessary because the variable to be explained (employment/non-employment) is a dummy variable with only two values (employment = 1; non-employment = 0).

The exercise we carry out is simple, starting with separate logit regressions for men and women in the two years so that we end with four different sets of results. We use 60 explanatory variables, all but one of which are dummy variables with values of 0 or 1. These include four education levels (3 dummy variables), five age groups (4 dummy variables), three veteran status groups (2 dummy variables), nine regions (8 dummy variables), three urbanization groups (2 dummy variables), 21 metropolitan location groups (20 dummy variables), six mobility status groups (5 dummy variables), three marital status groups (2 dummy variables), three number of adults in family groups (2 dummy variables), and four variables designating the number of chil-

Table A1.2: Non-Participation in the Labor Force of the Prime Working-Age Population as a Percent of the Total Cohort

Highest level of education	White males	Black males	Other males	White females	Black females	Other females	Total
March 1964							
High-school dropout	3.9%	5.4%	4.9%	60.6%	49.1%	71.7%	31.6%
High-school diploma	1.5	2.8	*	58.3	40.4	49.4	34.2
Some university	2.6	*	*	59.4	36.8	36.2	30.3
University degree	2.5	*	*	46.5	19.3	36.8	18.1
Total	2.7	4.2	5.1	58.3	44.6	55.8	31.0
March 1971							
High-school dropout	6.0	10.7	7.7	56.8	46.6	59.8	31.7
High-school diploma	2.2	6.0	*	50.8	32.0	48.5	29.4
Some university	4.0	7.2	*	50.0	28.9	34.9	25.9
University degree	2.4	8.8	8.4	41.0	10.4	31.5	16.4
Total	3.6	8.9	6.3	51.4	38.3	46.9	31.3
March 1979							
High-school dropout	8.5	17.7	14.0	51.7	45.3	57.8	31.7
High-school diploma	3.1	6.4	8.2	37.1	28.6	37.2	22.3
Some university	4.1	6.1	8.7	34.4	19.8	24.5	18.3
University diploma	2.8	5.0	8.7	25.5	11.8	27.1	11.9
Total	4.2	10.1	9.4	37.4	31.5	37.1	21.3

March 1990							
High-school dropout	13.1	25.3	22.1	45.2	50.8	59.1	30.8
High-school diploma	4.8	10.2	11.9	25.7	23.8	32.4	16.4
Some university	4.7	6.1	7.5	21.2	15.7	28.2	13.2
University degree	2.6	6.2	6.3	16.9	5.0	19.8	9.2
Total	5.3	11.7	10.2	24.9	24.8	32.0	19.8
March 1994							
High-school dropout	15.9	32.8	20.7	47.4	54.9	52.6	33.4
High-school diploma	6.9	15.4	9.3	24.7	28.0	28.6	17.1
Some university	5.0	9.6	11.8	20.8	16.8	29.3	13.7
University degree	2.9	5.7	8.3	14.9	6.7	23.3	8.9
Total	6.3	15.3	11.3	23.5	25.6	31.1	21.0

Notes: The non-participants in the labor force include those not looking for work (who are classified as unemployed) and not employed. The data come from the Current Population Survey discussed Appendix 1.1.

dren in family groups (3 dummy variables). Our one continuous variable is "other family income." We omit the probabilities calculated for some of these variables since they have little relevance for our discussion.

The results suggest that the location variables had a small impact on the probabilities of employment, other factors held constant. For both men and women, for instance, the coefficients for the variables indicating different parts of the metropolitan areas were not greatly different. The changes in the relative employment probabilities over the period were also not greatly different in the various parts of the metropolitan area. Of course, it is possible that unemployment probabilities in different areas within the central city, for instance, poor ghetto areas, did change dramatically over the period. Unfortunately, the CPS data are not sufficiently sensitive to such geographical subtleties to catch such differences. On the other hand the CPS does catch regional differences, but employment probabilities show no major differences between 1971 and 1994.

Family structure variables have some impact among men. In particular, married men are eight or nine percentage points more likely to be employed than those who are single. However, the number of children has little effect on these employment probabilities. For women, on the other hand, the differences are more complex. More specifically, in 1971 never-married women had considerably higher employment probabilities than married women, other things remaining the same. By 1994, however, these employment probabilities were the same. Thus it was the entry of married women into the labor force that provides the key to understanding the changes in female employment over the period. In both years women with no children living in the family had the highest probability of employment. Nevertheless, the differences narrowed between the two years.

Although this change in family structure has been extremely important for understanding the increased employment of women, in this study we will not explore the matter further. Clearly this trend is, in part, a result of exogenous forces such as changing attitudes of women toward work outside the home. But it is also, in part, a result of endogenous forces, for instance, a decline in their husband's earnings that paralleled the falling real income of less-educated males or the rising cost of a college education for their children.

The race variable also appears important. For men, employment probabilities were lower for blacks than for whites. Moreover, they fell more for the former than the latter so that the employment gap between the two races widened. In the various statistical experiments we found that these factors are particularly important among the less-educated. Among women, African Americans had the highest employment probabilities in 1971. Employment probabilities for white women rose considerably more than for black women so that by 1994 white women had slightly higher employment probabilities. As with men, these trends were exacerbated by what was happening among the less-educated.

Chapter 2

Note 2.1: The Data from the National Adult Literacy Study

We obtained the data disks containing the raw data for the National Adult Literacy Study (NALS) from the Department of Education, National Center for Education Statistics and, recently, they were placed on the Web. These data are relatively self-explanatory and need few additional comments.

For the raw scores on the examinations, we used "plausible value #1" and screened out those scores estimated from tests that were not completed. We also removed military personnel and all those without a specified occupation. In addition, we screened out all those whose sex, age, education, employment status, and other demographic characteristics were not specified. Finally, we excluded all those under 25 and over 49 so as to focus only on those in the prime working-ages.

Table A1.3: *Estimated Employment Probabilities of the Prime-Age Population, 1971 and 1994*

	Men			Women		
	1971	1994	Difference	1971	1994	Difference
Education variables:						
High-school dropouts	89.2%	73.6%	-15.6%	38.2%	47.3%	+9.1%
High-school diploma	95.2	86.7	-8.5	49.5	70.8	+21.3
Some university education	94.4	90.7	-3.7	51.4	76.8	+25.4
University degree	97.2	94.9	-2.2	59.8	83.8	+24.1
Race variables:						
White	94.4	90.6	-3.8	46.1	74.6	+28.5
Black	92.3	82.7	-9.5	56.2	71.8	+15.6
Other	93.0	85.8	-7.2	48.1	68.8	+20.8
Age variables:						
25–29 years	93.5	90.9	-2.6	39.8	71.0	+31.2
30–34 years	94.5	90.0	-4.4	46.7	73.3	+26.5
35–39 years	94.7	89.6	-5.0	52.7	75.1	+22.4
40–44 years	94.7	88.8	-5.9	51.2	77.1	+25.9
45–49 years	93.7	88.9	-4.8	47.6	72.9	+25.3
Location variables: Residence in metropolitan areas (MSA):						
Central city	93.3	88.0	-5.3	46.2	71.5	+25.3
Other parts of MSA	95.0	90.7	-4.3	46.2	75.1	+28.8
Not in MSA	93.9	88.0	-5.9	49.3	75.1	+25.8

Table A1.3 (cont.)

Location variables: Residence in regions (Census Bureau designations)

Northeast	92.4	88.0	-4.4	49.5	75.8	+26.3
Mid-Atlantic	94.2	87.7	-6.5	45.9	71.1	+25.1
East North Central	94.0	89.6	-4.3	46.7	76.3	+29.6
South Atlantic	95.6	91.9	-3.6	50.1	79.3	+29.2
East South Central	94.4	90.8	-3.6	48.0	71.3	+23.3
West South Central	95.0	90.0	-5.0	44.8	72.0	+27.2
Mountain states	94.2	90.7	-3.5	48.7	76.0	+27.3
Pacific states	91.9	87.9	-4.0	45.0	72.8	+27.8

Family structure variables: Married status

Never married	86.6	82.4	-4.1	65.8	73.2	+7.5
Married, spouse present	95.2	92.3	-2.8	43.5	73.3	+29.8
Other	88.8	83.8	-5.0	61.2	76.8	+15.6

Family structure variables: Own children living in family

No children	92.9	89.0	-3.8	63.5	81.4	+17.8
One child	94.3	91.3	-3.0	50.2	73.9	+23.7
Two children	95.3	90.0	-5.3	43.6	68.6	+25.0
Three of more	94.5	89.3	-5.2	35.6	57.4	+21.9

Notes: The employment probabilities are calculated from the logit regression coefficients and the average values for each variable. For estimating these probabilities for the variables within a related set (that is, where one variable is defined as the base), we assume that all variables in the equation other than the related set under examination are at their mean value. Then we focus on one variable, setting its value equal to one while the value of the other variables in the related set are equal to zero.

For men the samples sizes are 20,155 in 1971 and 24,515 in 1994; for women, 22,490 and 26,989. The pseudo R^2 (Nagelkerke adjusted generalized R^2 (SAS Institute, 1995)) for men are respectively .1539 and .1765; for women, .1539 and .1582 . For simplicity we do not include in this table all the variables in the regressions explaining the employment/non-employment variables. Differences may not add because of rounding. Related regressions using the National Adult Literacy Survey are reported in Chapter 2.

The data come from the March Current Population Survey for 1971 and 1994.

Since the detailed occupational listings carry the same census code used in the CPS, no serious problems were encountered in matching our "job tier rating" with the occupations.

Note 2.2: Notes on the Education Variable in the Current Population Survey

The level of formal education plays an important role in the statistical analysis in this book. Although the NALS data on education appear to be carefully collected, the education data from the Current Population Survey raise two sets of problems. The first concerns the consistency of the series over time. The second concerns the degree to which the respondents were telling the truth. After examining both sets of issues, we then explore some education trends of different racial/ethnic groups.

The Consistency of the CPS Data on formal education over time. In 1992 the Current Population Survey (CPS) changed slightly the wording of its questions on labor force participation and education. These differences are discussed in various articles in the September 1993 issue of *Monthly Labor Review.* The education question, which previously inquired about the highest number of years of school attended, subsequently asked whether the corresponding formal credential (such as a high-school diploma) had been received. Kominski and Siegel (1993) and Frazis, Ports, and Stewart (1995) discuss in detail these particular changes and their impact on time-series results.

We do not believe that the changes in the wording of the questions about education would have much impact on the number of those with a high-school degree or less. For those who have attended some college, differences may arise since earlier questions asked how many years of college the respondent completed without specifying whether the person had actually obtained a degree. By way of contrast, the later questions do not ask how many years the person attended college, but focus instead upon the degrees obtained. For these reasons we do not emphasize small changes in the various educational series between 1990 and 1994. Although it proved impossible to correct for these changes, we do not believe that, for our purposes, these changes substantially affect the conclusions we draw from the data.

The most problematic category in the earlier CPS classification of years of schooling is "some higher education." Some survey respondents may have included technical and trade school education, while others would have answered the question only in terms of college or university training.

Truthfulness of the replies. Some analysts such as John Bishop (1991) argue that an increasing share of the population reports more formal years of schooling than they actually have. Is this true and, if so, how does this affect our analysis? In the brief discussion below we find this argument has some merit, but its impact on our further results must not be exaggerated. It would be interesting to speculate on the motives of those overstating their education to a pollster, when they have absolutely nothing at stake. Nevertheless, the key questions are: How great is this overstatement? And has it changed over time to a sufficient degree to influence our calculations of trends in education?

For determining the bias introduced by respondents who overstate their educational credentials, it is necessary to estimate the population's total number of high-school diplomas and college degrees by another method. We made the estimates using a simple procedure:

We started with data on high-school graduates and university graduates with bachelor's degrees taken from Department of Education, National Center for Education Statistics (1995, Tables 98 and 236) and from Department of Commerce, Census Bureau (1975. Series 600, 601, 753, and 753). To obtain consistent series back to 1919, we had to make a series of minor interpolations, extrapolations, and other estimates. Assuming that all high-school students graduated at age 18 and all college students graduated at age 22, we estimated for each year the number of high-school diplomas and college degrees held by the population in the prime-age working years.

For estimating the General Educational Development (GED) credential, which is supposed to be the equivalent to a high-school diploma, we then utilized unpublished data and various annual reports of the GED Testing Service of the American Council on Education. Since the usual published data of the GED's include Canadians taking the test, we excluded these from our totals. Although the data also include those in U.S. trust territories taking the test, the number is small and we included these on the assumption that most taking the test eventually landed in the U.S.

Unfortunately, these GED data are quite incomplete since the age distribution of those who received such credentials are available only from 1989 to the present. Data on the age distribution of those taking the test are available to the mid 1970s, so we assumed that the success rates in the various age groups were the same as in the later years. Rougher estimates had to be made for earlier years. For the period from 1955 to the mid 1970s, we assumed that the age distribution of those successfully receiving a GED were the same as in the late 1970s. Since the GEDs began in 1942 and were designed primarily for current and past members of the armed forces, we assumed that all those taking the examination from 1942 to 1955 were under 35. Finally, we had to estimate those taking the test from 1942 through 1948 since data were totally unavailable. The estimates for each age taking the test in each year were aggregated for the entire prime working-age population in the same manner as the high-school degrees. Since the gender of those taking the examination or receiving a GED credential are unavailable, we assumed for simplicity that the breakdown was 50-50.

Finally, we estimated the number of immigrants with high-school diplomas and college degrees by starting from census data (U.S. Department of Commerce, Census Bureau, 1973, Table 1 and 1993, Table 3) on the highest educational attainment of the foreign-born in the two years. Assuming that the number increased exponentially between the two years, we made estimates for both sexes.

To these estimates of the prime working-age population with U.S.-issued diplomas and degrees, we added those with the GED credential as an equivalent to a high-school diploma. We combined this data set with our estimates of the educational credentials of immigrants into our overall estimate. Finally, we compared these with the series of claimed educational credentials from the CPS. Several problems arise in such a comparison aside from the approximations that were necessary to calculate the "actual" series. In particular, the "claimed series" is understated in comparison to the "actual series" because it excludes those who have died, the armed forces (who numbered 1.8 million in 1992), those civilians who are living abroad (in 1992 these comprised 6.3 million (U.S. Department of Commerce, Census Bureau, annual, 1992, p. 9)), and U.S. tourists abroad (who averaged, at a given point in 1992, 6.7 million in 1992 (*ibid*)).

Since we are interested in changes over time, it is necessary to see how the biases in the CPS might change. On the one hand, since the number of military is increasing more slowly than the population, this would overstate the rise in claimed credentials in comparison to the "actual." On the other hand, since some of the number of tourists abroad and the number of Americans living abroad have increased faster than the population (for instance, in 1970 about 1.7 million civilian Americans lived abroad (U.S. Department of Commerce, Census Bureau, 1975, Series A-11)), the amount of claimed credentials in the CPS should have risen more slowly than the "actual" series. The fact that some in the prime-age population have died – and mortality has been inversely related to education – would also tend to understate the growth of the claimed credentials.

The comparison of our estimated series of "actual" educational credentials issued to the prime-age population with the educational credentials claimed by respondents to the CPS yields the information we seek. For 1994 such comparisons suggest that the number of the prime working-age population holding high-school diplomas was understated by 7.1 percent, while the number of those holding college degrees was overstated by 2.6 percent. For the prime-age population the degree of overstatement was somewhat greater for men than women, and for those over 30 in comparison to those in their twenties.

Since the degree of over- or understatement varies somewhat in different years, the growth rates of those with a high-school diploma and college degree also differs from the CPS rates. For instance, between 1971 and 1994, the people claiming at least a high-school diploma increased 107 percent, while our estimates for actual diplomas granted increased 110 percent. Between the same years, the people claiming a college degree increased 203 percent, while our estimate of the number of actual college degrees issued increased 178 percent.

The degree of bias is most crucial in our calculations using the CPS to measure the displacement of less-educated by more-educated workers. Given the accuracy with which we are working, these biases should not affect our overall conclusions although, of course, they would influence the specific numerical outcomes.

Disaggregated trends in the formal education of prime-age workers. In Chapter 2 the discussion of Chart 2.1 covers the aggregate trends of formal education for the prime-age population. Table A2.1 provides some data on these trends when the aggregate data are divided by race/ethnicity and sex. The race/ethnicity groups are: Whites (including white Hispanics), Blacks (including black Hispanics) and "others," which includes certain Asians, native peoples of North and South America, and those declaring themselves as racially mixed. The data for "other races" are quite unreliable for the early years for reasons discussed below.

The major results can be quickly summarized. At the beginning of this time period, fewer men (white and black prime work-age) than women had a high-school diploma or less ("less-educated"). By 1994, however, the educational level of women (white and black prime working-age) had increased faster than men to close the gap. Indeed, among African Americans in 1994, there were fewer less-educated women than men.

Comparisons between whites and blacks yield a mixed picture. The fraction of blacks (men and women) who were high-school dropouts has converged with the similar fraction of whites. The gap between the fraction of blacks with just a high-school diploma or less and the similar fraction for whites remained fairly constant between 1964 and 1994. Thus, white prime-age workers have remained somewhat more educated than prime-age African Americans.

The reduction in the fraction of white males with less education has slowed down in the last decade. For black males, white females, and black females, the reduction in the fraction with less education has actually stayed the same or increased in the last decade. Several aspects of this deserve note. First, the increasing participation rate of all women in the prime working-ages is related to this rising share of more-educated women. Second, the decline in the share of males in the prime working-ages with little education is undoubtedly related in part to their declining participation in the labor force because the average level of abilities of those remaining in this low-education cohort has fallen as the more able obtain more education.

The results for "other races" must be interpreted cautiously for several reasons. First, the samples are quite small, especially for 1964. Second, the racial designations are self-identified (in contrast with the NALS). With the increase of racial pride over the years, some who previously identified themselves as white or black may now designate themselves as belonging to "other race." Third, many of these people are immigrants who may not be used to answering questions from Census Bureau workers. Indeed, some may avoid such encounters if they are in the country illegally. Fourth, the schooling equivalencies are quite different in other countries than in the USA so that, for instance, a year of a German gymnasium should really count for more than a year of schooling in the U.S. Finally, the results are highly dependent upon immigration, which has greatly increased during the 30 years covered in the table. As a result, those identifying themselves as some race other than white or black increased eight-fold from 1964 to 1994.

Among men from 1974 onward, the schooling level appears to have changed little: The share of high-school dropouts has risen slightly and the share of those with just a high-school diploma has somewhat fallen. This appears to reflect the increasingly bifurcated nature of the immigrant stream: A higher share of those with very little education, and also those with a great deal of for-

Table A2.1: *Education by Race and Gender of the Less-Educated Population in Prime Working-Ages as a Percent of the Relevant Cohort, 1964–1994*

Highest level of formal education

	High-school dropout	High-school diploma	Combined	High-school dropout	High-school diploma	Combined	High-school dropout	High-school diploma	Combined
	White males			*Black males*			*Other males*		
1964	38.4%	34.8%	73.2%	67.5%	21.0%	88.5%	40.4%	23.9%	64.3%
1974	24.7	37.2	61.9	46.1	34.8	80.9	13.0	30.0	43.0
1984	14.7	36.8	51.5	28.2	39.9	68.0	15.3	23.5	38.8
1994	12.2	32.2	44.3	17.1	40.9	58.0	15.5	24.0	39.5
	White females			*Black females*			*Other females*		
1964	35.3	45.9	81.2	63.6	25.8	89.4	39.2	42.7	81.9
1974	24.4	48.1	72.5	45.5	37.1	82.7	23.6	36.3	59.8
1984	14.6	44.6	59.2	25.0	43.5	68.5	17.8	32.5	50.3
1994	10.9	34.1	45.0	15.5	39.1	54.8	17.7	25.9	43.6

Total (men and women of all races)

	High-school dropout	High-school diploma	Combined
1964	39.7	38.8	78.5
1974	26.6	42.0	68.6
1984	16.0	40.5	56.6
1994	12.3	33.6	45.9

Notes: Totals may not add because of rounding. The data are calculated from the Current Population Surveys for March of each year.

Note 2.3: Recalculation of Table 2.4

Table A2.2: *Partial Discrete Changes in Employment Probabilities (PDCEP) of the Prime Working-Age Population When NALS Scores are Excluded From the Regression*

Dependent variable: Working (=1), not working (= 0)

| | *Calculated coefficients* | |
	Men PDCEP	Women PDCEP
Highest educational achievement (high-school diploma is basis of comparison)		
High-school dropout	-10.6*	-19.6*
GED	-11.6*	-5.9*
Trade/vocational school	-1.7	+1.7
Some university	-0.7	+6.7*
B.A. or B.S.	+4.0*	+9.3*
At least one graduate degree	+8.8*	+18.4*
Race/ethnicity variables (White, non-Hispanic is basis of comparison)		
Black, non-Hispanic	-7.2*	-5.9*
Hispanic	+0.8	-4.4*
Other races/ethnicities	-5.6*	-12.0*
Place of birth (foreign-born = 1; native-born = 0)	-1.5	-3.2
Region of residence (Northeast is basis of comparison)		
South	+4.6*	+3.2*
Midwest	+3.6*	+5.2*
West	+1.7	+4.8*
Live in metropolitan area (yes = 1; no = 0)	+0.7	-1.1
Age (age 25-29 is the basis of comparison)		
Age 30-34	-0.6	+0.5
Age 35-39	-1.1	+2.2*
Age 40-44	-2.0*	+1.5*
Age 45-49	-3.5*	+4.6*
Never-married person living alone (yes = 1, no = 0)	-6.7*	+11.6*
Pseudo R^2	.0900	.1205
Sample size	6085	7789

Notes: This table is the same as Table 2.4, but omitting the scores for the NALS test. The coefficients represent the percentage change in the probability of employment if the dummy variable for the variable moves from 0 to 1 (or, for the literacy score coefficients, whether the variable changes one standard deviation). An asterisk designates statistical significance at the .05 level. For each block of variables, the "comparison variable" is designated.

These are weighted regressions with the population weights provided by the data set. The pseudo R^2 is the Nagelkerke adjusted generalized R^2 (SAS Institute, 1995). The data come from the 1992 National Adult Literacy Survey.

mal education are coming to the United States. (Chiswick and Sullivan ,1995). In the last decade, the share of those with very little education has risen. Among women, on the other hand, the share of those with just a high-school education or less has been falling steadily over the years. By 1994 women of other races had a higher share of high-school dropouts, but a lower share of those with just a high-school education. As a result, the percentage of those with relatively less education was roughly the same as white women. Because of the unreliability of the samples of "other races," we focus our attention on whites and blacks in the discussion in Chapter 3.

Chapter 3

Note 3.1: Imputing 1994–95 Census Occupation Codes for the March 1971 and 1972 CPS Samples

We base much of the analysis in this book on a comparable series of occupations over a quarter-century period, so the derivation of this series is crucial for our results.

In preparing for the 1980 Census of Population, the U.S. Census Bureau developed a new occupation classification system which was significantly different from the 1960 and 1970 occupation classification systems used for previous censes. Because the differences were considerable, most 1980 detailed occupation categories are not comparable to earlier categories with similar names. For example, of the people who were classified as "accountants" according to the 1960 and 1970 systems, some would still be classified as "accountants and auditors" under the 1980 system, but others would be classified as "financial managers," "other financial officers," "inspectors and compliance officers, except construction," and "bookkeepers, accounting, and auditing clerks." A detailed description of the logic behind the changes is given in U.S. Department of Commerce, Census Bureau (1989).

This dramatic change in classification systems has made it difficult to compare post-1980 occupation data with previous occupation data. In particular, the March Current Population Surveys used the 1960 definitions from March 1964 through March 1970, the 1970 definitions from March 1971 through March 1982, the 1980 definitions from March 1983 through March 1991, and a slight revision of the 1980 definitions from March 1992 through March 1995. Thus, it is possible to compare occupation data within the 1964 through 1982 range, and within the 1983 to 1995 range, but not across the two ranges.

In response to this problem, the U.S. Census Bureau, in the late 1980s, took a subsample of 127,125 persons in the experienced civilian labor force from the 1970 Census of Population and "double coded" it. In other words, they went back to the original verbal descriptions of occupations recorded by the surveyors in 1970, and determined which category would have applied to the same respondent after the change in the occupational nomenclature. Thus, every person in the subsample now had two occupation classifications.

Then a group of government economists and statisticians, (see Clogg *et al.,* 1991, and Weidman, 1989) used this double coded sample to develop a separate statistical model for each 1970 occupation, based on a nested logit approach, of the probability of a person being classified into various 1980 occupation categories, given that person's 1970 occupation category, as well as his or her gender, race, age, education level, class of job, industry of job, average hours worked per week, average weeks worked per year, and earnings. Instead of reporting one set of parameters for each model, with some sort of standard errors attached, they reported five sets of parameters for each model, randomly generated from the asymptotic normal posterior distribution of the estimated parameters for each model. These five sets of parameter estimates can then be used for multiple imputation of 1980 occupation codes for any set of data using 1970 occupation codes.

We acquired these tens of thousands of parameter estimates from Lynn Weidman and John Priebe at the U.S. Census Bureau, and then applied them to the March 1971 CPS sample to impute five 1980 occupation codes for each employed person in our sample. We then did a few small manipulations to update each of these 1980 codes to the revised 1980 occupation codes used in the March 1994 CPS (see U.S. Census Bureau, 1994). All further calculations done with the March 1971 CPS data were done five times, once for each set of imputed occupation codes, and then averaged.

We did, however, introduce one additional element of uncertainty into the use of these models. Our data for each individual on average weeks worked per year and earnings, was based on his or her primary job during the previous calendar year (1970). However, we were trying to impute the occupation for their current (March, 1971) job. In a small number of cases, a person's current job was in a different 1970 occupation category from their primary job in the previous year. In these cases, we used the nested logit model for their current occupation, but used the weeks worked and earnings data from their primary job last year. Clearly, this is the best option available, but it does introduce an extra amount of uncertainty into the validity of the imputations.

We present a more full (and tedious) description of our methods in Pryor and Schaffer (1997).

Note 3.2: Biases in the Data on Occupations

The Census Bureau's determination of the occupation of a person is not an exact process and the bias in these data deserves a brief discussion. After looking at some previous studies, we then turn to the biases introduced in the wage regressions.

Previous studies. The basic method to determine the accuracy of these data is to compare two different ratings for the same person. For comparing the various studies we use the percentage of people for whom the same ratings are given in both studies.

The Census Bureau tried several different methods to establish the accuracy of their census results. In one study (1964, Table 38) the Bureau compared the records of the same people from the 1960 census and from the 1960 Current Population Survey. Weighing the results (by the census number) for the individual occupational groups we find that 79.6 percent of the same occupations at a one-digit level were reported for the same people. In another study (1965, Table 2) the Bureau compared the occupation reported by the respondent and the occupation listed in his employer's records at a one-digit level. At a one-digit level these corresponded in 81.1 percent of the cases. When listings of secondary occupations were included, the correspondence reached 83.2 percent of the cases (Table 3). In a final study (1972, Table 45) the Census Bureau reinterviewed the people and found that the occupations on a one-digit level were the same in 78.1 percent of all cases.

In a later study Mellow and Sider (1983) looked at occupational ratings from both workers and their employers. Comparing one-digit occupational listings from the Current Population Survey in 1977, they found an agreement in 81.0 percent of all cases; when the same exercise was carried out for occupations listings at a three-digit level (which we use in this book), correspondence occurred in only 57.5 percent of all cases. Similar results on a one-digit level were also found using the Employment Opportunity Pilot Project Survey in 1980.

Biases introduced in wage regressions. What differences do all these problems in obtaining correct occupational data by the Census Bureau really make in our results. Mellow and Sider (1983) compute a wage regression using a variety of characteristics about the people obtained from the workers and from their employers as explanatory variables. The results are virtually identical. On a one-digit level, the differences in the designation of occupation appear to wash out.

The impact of such errors in the designation of various occupations depends, of course, on the ways in which the data are applied. Although we calculate various statistics for the individual occupations, we usually aggregate these statistics into many fewer categories, for instance, the four educational tiers. All sorts of misunderstandings can occur in the designation of an occupation. For instance, a grinding operator (occupation #709, classified under the one-digit category of "operator occupations") might designate himself as a precision grinder (occupation # 644, classified under the one-digit category of "craft occupations"). Or an usher (occupation #461, classified under the one-digit category of "service occupation") might label himself as a guide (occupation #462, also a "service occupation"). Three quite different aspects of these errors deserve mention:

a. Some of the errors, for instance, mislabeling of an usher, might simply place people in an occupational class with people quite similar to themselves and in the same educational tier. This should make little difference to our results. Given the larger number of classification errors on a three-digit than a one-digit occupational level, this is clearly the most common type of error.

b. Some of the errors might be symmetric, that is, as many precision grinders might list themselves as grinding operators as the reverse. This has no net impact on the occupation data; it does, however, influence the averages of the other characteristics if they are greatly different in the two occupations. For instance, such symmetric errors would reduce average wage differences between the types of grinders and, as a result, understate the impact of education on wages. If, of course, both occupations are aggregated in the same larger analytic category, for instance, the same educational tier, then such a misclassification would have no impact on the final conclusions.

c. Some of the errors might be non-symmetric. For instance, more grinder operators might classify themselves as precision grinders than the reverse. Again, the impact of many such errors might make little difference since we group these occupations into four large categories. Any net impact of these errors would occur only if a large number of these errors concerned occupations in different educational tiers. More specifically, this would tend to increase the number of people in tier 4 and reduce the number of people in tier 1. Moreover, the average level of certain characteristics such as education would be lower in all educational tiers.

We conducted a number of numerical experiments to determine the degree of bias and our general conclusion can be simply stated: We really cannot determine the impact of misstating the occupation until we know the net bias of overstatement, not just of this characteristic, but of all other characteristics contained in the regression as well. Given the fact that we work primarily with four large groups of occupations, which is more aggregated than the Census Bureau's one-digit classification, it seems unlikely that errors in the recording of the person's occupation would lead to results greatly different from those we have obtained.

Note 3.3: Skill Ratings and Structural Changes in Skills

In our discussion in the text we focus primarily on cognitive skills. Other skills are, however, important in the employment process and it is useful to deal briefly with this problem. We can readily combine data on the number of workers in the various occupations with information on the skill requirements for each of these from various data sources. This allows us to chart the changing skills reflected in the employed labor force. Since such an exercise has been carried out elsewhere, for instance, Pryor (1996), Chapter 2; and Wolff (1995-a), it is not necessary to dwell at length on these issues. We turn first to the measurement of skills and then turn to particular calculations.

The measurement of skills. The most comprehensive measurement of skills required for various occupations is carried out by the U.S. Department of Labor and presented in the *Dictionary of Occupational Titles,* which is published irregularly by the Bureau of Labor Statistics (BLS). These ratings are determined by committees of specialists and, since there is an unavoidable subjective element in making these assessment, we can carp at many individual ratings. They are, nevertheless, the most comprehensive and detailed such attempt available. We must, however, exercise caution in using these data because these ratings were made for the period around 1970 and are somewhat outdated.

Miller *et al.* (1980) discuss in great detail these ratings of a large number of occupations according to various skills. Roos and Treiman (1980) average and arrange these data according to a 1970 occupational nomenclature covering almost 600 occupations. It proved necessary, however, to convert these ratings to the 1994 occupational nomenclature of roughly 500 occupations.

For our purposes it was not necessary to use the highly involved techniques that we have used with the CPS data. Therefore, we carried this task out by hand in a rather rough manner, averaging a number of occupations when the 1994 occupation appeared to cover two or more of the occupations listed by Roos-Treiman. In some cases we had to find analogous occupations with which to estimate the ratings. Since most of the ratings did not greatly vary over similar occupations, we do not believe that the errors introduced by this hand-procedure are sufficiently severe to invalidate the descriptive use we have made of these ratings in the table below or their use in other tables in the appendix. It should be added that the changes in the weighted averages of the ratings as we move up the educational scale conform with expectations, for instance, those occupations where the average practitioners have more years of formal education require more analytic skills.

Supplementing these data on skills, we also draw upon the National Adult Literacy Survey. For each occupation we calculate the weighted average functional literacy of full-time workers and then use these data to generalize about the entire economy.

The calculations. In Table A3.1 we present the results of such an investigation. For each skill or educational level we indicate the period for which the rating was made. These ratings, in turn, serve as the weights for the averages for 1971 and 1994 presented in the next two columns.

The shifts in the occupational structure occurring over time, brought about by the changes in technology and in the relative production of various industries, has led to a small increase in the requirements of functional literacy.

This has an important implication for less-educated workers. From Table 2.3 in the text we note that less-educated women (that is, with just a high-school diploma or less) have higher functional literacy scores than less-educated men along the prose and document scales. Indeed, this difference in most cases is at least as great as the four-to-six-point increase in the requirements for functional literacy occurring in the last quarter-century . In turn, this implies that over time less-educated women are increasingly able to out-compete men of the same educational level in the job market.

Roos and Treiman (1980) carry out a factor analysis of 46 specific skills defined for the various occupations and extract several general factors. Analytic skills (which they call substantive complexity) are correlated with general educational level, specific vocational preparation, ability to analyze data, and various intellectual aptitiudes. Motor skills are correlated with coordination, dexterity, and ability to carry out such manual work as setting up, feeding, and tending machines. The physical demands variable is correlated not just with requirements for physical strength, but also with demands placed on workers for stooping, climbing, eye-hand coordination, and other types of physical activities. As we might expect, the change in the occupational structure occasioned by new technology and shifts in the industrial structure have led to higher requirement for substantive skills, and lower requirements for motor skills or physical demands.

In the table we also include three specific skills. The interaction skills reflect the ability to work with people and are highest for such tasks as mentoring, teaching, and counseling and lowest for those jobs consisting of working alone or taking orders from others. The specific vocational training reflects the amount of education specifically devoted toward developing the skills needed in that occupation, in contrast to the general education received in primary and secondary schools or liberal arts colleges. As we might expect, the changes in the occupational structure of

Table A3.1: *Structural Upskilling for Various Skills Among Employed Prime-Age Workers*

Skill/educational level	Base year for index	1971–72	1994–95
Functional literacy			
Prose scale	1992	294	300
Document scale	1992	292	297
Quantitative scale	1992	297	302
Average: three scales	1992	295	300
Skill ratings: factor analysis: The scales are from 0 (low) to 10 (high)			
Analytic skills (substantive complexity)	1970	4.24	4.67
Motor skills	1970	5.04	4.80
Physical demands	1970	2.02	1.89
Skill ratings: individual skills (scale are from 0 to 10)			
Data skills	1970	4.82	5.33
Interaction (people) skills	1970	2.42	2.77
Specific vocational training	1970	5.34	5.68
Strength required	1970	3.14	2.85

Notes: We assume that the education or skill requirement remains the same for each occupation and measure only the impact of the changing structure of occupations. For all these calculations we use the 500 different occupations in the Bureau of Census nomenclature.

The functional literacy data come from the underlying data of the National Adult Survey. The skill ratings for each occupation are drawn from Roos and Treiman (1980).

the prime-age workers have led to an increase in the required interaction skills and specific vocational training and a decline in the physical strength required for various jobs.

In passing, it is worthwhile to note the relevance of these data for the strange debate about "deskilling of American workers." According to the early advocates of this position, the attempt by American employers to reduce each job to its simplest components ("Taylorism") and to structure the workforce in an assembly line under a centralized control ("Fordism"), has led to a loss of work skills. Such views are buttressed by various case studies of technological displacement of skilled workers. Moreover, some empirical evidence shows that faster technological growth in various industries is associated with an inverse relation between the growth of total factor productivity and the increase of various skills. (The most careful such study is by Wolff (1995-a)). Nevertheless, all these arguments are beside the point – the occupational structure has changed in a manner so that the required analytic and interaction skills have risen for the workforce as a whole over the decades. In the next appendix we show, however, that for certain subgroups such as white males (but not black males), some skills required for jobs in tiers 1 and 2 have declined.

One last question deserves brief attention: To what extent are the changes in the required skill/educational levels due to changes in the occupational mix for each industry or to changes in the mix of industries? Edward Wolff uses the entire labor force to examine census data and, with the aid of a decomposition method, explores this question for some skills listed in Table 3.2. He shows (his Table 5) that between 1970 and 1990, changes in the industrial mix accounted for about two-thirds of the increased requirements for analytic (substantive) skills, and about three-fifths of the increased requirements for people (interactive) skills. He also shows that such changes in the industrial mix accounted for about three-quarters of the declining requirements in motor skills. We take up these questions from a different perspective in Chapter 3.

Note 3.4: Occupational Deskilling by Educational Tier

Over the last four decades the skill level of the occupational mix of the workforce as a whole, as calculated from Labor Department ratings of the various occupations, has increased (Pryor, 1996, Table 3.1). This type of calculation holds the skills in each single occupation constant and examines the impact of the shifting occupational structure on the average level of skills for the economy as a whole. We also present the results of such a calculation in Table A3.1 in the previous appendix. All such exercises show a general upskilling of the labor force.

As noted in the text, it is more difficult to determine how particular skill levels in particular occupations have changed, and three quite different answers to this question can be found in the social science literature. Those arguing for upskilling claim that advanced technology eliminates the repetitive tasks of various occupations, requiring people to focus more on those tasks involving broader and deeper skill abilities. This should occur especially in those enterprises where competition has forced them to find small market niches requiring quick reactions to changing markets and that require a more flexible workforce. Those arguing for downskilling claim that technology changes introduced by capitalist enterprises have a bias toward downskilling so that employers can more easily control their employees and pay them low wages. A final group – the no-changers – argues that the net change of technology on the skill mix has been small – certain occupations have experienced upskilling while others have experienced downskilling. We discuss some of the empirical evidence pertaining to these issues in Chapter 3.

A change in the skills of the four occupational tiers can occur through two other mechanisms. First, the composition of occupations within a given occupational tier can change, a matter investigated in Table A3.2 below. Second, a redefinition of the tier can occur when, in a later year, certain occupations are reclassified into different tiers when their average level of education changes. In the calculations below we do not take this into account. The statistics presented in Table A3.2 divide the occupational data according to the criteria of race and gender, because some startling differences between these groups can be found.

Several results of this calculation leap to the eye. In almost all cases black men hold jobs requiring less mental skills and more physical skills, and the same can be said in a comparison of black and white women. Furthermore, in most cases men hold jobs requiring more mental and physical skills than women. A notable exception is that over the last quarter-century, among those with a high-school diploma, women are now holding jobs requiring more data skills. Furthermore, in many cases – particularly by 1995 – women hold jobs requiring more people skills.

In terms of analytic skills (substantive complexity), deskilling has occurred only among white males and the same can be said for data skills, general educational level, and specific vocational training. Indeed, for analytic skills, general educational level, and specific vocational training, the average levels decline for the sample as a whole, primarily because the situation among white males dominates the sample. Contrary to the conjecture by others, we have not found a significant deskilling among prime-age black men with a high-school education or less.

Table A3.2: Characteristics of Job Held by Less-Educated Workers in Their Prime Working-Ages in 1971 and 1995

	White males		Black males		White females		Black females	
	1971	1995	1971	1995	1971	1995	1971	1995
Occupation tier 1 (10.5 years or less of schooling)								
Factor-analysis based scales								
Analytic skills (substantive complexity)	3.33	2.96	2.38	2.56	2.68	2.75	1.81	2.30
Motor skills	5.30	5.32	5.05	5.18	5.12	4.87	4.56	4.86
Physical demands	3.62	4.04	3.96	3.72	1.61	1.88	2.37	2.19
Undesirable work conditions	0.45	0.50	0.71	0.65	0.35	0.38	0.59	0.47
Data skills	3.79	3.19	2.32	2.61	2.82	3.09	2.26	2.45
People skills	1.49	1.23	1.10	1.08	1.44	1.60	1.22	1.45
General educational level	4.39	4.10	3.64	3.76	4.07	4.10	3.66	3.84
Specific vocational training	4.93	4.63	3.86	4.08	3.76	3.87	3.13	3.46
Occupation tier 2 (10.6 to 12.0 years of schooling)								
Factor-analysis based scales								
Analytic skills (substantive complexity)	4.16	3.85	2.91	3.07	3.94	3.99	2.78	3.22
Motor skills	5.14	5.13	4.97	5.14	5.57	4.99	5.19	4.96
Physical demands	2.75	3.13	2.87	2.97	0.80	1.01	1.65	1.48
Undesirable work conditions	0.32	0.39	0.56	0.49	0.14	0.16	0.32	0.22
Data skills	5.10	4.58	3.23	3.38	4.30	4.64	3.04	3.56
People skills	2.05	1.87	1.45	1.54	2.06	2.35	1.56	1.97
General educational level	5.08	4.84	4.09	4.24	5.13	5.14	4.49	4.60
Specific vocational training	5.54	5.36	4.17	4.46	4.68	4.87	3.92	4.27

Notes: The occupational tiers are defined according to their education intensity in 1971–72. The 1970 skill ratings for each characteristic run from 0 (low) through 10 (high) and the final results represent a weighted average of the workers in the various occupations in the particular group under investigation. As noted in the discussion, these ratings of job characteristics are somewhat outdated and interpretations must be made cautiously. The data come from the same database as used in Table A3.1.

Note 3.5: More Data on Years of Education and Occupation of Prime-Age Workers

Table A3.3: Years of Education and Occupations of Prime-Age Workers, 1979 and 1987

Occupation	Educational tier of occupation				
Tiers defined by average education of those in occupation in 1971–72	Tier 1 10.5 years or less	Tier 2 10.6–12.0 years	Tier 3 12.1–14.5 years	Tier 4 >14.5 years	Total
Highest educational attainment					
Part A: Percentage by rows: 1979					
High-school dropout	41.4%	22.5%	5.8%	0.7%	17.1%
Only high-school diploma	44.7	52.3	41.7	6.1	39.7
Some university	10.8	18.7	27.4	9.9	19.0
University degree	3.0	6.6	25.2	83.2	24.2
Total	100.0	100.0	100.0	100.0	100.0
Part B: Percentages by columns: 1979					
High-school dropout	54.4	32.0	13.0	0.6	100.0
Only high-school diploma	25.3	32.1	40.3	2.3	100.0
Some university	12.9	24.0	55.5	7.7	100.0
University degree	2.8	6.6	40.0	50.6	100.0
Total	22.5	24.4	38.4	14.7	100.0

Table A3.3 (cont.)

Part C: Percentage by rows: 1987

					Total
High-school dropout	30.4	15.0	3.6	0.4	11.2
Only high-school diploma	52.6	54.9	37.2	6.9	39.7
Some university	12.9	21.4	29.3	11.2	21.4
University degree	4.1	8.8	30.0	81.5	27.7
Total	100.0	100.0	100.0	100.0	100.0

Part D: Percentages by columns: 1987

					Total
High-school dropout	55.8	30.4	13.1	0.6	100.0
Only high-school diploma	27.2	31.5	38.7	2.7	100.0
Some university	12.5	22.8	56.7	8.0	100.0
University degree	3.0	7.2	44.7	45.1	100.0
Total	20.6	22.8	41.3	15.3	100.0

Notes: This table parallels Table 3.4 in the text and has the same sources and interpretations.

Chapter 4

Note 4.1: More Data on Years of Education and Occupation of Prime-Age Workers

Table A4.1: Comparison of the "Scaled-Up" 1971 Matrix to the Actual 1995 Matrix (Data in 1000.)

Highest educational level	Jobless	Occupational tiers				Total
Scaled-up 1971 population		Tier 1	Tier 2	Tier 3	Tier 4	
White male, high-school dropout	1406.	5412.	3581.	1372.	55.	11826.
Black male, high-school dropout	419.	1497.	439.	110.	4.	2469.
White female, high-school dropout	7542.	2260.	1753.	881.	39.	12477.
Black female, high-school dropout	1467.	962.	251.	129.	12.	2821.
White male, high-school graduate	901.	3863.	5586.	4967.	498.	15816.
Black male, high-school graduate	136.	614.	342.	195.	28.	1315.
White female, high-school graduate	11376.	1407.	2606.	5692.	253.	21334.
Black female, high-school graduate	675.	416.	377.	375.	12.	1855.
White male, some university	439.	561.	1211.	3020.	687.	5918.
Black male, some university	36.	78.	103.	119.	12.	348.
White female, some university	2950.	120.	405.	1908.	248.	5630.
Black female, some university	136.	23.	75.	175.	40.	449.
White male, university degree	342.	85.	358.	2810.	4432.	8026.
Black male, university degree	22.	10.	20.	75.	118.	244.
White female, university degree	2000.	35.	98.	802.	1760.	4695.
Black female, university degree	41.	3.	3.	41.	184.	272.
Total	29887.	17348.	17208.	22670.	8383.	95496.

Table A4.1 (cont.)

1995 prime-age population	Jobless	Occupational tiers				Total
		Tier 1	Tier 2	Tier 3	Tier 4	
White male, high-school dropout	1227.	2260.	1039.	269.	22.	4817.
Black male, high-school dropout	421.	306.	125.	32.	0.	884.
White female, high-school dropout	2168.	991.	647.	397.	34.	4238.
Black female, high-school dropout	623.	226.	167.	57.	8.	1082.
White male, high-school graduate	1584.	4583.	4073.	2988.	156.	13383.
Black male, high-school graduate	428.	947.	508.	342.	20.	2245.
White female, high-school graduate	3920.	1537.	2731.	5239.	495.	13923.
Black female, high-school graduate	947.	440.	515.	596.	75.	2573.
White male, some university	986.	2074.	2912.	4225.	730.	10927.
Black male, some university	224.	385.	446.	404.	60.	1519.
White female, some university	2975.	518.	1823.	6368.	844.	12529.
Black female, some university	483.	143.	422.	967.	102.	2116.
White male, university degree	610.	436.	867.	5362.	5031.	12306.
Black male, university degree	106.	73.	104.	343.	307.	932.
White female, university degree	1881.	126.	416.	4139.	4469.	11031.
Black female, university degree	107.	11.	60.	450.	363.	990
Total	18690.	15055.	16854.	32179.	12718.	95496.

Difference between scaled-up and actual matrix

	Jobless	Occupational tiers				Total
		Tier 1	Tier 2	Tier 3	Tier 4	
White male, high-school dropout	-179	-3152	-2542	-1103	-33	-7009
Black male, high-school dropout	2	-1191	-314	-78	-4	-1585
White female, high-school dropout	-5374	-1269	-1106	-484	-5	-8238
Black female, high-school dropout	-844	-736	-84	-72	-4	-1740
White male, high-school graduate	683	720	-1513	-1979	-342	-2431
Black male, high-school graduate	292	333	166	147	-8	930
White female, high-school graduate	-7456	130	125	-453	242	-7412
Black female, high-school graduate	272	24	138	221	63	718
White male, some university	547	1513	1701	1205	43	5009
Black male, some university	188	307	343	285	48	1171
White female, some university	25	398	1418	4460	596	6897
Black female, some university	347	120	347	792	62	1668
White male, College Grad.	268	351	509	2552	599	4279
Black male, university degree	84	63	84	268	189	688
White female, university degree	-119	91	318	3337	2709	6336
Black female, university degree	66	8	57	409	179	719
Total	-11198	-2290	-353	9507	4334	0

Notes : The basic data come from the Current Population Survey.

Note 4.2: Using the Biproportional Matrix Technique for Decomposition

The biproportional matrix technique (or RAS technique) was originally developed as a way of updating input-output tables when new data are available on the row totals and column totals, but not on the individual values within the table. It was first developed by Richard Stone (1961, 1962) for use in his empirical work. The rationale behind this technique, as well as the assumptions implicit in it and the properties of its results have been thoroughly investigated by Michael Bacharach (1970).

The biproportional matrix technique works for any non-negative matrix, A, for which new positive values for all of the row totals, c_i, and column totals, c_j, are known. It involves finding a matrix, B, such that:

A1) $b_{ij} = r_i \, a_{ij} \, s_j$ *for all* $i = 1,...,M$ *and* $j = 1,...,N$

with the property that:

A2) $\sum_{j=1}^{N} b_{ij} = c_i.$ *for* $i = 1,...,M$ *and* $\sum_{i=1}^{M} b_{ij} = c_{\cdot j}$ *for* $j = 1,...,N$

where b_{ij} is the $(i,j)th$ element in matrix B, and a_{ij} is the $(i,j)th$ element in matrix A, and both matrices have M rows and N columns.

This technique involves the solution of a system of non-linear equations, equal in number to the sum of the two dimensions of the original matrix. However, one of its most attractive properties is that it can be computed by a fairly simple iterative technique which is guaranteed to converge in almost all cases. In step 1 of the iterative technique, each row is multiplied by an appropriate constant which will make each of the row totals equal to the desired row totals. In step 2, each column is multiplied by an appropriate constant which will make each of the column totals equal to the desired column totals. Then step 1 is repeated, and so on. For the simple 16 row by 5 column matrix used in this study, it usually took a few thousand iterations, and less than a minute of computing time, for the process to converge.

The feature of the biproportional matrix technique that makes it appropriate for the decomposition analysis in this paper is its distance-minimizing property. One way to measure the distance between two matrices, A and B, is by the "chi-squared distance" between them:

A3) $X^2 = \sum_{i=1}^{M} \sum_{j=1}^{N} (\frac{b_{ij} - a_{ij}}{a_{ij}})^2$

Bacharach (1970: 77-82) shows that the RAS technique (approximately) minimizes the Chi-squared distance between the derived matrix and the original one, given the constraints.

Another way to measure the distance between two matrices is by the "information distance" between them:

A4) $ID = \sum_{i=1}^{M} \sum_{j=1}^{N} b_{ij} \, \log (\frac{b_{ij}}{a_{ij}})$

Bacharach (1970: 83-5) also shows, as does Theil (1977), that the RAS technique minimizes this distance, which can be interpreted as the "expected information" of the message transforming the original matrix into the estimated matrix, subject to the constraints.

Since our original matrix represents important features of 1971 U. S. labor markets, when we use the RAS technique to update the matrix to the row and column totals for 1995, we are finding the derived matrix which is closest in distance to the original 1971 matrix, while still having the row and column totals for 1995. In other words, we are finding the matrix which least disrupts the relative sizes of the 80 terms in our original matrix while adjusting the whole matrix so as to have row and column totals equal to those in 1995.

This interpretation of the RAS result suggests the following decomposition method. Each term in the 1995 matrix, c_{ij}, can be written as:

A5) $\qquad c_{ij} = r_i \, a_{ij} \, s_j \; + \; e_{ij} \qquad for \; i = 1,...,M \; and \; j = 1,...,N$

where the first term on the right-hand side is the RAS "estimate" of the term in the 1995 matrix and the second term on the right-hand side is a residual term. Then the change between 1971 and 1995 can be written as:

A6) $\qquad \left(c_{ij} - a_{ij} \right) = \left(r_i \, s_j - 1 \right) a_{ij} \; + \; e_{ij}$

where the first term on the right-hand side is the "aggregate" change term and the second term on the right-hand side is the "structural" change term. The r_i and s_j terms are found by applying the RAS technique to the 1971 matrix and 1995 row and column totals. Then the e_{ij} term is found by using formula A5.

Note 4.3: Further Decomposition of the Structural Changes

The method for dividing the structural change component into two further subcomponents is straightforward. For the 16 terms in the non-employed column there is no further decomposition. For the 64 terms in the other four columns, the further decomposition is based on how accurate is the estimate of non-employment. Using the same notation as in Appendix 4.2, we have:

A7) $\qquad e_{ij} = -e_{i1} \left(\dfrac{r_i \; a_{ij} \; s_j}{\displaystyle\sum_{k=2}^{N} r_i \, a_{ik} \, s_k} \right) + \mu_{ij} \quad for \; i = 1,...,M \; and \; j = 2,...,N$

The first term on the right-hand side is what we call the "proportional employment" change. This term allocates a fraction of the residual in estimating non-employment to each of the employed categories. The fraction is based on the share in total employment of each occupation tier. The second term on the right-hand side is what we call the "occupation shifting" change. This is the residual left in each employment category after the "aggregate" and "proportional employment" changes have been calculated. It represents movements across the occupation tiers.

Based on the material in this appendix and the previous one, the overall decomposition into three pieces can be written as:

A8a) $(c_{il} - a_{il}) = (r_i s_l - 1) a_{il} + e_{il}$ $for\ i = 1,...,M$

A8b) $(c_{ij} - a_{ij}) = (r_i s_j - 1) a_{ij} + e_{il} \left(\dfrac{r_i a_{ij} s_j}{\displaystyle\sum_{k=2}^{N} r_i a_{ik} s_k} \right) + \mu_{ij}$

$for\ i = 1,...,M\ and\ j = 2,...,N$

where r_i and s_j are chosen so as to minimize:

A9) $ID = \displaystyle\sum_{i=1}^{M} \sum_{j=1}^{N} r_i a_{ij} s_j \log (r_i s_j)$

subject to:

A10) $\displaystyle\sum_{j=1}^{N} r_i a_{ij} s_j = c_i.$ for $i = 1,...,M$ and $\displaystyle\sum_{i=1}^{M} r_i a_{ij} s_j = .j$ for $j = 1,...,N$

In Table A4.2 we show the results of the decomposition of all of the structural change numbers from Panel C of Table 4.3. Bold and light arrows are added to emphasize the directions of the flows. The arrows always indicate movement from negative numbers (the sources of the flows) toward positive numbers (the targets of the flows). The bold arrows are for larger flows (greater than 100 thousand for white males and white females, greater than 16 thousand for black males and black females), and the light arrows are for smaller flows. The top set of arrows within each demographic-education group is for the proportional employment changes. The other arrows are for the occupation shifting changes.

When both sets of arrows point to the left, as they do for white male high-school graduates, it indicates that some employed people in this demographic-education group lost employment while other employed people were bumped down the job ladder. This means that the losses of jobs were disproportionately in the jobs with higher education intensiveness (i.e., tier 3 and tier 4). When the top set of arrows point to the left and the bottom set points to the right, as they do for white female high-school dropouts, it indicates that some employed people in this demographic-education group left employment while other employed people moved up the job ladder. This means that the losses of jobs were disproportionately in the lower tier occupations (i.e., tier 1 and tier 2).

Table A4.2: *Decomposition of Structural Changes into Proportional Employment Component and Occupation Shifting Component*

Total Prime-Age Population						
Race/Gender	Education	Jobless	Tier 1 Occupations	Tier 2 Occupations	Tier 3 Occupations	Tier 4 Occupations
White males	High-school dropouts	939	-528 245	-301 -11	-107 -142	-3 11
Black males	High-school dropouts	346	-264 -46	-67 36	-15 11	0 -1
White females	High-school dropouts	378	-190 -47	-127 -49	-59 72	-2 24
Black females	High-school dropouts	264	-197 -116	-45 91	-21 20	-1 5
White males	High-school diploma	1,189	-355 1,063	-443 -327	-366 -648	-25 -88
Black males	High-school diploma	311	-177 -85	-85 12	-45 79	-4 -6
White females	High-school diploma	-1,268	213 -145	341 39	693 -227	21 333
Black females	High-school diploma	383	-152 -204	-119 10	-110 130	-2 65
White males	Some university	530	-68 806	-126 -550	-292 -1,253	-44 -103
Black males	Some university	140	-41 8	-46 20	-50 -55	-3 28
White females	Some university	-1,740	98 -19	285 258	1,249 -488	108 249
Black females	Some university	78	-7 -9	-20 -2	-44 49	-7 -38
White males	University graduates	255	-4 239	-16 148	-114 115	-121 -502
Black males	University graduates	51	-3 18	-6 7	-20 13	-22 -38
White females	University graduates	-1,849	38 -63	91 -36	697 690	1,022 -591
Black females	University graduates	-7	0 -8	0 41	2 237	5 -271

Chapter 5

Note 5.1: More Data on Median Hourly Wages

Table A5.1: Median Hourly Wages of Prime-Age Workers, 1978 and 1986

Occupational tier (defined by average education of practitioners in 1971)	Tier 1 10.5 years of less	Tier 2 10.6 to 12.0 ye	Tier 3 12.1 to 14.5 years	Tier 4 14.6 years or more	Total
Highest educational attainment					
Panel A: Men, 1978 median hourly wages (1994 prices)					
High-school dropout	$10.47	$12.52	$12.61	$11.76	$11.44
High-school diploma or equivalent	13.33	15.04	15.74	18.14	14.65
Some university or trade/vocational school	13.48	14.74	15.70	16.97	15.25
One or more university degrees	12.67	12.98	18.86	19.14	18.36
Total	12.37	14.42	16.70	18.76	15.03
Part B: Men, 1986 median hourly wages (1994 prices)					
High-school dropout	8.52	10.78	10.63	14.35	9.42
High-school diploma or equivalent	11.15	13.81	14.26	17.52	12.95
Some university or trade/vocational school	12.43	13.64	15.55	18.12	14.57
One or more university degrees	11.19	13.78	19.43	20.19	18.78
Total	10.48	13.23	16.19	19.78	14.19

Panel C: Women, 1978 median hourly wages (1994 prices)

High-school dropout	6.51	6.26	7.41	7.82	6.51
High-school diploma or equivalent	6.72	7.08	9.05	10.20	8.20
Some university or trade/vocational school	6.11	7.83	10.09	9.74	9.39
One or more university degrees	6.52	7.92	10.88	12.75	11.76
Total	6.63	6.97	9.51	12.33	8.61

Part D: Women, 1984 median hourly wages (1994 prices)

High-school dropout	5.98	5.82	7.43	6.67	6.21
High-school diploma or equivalent	6.73	6.81	9.50	10.35	8.33
Some university or trade/vocational school	6.83	7.87	10.83	10.90	10.03
One of more university degrees	6.84	8.43	13.60	14.39	13.60
Total	6.47	6.97	10.36	13.50	9.39

Notes: See notes to Table 5.1 in the text

Note 5.2: Estimating Hourly Wage Data

The methods for estimating hourly wage data from the March CPS data sets are somewhat different for the two years under examination, 1970 and 1994. The more recent years of the March CPS, dating back to March 1976, contain data on each person's annual earnings in the previous year, the number of weeks they worked in the previous year, and the usual hours per week they worked in the previous year. Dividing annual earnings by the product of weeks-worked and usual-hours-worked gives an estimate of the effective hourly wage rate each person earned in the previous year.

One potential difficulty is introduced by the fact that annual earnings for 1994 are "top-coded" in the March 1995 CPS at $100,000. In other words, any person who reported their annual earnings as greater than or equal to $100,000 was listed as having annual earnings of exactly $100,000. Thus, it is impossible to know whether such a person earned exactly $100,000, or perhaps much more than this in the previous year. In the March 1995 CPS, 1.6 percent of all persons who were employed during at least part of 1994 have their annual earnings top-coded. However, this number is significantly larger for some sub-populations. For persons with a college degree or higher, 5.4 percent are top-coded. For white males with a college degree or higher, 9.3 percent are top-coded. Sixteen of the approximately 500 detailed occupations have more than 10 percent of their sample top-coded.

The tables on wage rates presented in the text were calculated several different ways, first with no adjustment for top-coding, then with several alternative adjustments for top-coding. The different methodology altered some of the wage results at the very high end of the earnings distribution. The results emphasized in this paper, however, were not particularly sensitive to the method used for dealing with top-coded annual earnings.

For the March 1971 CPS, the methods used to estimate hourly wage data are significantly more complex than those used for the March 1995 CPS. For all the March CPS data sets prior to March 1976, the data on weeks-worked last year and usual-hours-worked per week is much less precise than in the later years. Although the interviewed persons were asked the exact number of weeks they worked and the usual hours they worked per week, the Census Bureau surveyors only recorded these answers by indicating what range the numbers fell into. For weeks-worked last year, the ranges were 1–13 weeks, 14-26 weeks, 27-39 weeks, 40-47 weeks, 48-49 weeks, and 50-52 weeks. For usual-hours-worked per week, the ranges were 1-34 and 35+. Annual earnings, fortunately, were recorded as an actual number. However, the problem is how to estimate total hours worked last year from just the two-coded responses.

Some researchers have simply used the midpoints of the indicated ranges as their estimate of these numbers. This may be a reasonable approach for the weeks-worked data, but it is much less satisfactory for the usual-hours-worked per week data, where there are only two ranges and the top one has no midpoint. To get around this problem, a more complex approach is used, similar in spirit but not in all of the details, to that used by Juhn, Murphy, and Topel (1991). The basic approach is to use the complete data from the more recent March CPS data sets to estimate an econometric model for inferring weeks-worked and usual-hours-worked data from the set of variables available on each individual in the March 1971 sample. An outline of the details follows.

The first step is to choose the data set to use for estimation of the model. Juhn, Murphy, and Topel use the maximum number of observations available to them by pooling all of the individual observations from the March 1976 through March 1990 CPS samples. This gives them over a million observations to use in their regressions. However, their choice raises the question of whether the underlying behavior, as well as the precise definitions of economic variables, used in March 1990 are consistent with those in March 1971. In particular, since the definitions of most detailed occupations were radically changed after March 1982, it is problematical to use occupation categories as one of the estimating variables. Perhaps for this reason, Juhn, Murphy, and Topel do not use occupation categories in their model. However, our calculations, based just on the March 1976 through March 1982 data, suggest that occupation category is one of the more important predictors of weeks-worked and usual-hours-worked per week. Therefore, we pool only the individual observations from the March 1976 through March 1982 CPS samples. This still gives us several hundred thousand observations to work with, as well as more consistent definitions and less likelihood of behavioral changes.

The second step is to separate the data into subgroups based on the most important characteristics. We divided our data into 48 subcategories. Each person was assigned to one of the groups based on (a) in which of the six weeks-worked categories; (b) in which of the two usual-hours-worked per week categories; and, for the week before the March survey, (c) in which of the four employment status categories (employed and at work last week, employed but not at work last week, unemployed, or not in the labor force) the respondent was classified. For the estimation of usual-hours-worked we pooled the data across the six weeks-worked categories and therefore had only eight separate models to estimate.

In the two largest of these eight sub-categories, consisting of people currently employed and at work last week, we had data on the number of hours they had worked in the previous week. Since this correlates well with usual-hours-worked per week last year, we followed Juhn, Murphy, and Topel's strategy of using the other variables to estimate the gap between usual-hours-worked per week last year and hours worked last week, rather than estimating usual-hours-worked per week last year directly. For those individuals who usually worked 35+ hours per week last year, we regressed the log of this gap on 50 dummy variables for weeks-worked last year (5 dummy variables), years of education (5), real earnings in 1976 dollars (7), occupation category (11), industry category (10), class of job (2), gender/race category (3), marital status (3), and potential years of experience (4). After dropping industry category, gender/race category, and marital status (due to lack of statistical significance), we ended up with a coefficient of determination (R^2) of about .48.

For those individuals that usually worked one to 34 hours per week last year, we followed a similar procedure, except that we used the gap instead of the log of the gap as our dependent variable. After dropping industry category, class of job, and marital status from this regression, we ended up with an R^2 of about .51. In applying these two sets of results to individuals in the March 1971 data, we used as our estimate of usual-hours-worked per week last year the number of hours worked in the previous week by that individual plus the likely gap between the two, given that person's characteristics. Since hours-worked last week is already a good estimator of usual-hours-worked per week last year, and since we were able to explain half of the remaining difference as well, the overall fit of these two models was very good.

For the other six, much smaller, subcategories, the individuals did work last year, but they did not work in the week before the survey, so we could not use the same approach as above. Instead we regressed either the level of usual-hours-worked per week last year, or the log of this level, on the same set of 50 dummy variables described above. We then dropped those variables which had relatively little statistical significance and re-estimated the model. For the three subcategories where the individuals usually worked 35+ hours per week last year, we used the log of usual-hours-worked as the dependent variable. For the three subcategories where the individuals usually worked one to 34 hours per week last year, we used the level of usual-hours-worked as the dependent variable. The R^2 values for these six regressions ranged from .12 to .26.

For the estimation of weeks-worked last year we pooled the data across the two usual-hours-worked per week categories and the four current employment status categories. We had, therefore, only six separate models to estimate. For each of these categories, we regressed the log of weeks-worked last year on one continuous variable and 48 dummy variables. The continuous variable was the log of real earnings in 1976 dollars, and the dummy variables were for full-time/part-time status last year (1 dummy variable), years of education (5), real earnings in 1976 dollars (2), occupation category (11), industry category (10), class of job (2), sex/race category (3), marital status (3), potential years of experience (4), and real non-labor income in 1976 dollars (7). After dropping insignificant variables, the R^2 value for the 1–13 weeks-worked category was .40, but the R^2 values for the other cases ranged only from .04 to .08. Thus, for all but the first category, these results were not much better than just using subcategory means from the March 1976 to March 1982 CPS samples as the weeks-worked estimate within each range.

After estimating the missing weeks-worked last year and usual-hours-worked per week last year values in the 1970 sample, we then calculated the average hourly wage rate by the same method used on the 1994 sample. In addition, we had to deal with a similar top-coding problem. However, the degree of top-coding was less severe in 1970 than in 1994. In the 1970 data, annual earnings are top-coded at $50,000. In 1994 dollars, this would be $186,211. Therefore, only 0.2 percent of all persons who were employed during at least part of 1970 have their annual earnings top-coded. This number is 0.7 percent for persons with a college degree or higher and 1.1 percent for white males with a college degree or higher. Only one detailed occupation, physicians, has more than 6 percent of its observations top-coded.

There are several different ways to deal with the "top-coding problem," which we discuss in Pryor and Schaffer (1997). We have adopted the unusual method of estimating statistically from the CPS data itself, the missing or truncated right side tail of the earnings distribution within each detailed occupation. This can be done using the modified maximum likelihood method of West (1986, 1987) applied to each occupation separately. Then the mean earnings level within each of these estimated tails can be calculated and assigned to everyone in that occupation who is top-coded. This eliminates the bias in calculating the mean earnings level over the entire population. It also reduces, but does not eliminate, the bias in calculating the variance in the mean earnings level over the entire population. Finally, and most importantly for our work, it eliminates the bias in calculating occupation-specific mean earnings levels.

In order to implement this strategy, we had to deal with two problems. First, West's research suggests the following three-step strategy for estimating the right side tail of an earnings distribution. First, calculate the mean value of earnings over the entire (non-truncated) distribution. Second, assume that the distribution, from the mean point on, follows a simple Pareto distribution. Third, use the data from the mean point on to estimate the single critical parameter of this simple Pareto distribution. A severe problem arose with the first step. We could not calculate the mean value of earnings over the entire distribution because all the distributions were truncated. West correctly points out that if only the top two or three percent of the sample is truncated, then the "Windsorized mean" can be substituted for the actual mean. The Windsorized mean is just a standard mean calculated over all the observations using the truncated or top-coded values of earnings wherever they occur. No attempt is made to adjust the top-coded values upward.

Unfortunately, in some of our detailed occupation samples, more than five percent of the observations are top-coded. In these cases, the Windsorized mean becomes a less acceptable approximation of the true mean. We dealt with this by using information on the median value of earnings. As long as the truncation is less than 50 percent of the entire sample, the calculated median is unaffected by the degree of truncation. It is also clear that with a typical skewed-right earnings distribution, the median value of earnings is less than the mean value; in point of fact, it is usually between 85 to 95 percent of the mean value. Thus, if the calculated Windsorized mean is below or slightly above the median, some multiple (something between 100/85 and 100/95) of the median may be a better predictor of the true mean than the Windsorized mean.

To use a slightly cautious version of this procedure, we used as our estimate of the true mean level of earnings in each detailed occupation, the maximum of: (a) the Windsorized mean level of earnings in that occupation, (b) (100/95) times the median level of earnings in that occupation, and

(c) the median value of earnings in the entire population. This last term was included as a final defense against perverse results, since the modified maximum likelihood method fails much more dramatically if the starting point of the distribution is too far to the left rather than too far to the right. After estimating the mean earnings level for each occupation in this way, we then estimated the shape of the missing part of the tail using West's modified maximum likelihood method. Finally, from the estimated tail we calculated the estimated mean value of the top-coded cases within each occupation and imputed this value to each person with top-coded earnings within that occupation.

The second problem in implementing our strategy was that we had too few observations on some of our detailed occupations to generate reliable results. To deal with this problem, we estimated the mean value of earnings in the top-coded cases at two different levels: once at the most detailed occupation level (that is, "three-digit" or "500-category"), and once at a slightly more aggregated level (that is, "two-digit" or "50-category"). For every detailed occupation for which there were at least 300 observations, we used the estimated value for that occupation. For every detailed occupation for which there were less than 300 observations, we used a weighted average of the value calculated for that detailed occupation and of the value calculated for the two-digit occupation of which that detailed occupation was a part. The weight given to the estimate from the detailed occupation was equal to the number of observations divided by 300. In addition, if one of the two estimates was greater than $200,000 (in March 1971 and 1979) or $400,000 (in March 1987 and 1995), then only the remaining estimate was used. Finally, if both of the estimates were greater than $200,000 or $400,000, then the estimated mean value of the top-coded cases was set at $200,000 or $400,000. This last case occurred between zero and three times over the four years examined.

Note: 5.3: The Impact of Other Cognitive Skills on Wages

Functional literacy is but one of several cognitive and other skills influencing wages. Since some of these skills may be correlated with functional literacy, the calculated coefficient relating functional literacy to employment and wages may be overstated. The purpose of this appendix is to gain some insights into the quantitative dimensions of this problem.

Since the NALS data set does not include suitable data for such an investigation, we have combined it with another data set focusing exclusively on skills necessary for particular occupations. This forces us to calculate the regressions by occupation, rather than person. The first step, therefore, is condensing the NALS data by calculating for each occupation the weighted average functional literacy scores, wages, racial and gender composition, and other variables. The second step is to merge these with data on a variety of skill ratings for different occupations from the U.S. Department of Labor's *Dictionary of Occupational Titles*, which we discuss briefly in Appendix A3.3. As in Table A3.1 we rescale these skill ratings so they all run from zero (low) to 10 (high).

Before proceeding, however, several words of caution are necessary. For some occupational groups within the NALS, the number of cases is very small, so that there is considerable statistical noise in the condensed data. The skill ratings of various occupations from *Dictionary of Occupational Titles* also give rise to many problems. First, as noted in Appendix 3.3, the original ratings are somewhat subjective. For instance, the degree to which the various committees actually used a common scale to make their judgements is unknown. Second, these data are outdated since they were made more than 20 years ago. In many cases, skill ratings from even earlier years were carried over without review. Third, the data also do not include such skills as ability to work in groups or special leadership skills. Although these skill ratings by the U.S. Department of Labor are problematic in many cases and contain considerable statistical noise, they are nevertheless the best data on occupational skill requirements that are available.

Table A5.2: *Average Weekly Wages in 1992 in Different Occupations of Full-Time Prime-Age Workers as a Function of Particular Occupational Characteristics*

	Sample means	Model 1 Calculated regression	Standard error	Model 2 Calculated regression	Standard error
Dependent variable: logarithm of average weekly wages in the occupation					
Intercept		+3.991*	0.201	+4.591*	0.241
Independent variables					
Characteristics of those in occupation					
Average functional literacy score	295.5	+0.0039*	0.0007	+0.0031*	0.0007
Average years of education	13.9	+0.075*	0.011	+0.048	*0.012
Percent of women	37.7	-0.409*	0.044	-0.418*	0.048
Percent of black, Non-Hispanics	10.3	-0.086	0.090	-0.086	0.089
Percent of Hispanics	8.5	-0.029	0.101	-0.080	0.100
Percent of "other races"	2.8	-0.371*	0.178	-0.430*	0.174
Average weeks worked in year	46.8	+0.005	0.003	+0.003	0.003
Necessary skills for occupation (scale 0 to 10)					
Structural complexity (analytic skills)	4.6	—	—	+0.036*	0.011
Strength required	3.3	—	—	-0.021*	0.011
Adjusted coefficient of determination (R^2)		.5040		.5255	
Size of sample		433		433	

Notes: The data on the characteristics of those in the occupation come from the NALS; the data on necessary skills for the occupation come from Roos and Treiman (1980).

Appendix Notes

Note: 5.4: Wage Regressions at Different Points in Time

Table A5.3: *CPS Wage Regressions in 1994 dollars*

| | Calculated regression coefficients | | | |
| | Men | | Women | |
	1971	1995	1971	1995
Dependent variable = natural log of median weekly wage				
Intercept	+5.889*	+6.039*	+5.539	+5.807*
Highest educational level: High-school diploma is the basis of comparison				
High-school dropout	-0.139*	-0.217*	-0.082*	-0.145*
Some university or trade/voc. school	+0.057*	+0.082*	+0.101*	+0.106*
At least one university degree	+0.241*	+0.242*	+0.305*	+0.395*
Race/ethnicity variables: White is the basis of comparison				
Black	-0.236*	-0.138*	-0.021	-0.038*
Other races/ethnic groups	-0.169*	-0.059*	-0.017	-0.030*
Occupational groups by level of educational intensiveness in 1971-72. tier 4 occupations (>14.5 years of schooling) is the basis of comparison				
Tier 1 occupations: 0–10.5 years	-0.275*	-0.419*	-0.344*	-0.413*
Tier 2 occupations: 10.6–12.0 years	-0.176*	-0.319*	-0.244*	-0.344*
Tier 3 occupations: 12.1–14.5 years	-0.060*	-0.137*	-0.112*	-0.098*
Region of residence: Northeast is basis of comparison				
South	+0.046*	-0.066*	-0.032*	-0.106*
Midwest	-0.086*	-0.105*	-0.107*	-0.120*
West	+0.022*	-0.076*	+0.000	-0.069*
Residence: Live in metropolitan area is basis of comparison				
Not live in MSA	-0.115*	-0.087*	-0.124*	-0.138*
MSA not designated	—	-0.070*	—	-0.142*
Age: 25–29 is basis of comparison				
Age 30–34	+0.104*	+0.145*	+0.012	+0.110*
Age 35–39	+0.172*	+0.253*	+0.018	+0.155*
Age 40–44	+0.181*	+0.293*	+0.032*	+0.179*
Age 45–49	+0.186*	+0.340*	+0.045*	+0.188*
Weeks worked last year	+0.003*	+0.003*	+0.005*	+0.005*
Dummy variables for 21 industries	Yes	Yes	Yes	Yes
Adjusted coefficient of determination (R^2)	.2977	.3027	.3144	.3356
Size of sample	18794	22489	8229	16923

Notes: The data come from the Current Population Survey, March 1971 and March 1995. An asterisk denotes a calculated coefficient that is statistically significant at the .05 level. Only full-time workers earning between $80 and $4000 a week are included in the regression.

Chapter 6

Note 6.1: More Charts on the Wage Distribution

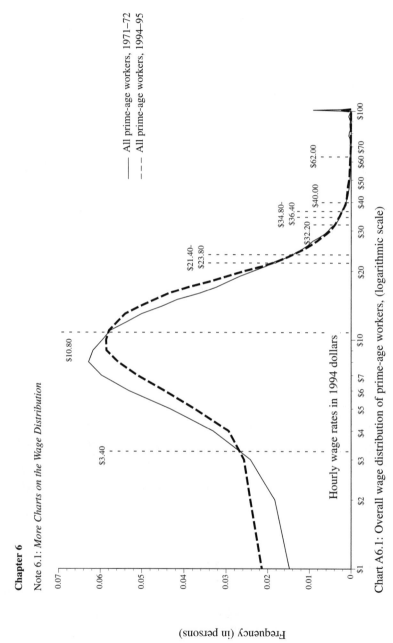

Chart A6.1: Overall wage distribution of prime-age workers, (logarithmic scale)

Notes: Data come from Current Population Survey.

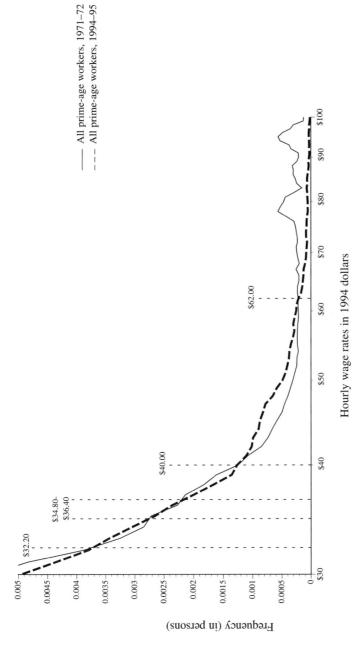

Chart A6.2: High end of the overall wage distribution of of prime-age workers (logarithmic scale)

Notes: See notes for Chart A6.1

The results of the regression experiments are reported in Table A5.2. Since all of the independent variables representing characteristics of the occupations might have an impact on wages, it is necessary to proceed by trial and error.

The demographic and other variables employed throughout the discussion explain about half of the variation in the logarithm of the weekly wage. As before, functional literacy and education have independent and positive impacts on wages. A change in one standard deviation of functional literacy is associated with a 26 percent change in weekly wages, other variables held constant.

Wages are significantly lower in those occupations where the percentage of women is higher. The same also holds true with those occupations where the percentage of those of "other races" is higher, but this is such a heterogeneous category that it is difficult to determine what is happening. The other demographic variables play no significant role.

We added 12 variables, drawn from Roos and Treiman (1980), which represent other necessary skills for the various occupations. These only raised the coefficient of determination about 2.4 percentage points. Without the demographic variables, they explain 37 percent of the variation of the logarithm of the weekly wage. When individually added, several skills proved to have a statistically significant explanatory power including: data skills, people skills (interpersonal skills), substantive complexity (analytic skills), physical strength requirements, specific vocational preparation, and general educational level. Nevertheless, these did not seem to be very robust relationships and, when taken two at a time, only the regression coefficients for the requirements for analytic skills and physical strength proved statistically significant. Average wages fall as the strength required for the job rises. We would expect such results since these occupations are declining in relative importance and there are still many who have little to offer the job market other than their muscles. Average wages rise as the analytic skills necessary for the job increase. These analytic skills are different from either education or functional literacy, so that we really have three cognitive dimensions to take into account for understanding differences in wage rates of various occupations.

As expected, the calculated coefficient relating functional literacy to wages is lower in Model 2 than Model 1, when the other skill variables are included. The difference in the calculated coefficient in the two models is about 20 percent, which we use as a rough approximation of the bias when discussing the results from Table 5.3.

In sum, functional literacy plus the demographic and other variables used throughout this essay appear the most important explanatory variables for wages. The addition of other skills – particularly requirements of physical strength and analytic abilities – adds additional explanatory power to the regressions, as well as reducing the impact of functional literacy alone.

Chapter 7

Note 7.1: The Impact of Immigration on the Employment of Native-Born Workers

Two separate questions must be asked in determining the impact of immigrants on employment of native workers: Are immigrants pushing the native-born out of specific labor markets? And what impact on overall employment does such immigration have? The second question has received considerable attention in the economic literature, and in our discussion, we only summarize some of the most important results of others.

Displacement of natives by immigrants in specific labor markets. Immigration can have quite different effects on native workers in local and national labor markets. For instance, immigrants might displace native workers in a particular labor market or, more subtly, high inflows of foreign immigrants may discourage migration to that area by native workers. Despite events on local labor markets, in both cases immigration might or might not have an affect on employment for the nation as a whole.

Since considerable recent work has focused on this displacement effect (for instance, Borjas, Freeman, and Katz (1997)), it is not necessary to present our results in detail. One of our calculations, however, deserves brief mention. In this investigation we arranged data on the various metropolitan areas according to the change in the number of foreign-born between 1970 and 1980. In the top five metropolitan areas of immigrant flow (Los Angeles area, Miami, New York City, Anaheim-Santa Ana-Garden Grove, and Houston), the foreign-born increased 4.1 million while the native population decreased 2.3 million. Clearly population displacement occurred and is like to occur in these areas in the future, since immigrants often choose to live with others sharing their ethnic background. These issues are discussed in greater detail by many including Borjas, Butcher and Card (1991), Lalonde and Topel (1992) and Altonji and Card (1991).

By way of contrast, in the next five ranking metropolitan areas the foreign-born increased 1.5 million and the native-born increased 1.7 million. Moreover, in the remaining 192 metropolitan areas, the foreign-born increased 2.5 million, while the native-born increased 19.5 million..

Looking at the U.S. as a whole, one important result emerges from several extensive studies such as those by Frey (1994, 1996), Filer (1992) and Borjas, Freeman and Katz (1997). Briefly, less skilled native workers living in states or metropolitan areas receiving large number of immigrants in the late 1980s were more likely to migrate elsewhere. This result also indicates potential difficulties of interpretation when comparing employment rates in cross-section analyses of U.S. metropolitan areas.

Such studies raise a question: What is the relevant labor market for making such comparisons of labor displacement? A recent study of the wage impact of immigrants by Borjas, Freeman, and Katz (1996) argues that the relevant size of the labor market may not be the metropolitan area, but rather the state or the region. Their regressions showing the impact of a changing number of immigrants on wage changes, while holding education and area effects constant, show no impact in various metropolitan areas. By way of contrast, they do find a statistically significant and negative effect if the empirical focus is changed to the state or the region.

Job displacement for the nation as a whole. To avoid a confusion sometimes found in discussions about the impact of immigration, the problem of the time-period of analysis deserves brief attention. If all markets functioned perfectly, an influx of low-skilled immigrants would, in the short-run, lead to a certain displacement of native low-skilled workers, as well as a decline in wages. In the long-run, however, managers would have time to adjust their technologies to absorb such unskilled workers. Moreover, as long as relative prices of unskilled-labor intensive goods do not fall, the wages of unskilled workers will not decline.

Markets do not, however, function perfectly and a long-run equilibrium may never be achieved if immigration into the area continues. So wage and employment effects of immigration may in this restricted sense be permanent.

At first glance it appears easy to determine the impact of immigrants on the share of less-educated native workers employed in the various metropolitan areas. One need merely examine the determinants of the employment rate of native-born workers and include as an explanatory variable the percentage of foreign-born in the population. Unfortunately, such a method does not take into account a statistical bias arising because immigrants may be attracted to some cities with low initial rates of unemployment.

Several methods of circumventing the problem can be found in the economic literature, although each of the various solutions raises its own set of problems, all of which are discussed by Altonji and Card (1991). Some have looked at first differences, that is, the change in unemployment related to the change in the number of immigrants. Others have used an instrumental variables technique, by which a particular labor market's attractiveness to immigrants is approximated by some variable, such as the number of immigrants already in the area. Although both techniques can be justified, some obvious objections can also be raised. We tried a different technique, namely focusing our attention on employment of the less-educated native population while holding constant certain employment data of the more-educated. This allows us to account for the fact that if non-employment of the more-educated is higher in a particular labor market, then we would expect non-employment of the less-educated to be higher as well. The results we obtained were little different from those of others.

The various studies in the economic literature are competently and clearly reviewed by Borjas, (1994), so there is little need to replicate his analysis. Almost all studies show that immigration has a weak effect on the employment of native-born workers. Of these, a study by Altonji and Card (1991) shows the greatest adverse impact of immigration on employment of less-educated workers. Without taking into account the statistical bias discussed above, they conclude that a 10 percent point increase in the fraction of immigrants in an MSA would lead to a reduction of the employment rate of less-educated natives of roughly two percent in 1970. For 1980 they found a much smaller decline. When they attempted to take account of the statistical bias, this negative impact on native employment was eliminated. They conclude: "On balance . . . the effect of immigrant densities on the employment and participation rates of (low-skilled) natives is small and potentially zero." More recently, Borjas, Freeman, and Katz (1997, p. 25) conclude from their econometric study: "The one valid inference from an analysis of spatial correlations is that immigration is not a major determinant of the regional structure of labor market outcomes (employment and wages) for natives."

An interesting natural experiment occurred in 1980 when Fidel Castro permitted the emmigration of Cuban nationals. Roughly 125,000 Cubans, mostly unskilled, arrived in Florida and Miami's labor force increased seven percent. David Card's (1990) study of the impact of this shock shows that within a relatively short time, the impact on wages and employment of various competing groups of Miami workers barely changed. Borjas (1994) reviews other studies of a like nature in other locations and finds similar results. Such studies, however, usually do not focus directly on the outflow of native workers, but rather on the employment of native workers who remain.

Other empirical approaches to the impact of immigration on the employment rates of native-born workers do not rely on regression techniques but instead apply alternative types of statistical analyses, for instance, the use of similarity indices by Rearnon (1997 forthcoming). Although we can discuss these at much greater length, we must always return to the conclusion of the analysis in Chapter 3, namely, for the nation as a whole, the number of jobs requiring few educational credentials have increased faster than the prime-age workers with just a high-school education or less. It does not seem likely, therefore, that immigration is the key cause for increasing joblessness among less-educated males.

Chapter 8

Note 8.1: Determinants of Hiring Criteria and of Labor Force Composition

If we hold the cynical view that the stated hiring criteria are simply a rationalization of who is hired, then the statistical analysis is clear. We should use the various hiring criteria as the dependent variable and the various attributes of the workplace as the independent variables in any kind of regression analysis. Such an exercise is carried out in Table A8.1.

Table A8.1: *Determinants of hiring criteria*

Dependent variable (Scale 1 to 5)	Work attitudes		Communication skills	
	Coefficient	Standard error	Coefficient	Standard error
Independent variables				
Constant	+4.0136*	0.1981	+3.9197*	0.2340
Percent full-time workers in establishment	-0.0007	0.0980	-0.1173	0.1158
Percent production workers	-0.0004	0.0006	-0.0039*	0.0007
Average education in years of production workers	+0.0086	0.0105	+0.0525*	0.0124
Percent full-time workers who are women	+0.0019*	0.0008	+0.0028*	0.0009
Percent full-time workers who are minorities	-0.0008	0.0006	-0.0021*	0.0007
Percent of full-time workers with less than one year at firm	-0.0023*	0.0010	-0.0044*	0.0012
Establishment adopted total quality management program	+0.0072	0.0325	-0.1668*	0.0384
Percent of non-managerial workers who attend regular staff meetings	+0.0006	0.0004	+0.0015*	0.0005
Job sharing between employees	+0.0512	0.0358	+0.0219	0.0423
Percent non-managers/supervisors in job rotation	+0.0014*	0.0006	+0.0007	0.0007
Percent non-manager/supervisor in self-managed teams	+0.0003	0.0006	+0.0017*	0.0007
Level of wages	-0.0337*	0.0171	-0.0493*	0.0202
Union representation	+0.0756*	0.0365	+0.0331	0.0431
19 dummy variables for industries	Yes		Yes	
Adjusted coefficient of determination	.0325		.1609	
Sample size	2319		2317	

Notes: The data come from the Educational Quality of the Workforce data bank. The asterisks designate statistical significance at the .05 level. A more exact source reference is given in the footnote to Table 8.1.

Table A8.2: *Labor Force Composition as a Function of Hiring Criteria*

Dependent variable	Percent of minority workers		Percent of female workers	
	Coefficient	Standard error	Coefficient	Standard error
Independent variables				
Constant	+41.79*	3.63	+21.79*	3.75
Importance of previous work experience	-0.9275	0.5197	+0.0963	0.5374
Importance of boss's recommendation	+0.6880	0.4453	+1.1369*	0.4605
Importance of years of education	-2.0404*	0.5503	-0.7575	0.5691
Importance of academic performance	-0.5094	0.6292	-0.5671	0.6506
Importance of teacher's recommendation	-0.5204	0.5428	+1.6730*	0.5612
Importance of co-worker's recommendation	+0.5179	0.4822	-1.1610	0.4986
Importance of reputation of applicant's school	+0.4511	0.5163	+0.0374	0.5339
Importance of applicant's attitude	-0.0034	0.7870	-0.6032	0.8138
Importance of communication skills	-1.1332	0.6517	+4.8871*	0.6739
Importance of interview test scores	+0.3384	0.3439	+0.1142	0.3556
Importance of industry-based credentials	-1.2085*	0.4253	-0.6631	0.4398
Adjusted coefficient of determination	0.0222		.0304	
Sample size	2544		2544	

Notes: The data come from the Educational Quality of the Workforce data bank. The asterisks designate statistical significance at the .05 level. A more exact source reference is given in the footnote to Table 8.1.

The results show that such an approach has very limited success. For some hiring criteria such as work attitudes, the characteristics of the firm explain relatively little of the variation. For other hiring criteria such as communication skills, the characteristics of the firm explain somewhat more, although the degree of explanatory power is hardly impressive.

By way of contrast, if we believe that the employment criteria can help us explain the composition of the workforce, then we should use particular labor force characteristics such as the racial or gender composition of the labor force of the enterprise as the dependent variable and the various work criteria as the independent variables. Such an experiment is carried out in Table A8.2.

The results of this experiment to explain the share of women and minorities in the labor force are even less impressive, since both regressions have very low explanatory power. When dummy variables representing the various industries are added, the statistical significance of the criteria variables for minority workers does not greatly change, but for female workers their statistical significance is reduced.

From these two types of experiments we must conclude that the relationships between who is hired (defined in terms of race and gender) and the hiring criteria are not strong.

Bibliography

Abowd, John M. and Richard B. Freeman, editors. 1991-a. *Immigration, Trade, and the Labor Market*. Chicago: University of Chicago Press.

Abowd, John M. and Richard B. Freeman. 1991-b. "Introduction and Summary," in Abowd and Freeman, editors (1991-a): pp. 1–29.

Abraham, Katharine G. 1991. "Mismatch and Labour Mobility: Some Final Remarks," in Padoa-Schioppa (1991): pp. 453–80.

———. 1997. "Comment on Farber," *Brookings Papers on Economic Activity: Microeconomics*: pp. 135–41.

Altonji, Joseph G. and David Card. 1991. "Immigration and the Labor Market Outcomes of Less-skilled Natives," in Abowd and Freeman (1991): pp. 201–35.

Amsden, Alice H. 1996. "Convergence, Technological Competition, and Transmission of Long-run Unemployment," in Eatwell (1996-a): pp. 41–58.

Anderson, Elijah. 1990. *Street Wise*. Chicago: University of Chicago Press.

Anon. 1990. "Americans at Work," *The Public Perspective* 1, No. 6 (`November/December): p. 82.

Anon. 1992. "The American Worker," *The Public Perspective* 3, No. 4 (May/June): pp. 111–16.

Autor, David H., Lawrence F. Katz, and Alan Krueger. 1997. "Computing Inequality: Have Computers Changed the Labor Market?" National Bureau of Economic Research, *Working Paper* 5956. Cambridge, Massachusetts.

Bacharach, Michael. 1970. *Biproportional Matrices and Input-Output Change*. Cambridge, England: Cambridge University Press.

Badgett, M. V. Lee and Heidi I. Hartman. 1995. "The Effectiveness of Equal Employment Opportunity Policies," in Margaret C. Simms, editor. *Economic Perspectives on Affirmative Action*. Washington, D.C.: Joint Center for Political and Economic Studies.

Barlett, Don and Jim Steele. 1996. *America: Who Stole the Dream?* Kansas City, Missouri: Andrews and McMeel.

Bartelsman, Eric J. and Wayne B. Gray. 1996. "The NBER Manufacturing Productivity Database," National Bureau of Economic Research, *Technical Working Paper* 205. Cambridge, Massachusetts.

Baumol, William J. and Edward N. Wolff. 1996. "Protracted Frictional Unemployment as a Heavy Cost of Technical Progress, "The Jerome Levy Economic Instituter of Bard College, *Working Paper* 179. Annandale-on-Hudson, New York.

Bayoumi, Tamim. 1990. "Saving-Investment Correlations," International Monetary Fund, *Staff Papers* 37, No. 2 (June): pp. 360–87.

Bergmann, Barbara R. 1996. *In Defense of Affirmative Action*. New York: HarperCollins.

Bergstrand, Jeffrey H., *et al.*, editors. 1994. *The Changing Distribution of Income in an Open U.S. Economy*. Amsterdam: North-Holland.

Berman, Eli, John Bound, and Zvi Griliches. 1994. "Changes in the Demand for Skilled Labor within U.S. Manufacturing: Evidence From the Annual Survey of Manufactures," *Quarterly Journal of Economics* 109, No. 2 (May): pp. 367–98.

Berman, Eli, Stephen Machin, and John Bound. 1996. "Implications of Skill-Biased Technological Changes: International Evidence," processed.

Betts, Julian R. 1995. "Does School Quality Matter? Evidence from the National Longitudinal Survey of Youth," *Review of Economics and Statistics* 77, No. 2 (May): 231–50.

Bhagwati, Jagdish and Marvin H. Kosters, editors. 1994. *Trade and Wages: Leveling Wages Down?* Washington, D.C.: AEI Press.

Bishop, John. 1991. "Achievement, Test Scores, and Relative Wages," in Kosters (1991): pp. 146–87.

Blackburn, McKinley L., David E. Bloom, and Richard B. Freeman. 1990. "The Declining Economic Position of Less-Skilled American Men," in Gary Burtless, editor. *A Future of Lousy Jobs: The Changing Structure of U.S. Wages*. Washington, D.C.: Brookings Institution, pp. 31–77.

Blackburn, McKinley and David Neumark. 1993. "Omitted-Ability Bias and the Increase in the Return to Schooling," *The Journal of Labor Economics* 11, No. 3 (July): pp. 521–544.

Blanchflower, David G. and Andrew J. Oswald. 1994. *The Wage Curve*. Cambridge, Massachusetts: MIT Press.

Blank, Rebecca M. 1997. *It Takes a Nation: A New Agenda for Fighting Poverty*. New York: Russell Sage Foundation.

Blau, Francine, and Lawrence M. Kahn. 1996-a. "International Differences in Male Wage Inequality: Institutions versus Market Forces," *Journal of Political Economy* 104, No. 4 (August): pp. 791–836.

———. 1996-b. "Wage Structure and Gender Earnings Differentials: An International Comparison," *Economica* 63, No. 250 (Supplement): pp. S29–S62.

———. 1994. "Rising Wage Inequality and the U.S. Gender Gap," *American Economic Review* 84, No. 2 (May): pp. 23–8.

Borjas, George J. 1995. "The Internationalization of the U.S. Labor Market and the Wage Structure," Federal Reserve Bank of New York, *Economic Policy Review*, 1, No. 1 (January): pp. 3–8.

———. 1994. "The Economics of Immigration," *Journal of Economic Literature* 33, No. 4 (December): pp. 1667–1718.

Borjas, George J. and Richard B. Freeman, editors. 1992. *Immigration and the Work Force*. Chicago: University of Chicago Press.

Borjas, George J., Richard B.. Freeman, and Lawrence F. Katz. 1992. "On the Labor Market Effects of Immigration and Trade," in George J. Borjas and Richard B. Freeman, editors (1992): pp. 213–44.

———. 1996. "Searching for the Effect of Immigration on the Labor Market." National Bureau of Economic Research, *Working Paper* 5454. Cambridge, Massachusetts.

———. 1997. "How Much Do Immigration and Trade Affect Labor Market Outcomes?" *Brookings Papers on Economic Activity* No. 1: pp. 1–67.

Borjas, George J., Richard B. Freeman, and Kevin Lang. 1991. "Undocumented Mexican-born Workers in the United States: How Many, How Permanent?" in Abowd and Freeman (1991-a): pp. 77-101.

Borjas, George J., and Valerie A. Ramey. 1995. "Foreign Competition, Market Power, and Wage Inequality," *Quarterly Journal of Economics* 110, No. 4 (November): pp. 1075–1110.

———. 1994. "Time-Series Evidence on the Sources of Trends in Wage Inequality," *American Economic Review* 81, No. 2 (May): pp. 292–296.

Bound, John, and George Johnson. 1995. "What Are the Causes of Rising Wage Inequality in the United States?" Federal Reserve Bank of New York, *Economic Policy Review* 1, No. 1 (January): pp. 9–17.

————. 1992. "Changes in the Structure of Wages in the 1980s: An Evaluation of Alternative Explanations," *American Economic Review* 82, No. 3 (June): pp. 371–392.

Bradbury, Katharine L. 1996. "The Growing Inequality of Family Incomes: Changing Families and Changing Wages," *New England Economic Review*, (July/August): pp. 55–82.

Bradbury, Katharine L., Yolanda K. Kodrzycki, and Christopher J. Mayer. 1996. "Spatial and Labor Market Contributions to Earnings Inequality: An Overview," *New England Economic Review*, (May/June): pp. 1–10.

Brauer, David A., and Susan Hickok. 1995. "Explaining the Growing Inequality in Wages Across Skill Levels," Federal Reserve Bank of New York, *Economic Policy Review* 1, No. 1 (January): pp. 61–75.

Brenner, M. Harvey 1973. *Mental Illness and the Economy*. Cambridge, Massachusetts: Harvard University Press.

Brigger, John E. and Steven E. Haugen. 1995. "BLS Introduces a New Range of Alternative Unemployment Measures," *Monthly Labor Review* 118, Number 10 (October): pp. 19–27.

Brown, James N. and Audrey Light. 1992. "Interpreting Panel Data on Job Tenure," *Journal of Labor Economics* 10, Number 3 (July): pp. 219–57.

Buchholz, Rogene A. 1978. "The Work Ethic Reconsidered," *Industrial and Labor Relations Review* 31, No. 4 (July): pp. 450–60.

Buron, Lawrence, Robert Haveman, and Owen O'Donnell. 1995. "Recent Trends in U.S. Male Work and Wage Patterns: An Overview," University of Wisconsin-Madison, Institute for Research On Poverty, *Discussion Paper* No. 1060-95.

Burtless, Gary. 1996. "Trends in the Level and Distribution of U.S. Living Standards: 1973–93," *Eastern Economic Journal* 22, No. 3 (Summer): pp. 271–190.

————. 1995. "International Trade and the Rise in Earnings Inequality," *Journal of Economic Literature* 33, No. 2 (June): pp. 800–816.

Butcher, Kristin and David Card. 1991. "Immigration and Wages: Evidence from the 1980's," *American Economic Review* 81, No. 2 (May): pp. 292–6.

Cameron, Stephen V. and James J. Heckman. 1993. "The Nonequivalence of High School Equivalents," *Journal of Labor Economics* 11, No. 1 (January): pp. 1–47.

Campbell, Anne, Irwin S. Kirsch, Andrew Kolstad. 1992. *Assessing Literacy*. Washington, D.C.: U.S. Department of Education, National Center for Educational Statistics.

Cappelli, Peter. 1993. "Are Skilling Requirements Rising? Evidence from Production and Clerical Jobs," *Industrial and Labor Relations Review* 46, No. 3 (April): pp. 515–30.

————. 1996. "Technological and Skill Requirements: Implications for Establishing Wage Structures," *New England Economic Review*, Special Issue, *Earning and Inequality*. May/June: pp. 139–54.

————. n.d. "Is the 'Skills Gap' Really about Attitudes," EQW, *Working Papers* 5. Philadelphia, Pennsylvania: National Center on the Educational Quality of the Labor Force.

Card, David and Alan B. Krueger. 1995. *Myth and Measurement: The New Economics of the Minimum Wage*. Princeton, New Jersey: Princeton University Press.

Chiricos, Theodore G. 1987, "Rates of Crime and Unemployment: An Analysis of Aggregate Research Evidence," *Social Problems* 34, No. 2 (April): pp. 187–204.

Chiswick, Barry R. and Teresa A. Sullivan. 1995. "The New Immigrants," in Farley (1995): pp. 211–71.

Cline, William R. 1997. *Trade and Wage Inequality*. Washington, D.C.: Institute for International Economics.

Clogg, Clifford C., Donald B. Rubin, Nathaniel Schenker, Bradley Schultz, Lynn Weidman. 1991. "Multiple Imputation of Industry and Occupation Codes in Census Public-use Samples Using Bayesian Logistic Regression," *Journal of the American Statistical Association* 86, No. 413 (March): pp. 68–78.

Cohany, Sharon R., *et al.* 1994. "Revisions in the Current Population Survey Effective January 1994," *Employment and Earnings* 41, No. 2 (February): pp. 13–38.

Constantine, Jill, and David Neumark. 1996. "Training and the Growth of Wage Inequality," *Industrial Relations* 35, No. 4 (October): pp. 491–510.

Council of Economic Advisors. Annual. *Economic Report of the President*. Washington, D.C.: G.P.O.

Danziger, Sheldon and Peter Gottschalk. 1995. *America Unequal* (Cambridge, MA: Harvard University Press.

Danziger, Sheldon and Peter Gottschalk, editors. 1993. *Uneven Tides: Rising Inequality in America*. New York: Russell Sage Foundation.

Davis, Steven J. and John Haltiwanger. 1992. "Gross Job Creation, Gross Job Destruction, and Employment Reallocation," *Quarterly Journal of Economics* 103, No. 3 (August): pp. 819–63.

Davis, Steven J., John Haltiwanger, and Scott Schuh. 1996. *Job Creation and Destruction*. Cambridge: MIT Press.

Day, Jennifer Cheeseman. 1993. *Population Projections of the United States, By Age, Sex, Race, and Hispanic Origin: 1993 to 2050*. U.S. Department of Commerce, Census Bureau, *Current Population Report* P25-1104. Washington, D.C.: G.P.O.

Devenow, Andrea, and Ivo Welch. 1996. "Rational Herding in Financial Economics," *European Economic Review*, 40, No. 3-5 (April): pp. 603–15.

Diebold, Francis X., David Neumark, and Daniel Polsky. 1994. "Job Stability in the United States," National Bureau of Economic Research, *Working Paper* 4859. Cambridge, Massachusetts.

———. 1995. "Is Job Stability Declining in the U.S. Economy? Comment," *Industrial and Labor Relations Review* 49, Number 2 (January): pp. 348–52.

DiNardo, John, Nicole M. Fortin, and Thomas Lemieux. 1996. "Labor Market Institutions and the Distribution of Wages, 1973–1992: A Semiparametric Approach," *Econometrica* 64, No. 5 (September): pp. 1001–44.

DiNardo, John E. and Jörn-Steffen Pischke. 1997. "The Returns to Computer Use Revisited: Have Pencils Changed the Wage Structure Too," *Quarterly Journal of Economics* 112, No. 1 (February): pp. 291–303.

Dunlop, John T. 1957. "The Tasks of Contemporary Wage Theory," in Dunlop, editor, *The Theory of Wage Determination*. London: Macmillan: 3–27.

Eatwell, John, editor. 1996-a. *Global Unemployment: Loss of Jobs in the '90s*. Armonk, New York: M.E. Sharpe.

Eatwell, John, 1996-b. "Introduction," in Eatwell (1996-a): pp. 3–20.

Engen, Eric M., William G. Gale, and John Karl Scholz. 1996. "The Illusory Effects of Saving Incentives on Savings," *Journal of Economic Perspectives* 10, No. 4 (Fall): pp. 113–138.

Eissa, Nada. 1996. "Tax Reforms and Labor Supply," *Tax Policy and the Economy* 10, Cambridge, MIT Press for National Bureau of Economic Research .

Farber, Henry S. 1993. "The Incidence of Job Loss: 1982–91," *Brookings Papers on Economic Activity: Microeconomics* 1. Washington, D.C.

———. 1995. "Are Lifetime Jobs Disappearing: Job Duration in the United States, 1973–93," Industrial Relations Section, Princeton University, *Working Paper* No. 341. Princeton, New Jersey.

———. 1996. "The Changing Face of Job Loss in the United States, 1981–93," National Bureau of Economic Research, *Working Paper* 5596. Cambridge, Massachusetts.

———. 1997. "The Changing Face of Job Loss in the United States, 1981–95," *Brookings Papers on Economic Activity: Microeconomics*: pp. 55–128.

Farley, Reynolds, editor. 1995., *State of the Union: America in the 1990's*, Volume 2, *Social Trends*. New York: Russell Sage.

Feenstra, Robert C. 1996. "U.S. Imports, 1972–94: Data and Concordances," National Bureau of Economic Research, *Working Paper* 5515. Cambridge, Massachusetts.

———. 1997. "U.S. Exports, 1972–94: Data and Concordances," National Bureau of Economic Research, *Working Paper* 5910. Cambridge, Massachusetts.

Feenstra, Robert C. and Gordon H. Hanson. 1996. "Globalization, Outsourcing, and Wage Inequality," *American Economic Review* 86, No. 2 (May): pp. 240–5.

Ferguson, Ronald F. 1993. "New Evidence on the Growing Value of Skill and Consequences for Racial Disparity and Returns to Schooling," John F. Kennedy School of Government, Harvard University, Faculty Research, *Working Paper,* Series R93-34. Cambridge, Massachusetts.

Filer, Randall K. 1992. "Immigrant Arrivals and the Migratory Patterns of Native Workers," in Borjas and Freeman (1992): pp. 245–69.

Frank, Robert H. and Philip J. Cook. 1995. *The Winner-Take-All Society: How More and More Americans Compete for Ever Fewer and Bigger Prizes, Encouraging Economic Waste, Income Inequality, and an Impoverished Cultural Life*. New York: Free Press.

Frazis, Harley, Michelle Harrison Ports, and Jay Stewart. 1995. "Comparing Measures of Educational Attainment in the CPS," *Monthly Labor Review* 118, No. 9 (September): pp. 40–4.

Freeman, Richard B. 1996-a. "Labor Market Institutions and Earnings Inequality," *New England Economic Review*, (May/June): pp. 157–168.

———. 1996-b. "Why Do So Many Young American Men Commit Crimes and What Might We Do About It?" *Journal of Economic Perspectives* 10, No. 1 (Winter): pp. 25–42.

———. 1994. "The Labor Market," in James Q. Wilson, editor. *Crime and Public Policy*. San Francisco: ICS Press: pp. 171–91.

Freeman, Richard B, and Lawrence F. Katz, editors. 1995. *Differences and Changes in Wage Structures*. Chicago, Illinois: University of Chicago Press.

———. 1994-a. "Rising Wage Inequality: The United States Vs. Other Advanced Countries," in Freeman and Katz (1994-b).

———. 1994-b. Editors. *Working Under Different Rules*. New York, New York: Russell Sage Foundation.

Frey, William H. 1994. "The New White Flight," *American Demographics* 16, No. 4 (April): pp. 40–8.

———. 1996. "Immigration and Internal Migration 'Flight' from US Metropolitan Areas: Toward a New Demographic Balkanisation," *Urban Studies* 32, No. 4/5 (May): pp. 733–59.

Friedlander, Daniel and Gary Burtless. 1994. *Five Years After: The Long-Term Effects of Welfare-to-Work Programs*. New York: Russell Sage Foundation.

Gale, Douglas, 1996. "What Have We Learned from Social Learning?" *European Economic Review*, 40, Nos. 3-5 (April): pp. 617–28.

Gardner, Jennifer M. 1995. "Worker Displacement: A Decade of Change," *Monthly Labor Review* 188, No. 4 (April): pp. 45–57.

Ginzberg, Eli, editor. 1994. *The Changing U.S. Labor Market*. New York: Eisenhower Center for the Conservation of Human Resources, and Boulder, Colorado: Westview Press.

Grogger, Jeff. 1996. "Does School Quality Explain the Recent Black/White Wage Trend," *Journal of Labor Economics* 14, No. 2 (April): 231–54.

Grubb, W. Norton. 1996. *Learning to Work: The Case for Reintegrating Job Training and Education*. New York: Russell Sage.

Haltiwanger, John, 1997. "Comment on Farber," *Brookings Papers on Economic Activity: Microeconomics*: pp. 129–35.

Hamermesh, Daniel S. 1989. "What Do We Know About Worker Displacement in the U.S.?" *Industrial Relations* 28, No. 1 (Winter): pp. 51–9.

Hanushek, Eric A. and Dongwook Kim. 1995. "Schooling, Labor Force Quality, and Economic Growth," National Bureau of Economic Research, *Working Paper* 5500. Cambridge, Massachusetts.

Hecker, Daniel E. 1992. "Reconciling Conflicting Data on Jobs for College Graduates," *Monthly Labor Review* 115, No. 7 (July): pp. 3–13.

——. 1995. "College Graduates in 'High School' Jobs: A Commentary," *Monthly Labor Review* 118, No. 12 (December): p. 28.

Heckman, James J., Lance Lochner, Jeffrey Smith, and Christopher Taber. 1997. "The Effects of Government Policy on Human Capital Investment and Wage Inequality," processed.

Heckman, James J., Rebecca L. Roselius, and Jeffrey A. Smith. 1994. "U.S. Education and Training Policy: A Re-evaluation of the Underlying Assumptions behind the 'New Consensus'," in Solmon and Levenson (1994}: pp. 83–121.

Holzer, Henry J. 1991. "The Spatial Mismatch Hypothesis: What Has the Evidence Shown," *Urban Studies* No. 1 (February): pp. 105–22.

——. 1994. "Black Employment Problems: New Evidence, Old Questions," *Journal of Policy Analysis and Management* 13, No. 4: pp. 699–722.

——. 1996-a. "Employer Skill Needs and Labor Market Outcomes," processed.

——. 1996-b. *What Employers Want: Job Prospects for Less-Educated Workers.* New York: Russell Sage.

Horowitz M. and I. Herrnstadt. 1966. "Changes in Skill Requirements of Occupations in Selected Industries," in National Commission on Technology, *Technology and the American Economy*, Appendix, Volume 2, *Changes in the Skill Requirements of Occupations in Selected Industries*. Washington, D.C.: G.P.O.

Howell, David R. 1997. "Institutional Failure and the American Worker: The Collapse of Low-Skill Wages," Jerome Levy Economics Institute of Bard College, *Working Paper* 29-1997. Annandale-on-Hudson, New York.

Howell, David R. and Edward Wolff. 1991. "Trends in the Growth and Distribution of Skill in the U.S. Workplace, 1960–1985," *Industrial and Labor Relations Review* 44, No. 3 (April): pp. 481–501.

Hubbard, R. Glenn and Jonathan S. Skinner. 1996 . "Assessing the Effectiveness of Saving Incentives," *Journal of Economic Perspectives* 10, No. 4 (Fall): pp. 73–90.

Hughes, Mark Alan. 1989. "Misspeaking Truth to Power: A Geographical Perspective on the 'Underclass' Fallacy." *Economic Geography* 65, No. 3 (July):187–207.

Hunt, Earl. 1996. *Will We be Smart Enough: A Cognitive Analysis of the Coming Workforce.* New York: Russell Sage Foundation.

Inter-University Consortium for Political and Social Research (ICPSR). 1996. *Guide to Resources and Services, 1996–1997.* Ann Arbor, Michigan.

Jargowsky, Paul A. 1997. *Poverty and Place: Ghettos, Barrios and the American City.* New York: Russell Sage.

Jencks, Christopher S. and Susan E. Mayer. 1990. "Residential Segregation, Job Proximity, and Black Job Opportunities," in Lawrence E. Lynn, *et al. Inner-city Poverty in the United States.* Washington, D.C.: National Academy Press, pp. 187–222.

Jenkins, Stephen. 1991. "The Measurement of Income Inequality," in Lars Osberg, editor, *Economic Inequality and Poverty: International Perspectives.* Armonk, New York: M. E. Sharpe, Inc.

Johnson, George E. and Richard Layard. 1986. "The Natural Rate of Unemployment: Explanation and Policy," in Orley Aschenfelter and Richard Layard, editors. *Handbook of Labor Economics*, 2. Amsterdam: North Holland Press: pp. 921–99.

Juhn, Chinhui. 1992. "Decline in Male Labor Market Participation: The Role of Declining Market Opportunities," *Quarterly Journal of Economics* 197, No. 1: pp. 79–121.

Juhn, Chinhui, and Kevin Murphy. 1995. "Inequality in Labor Market Outcomes: Contrasting the 1980s and Earlier Decades," Federal Reserve Bank of New York. *Economic Policy Review* 1, No. 1 (January): pp. 26–32.

Juhn, Chinhui, Kevin M. Murphy, and Brooks Pierce. 1993. "Wage Inequality and the Rise in Returns to Skill," *Journal of Political Economy* 101, No. 3 (June): pp. 410–43.

Juhn, Chinhui, Kevin M. Murphy, and Robert H. Topel. 1991. "Why Has the Natural Rate of Unemployment Increased Over Time?" *Brookings Papers on Economic Activity*, Number 2: pp. 75–126.

Kain, John F. 1992. "The Spatial Mismatch Hypothesis: Three Decades Later," *Housing Policy Debate* 3, No. 2: pp. 371–460.

Kaplan, David and Richard L. Venezky. 1993. "What Can Employers Assume about the Literacy Skills of GED Graduates," National Center for Adult Literacy, *Technical Report* TR93-5. Philadelphia.

Karoly, Lynn A. 1993. "The Trend in Inequality Among Families, Individuals, and Workers in the United States: A Twenty-Five Year Perspective," in Danziger and Gottschalk (1993): pp. 19–97.

Kasarda, John D. 1995. "Industrial Restructuring and the Changing Location of Jobs," in Raymond Farley, editor. *State of the Union: America in the 1990s*, Volume 1, *Economic Trends*. New York: Russell Sage Foundation.

Katz, Lawrence F., Gary W. Loveman, and David G. Blanchflower. 1995. "A Comparison of Changes in the Structure of Wages in Four OECD Countries," in Freeman and Katz (1995).

Katz, Lawrence F., and Kevin M. Murphy. 1992. "Changes in Relative Wages: 1963–87: Supply and Demand Factors," *Quarterly Journal of Economics* 107, No. 1 (February): pp. 35–78.

Kim, Il-Joong, Bruce L. Benson, David W. Rasmussen, Thomas W. Zuehlke. 1989. "An Economic Analysis of Recidivism among Drug Offenders," *Southern Economic Journal* 29, No. 1: pp. 169–83.

Kirsch, Irwin S and Ann Jungeblut. 1986. *Literacy Profiles of America's Young Adults*, Educational Testing Service, *Report* 16-L-02. Princeton, New Jersey.

Kirsch, Irwin S., Ann Jungeblut, and Anne Campbell. 1992. *Beyond the School Doors: The Literacy Needs of Job Seekers Serviced by the U.S. Department of Labor*. Washington, D.C.: U.S. Department of Labor and Princeton, New Jersey: Educational Testing Service.

Kirsch, Irwin S., Ann Jungeblut, Lynn Jenkins, and Andrew Kolstad. 1993. *Adult Literacy in America: A First Look at the Results of the National Adult Literacy Survey*. National Center for Educational Statistics. Washington, D.C.: G.P.O.

Kirschenman, Joleen, Philip Moss, and Chris Tilly. 1995. "Employer Screening Methods and Racial Exclusion," Russell Sage Foundation, *Working Paper* 77. New York, New York.

Kodrzycki, Yolanda K. 1997. "Training Programs for Displaced Workers: What do They Accomplish?" *New England Economic Review*. May/June: pp. 39–58.

———. 1996. "Labor Markets and Earnings Inequality: A Status Report," *New England Economic Review*. May/June: pp. 11–25.

Kominski, Robert and Andrea Adams. 1991. *Educational Attainment in the United States*, U.S. Census Bureau, *Current Population Report*, Series P-20, Number 462. Washington, D.C.: G.P.O.

Kominski, Robert and Paul M. Siegel. 1993. "Measuring Education in the Current Population Survey," *Monthly Labor Review* 116, No. 9 (September): pp. 34–8.

Kortian, Tro. 1995. "Modern Approaches to Asset Price Formation: A Survey of Recent Theoretical Literature." Reserve Bank of Australia, *Discussion Paper* 9501 (March).

Kosters, Marvin H. 1991-a. "Wages and Demographics," in Kosters (1991-b): pp. 1–33.

———. Editor, 1991-b. *Workers and their Wages*. Washington, D.C.: AEI Press.

LaLonde, Robert J. and Robert H. Topel. 1992. "The Assimilation of Immigrants in the U.S. Labor Markets," in Borjas and Freeman (1992): pp. 67–92.

Lave, Jean. 1988. *Cognition in Practice*. New York: Cambridge University Press.

Lazear, Edward P. 1995. *Personnel Economics* Cambridge, Massachusetts: MIT Press.

Lazear, Edward P. and Sherwin Rosen. 1981. "Rank-order Tournaments as Optimum Labor Contracts," *Journal of Political Economy* 89, No. 5 (October): pp. 841–64.

Leamer, Edward E. 1996. "Wage Inequality from International Competition and Technological Change: Theory and Country Experience," *American Economic Review* 86, No. 2 (May): pp. 309–314.

Lebrecht, Norman. 1997. *Who Killed Classical Music: Maestros, Managers, and Corporate Politics*. Secaucus, New Jersey: Carol Publishing Group.

Levitan, Sar A., Frank Gallo, and Isaac Shapiro. 1993. *Working But Poor: America's Contradiction*. Baltimore, Maryland: The Johns Hopkins University Press, Revised Edition.

Levy, Frank. 1995. "The Future Path and Consequences of the U.S. Earnings Gap," Federal Reserve Bank of New York, *Economic Policy Review* 1, No. 1 (January): pp. 35–41.

Levy, Frank and Richard C. Michel. 1991. *The Economic Future of American Families: Income and Wealth Trends*. Washington, D.C. Urban Institute Press.

Levy, Frank and Richard J. Murnane. 1992. "U.S. Earnings Levels and Earnings Inequality: A Review of Recent Trends and Proposed Explanations," *Journal of Economic Literature* 30, No. 3 (September): pp. 1333–81.

Lilien, David M. 1982. "Sectoral Shifts and Cyclical Unemployment," *Journal of Political Economy* 70, No. 4 (August): pp. 777–93.

Lipset, Seymour Martin. 1992. "The Work Ethic, Then and Now," *Journal of Labor Research* 13, No. 1 (Winter): pp. 45–54.

McKenzie, Martha Nolan. 1997. "Secretaries Go from 'Take a Letter' to Taking Charge," *New York Times*, January 26.

Mallinckrodt, Brent and Bruce R. Fretz. 1988. "Social Support and the Impact on Job Loss on Older Professionals," *Journal of Counseling Psychology* 35, No. 3: pp. 281–6.

Marcotte, Dave E. 1995. "Declining Job Stability: What We Know and What It Means," *Journal of Policy Analysis and Management* 14, Number 4 (Fall): pp. 590–9.

Marshall, Roy. 1994. "Jobs and Skill Demands in the New Economy," in Solmon and Levenson (1994): pp. 21–57.

Massey, Douglas S. and Nancy A. Denton. 1993. *American Apartheid: Segregation and the Making of the Underclass*. Cambridge, Massachusetts: Harvard University Press.

Maxwell, Nan L. 1994. "The Effect on Black-White Wage Differences of Differences in the Quantity and Quality of Education," *Industrial and Labor Relations Review* 47, No. 2 (January): pp. 249–64.

Mellow. Wesley and Hal Sider. 1983, "Accuracy of Response in Labor Market Surveys: Evidence and Implciations," *Journal of Labor Economics* 1, No. 4 (October): pp. 331–345.

Miller, Ann R. *et al.*, editors. 1980. *Work, Jobs, and Occupations*. Washington, D.C.: National Academy Press.

Mishel, Lawrence and Jared Bernstein. 1994. "Is the Technology Black Box Empty?" Economic Policy Institute, *Technical Paper*. Washington, D.C.

Mishel, Lawrence, Jared Bernstein, and John Schmitt, 1997. *The State of Working America, 1996–1997*. Armonk, NY: M. E. Sharpe.

Mishel, Lawrence and Ruy A. Teixeira. 1991. "The Myth of the Coming Labor Shortage," *The American Prospect*, No. 4 (Fall): pp. 98–103.

Morrow, Paula. 1993. *The Theory and Measurement of Work Commitment*. Greenwich, Connecticut: JAI Press.

Moss, Philip and Chris Tilly. 1995. "Skills and Race in Hiring: Quantitative Findings from Face-to-Face Interviews," *Eastern Economic Journal* 21, No .3 (Summer): pp. 357–373.

Mullis, Ina V. S. *et al.* 1994. *NAEP 1993: Trends in Academic Progress*. Washington, D.C.: National Center for Education Statistics.

Murnane, Richard J. and Frank Levy. 1997. *Teaching the New Basic Skills*. New York: Free Press.

Murnane, Richard J., John B. Willett, and Frank Levy. 1995. "The Growing Importance of Cognitive Skills in Wage Determination," *Review of Economics and Statistics* 77, No. 3 (May): pp. 251–66.

Murphy, Kevin M., and Finis Welch. 1993-a. "Inequality and Relative Wages," *American Economic Review* 83, No. 2 (May): pp. 104-9.

———. 1993-b. "Occupational Change and the Demand for Skill, 1940–1990," *American Economic Review* 83, No. 2 (May): pp. 122-6.

———. 1992. "The Structure of Wages," *Quarterly Journal of Economics* 107, No. 1 (February): pp. 215–326.

———. 1991. "The Role of International Trade in Wage Differentials," in Kosters (1991-b): pp. 39–77.

Neal, Derek A. and William R. Johnson. 1996. "The Role of Premarket Factors in Black-White Wage Differences," *Journal of Political Economy* 104, No. 5 (October): pp. 869–96.

O'Neill, June. 1990. "The Role of Human Capital in Earnings Differences between Black and White Men," *Journal of Economic Perspectives* 4, No. 4 (Fall): 25–47.

Orfield, Gary. 1993. *The Growth of Segregation in American Schools: Changing Patterns of Separation and Poverty Since 1968.* Washington, D.C.: National School Boards Association.

Organization of Economic Cooperation and Development (O.E.C.D.) Annual. *Labour Force Statistics.* Paris.

———. 1995. *Literacy, Economy, and Society.* Paris.

———. 1996. *Employment Outlook,* June.

Orlean, Andre. 1995. "Bayesian Interactions and Collective Dynamics of Opinion: Herd Behavior and Mimetic Contagion," *Journal of Economic Behavior and Organization* 28, No. 2 (October): pp. 257–74.

Orr, Larry L., *et al.* 1995. *Does Training for the Disadvantaged Work? Evidence from the National JTPA Study.* Washington, D.C.: Urban Institute Press.

Padoa-Schioppa, Fiorella, editor. 1991. *Mismatch and Labour Mobility.* New York: Cambridge University Press.

Parker, Jeffrey. 1992. "Structural Unemployment in the United States: The Effects of Interindustry and Interregional Dispersion," *Economic Inquiry* 30, No. 1 (January): pp. 101–16.

Perelman, Michael. 1996. *The Pathology of the U.S. Economy: The Costs of a Low-Wage System.* New York, NY: St. Martin's Press.

Phelps, Edmund S. 1994. *Structural Slumps.* Cambridge, Massachusetts: Harvard U. Press.

———. 1997. *Rewarding Work: How to Restore Participation and Self-Support to Free Enterprise.* Harvard University Press.

Pierce, Brook and Finis Welch. 1994. "Dimensions of Inequality in Labor Income," in Bergstrand (1994): pp. 145–179.

Poterba, James M., Steven F. Venti, and David A. Wise. 1996. "How Retirement Saving Programs Increase Saving," *Journal of Economic Perspectives* 10, No. 4 (Fall): pp. 91–112.

Pryor, Frederic L. 1983. "Some Economics of Sloth," *The Social Science Review* 5, No. 1 (Fall): pp. 82–192.

———. 1996. *Economic Evolution and Structure: The Impact of Complexity on the U.S. Economic System.* New York: Cambridge University Press.

———. 1998. "The Impact of Foreign Trade on the Employment of Unskilled U.S. Workers: Some New Evidence," *Southern Economic Journal,* forthcoming, 1998.

Pryor, Frederic L. and David Schaffer. 1997. "Wages and the College Educated: A Paradox Resolved," *Monthly Labor Review* 120, No. 7 (July): pp. 3–14.

———. 1998. "Expected Wages of Workers by Race/Ethnicity: The Impact of Education and Cognitive Skills," processed.

Reardon, Elaine. 1997. "Demand-side Changes and the Relative Economic Progress of Black Men: 1940–1990." *Journal of Human Resources* 32, No. 1 (Winter): pp. 69–97.

Rifkin, Jeremy. 1995. *The End of Work: The Decline of the Global Labor Force and the Dawn of the Post-Market Era.* New York: G.P. Putnam's Sons.

Rivera-Batiz, Francisco L. 1992. "Quantitative Literacy and the Likelihood of Employment Among Young Adults in the United States," *Journal of Human Resources* 27, No. 2 (Spring 1992): pp. 313–28.

———. 1995. "Vocational Education and General Equivalency Diploma, and Urban and Minority Populations," *Education and Urban Society* 27, No. 1 (May 1995): pp. 313–28.

Roos, Patricia A. and Donald J. Treiman. 1980. "DOT Scales for the 1970 Census Classification," in Miller, *et al.* (1980): pp. 336–89.

Rose, Stephen J. 1995. *Declining Job Security and the Professionalization of Opportunity*, National Commission for Employment Policy, *Research Report* 95-04.

SAS Institute. 1995. *Logistic Regression Examples: Using the SAS System*. Cary, North Carolina.

Sachs, Jeffrey D. and Howard Shatz. 1994. "Trade and Jobs in U.S. Manufacturing," *Brookings Papers on Economic Activity*, No. 1. Washington, D.C.: pp. 1–84.

Schaffer, David L. 1995. "The Natural Rate of Unemployment Revisited: A Disaggregated Analysis." Unpublished manuscript presented at the Atlantic Economic Society Meetings in Williamsburg, Virginia, October.

Schaffer, David and Frederic L. Pryor. 1998. "Changes in the Distribution of Wages," processed.

———. 1998. Increasing Joblessness and Lower Wages Among Less Educated Men: Are Women the Cause," processed.

Shiller, Robert J., 1995. "Conversation, Information, and Herd Behavior," *American Economic Review* 85, No. 2 (May): pp. 181–185.

Sicherman, Nachum. 1991. " 'Overeducation' in the Labor Market," *Journal of Labor Economics* 9, No. 2 (April): pp. 101–22.

Simon, Marlise. 1995. "France Finds Reading Tests Incomprehensible," *New York Times*, December 12: p. 3.

Smeeding, Timothy M., and John Coder. 1995. "Income Inequality in Rich Countries during the 1980s," *Journal of Income Distribution* 5, No. 1: pp. 13–29.

Smith, James P. and Barry Edmonston, editors. 1997. *The New Americans: Economic, Demographic, and Fiscal Effects of Immigration*. Washington, D.C.: National Academy Press.

Solmon, Lewis C. and Alec R. Levenson, editors. 1994. *Labor Markets, Employment Policy, and Job Creation*. Washington, DC: Milken Institute for Job and Capital Formation, and Boulder, Colorado: Westview Press.

Spence, A. Michael. 1974. *Market Signaling*. Cambridge, Massachusetts: Harvard University Press.

Spenner, Kenneth I. 1983. "Deciphering Prometheus: Temporal Change in Work Content," *American Sociological Review* 48, (December): pp. 824–37.

———. 1988. "Technological Change, Skill Requirements, and Education: The Case for Uncertainty," in Richard M. Cyert and David C. Mowery, editors. *The Impact of Technological Change on Employment and Economic Growth*. Cambridge: Ballinger Publishing Company: pp. 131–84.

Steele, Claude and Joshua Aronson. 1995. "Stereotype Threat and the Intellectual Test Performance of African Americans," *Journal of Personality and Social Psychology* 69, No. 5 (November): 797–811.

Stone, Richard. 1961. *Input-Output and National Accounts*. Paris: OECD.

———. 1962. "Multiple Classifications in Social Accounting," *Bulletin de l'Institut International de Statistique* 39, No. 3, pp. 215–233.

Swinnerton, Kenneth and Howard Wial. 1995. "Is Job Stability Declining in the U.S. Economy?" *Industrial and Labor Relations Review* 48, No. 2 (January): pp. 293–304.

———. 1996. "Is Job Stability Declining in the U.S. Economy? A Reply to Diebold, Neumark, and Polsky," *Industrial and Labor Relations Review* 49, Number 2 (January): pp. 352–6.

Theil, Henri. 1977. "The Informational Analysis of Changes in Regional Distributions," in Cornelis A. van Bochove, *et al.*, editors, *Modeling for Government and Business*. Leiden: Martinus Nijhoff: pp. 9–32.

Theil, Henri and Riddhi Ghosh. 1980. "A Comparison of Shift-Share and the RAS Adjustment," *Regional Science and Urban Economics* 10: pp. 175–180.

Thurow, Lester C. 1973. *Generating Inequality*. New York: Basic Books.

———. 1996. *The Future of Capitalism: How Today's Economic Forces Shape Tomorrow's World*. New York: William Morrow and Company.

Tilgher, Andriano. 1931. *Work: What It has Meant to Men Through the Ages*, translated. by Dorothy C. Fisher. New York: Harcourt, Brace, and Company.

Tyler, John, Richard J. Murnane, and Frank Levy. 1995. "Are More College Graduates Taking 'High School' Jobs? A Reconsideration of the Evidence." *Monthly Labor Review* 118, No. 12 (December): pp. 18–27.

U.S. Department of Commerce, Bureau of Economic Analysis. 1986. *The National Income and Product Accounts of the United States, 1929–82*. Washington, D.C.: G.P.O.

———. 1992, 1993. *National Income and Product Accounts of the United States*. Washington, D.C.: G.P.O.

———. 1995. *Gross Production by Industry, 1947–93*. Computer Diskette Number BE-51.

U.S. Department of Commerce, Census Bureau. Annual. *Statistical Abstract of the United States*. Washington, D.C.: G.P.O.

———. 1964. *Evaluation and Research Program of the U.S. Census of Population and Housing: 1960. Accuracy of Data on Population Characteristics as Measured by CPS-Census Match*. Series ER 60, No. 5. Washington , DC: GPO.

———. 1965. *Evaluation and Research Program of the U.S. Census of Population and Housing: 1960. The Employer Record Check*. Series ER 60, No. 6. Washington, D.C.: GPO.

———. 1971. *Current Population Survey, March 1971: Technical Documentation*. Washington, D.C.: G.P.O.

———. 1972-a .*Evaluation and Research Program of the U.S. Census of Population and Housing: 1960. Effects of Different Reinterview Techniques on Estimates of Simple Response Variance*. Series ER 60, No. 11. Washington, D.C.: GPO.

———. 1972-b. *Public Use Samples of Basic Records from the 1970 Census: Description and Technical Documentation*. Washington, D.C.: G.P.O.

———. 1972-c. *Current Population Survey, March 1971: Technical Documentation*. Washington, D.C.: G.P.O.

———. 1973. *1970 Census of Population*. Subject Report. *Educational Attainment*, PC (2)-5B. Washington, D.C. G.P.O.

———. 1975. *Historical Statistics of the United States: Colonial Times to 1970*. Washington, D.C.: G.P.O. .

———. 1989. *The Relationship Between the 1970 and 1980 Industry and Occupation Classification Systems*. Technical Paper 59. Washington, D.C.

———. 1992. *1990 Census of Population: General Population Characteristics, United States, Metropolitan Areas*, 1990 CP-1-1B. Washington, D.C.: G.P.O.

———. 1993-a. *1990 Census of Population: Social and Economic Characteristics: United States*, CP-2-1. Washington, D.C.: G.P.O.

———. 1993-b. 1990 *Census of Population and Housing: Population and Housing Unit Count, United States*, CPH-2-1. Washington, D.C.: G.P.O.

———. 1993-c. *1990 Census of Population, The Foreign-Born Population in the United States, 1990*, CP-3-1. Washington, D.C.: G.P.O.

———. 1994. *Current Population Survey, March 1994: Technical Documentation*. Washington, D.C: G.P.O.

———. 1995. *Current Population Survey, March 1995: Technical Documentation*. Washington, D.C.: G.P.O.

————. 1996. "Population Projections of the United States by Age, Sex, Race, and Hispanic Origin: 1995 to 2050," *Current Population Reports* P25-1130. Washington, D.C. G.P.O.

U.S. Department of Education National Center for Education Statistics. 1993. *Adult Literacy in America*. Washington, D.C. G.P.O.

————. 1995. *Digest of Education Statistics 1995*, NCES Paper 95-029. Washington, D.C.: G.P.O.

Uchitelle, Louis. 1997. "Welfare Recipients Taking Jobs Often Held by the Working Poor," *New York Times*, April 1: p. A1.

Valletta, Robert G. 1997. "The Effects of Industry Employment Shifts on the U.S. Wage Structure, 1979–1995," Federal Reserve Bank of San Francisco, *Economic Review*, Number 1: pp. 16–32.

Warr, Peter. 1987. *Work, Unemployment, and Mental Health*. Oxford: Clarendon Press.

Warren, Robert and Jeffrey S. Passel. 1987. "A Count of the Uncountable: Estimates of Undocumented Aliens Counted in the 1980 United States Census," *Demography* 24, No. 3 (August): pp. 375–93.

Wattenberg, Ben. 1991. *The First Universal Nation: Leading Indicators and Ideas about the Surge of America in the 1990s*. New York: Free Press.

Weidenbaum, Murray. 1994. "How Government Reduces Employment," in Solmon and Levenson (1994): pp. 279–97.

Weidman, Lynn. 1989. "Final Report - Industry and Occupation Imputation," U.S. Census Bureau, Statistical Research Division, *Report Series*, Number 3: Census SRD/89/03 (April). Washington, D.C.: G.P.O.

Weigand, Bob. 1997. "Corning Inc. Says People With Only High School Diploma Need Not Apply for Jobs," *Buffalo News*, October 3, 1997, p. A-13.

West, Sandra A. 1986, "Estimation of the Mean from Censored Income Data," *Proceedings of the 1986 Annual Meeting of the American Statistical Association,* Volume 2, *Survey Research Methods*: pp. 665–670.

————. 1987. "Measures of Central Tendency for Censored Earnings Data from the Current Population Survey," *Proceedings of the 1987 Annual Meeting of the American Statistical Association*, Volume 4, *Business and Economic Statistics Section*: pp. 751–756.

Wilson, William Julius. 1996. *When Work Disappears: The World of the New Urban Poor*. New York: Knopf.

Wolff, Edward N. 1995-a. "Technology and the Demand for Skills," New York University Department of Economics, *Working Paper* No. 152. New York.

————. 1995-b. *Top Heavy: A Study of the Increasing Inequality of Wealth in America*. New York, NY: Twentieth Century Fund Press.

Wood, Adrian. 1994. *North-South Trade, Employment and Inequality*. Oxford: Clarendon Press.

————. 1995. "How Trade Hurts Unskilled Workers," *Journal of Economic Perspectives* 9, Number 3 (Summer): pp. 57–80.

Zemsky, Robert, Amy Johnson, *et al.* 1996. "In Search of a Logic: A Report on Work Relations, School Effectiveness, and Employer Satisfaction in Five Metropolitan Areas," National Center on the Educational Quality of the Workforce, processed.

Zemsky, Robert, Daniel Shapiro, Barbara Gelhard and Maria Iannozzi. 1996. "The Education and Training Nexus: Employers' Use of Academic Screens and the Provision of New-Hire Training," EQW *Working Papers* 38. Philadelphia: National Center on the Educational Quality of the Labor Force.

Name Index

Abowd, John M., 194
Abraham, Katharine G., 174, 178
Altonji, Joseph G., 275-6
Amsden, Alice H., 220
Anderson, Elijah, 205
Aronson, Joshua, 30
Autor, David H., 120
Bacharach, Michael, 81, 260-61
Badgett, M. V. Lee, 90
Barlett, Don, 1
Bartelsman, Eric J., 186, 191
Baumol, William J., 214
Bayoumi, Tamim, 232
Bergmann, Barbara R., 91
Berman, Eli, 171
Bernstein, Jared, 1
Betts, Julian, 30
Bhagwati, Jagdish, 1
Bishop, John, 60, 61, 120, 243
Blackburn, McKinley L., 33, 120
Blanchflower, David G., 103, 133, 135
Blank, Rebecca M., 200
Bloom, David E., 33
Borjas, George J., 50, 183, 194, 197, 275-6
Bound, John, 138, 171
Bradbury, Katharine L., 138
Brauer, David A., 138
Bregger, John E., 7
Brenner, M. Harvey, 1
Brown, James N., 177
Buchholz, Rogene A., 211
Burtless, Gary, 33, 138, 183, 227
Butcher, Kristin, 275
Cameron, Stephen V., 29
Campbell, Anne, 21
Cappelli, Peter, 53, 206
Card, David, 215, 275-6
Castro, Fidel, 276
Chiricos, Theodore G., 5
Chiswick, Barry R., 248

Clogg, Clifford, 248
Cohany, Sharon R., 6
Cook, Philip J., 1, 139-40
Danziger, Sheldon, 1
Davis, Steven J., 174-7
Devenow, Andrea, 139
Diebold, Francis X., 177
DiNardo, John E., 120, 141
Dunlop, John, 110
Eatwell, John, 219
Edmonston, Barry, 193, 195
Eissa, Nada, 213
Engen, Eric M., 232
Farber, Henry S., 177
Farley, Reynolds, 1
Feenstra, Robert C., 185-6, 191
Ferguson, Ronald F., 120
Filer, Randall K., 275
Fortin, Nicole M., 142
Frank, Robert H., 1, 139-40
Frazis, Harley, 243
Freeman, Richard B., 5, 33, 50, 138, 183, 194, 197, 275
Fretz, Bruce R., 5
Frey, William H., 277
Friedlander, Daniel, 227
Gale, William G., 232
Gale, Douglas, 139
Gallo, Frank, 1
Gardner, Jennifer M., 177
Ghosh, Riddhi, 77, 81
Ginzberg, Eli, 1
Gottschalk, Peter, 1
Gray, Wayne B., 186, 191
Griliches., Zvi, 171
Grogger, Jeff, 30
Grubb, W. Norton, 227
Haltiwanger, John, 174-7
Hamermesh, Daniel S., 177
Hanson, Gordon, 185

292

Hanushek, Eric A., 26
Hartman, Heidi I., 90
Haugen, Steven E, 7
Hecker, Daniel E., 59, 60, 61, 63
Heckman, James J., 29, 227
Hickok, Susan, 138
Holzer, Henry J., 1, 27, 115, 199, 206
Howell, David R., 52, 171
Hubbard, R. Glenn, 232
Hughes, Mark Alan, 199
Hunt, Earl, 20
Jargowsky, Paul A., 199
Jencks, Christopher S., 199
Jenkins, Stephen, 144
Jenkins, Lynn, 144
Johnson, Amy, 57
Johnson, George E., 138
Johnson, William R., 33, 106, 109
Juhn, Chinhui, 33, 57, 122, 150, 266-7
Jungeblut, Ann, 21
Kain, John F., 199
Kaplan, David, 29
Karoly, Lynn A., 138
Kasarda, John D., 200
Katz, Lawrence F., 33, 120, 138, 183, 275
Kim Dongwook, 26
Kim, Il-Joong, 5
Kirsch, Irwin S., 17, 21, 23, 34
Kirschenman, Joleen, Philip, 208
Kodrzycki, Yolanda K., 138, 227
Kominski, Robert, 243
Kortian, Tro, 139
Kosters, Marvin H., 1, 33
Krueger, Alan B., 120, 215
LaLonde, Robert J., 275
Lang, Kevin, 50, 194, 197
Lave, Jean, 22
Layard, Richard, 174
Lazear, Edward P., 140
Lebrecht, Norman, 139
Lemieux, Thomas, 142
Levenson, Alec R., 1
Levitan, Sar A., 1
Levy, Frank, 32, 59, 60, 63, 120, 138, 206, 227
Light, Audrey, 177
Lilien, David M., 174
Lipset, Seymour Martin, 212
Lochner, Lance, 227
Machin, Stephen, 171
McKenzie, Martha Nolan, 53

Mallinckrodt, Brent, 5
Marcotte, Dave E., 177
Marshall, Roy, 206
Maxwell, Nan L., 106, 115
Mayer, Susan E., 199
Mellow. Wesley, 249
Miller, Ann R., 251
Mishel, Lawrence, 1, 60
Morrow, Paula, 211
Moss, Philip, 205
Mullis, Ina V. S., 32
Murnane, Richard J., 32, 59, 60, 63, 106, 114, 120, 138, 206, 227
Murphy, Kevin M., 33, 57, 122, 138, 150, 266-7
Neal, Derek A., 33, 106
Neumark, David, 120, 177
O'Neill, June, 30, 106, 109, 114
Orlean, Andre, 139
Orr, Larry L., 227
Oswald, Andrew J., 103, 133, 135
Padoa-Schioppa, Fiorella, 174
Parker, Jeffrey, 174
Passel, Jeffrey S., 197
Perelman, Michael, 1
Phelps, Edmund S., 228
Pierce, Brook, 33
Pischke, Jörn-Steffen, 120
Polsky, Daniel, 177
Ports, Michelle Harrison, 243
Poterba, James M., 232
Priebe, John, 249
Pryor, Frederic L., 52, 55, 114, 142, 171-2, 175, 182, 188-9, 203, 211-12, 249-50, 253, 268
Rawls, John, 144
Reardon, Elaine, 276.
Rifkin, Jeremy, 219
Rivera-Batiz, Francisco L., 37
Roos, Patricia A., 70, 111, 251-2, 270, 274
Rose, Stephen J., 177
Roselius, Rebecca L., 227
Rosen, Sherwin, 140
Sachs, Jeffrey D., 192
Schaffer, David, 55, 114, 142, 249, 268
Schmitt, John, 1
Scholz, John Karl, 232
Schuh, Scott, 175-7
Shapiro, Isaac, 1
Shapiro Daniel, 207
Shatz, Howard, 192

Shiller, Robert J., 139
Sicherman, Nachum, 57
Sider, Hal, 249
Siegel, Paul M., 243
Simon, Marlise, 26
Skinner, Jonathan A., 232
Smith, Jeffrey A., 227
Smith, James P., 193, 195
Smith, Thomas, 212
Solmon, Lewis C., 1
Spenner, Kenneth I., 53
Steele, Jim, 1, 30
Stewart, Jay, 243
Stone, Richard A., 77, 260
Sullivan, Teresa, 248
Swinnerton, Kenneth, 177
Taber, Christopher, 227
Teixeira, Ruy A., 60
Theil, Henri, I, 77, 81, 145, 261
Thélot, Claude, 26
Thurow, Lester C., 1, 75
Tilgher, Andriano, 211
Tilly, Chris, 206
Topel, Robert H., 266-7, 275
Treiman, Donald J., 70, 111, 251-2, 270, 274
Tyler, John, Richard J., 59, 60, 61, 63
Uchitelle, Louis, 229
Valletta, Robert G., 142
Venezky, Richard L., 29
Venti, Steven F., 232
Vernon, Raymond, 220
Warr, Peter, 5
Warren, Robert, 197
Wattenberg, Ben, 223
Weidenbaum, Murray, 214
Weidman, Lynn, 248-9
Weigand, Bob, 43
Welch, Ivo, 139
Welch, Finis, 33
West, Sandra A., 268
Wial, Howard, 177
Willett, John B., 32, 120
Wilson, William Julius, 1, 115, 206
Wise, David A., 232
Wolff, Edward N., 1, 52, 171, 198, 214, 250,
    252-3
Wood, Adrian, 188
Zemsky, Robert, 57, 207, 211

Subject Index

Absenteeism, 211-3
Affirmative action policies, 75, 90
African-Americans, *see* race/ethnicity
Armed Forces Qualification Test (AFQT),
    see cognitive skills
Age, *see also* employment, age determinants
    impact on employment, 12, 39, 41, 223
    impact on functional literacy, 28, 31, 32
    impact on occupation, 60-63
    impact on wages, 111, 113-4, 126, 271
Aggregate changes, *see* decomposition
    analysis
Attitudes toward work, *see* employment
Average absolute deviation from median
    (AADM), 168
Baby boom generation, 100, 223
Balance of payment effects, *see* trade, foreign
Biproportional matrix technique, *see*
    decomposition analysis
Blanchflower-Oswald hypothesis, 133-5
Cognitive skills, *see also* functional literacy
    Armed Forces Qualification Test (AFQT)
        23, 33, 114-5
    as sorting mechanism, 3
    definition, 11, 20
    determinant of education, 11, 33
    functional literacy, 20, 21
    impact on employment, 11, 34-8, 39, 41
    impact on productivity, 110
    impact on wages, 106-8, 111-3, 116-29
    innate intelligence, 22, 46
    measurement problems, 20-2
    other types of skills, 30
    productivity, 110
    Scholastic Aptitude Test (SAT), 20, 30, 32
Communication skills, *see* employment
Conditional weighted density estimation, 141
Consumption structure, *see* production
Competition for jobs, 94-5 *see also*
    displacement mechanisms
    head-to-head competition, 94-5

Credentials, educational, 43
    creep, 58
Current Population Survey (CPS), 2, 6, 9, 15-6,
    234
    description, 15, 234
    imputing detailed occupations, 248-50
Decomposition analysis
    aggregate changes, 2, 76, 82-3, 85-6
    biproportional matrix technique, 77-81,
        260-1
    changes in wage inequality, 2
    definition, 76
    demographic-education multiplier, 80-4
    employment-occupation multiplier, 80-4
    general explanation, 77
    information distance, 80-1, 86
    occupational shifting component, 91-4
    proportional employment component, 91-4
    RAS multipliers, 76-7, 80-4
    RAS technique, 77-81
    structural change, 76, 85-94, 261-3
    Theil technique, 77-81
    timing, 97-8
Dictionary of Occupational Titles, 53, 69-70,
    111, 241-2, 269
Displacement mechanisms, 74-101, 108-9
    black females with college degrees, 91, 93,
        99
    determinants, 12, 59-67, 74-101, 108-9, 111
    head-to-head competition, 94-5
    indirect versus direct, 96-98
    induced by labor market policies, 228
    impact of immigration, 275-6
    impact of productivity differences, 90, 98-9
    impact of wage differences, 90, 98-9, 108-9
    less-educated by more-educated, 12-3,
        87-9, 90, 94
    low-cognitive-skilled people by
        high-cognitive skilled people, 59-67
    men by women, 4-5, 12, 74-101, 157-62,
        166-8

overview, 216-9
trends, 17, 97-8
Downsizing, *see* employment, downsizing
Downward occupational mobility, *see*
    occupational mobility
Economic stagnation, 219-22
Education
    and gender, 43
    and race/ethnicity, 43
    data, 242-5
    cognitive skills, 11, 27-9
    cross-section and time-series results, 45
    GED, 24, 27, 28, 29, 35, 39, 40
    graduate degree, 28, 35. 39
    high-school dropouts, 24, 28, 35, 39
    impact on functional literacy, 23-9
    impact on employment, 9-12, 35, 37-41,
        207-11
    impact on occupation, 61-8
    impact on wages, 11, 57, 104-8, 112-4,
        116-9, 121-8, 271
    intensity, 2, 48-9, *see also* occupations, tiers
    levels, 42
    measurement problems, 243-6
    mother's education on functional literacy,
        28, 31
    trends, 42, 225-6
Educational upgrading
    definition, 43-4
    occupations with greatest increases, 54-7
    previous studies, 53-4
    real versus pseudo, 43, 52, 54, 56
    structural, 43-4
Efficiency wages, *see* wages
Employment, *see also* displacement,
    joblessness, labor market,
    unemployment
    attitudes toward work, 14, 206-7, 212-4
    data, 8, 77-8, 246, 255-6
    definition, 6-7
    determinants, 19, 34-42, 207, 216-9, 237,
        240, 247-8
    definition, 6
    downsizing, 173, 220
    hiring criteria, 206-12, 276-8
    impact of age, 12, 39, 41, 223
    impact of cognitive skills, 11
    impact of education, 9-12, 35, 37-41, 207-11
    impact of family structure, 12, 37-9, 41
    impact of foreign trade, 2, 3, 14, 171-2,
        182-93

impact of functional literacy, 34-8, 39, 41
impact of gender, 11, 37. 38-41, 209-11
impact of labor/capital ratios, 186-8
impact of immigration, 2, 3, 14, 37-40,
    193-8, 274-6
impact of marital status, 38, 41
impact of metropolitan area, 37, 39, 41,
    198, 200-3
impact of place of birth, 37-40
impact of race/ethnicity, 9, 12, 37-40, 200-3,
    209-11
impact of region, 37, 39-41, 198
impact of structural shifts of production,
    179-82
impact of structural shifts of productivity,
    179-82
impact of subjective factors, 206-14, 216
institutional influences, 213-6
job creation, 173-7, 180, 184, 232-3
job destruction, 173-7, 180, 183-4
job security, 173-4, 177, 213
job tenure, 177-80
men, 34-5, 58
probabilities, 241-2
spacial mismatch of jobs, 14, 198-203
status and functional literacy, 34-6
structural change, 14
technical change, 12, 48-68, 170-80
trends, 3-4, 7-11, 13, 219-26
turbulence, 171-80
women, 34-5, 52, 58, 222-3
Ethnicity, *see* race/ethnicity
Exports, *see* trade, foreign
Fairness norms, 110
Family structure
    impact on employment, 12, 37-9, 41
Fiscal policy, 220-21
Foreign birth, *see also* immigration
    impact on functional literacy, 28
    impact on employment, 37-40
    impact on wages, 111, 115
Foreign trade and exchange, 1, 2, 14, 183-93
    balance of payments, 183
    foreign exchange market, 218
    impact on employment, 171-2, 183-93
    non-competitive imports, 188
    shift-share analysis, 189-93
Functional literacy, *see also* cognitive skills,
    displacement
    data, 17, 23-5
    definition, 20-3

determinants, 27-34
document scale, 22
employment status, 35
foreign scores, 26
GED, 24, 28
graduate degree, 24, 28
high school, 24, 28
impact of age, 28, 31-2
impact of education, 23-9, 34-5
impact of employment status, 34-5
impact of gender, 23-9, 34-5
impact of race/ethnicity, 27-31
impact on employment, 34-8, 39, 41
impact on occupational tier, 66-68
impact on productivity, 110
impact on wages, 13, 106-8, 111-3, 116-28
international comparisons, 26
men, 26-7, 34-6
National Adult Literacy Study, 17, 21-34,
    240, 243
prose scale, 21-2
quantitative scale, 22
scores, 23-5
trade/vocational school, 24, 28
university degree, 24, 28
women, 26-7, 34-6
GDP growth, 172
Generalized entropy coefficient,
    see inequality indices
Gender, *see also* displacement
employment, 7, 9-10, 12
functional literacy, 26, 27
impact on cognitive skills, 23-9
impact on employment, 37-41, 209-11
impact on occupation, 60-1
impact on wage distribution, 138
impact on wages, 11, 13, 103-6, 112-4,
    126, 147-50, 157-68
jobless rates, 8
productivity differences, 75, 90
Generalized entropy index, *see also* wage
    inequality
decomposibility, 147-53
definition, 142-5
results, 147-53
Gini coefficient, 144
Health industry, 4, 140, 154-7, 160-2
Heckscher-Ohlin theorem, 182
High school jobs, *see also* occupations,
    occupational mobility
data, 62-3

definitions, 61-3
history of discussion, 59-61
High skill jobs, *see* skills
Hiring criteria, *see* employment
Immigration, 193-98, *see also* foreign birth,
    labor force
effect on employment, 2, 14, 37-40, 193-8,
    274-6
effect on wages, 111, 115
immigrants as share of employed, 194-7
Implicit contracts, 3
Imports, *see* trade, foreign
Income tax rates, 213-4
Industries, *see* production
Inequality indices, 141-4
comparisons, 144-53
decomposibility, 143-4, 147-53
generalized entropy coefficient, 142-4
Gini coefficient, 144
percentile, 141-5
properties, 141-3
Theil coefficient, 142-4
Information age, 223
Information distance, *see* RAS technique
International trade, *see* foreign trade and
    exchange
Investment, 224
Jobs, *see* employment, occupations
Joblessness non-employment, *see also*
    employment
data, 7-11
definition, 6-7
impact of cognitive skills, 11-2, 34-8
impact of education, 8-12, 37, 39-40
non-participation rates, 238-40
policies aimed at, 226-33
social impact, 5
trends, 3, 7-11, 219-26, 234-40
Labor force, *see also* employment,
    unemployment
baby boomers, 100
by gender, race, occupational tier, and
    education, 78-9
data, 78-9
immigrants, 193-98
participation rates, *see* employment
prime-age, definition, 6
Labor market, 1, 17, *see also* wage level
    changes
demand factors, 48-52, 228-33
dual labor market, 110

market functioning policies, 229, 231
Phillips curve, 133-5, 222
policies, 226-33
supply factors, 49-52, 226-8, 230
tightness, 222
Labor mobility, 194, 198-200, *see also* occupational mobility
Labor unions, 4, 138, 165-6
Legal services industry, 4, 140, 154-7, 160-2
Literacy, *see* functional literacy
Lognormal wage distribution, 141
Logit analysis, 36-7
Low-skill jobs, *see* skills
Manufacturing sector, 1
Metropolitan statistical areas, 200-3
    impact on functional literacy, 28
    impact on employment, 37, 39, 41, 198, 200-3
    impact on wages, 113, 271
    spatial mismatch of jobs, 1-2, 14, 198-203
Minimum wage laws, 138, *see also* wage levels, minimum
    public policy, 227
    sources of wage stickiness, 3, 58, 74
Monetary policy, 220-21
Multipliers, *see* decomposition analysis
National Adult Literacy Study, *see* cognitive skills, functional literacy
Natural rate of unemployment, *see* unemployment
Non-employment, *see* joblessness
Occupations, *see also* wage levels, wage distribution
    definition, 15-6
    demand factors, 50-52
    dentists, 154, 161
    deskilling, 252-4
    educational intensity, *see* occupations, tiers
    educational upgrading, *see* educational upgrading
    high-school jobs, 3, 59-65
    impact of education, 61-8
    impact of age, 60-3
    Impact of functional literacy, 66-8
    impact on wages, 104-6, 109-10, 112-3, 115, 271
    inputing detailed occupations, 248-50
    lawyers, 129, 131, 154, 161
    measurement, 15-6, 48-52, 248-50
    pharmacists, 154, 161

physicians, 129, 131, 154, 161
    skill requirements, 48-57, 60
    structural changes, 43-4
    supply, 50-2
    tiers, 2, 48-52, 257-60
    trends, 48-52, 257-60
    upskilling, *see* skill
Occupational mobility, *see also* displacement
    changes, 61-6
    downward, 3, 12-3, 45, 58-63
Occupational discrimination
    black women with university degrees, 99
Partial discrete change statistic, 36-7, 39
    definition, 36
Percentile range index, 142
Phillips curve, 133-5, 222
Place of birth, see foreign birth
Policy implications, 18, 226-33, *see also* labor market, policies
    demand-side policies, 228-33
    market functioning policies, 229, 231
    subsidies, 228-9
    supply-side policies, 226-8, 230
Population, *see* labor force
Prime age
    definition, 6
Production, *see also* technical change
    efficiency wages, 58, 74, 110, 216
    industries, 189-93
    labor/capital ratios, 184-7
    productivity, 171, 180-2, 189-93
    skill intensities, 184-9
Productivity trends, 172-3
Public opinion surveys, 173, 177, 213
Race/ethnicity, *see also* joblessness, wage level
    education, 43
    impact on cognitive skills, 27-31
    impact on employment, 9-10, 37-40, 43, 200-3, 209-11
    impact on wages, 13, 112-5, 126, 137
    impact on wage distribution, 147-50
RAS technique, *see* decomposition analysis
Rate of return
    to cognitive skills, 13, 116-32
    to education, 11, 106, 112, 116-9, 121-8
Regression analysis, 2
Regions, *see also* metropolitan areas
    impact on functional literacy, 28, 31
    impact on employment, 37, 39-41, 198, 200-3

impact on wages, 113, 271
spatial mismatch, 2
Residence, *see* regions
Service sector, 1
Skills, 111, see also occupation
deskilling, 252-4
different types, 68-70, 251-4
measurement, 48, 53, 250-54
upskilling, 44, 52-57, 68-9, 119-21, 128-9
tiers, 68 - 70
Spatial mismatch, 2, 198-203, *see also*
employment. regions and employment,
metropolitan areas
Stagnation, *see* economic stagnation
Structural changes, *see* decomposition analysis
Subsidies, 230
Technical change, 1, 170-80
skill-biased, 43-4, 58, 116-32, 138-9,
170-81, 220, 223-25
Theil coefficient, *see* inequality indices
Tiers, *see* occupations, tiers
Trade, foreign, *see* foreign trade and exchange
Turbulence in labor market, *see also*
employment
data, 170-80, 183
index, 174-5
Unemployment, *see also* joblessness
compensation, 214-5
data, 10, 134-5, 235-7
definition, 6-7
impact on wages, 133-5
insurance, 214
measurement, 6-8
natural rate, 8-9
OECD nations, 10
Phillips curve, 133-5, 222
trends, 10, 134-5
Unions, *see* labor unions
Upgrading, *see* education, upgrading
Upskilling, *see* skills
Wage distribution, 137-69, *see also* wage
level, displacement mechanisms,
inequality indices
by subgroups, 147-69
conditional weighted density estimation, 141
data, 13, 144-7, 152-3, 272-3
decomposing, 147-53
determinants, 138-40, 216-9
generalized entropy measures, 142-5,
147-53

impact of cognitive skills, 11, 13-4, 156-7,
162
impact of education, 11, 148-51, 165-8
impact of gender, 11, 103-6, 112-4, 126,
147-50, 157-68
impact of industry, 138, 140, 155-7
impact of occupation, 148-50, 154-62
impact of race/ethnicity, 147-50
impact of technological change, 138-9
impact of winner-take-all wage setting, 5,
138-40, 162-3
impact of women's increased labor force
participation, 138
increased variance in education, 93, 168
inequality at a single point in time, 147,
152-3
inequality over time, 4
measurement, 141-4
percentile range measure, 142
technological change, 5
trends, 3-4, 13, 144-69, 222-5
winner-take-all, 5, 138-40
within tier 4 occupations, 151-64
Wage level, 102-36, *see also* wage distribution
combination effects, 132-3
contours, 10
data, 61, 103-6, 265-6
determinants, 109-115, 216-9, 271
efficiency wage, 58, 74, 110, 216
estimation, 266-9
impact of age, 111, 113-4, 126, 271
impact of cognitive skills, 11, 106-8, 111-3,
116-23, 124-8
impact of education, 11, 57, 104-8, 112-4,
116-9, 121-8, 271
impact of functional literacy, 13,106-8,
111-3, 116-9, 120-9
impact of gender, 11, 13, 103-6, 112-4,
126, 271
impact of industry, 111, 113
impact of metropolitan area, 113, 271
impact of occupational tier, 104-6, 109-10,
112-3, 115, 117-9, 271
impact of place of birth, 111-3, 115
impact of race/ethnicity, 13, 112-5, 126,
133
impact of region, 113, 271
impact of non-cognitive skills, 111, 120-3,
269-70
minimum wage, 3-4, 214-5

part-time worker, 126
part-year worker, 126
Phillips curve, 133-5, 222
predicted versus actual, 128-31
relationship to unemployment, 133-5
stickiness, 3, 58, 74
subgroups, 61
technical change, 120
trends, 13, 103-6, 116-32, 221-4
Wage inequality, *see* wage distribution
Wage stickiness, 3, 74, 57-8, 108, 215-7, *see*
    also implicit contracts; wage, minimum
Work attitudes/ethic, 204-5, 208, 211-3
Winner-take-all, *see* wage distribution